THE GOLDEN AGE *of the* LITHUANIAN YESHIVAS

BEN-TSIYON KLIBANSKY

THE GOLDEN AGE *of the* LITHUANIAN YESHIVAS

TRANSLATED BY
NAHUM SCHNITZER

INDIANA UNIVERSITY PRESS

The English-language edition is licensed from the original Hebrew-language publisher, The Zalman Shazar Center, Jerusalem.

This book is a publication of

Indiana University Press
Office of Scholarly Publishing
Herman B Wells Library 350
1320 East 10th Street
Bloomington, Indiana 47405 USA

iupress.org

Manufactured in the United States of America

First printing 2022

Library of Congress Cataloging-in-Publication Data

Names: Klibansky, Ben-Tsiyon, author. | Schnitzer, Nahum, translator.
Title: The Golden age of the Lithuanian yeshivas / Ben-Tsiyon Klibansky ; translated by Nahum Schnitzer.
Other titles: Ke-tsur ḥalamish
Description: Bloomington : Indiana University Press, 2022. | Includes bibliographical references and index.
Identifiers: LCCN 2021030856 (print) | LCCN 2021030857 (ebook) | ISBN 9780253058492 (hardback) | ISBN 9780253058508 (paperback) | ISBN 9780253058522 (ebook)
Subjects: LCSH: Yeshivas—Lithuania—History—20th century. | Jews—Education—Lithuania—20th century. | Lithuania—Religious life and customs.
Classification: LCC BM85.L57 K5413 2013 (print) | LCC BM85.L57 (ebook) | DDC 296.071/1—dc23
LC record available at https://lccn.loc.gov/2021030856
LC ebook record available at https://lccn.loc.gov/2021030857

This book is published with the assistance of:

The Eisenberg Family (Israel)
in memory of their family, born in Verzhan (Veivirženai), Lithuania

The Davidow Family (USA)
in memory of their ancestors from Shaki (Šakiai), Lithuania
whose descendants have accomplished great things
and live throughout the world

To the memory of my father,
a student of Slabodka Yeshiva in Lithuania,
whose virtues inspire me to this day

CONTENTS

THE GOLDEN AGE *of the* LITHUANIAN YESHIVAS

INTRODUCTION

THIS BOOK describes the world of Lithuanian yeshivas in Eastern Europe in the last phase of their existence, from the end of the First World War until the first days of the Holocaust—an era that the collective memory of the Torah world defines as the "golden age" of its history. Upon examination of photos and memories of those years, and even from a few decades earlier, this yeshiva world may seem modern and familiar from a number of aspects. Even so, how this world came into being is unclear, and the research up until this point has not exhaustively investigated its origins. It would seem possible to learn about the early history of the world of the Lithuanian yeshivas from the testimony of Yosef, rabbi of the town of Krinik in Grodno Province and a student of Rabbi Ḥayim of Volozhin (1749–1821), regarding the early nineteenth century: "The world was desolate, absolute chaos, because even the word 'yeshiva' was unknown in the world, or the idea of a yeshiva, or what one does there."[1] His words have been criticized, sometimes sharply, but it is accepted in the research that the Lithuanian yeshiva world as we know it came into being or was reconstituted only after this time.[2]

In order to understand the break in continuity between the world of the renewed yeshivas and the yeshiva world in earlier times, one has to examine the history of the area where the Lithuanian yeshivas were located. This region had previously been within the borders of the Grand Duchy of Lithuania, which in the fourteenth and fifteenth centuries had been the largest country in Europe and stretched from the Baltic Sea in its northwest to the Black Sea in the south. In 1569 the Grand Duchy united with the Kingdom of Poland into the Polish-Lithuanian Commonwealth in a pact signed in Lublin. As a consequence of the unification, the southern portions of the duchy were transferred to Polish control, whereas in its reduced territory the Grand Duchy still retained a degree of military and economic autonomy. The Jews there developed their own autonomous rule, with the Council of the Land of Lithuania as its head. This council had judicial authority and the right to enact rules that obligated the entire Jewish Lithuanian community, as well as the right to represent that community before the duchy's authorities.[3]

Rabbis and scholars began to immigrate to the Grand Duchy, and similar to the large cities in Poland, several of the duchy's cities became renowned centers of Torah learning. In the middle of the seventeenth century, these centers were severely damaged. One of the armies of Bogdan Chmelnitsky (1595/6–1657), who led the Cossack rebellion against the Polish-Lithuanian Commonwealth, went as far north as the Grand Duchy of Lithuania and brought ruin and desolation to the Jewish communities in its center and south. The armies of the Tsardom of Russia from the east and Sweden from the west caused further damage of their own to the Jewish communities in the northern part of the duchy. Only in 1661, when the Polish-Lithuanian Commonwealth was released from the subjugation of foreign armies, did relief come to the Jewish Lithuanian communities as well. The Council of the Land of Lithuania took the rehabilitation of spiritual life upon itself, and its first decision toward the end of that year concerned yeshiva students and youngsters who studied. This cultivation of Torah scholarship and its students contributed to the preservation of the Grand Duchy of Lithuania as a Torah center even after the years of destruction and ruin. The Lithuanian center continued to develop, and it achieved impressive success in the eighteenth century at the time of Rabbi Eliyahu, the "Gaon of Vilna" (1720–1797).[4] Torah scholarship was prevalent among the Jews of the Grand Duchy and became one of the marks of the unique culture and tradition that shaped these Jews into what is referred to as Lithuanian Jewry. This title continued to accompany them in the Lithuanian region even when its political borders and regime changed, practically up to the time of the Holocaust.[5]

One of the salient signs of widespread learning in the Grand Duchy of Lithuania and the development of the duchy into a center of Torah was the large number of yeshivas there. At the head of each yeshiva was usually the local rabbi, who received his salary from the community. Many of the students were not local because the Lithuanian Jews abided by the rule "Exile yourself to a place of Torah," and their sons preferred to study far away from home.[6] Because the students were isolated from their parents' support, the local community also took their material maintenance upon itself in the form of "days": community members donated daily meals to the yeshiva, each one on the day convenient to him among the days of the week, and the yeshiva *gaba'im* (beadles) took care of dividing these days among the needy students so that they could study without having to worry about food. For sleeping, these *talmidim* (students) made do with the benches of the *beit-midrash* (study hall) where they studied or the women's section of the local synagogue, which was otherwise unused over the course of the week. This basic maintenance, donated by householders of limited means due to the importance they saw in Torah learning and their desire to have a part in it, at least in its material aspect, made it possible for the talmidim to dedicate themselves to their studies in the yeshiva far away from their homes and grow into scholars and eventually even into rabbis.

This picture of Torah study in the Grand Duchy of Lithuania changed at the end of the eighteenth century. The change occurred probably due to the great geopolitical shifts that took place in Eastern Europe. The Polish-Lithuanian Commonwealth was beset by crisis at the time; its stronger neighbors took advantage of its precarious situation and decided to take it over and divide its lands. The eastern territories were taken over by Catherine II (1729–1796), the Russian Tsarina, for her empire. These areas were defined as the Pale of Settlement, and only there were local Jews allowed to continue to reside. Among these were the over two hundred thousand Jews who had lived in the former Grand Duchy of Lithuania. The damage to the economy that accompanied this change of rulers harmed the ability of the Jews to continue to support and maintain the yeshiva students. This can explain the picture described by Rabbi Yosef of Krinik in the beginning of the nineteenth century, in which no active yeshivas were extant.[7]

It pained rabbis to see the dire condition of Torah study in Lithuanian Jewish society. One who acted to ameliorate this was Rabbi Ḥayim of

Volozhin, the disciple of the Gaon of Vilna. Rabbi Ḥayim served as town rabbi in Volozhin, which after the partitions of the Polish-Lithuanian Commonwealth was located in Vilna Province in the western part of the Russian Empire. There he established a yeshiva in 1802 and developed for it an economic model that was different from that which was customary in the "community yeshivas" of the eighteenth century. In his desire to avoid being dependent on the leaders of his small community, he set up the support of the yeshiva based on the contributions of Jews outside Volozhin. To that end, he appointed emissaries who went out to Jewish communities throughout the Pale of Settlement and the newly shrunken borders of Poland and collected funds for his yeshiva. In this way, Rabbi Ḥayim established a new and innovative model for the Torah-study institution—the model of the supracommunity yeshiva. This transformation significantly deviated from a mere economic-structural change. The community, which up until that time had exercised total control over the yeshiva that was located in its town, became substantially dependent upon the supracommunity yeshiva, which provided a livelihood to many of the town's inhabitants through students either renting rooms, buying food, or ordering daily meals from them. This highly significant change had an influence on the image of the yeshiva student as well. Instead of the image of the community yeshiva student who was in need of the kindness of the town's householders, a new image arose of the scholarly *baḥur* (young man) who enjoyed the economic backing of the yeshiva and was no longer dependent on the local community. This young man had self-respect and could voice his opinions in the town without fear of this harming his economic support. The status of the yeshiva head, the *rosh-yeshiva*, also underwent transformation. His concern for his yeshiva and its reputation brought him renown as well, and this even caused the Jewish public to expect his involvement in the burning issues of the day. From the position of a rosh-yeshiva dependent upon his community, he was raised to that of a communal leader thanks to the supracommunity yeshiva.

The establishment of the Volozhin Yeshiva and the relative recovery that took place after the far-reaching geopolitical changes occurred encouraged the establishment of additional yeshivas in the cultural space of Lithuanian Jewry. Most of these were community yeshivas, among them a yeshiva in Mir, Minsk Province, that later on would become supracommunity. The studies in most of these yeshivas followed a uniform pattern. The year was divided into a winter semester that stretched from the beginning of the month of Ḥeshvan (October–November) until Nisan (March–April) and a summer term from the beginning of Iyar (April–May) until the ninth of Av (July–August). Every weekday, studies were held during two *sedarim* (sessions), morning and afternoon, when the talmidim would independently delve into a common Talmudic tractate. There were also those who would study an additional tractate of their own when they had the time. Those who were especially *matmidim* (diligent) were accustomed to hold a third study session in the evening after dinner until late at night. Besides their independent study, the talmidim would hear a weekly, or even daily, lecture from the rosh-yeshiva; each yeshiva operated in its own fashion. Many of the yeshivas began to concentrate on abstract, theoretical Talmudic scholarship—*Torah liShma* (Torah for its own sake)—without any orientation toward rendering legal decisions or professional preparation for the rabbinate.[8]

Parallel to these yeshivas, there was a common phenomenon that took place in the batei-midrash of Lithuanian towns: study outside an institutional framework. Like those baḥurim who left their homes for the yeshivas, there were those who preferred to study without a rosh-yeshiva or constant supervision; in their wanderings they would take a seat in a beit-midrash in some town and begin to study a Talmudic subject on their own. They received their sustenance from local residents who volunteered to provide them with food and drink. If several other out-of-town baḥurim gathered in the beit-midrash, the gaba'im would take care of regularly supplying them with meals. Groups like this were called study *kibbutzim*—study groups. These were, in practice, a noninstitutional parallel to community yeshivas because they usually lacked a set daily schedule, a defined curriculum, and a formal Talmud instructor.[9]

By the middle of the nineteenth century, in the renewed Torah world there already were institutions of various types that were intended for young men with advanced Talmudic knowledge: town and city community yeshivas, a few private yeshivas, the supracommunity yeshivas in Volozhin and Mir, and many study kibbutzim. This gathering of talented and ambitious young men to study Torah was an accepted phenomenon at that time and a recognizable sign of the love and appreciation for Torah scholarship by the Jewish Lithuanian masses, attested to by the fact that these towns' Jews supported the young scholars in a decent fashion. This widespread phenomenon of learning brought renown to the Lithuanian cultural space and strengthened the image of Lithuanian Jewry as a particularly scholarly Jewish community.[10]

From the 1840s, cultural, social, and economic changes began to take place among the Jews of Eastern Europe that resulted chiefly from the governmental reforms of the Russian Empire. Modernization slowly spread into the cities and even into the small towns of the Pale of Settlement. Practical ambitions of shortening service in the Russian army or of making a decent livelihood began to find their place among the traditionally observant, who were the vast majority of the Jews in the Pale of Settlement, and their sons turned to the pursuit of non-Torah studies. New priorities were being accepted in Jewish society, and these weakened the elevated status of those young men who clung to classical Talmudic scholarship and even diminished the demand for the exceptional scholars among them. The spreading *Haskalah* (Enlightenment) movement influenced the concentrations of Torah students as well. Those effects were especially felt in the study kibbutzim, which were noninstitutional in nature; their presence diminished, and few remained by the end of that century.[11] The yeshivas also experienced change. The diminution of their previous glory brought increasing economic difficulty on the part of the communities to support them. Consequently, some chose to imitate the supracommunity yeshivas of Volozhin and Mir. Indeed, toward the end of the nineteenth century, in addition to the community yeshivas, there were a number of supracommunity institutions.[12]

These rapid changes within Jewish society began to rouse rabbis and community activists in Eastern Europe. One of the individuals able to recognize the changes in Jewish society early on was Rabbi Yisrael Lipkin. Upon observing those trends, he decided to struggle against them by promoting traditional values that had been neglected in Jewish society in Eastern Europe. In the 1840s he began to form a new movement, the Musar movement, which made improving traits related to interpersonal relationships its supreme goal. He even developed an organized system of study aimed at achieving these goals. However, his demanding and unusual system was not appropriate for the wider community and did not succeed within it.[13]

Only years later did other rabbis and social activists in Eastern Europe come to the realization that a clear drift had already occurred in parts of Jewish society away from its traditional moorings, and they began to seek ways to reverse that tide. They soon saw that words and polemics directed toward the forces that were stirring up Jewish society were insufficient, and they realized that they needed to take practical steps to fundamentally change the situation. Their comprehension of the dangers that faced the very foundations of traditional society and the discussion about the proper ways to react to them created a new entity: Eastern European Orthodoxy. Orthodoxy quickly learned the modern methods of the new and threatening forces and even adopted some of them in its reactions to the processes of modernization and secularization. Among these reactions were organizing to establish political organizations, attempts at creating an independent press, and making modifications in Torah education.[14]

The attempts of Orthodoxy to find answers and solutions to the dynamic situation were often focused on the yeshivas. There was a reason for this: the talmidim were talented young men who had been trained to become spiritual leaders, and it was natural that they were the most sensitive to both internal and external influences and to the new trends. Indeed, within the yeshiva world there were attempts at various responses to this reality; the common denominator among them was the addition of new and atypical areas of learning to the traditional study of Talmud. Rabbi Yitzḥak-Ya'akov Reines chose to add basic secular studies to the curriculum of the yeshiva he established in 1882 in Sventchian, Vilna Province, where he served as rabbi. By this he aspired to prepare his students to serve as community rabbis and at the same time be eligible to be government-appointed rabbis who could present the needs of their communities before the authorities in the Russian language. In contrast, at the same exact time, several talmidim of Rabbi Yisrael Lipkin and their students decided to add elements of their rabbi's Musar system, which had been unsuccessful up until that point, to the curriculum of the yeshivas they had established in the early 1880s. The declared purpose of this addition to the daily study schedule of these Musar yeshivas was to improve the character of their students and educate them in "fear of Heaven," but it was also unconsciously directed at training them to concentrate on their own inner lives rather than seeking to "save" the outside world through foreign ideologies.

These innovative responses were considered unusual in their time and unacceptable to the majority of Orthodox leaders, but the very fact that they were raised and provoked internal arguments shows that Orthodoxy regarded the yeshivas as one of the principal arenas for winning the struggle with modernity and secularization.[15]

The great changes rocking Tsarist Russia were intensified in the late nineteenth and early twentieth centuries. The power of the radical Russian socialist movements grew in those years, and their revolutionary influence was felt keenly in the Jewish street. This influence was joined by that of new movements within Jewish society: the Bund, which gained adherents among the proletarian Jewish youth who hoped for a change in their condition and status, and Zionism, which began to awaken submerged national hopes in the Jewish public. The influence of these avant-garde movements grew as the winds of rebellion that buffeted the Tsarist Russian Empire strengthened, reaching its peak with the 1905 revolution. At the same time that Russian society seethed with rebellion, Jewish communities were in internal turmoil as well, and many of their young people were drawn into the fracas by the significant movements of the time. The yeshivas were located in the midst of this dynamic arena of events and naturally were influenced by them. The burning winds from the outside blew in through the yeshiva walls.[16] In an attempt to prevent talmidim from deviating from the yeshiva's path and spirit, the supervisors of the yeshivas tried to search for non-Torah literature among their belongings and occasionally caught students in their disgrace. But quite a few talmidim were undeterred; they crossed the line and were drawn into the radical movements. There were yeshivas that could not bear the pressure and dissolved.[17]

The solution chosen by some roshei-yeshiva to save their Torah-study institutions from collapse during the tempestuous revolt of 1905 was to imitate to a degree the Musar yeshivas, that is, moderate integration of Musar studies in the yeshiva curriculum. In this framework, students independently studied the classic Musar works for half an hour each day, and Musar talks were given by the Musar-mashgiḥim (Musar supervisors), a new position in those yeshivas. This solution on the part of the yeshiva heads was surprising because only a few years previously, the establishment of Musar yeshivas was the source of a great and bitter controversy among Lithuanian rabbis. However, the dire situation of the yeshivas demanded a radical solution from their heads, and they regarded the integration of Musar studies into their institutions to be such a solution. In spite of the difficulty of implementation, Musar study began to show signs of success as it strengthened the yeshivas from within. At the same time, the trend of the diminishment of the yeshivas subsided as reactionary policies appeared in Russia when the authorities sought to rid the streets of revolution. These influences from within and from without were effective in quieting the stormy winds that buffeted the yeshivas and in bringing about the gradual return to regular studies.

The beginning of the second decade of the twentieth century was marked by the stabilization of the Lithuanian yeshivas as they underwent processes of renewal and flourishing. This stabilization also brought about the crystallization of their characteristics: in the sphere of study, besides theoretical Talmud learning, an element of Musar was added in many of them, and the presence of a Musar supervisor was well accepted. In terms of their organizational structure, a significant number were now supracommunity institutions, alongside the traditional community yeshivas. In order to maintain these supracommunity institutions, it was necessary for their heads to go out on fundraising journeys. Because the roshei-yeshiva were recognized personalities among the Jewish public, each of their visits in important communities and large cities not only increased the donations to their yeshivas but also added to their reputation among both adults and the younger potential students.[18]

In those last years before the First World War, the Lithuanian Torah-study institutions numbered more than thirty yeshivas for mature students. Most of them were located in the "Lithuanian" provinces of Kovna, Vilna, Grodno, Minsk, and Mohilev in the Pale of Settlement, and some were in the neighboring areas of the northeastern provinces of Poland, Suvalk and Lomzhe, where a significant Lithuanian Jewish population lived. Only a few yeshivas of the Lithuanian style were located outside the culture space of Lithuanian Jewry, either within central Poland or in the Ukrainian Vohlin Province in the Pale of Settlement. Map I.1 shows the locations of the Lithuanian Torah-study institutions in those years. A conservative estimate puts the number of students in a third of the yeshivas as two hundred or more in each. Indeed, some of them rejected

MAP I.1.

Deployment of the Lithuanian yeshivas prior to the First World War.

students due to a lack of space, and quite a few were forced to expand their facilities because of the congestion in their existing buildings. There is no reliable statistical data on most of these Lithuanian yeshivas, but a careful count yields a student population of some five thousand in all of them combined. This figure is moderate, but because most of the yeshivas were located in small or fair-sized towns, the material and spiritual impact that hundreds of students made on their surroundings was disproportionate to their number.[19]

This quasi-idyllic picture of the Lithuanian yeshivas changed unrecognizably with the outbreak of the First World War on August 1, 1914. This time they were faced with a crisis unparalleled in the entire century of the existence of the modern yeshiva world. Immediately at the start of the state of emergency at the war's outbreak, many students left to join their families or escape conscription by the Russian army. The size of these yeshivas was significantly reduced, and their economic situation worsened. Before long, about one-third closed their doors, most of them small community yeshivas that were expected to be closed and dissolved in times of trouble, but also a few more significant institutions where dozens of talmidim studied did not succeed in surviving.[20]

Following the early Russian military successes, relative calm returned to the yeshivas that remained, and the talmidim renewed their studies. However, this was for but a short time; by the end of winter and the beginning of the spring of 1915, the Russian front collapsed. The tsar's army began to retreat, and the Jews living near the front were falsely accused of collaboration with the German enemy. In punishment, in May 1915 approximately two hundred thousand Jews were expelled from the provinces of Kovna, Courland, and Grodno; among those expelled were yeshiva students, as well as roshei-yeshiva who went into exile with their families and closest students.[21]

The progress of the German army eastward and the occupation of the capitals of Grodno, Kovna, and Vilna Provinces in August–September 1915 spurred a hasty Russian retreat. Tens of thousands of Jews abandoned their homes in fear.[22] After a long and exhausting period of wandering, they were able to rest either in the regions of White Russia, Ukrainian provinces, or the New Russian provinces in the south of the Pale of Settlement, or the interior regions of Russia (which was forced to open its gates to the masses of exiles). In the prevailing panic, several yeshivas preferred flight rather than remaining in their places. This exodus was different from the first wave of expulsion because it was by choice on the part of the yeshiva heads and not forced upon them by the authorities. The yeshiva administrators chose to set off for unknown destinations throughout anti-Semitic Russia, where it was questionable whether they would be able to maintain their yeshivas. This was because of their fear of the new and unfamiliar authorities and their desire not to be separated from the significant sources of funding in Russia.[23]

Another wave of movement of the yeshivas from their place, apparently the most severe one, occurred in summer 1916 after the front warmed up following the counterattack of Russia, which came to aid her allies in the west. This time, not only yeshivas that had been exiled for the first time but also those that had already experienced migration to the provinces of White Russia in previous waves left these temporary locations.[24]

Examination of the migrations in the yeshiva world shows that from the beginning of the war, eleven yeshivas were uprooted and went into

MAP I.2.

Migration of Lithuanian yeshivas during the First World War.

exile; in some cases they even migrated from place to place. By the end of 1916, most had already settled in Ukrainian and New Russian provinces. Map I.2 shows the wandering, migratory paths that the yeshivas took. This phenomenon of the migration of educational institutions in times of trouble was unique, especially considering that these were institutions that lacked income, and their migration to new and unknown places was economically unpromising. Moreover, the heads of these exiled yeshivas could have received comfortable rabbinical positions in the towns where they had settled in Russia, sparing themselves the trials and tribulations of maintaining their yeshivas in times of war and shortages. In their commitment to the commandment to study Torah, independent of time and place, and in their view that teaching Torah to their students was the very essence of their lives, several roshei-yeshiva chose to continue to bear the heavy economic and administrational burden of their schools. Likewise, the unique phenomenon of talmidim who left their families under difficult conditions of exile and made great efforts to join their rabbis and their yeshivas is especially noteworthy. This can be attributed only to the fact that yeshiva study among their friends was a significant part of their very existence, and they saw the yeshiva as their natural habitat, whether in times of peace and calm or in trouble, war, and hunger.[25]

In their exile, the Jewish refugees faced two opposing trials. They were exposed to new and previously unknown worlds of Russian and Ukrainian culture, and they were even drawn into the vortex of democracy and freedom after the fall of the tsar in March 1917.[26] Soon afterward, from the time that the Red Bolsheviks took power in November 1917 and the outbreak of the civil war between them and their White opponents, they experienced the more familiar occurrences of degradation and attacks: harsh spiritual oppression by the Bolshevik authorities—and pogroms from their opponents. In 1919, these sporadic attacks on communities even turned into mass murder and total extermination in Ukraine. The Lithuanian yeshivas were part of this experience, and the unique historic events made their mark upon them as well. In that troubled period, about half of the migrant yeshivas permanently closed. Those yeshivas that survived the dreadful years were successful in preserving their character as institutions in the most difficult environmental and economic conditions.[27]

After the war, while the Eastern European countries still continued in their conflicts, the surviving yeshivas returned to their original locations—sometimes at a risk to the lives of their students—to areas that were no longer under Russian control, in the young and independent states of Lithuania and Poland. Similar to when these yeshivas went into exile, when they returned and settled in their places, they demonstrated solidarity in a manner that was incomparable to any other educational institutions. The dominant characteristic of this solidarity was the value of Torah study in every situation and under all conditions. When they began to function anew in the new recently established states, they were not alone. Alongside them were six veteran yeshivas that had not been forced to leave their places and remained there under the German occupational forces, two new yeshivas that had been established during the war itself, and two yeshivas that had been originally set up in White Russian and Ukrainian provinces but had fled to Poland when the Bolsheviks took over their towns.[28] The common factor among all these yeshivas—those that had migrated and those that remained in situ—was the harsh suffering and shortages that each had experienced during the war. This unique formative period of the First World War strengthened the yeshivas and their students and prepared them for the complex economic and social conditions that would prevail after the war. Indeed, some of these yeshivas became the supporting pillar of the renewed yeshiva world, the topic of this book.[29]

At first glance, it would seem that no change took place in the yeshivas' image in their locations in Lithuania and Poland during the interwar period in comparison with their image in the period before the First World War. Seemingly, there was no specific reason for any changes at all because these yeshivas hardly ceased their activities during the war, and therefore study went on continuously from the years before the war to the period starting after it. Indeed, all the yeshivas continued to learn the Talmudic tractates of a more theoretical nature without significantly increasing the study of *halachic* rulings, and most of them added an element of Musar teachings to their curriculum. Nevertheless, the yeshivas were obliged to undergo substantial changes due to their changed surroundings. They were no longer the only Jewish elitist intellectual institutions as they had been before the war. The countries of Lithuania and Poland gave their Jewish citizens cultural autonomy and made it possible for them to establish their own institutions of learning with government support. The Jews of Lithuania and Poland took advantage of this privilege and established expansive educational networks. Young Jews, who besides academic or professional training wanted a homelike feeling in their schools, could find this in one of the new Jewish educational frameworks rather than only in a yeshiva. This competition over the heart of the young Jew forced the yeshivas to adapt to the new reality. As previously mentioned, they did not revamp their program of study or introduce new and attractive subjects in their curriculum, but they did change their archaic pedagogical and organizational framework, where adults in their twenties studied with young boys. They divided the yeshiva institution into a *yeshiva-ketana* for beginning students aged twelve to sixteen and a *yeshiva-gedola* for adult students aged seventeen and older, who could study Talmudic subjects independently and did not require continuous direction by the rosh-yeshiva.

This new organizational framework, which was practically equivalent to the accepted division by age in the general educational system, where students studied in gymnasia or universities, was meant to be more attractive to talented young people who had completed elementary school and stood at the crossroad of deciding their future. Naturally, there were those who were the sons of religious functionaries and who wished to continue along the path that their fathers had chosen. However, among the youth joining the yeshiva world were also those who did so for economic reasons. At the same time that studies in the Jewish gymnasia received nearly no support from the authorities and consequently required high tuition fees, studying in the yeshivas was possible at no cost; moreover, the yeshivas funded, to the best of their ability, room and board for their talmidim. These conditions were likely to convince traditional parents from the lower middle socioeconomic class—and this group became larger owing to the worsening economic situation in Eastern Europe—to choose the yeshiva as place to continue the education of their gifted sons in the desire to provide them with a good reputation and a better future. The alternative, which was less promising from their standpoint, was work for the lads as artisan's apprentices or as simple workmen. In contrast, the number of young men from the higher socioeconomic classes in the yeshivas was small, because many of the members of these classes found their needs met in the Jewish gymnasia, and some even went on to study in universities.

The possibility of choice between different educational streams pushed aside the matter of reading Enlightenment and secular books, which was present in the yeshivas from the nineteenth century until the First World War. The persecution and detective work to find this type of literature in the students' rooms almost completely ceased, and there were even yeshivas where reading newspapers in public was permitted. In contrast, the influence of Musar supervisors in the yeshivas grew. This position had already existed in yeshivas before the First World War, but at that time the Musar-mashgiaḥ was received by the talmidim with suspicion, and many tried to avoid meeting him face-to-face.[30] In the interwar period, his position underwent a significant change, and in many instances he became the leading figure in the yeshiva. The talmidim waited for his pronouncements, participated in his Musar talks, and were influenced by them. Besides delving deeply into character improvement, the mashgiaḥ spoke about the role of the yeshiva student when he left the confines of his yeshiva and his goals in life. These talks were instrumental in strengthening the desire of the talmidim to continue their yeshiva studies and also their desire to cleave to the path of Torah and the fear of God, even after they completed their studies and started a family. The yeshiva in the period between the wars was therefore not only an institution of learning but also one of ideological education, which set as its goal producing graduates who were both scholars and religious personalities who would be guided by Torah throughout their lives.

Like other educational institutions, the yeshivas were in need of economic support to continue to exist. The proliferation of students of little means in the yeshivas required large monthly expenditures for their maintenance.[31] Because no tuition was paid, the yeshivas lacked income, and they were obliged to turn to the Jewish community to raise the necessary funds. When the economic condition of Eastern European Jewry worsened, the hope of the yeshivas was directed at fundraising overseas.

The difficult financial situation of the yeshivas prevented them at times from accepting new students, and at the end of the 1920s, most closed their doors to new talmidim because they were unable to support them. Only long fundraising campaigns on the part of their roshei-yeshiva in the centers of Orthodox Jewry overseas saved their institutions from heavy deficits and made it possible for regular study to continue. Indeed, for most of the interwar years, the yeshivas suffered from severe economic difficulties, and this situation expressed itself in meager financial support for the talmidim and even poor food in yeshivas that provided common meals in their dining rooms. However, these difficulties did not cause significant numbers of talmidim to abandon their yeshivas. The students continued to show solidarity and go in the path that the yeshiva had determined for them, without undue attention to the distressing material conditions.[32]

A clear expression of this solidarity among the talmidim under the difficult material conditions can be seen in the fact that the yeshivas were full. In the second half of the 1930s, there were thirty Lithuanian yeshivas in Poland, with the majority in the eastern frontier region, Kresy, and four yeshivas in Lithuania and two in Latvia. In all of them put together were more than four thousand talmidim, most of them from the age of eighteen and older, with some even in their late twenties. In not a few yeshivas, entirely new groups of students stood out—groups that were unknown in the time prior to the First World War. Before the war, most talmidim came from the cultural space of Lithuanian Jewry, a minority came from Poland, and even a few came from the Russian interior or neighboring Germany. In the years after the First World War, many students from Russia and Ukraine, who had studied in the yeshivas when those were in exile during the war and joined them when they returned to their original locations after the war, stood out. In addition to these talmidim, new groups of students from central European countries, especially from Germany, and even from the United States, began to study in the yeshivas. The desire of these Western students was to receive rabbinical ordination, a sort of degree, which was meant to promise them rabbinical positions in their countries. They absorbed classical yeshiva education in the yeshivas and shared their broad general knowledge with the local talmidim, many of whom came from provincial towns. The appearance of these young men, many of whom were graduates of gymnasia or even universities, added to the renown of the yeshivas and to their attractiveness in the eyes of local young people.

Significant changes also took place in the geopolitical deployment of the yeshivas in relation to the years before the First World War. Yeshivas that had been under the rule of the Russian Empire were in the independent states of Poland and the Baltic countries in the interwar period, whereas those that had remained in Russia and Ukraine after the war were closed. In Poland itself, changes took place as well, and a number of Lithuanian yeshivas now appeared in Hasidic areas such as Vohlin and the Kongresówka. Nevertheless, most of the Lithuanian yeshivas in Poland were concentrated in the Lithuanian areas in Kresy, and a new type of yeshiva was even established there: Hasidic yeshivas in the Lithuanian pattern.[33]

When the Second World War broke out, Poland was divided by the Ribbentrop-Molotov Pact between Nazi Germany and the Soviet Union. The Kresy region was supposed to fall under control of the Russians. They fulfilled their part in the pact within three weeks of the war's outbreak. Soon afterward, they signed a mutual-assistance treaty with Lithuania and committed to cede Vilna and its surroundings, which had been just taken from the Poles, to Lithuania. Once more an emergency situation arose, and similar to the period of the previous war, the yeshivas were required to reconsider their future plans. Many of those that were located in Soviet-occupied eastern Poland made the same decision: to leave. Similar to the First World War, but this time in a more organized fashion, these yeshivas fled with their heads and most of their students. They migrated toward Vilna, which was still in the area under Soviet occupation. Students who delayed due to visiting their homes decided to leave their families behind in Poland; though they felt they would never see them again, they set off on their journey as well. They risked stealing over the border in the extreme, record-breaking cold, and they joined their teachers and fellow students in Vilna after it had been ceded to Lithuania.

The yeshiva students did not make their way to Vilna alone. About fourteen thousand Jewish refugees from Poland moved on those same roads and gathered in that city. Nevertheless, two organized groups stood out among them: members of the youth movements and yeshiva students. The common elements shared by these two groups were the youth of their members and their lack of familial obligations. Among the approximately 3,300 baḥurim who studied in Lithuanian yeshivas in Poland at the end of the 1930s, more than two thousand reached Vilna during the war, along with their rabbis' families. In this way, eighteen Lithuanian yeshivas moved to Vilna.[34] The rare phenomenon of educational institutions migrating in times of trouble and their relocation from place to place occurred anew. Once again, solidarity and determination were shown by the yeshiva baḥurim.

In Vilna, and afterward in Lithuanian towns, these migrating yeshivas continued to operate as independent institutions alongside of the local yeshivas. Following the Soviet domination of Lithuania on June 15, 1940, most of the yeshivas with large student populations (either local or migrant) were forced to divide up into small groups and scatter to tiny towns. However, this did not succeed in breaking the spirit of most of the yeshiva students. They remained at their posts and persevered in their studies under the difficult conditions, until the time of deportation of some Polish refugees to Siberia and the annihilation of all the others soon after the German invasion of Lithuania.

This yeshiva world, which had been wiped out in Eastern Europe just few generations ago, had its own traditions, myths, legends, and fragments of stories, and the survivors passed them down to the next generation and sometimes put them in writing. Even if we accept these as historically accurate, they can present only a partial picture of the history of the yeshivas; they are insufficient in showing us the entire story or to explain the Lithuanian yeshivas' uniqueness. Surprisingly, the impressive regeneration of the Lithuanian yeshiva world in our time and its exemplary strength have not awakened or encouraged critical academic research regarding the history of even one of the yeshivas in Eastern Europe in the period between the two world wars, nor even one scholarly biography of one of their heads. These were not anonymous figures at all. They were individuals known in Orthodox circles all over the Jewish world whose lessons or Musar talks are studied in yeshivas to this day. Among the best known are roshei-yeshiva Shim'on Shkop, Naftali Trop, Baruch-Ber Leibowitz, and spiritual supervisors Notte-Hirsch Finkel and Yeruḥam Levovitz. Even if one attempts to interpret the overlooking of these personalities by researchers as due to the fact that for most of the year they were hidden in their own little world and their activities were limited to within the walls of the yeshiva, one will be surprised to see that so far, no scholars have researched even the world-renowned leaders of the Lithuanian yeshivas in Poland in the interwar period: Rabbis Ḥayim-Ozer Grodzensky and Yisrael-Meir HaCohen, known as the Ḥafetz-Ḥayim. Their involvement in Jewish public activity transcended the borders of Poland, and their influence even reached the Land of Israel and the United States. They definitely deserve multifaceted and in-depth study.[35]

As a result, this field is open to anthologies that are far from exhaustive and critical research. The unreasonable situation, in which nice stories have often overcome historical truth and anecdotes are stronger than facts, has created an unbalanced picture of the figures and events described, and it has inserted into the character of the interwar yeshiva world a number of anachronistic images that have nothing in common with reality. For example, one has become used to reading in such works that hundreds of students attended each of the yeshivas at the same time, and one has a mental picture of crowded study halls filled to the limit. As a rule, this picture fits only the later years of the period between the wars. In contrast, it is difficult to believe that in Volozhin, "mother of the Lithuanian supracommunity yeshivas," for most of that time there were not more than fifty-five students!

This book attempts to correct mistaken impressions and portray a more balanced picture, based on historical facts. It presents a lateral view of the world of Lithuanian yeshivas in its historical, organizational, economic, educational, social, and statistical aspects from the years after the First World War until the time of its destruction two decades later. This presentation is based on individual research of the history of each of the Lithuanian yeshivas in Eastern Europe. Knowledge of what was static and dynamic in their existence allows, on one hand, examination of the common processes they underwent from each of the aforementioned aspects, and on the other, identification of that which was unique to each one. Due to the lack of space, this book cannot include monographs about each yeshiva; nevertheless, it reveals a small portion of the events that occurred within some yeshivas to give examples of lateral processes or to highlight exceptional phenomena.

It is not easy to decide which institutions should be included in the interwar world of Lithuanian yeshivas. Up until the First World War, the yeshivas were located in their natural environment, regions of Lithuanian Jewish settlement under direct Russian rule or in neighboring Polish provinces, with only a few located outside this area. They were homogeneous in nature; their heads were products of the same schools, and most of their students came from a common cultural milieu. After the war, a significant change took place. The majority of the yeshivas fell under Polish rule, and a minority were located in independent Lithuania.[36] There was a complete break between these two new states. Hence their yeshivas differed due to geographic and political factors, which had influence chiefly in the area of organization: the many Lithuanian yeshivas in Poland were organized under a central yeshiva council, whereas the few in Lithuania functioned on their own, without any umbrella organization. Even the incorporated yeshivas in Poland were divided into special subgroups, such as those that belonged to the Novardok network, yeshivas established in Vohlin among the Hasidic population, or yeshivas under the authority of Hasidic *rebbes* (*admorim*). Despite the obvious differences between these groups, their yeshivas had common identifying characteristics that undoubtedly define them as "Lithuanian yeshivas" and permit their inclusion in the yeshiva world upon which this study centers. The exceptions are Torah educational institutions that are not included in this volume:

- Yeshivot-ketanot: Extensive networks of yeshivas for younger students were established in Lithuania and Poland in the interwar period and were oriented at preparing their students to study in the yeshivot-gedolot. In addition to their larger number, the yeshivot-ketanot were distinguished by their geographical spread, administration, and economic support. A separate study is needed to research them. This volume will deal only with them insofar as their connection to the yeshivot-gedolot.
- Branches: During the period between the wars, a trend of institutional expansion began by virtue of the initiatives of talented yeshiva graduates who migrated to the West and wished to establish similar education in the places where they had settled and of the heads of yeshivas who chose to establish branches in the Land of Israel. These new Torah-study institutions that were outside the traditional habitat preserved to a great extent the character of the mother yeshivas, although environmental influences and unknown outside forces require special research that is not within the purview of this book.[37]
- *Kollelim*: These Torah educational institutions were meant for outstanding married graduates of the yeshiva world. The kollelim stood out to a degree during the latter years of the nineteenth and the early twentieth centuries as completely independent institutions, or ones that functioned alongside some of the more famous yeshivas. At the end of the First World War, a number of organizational changes were made in these institutions, and this deserves further exhaustive and separate research.

In addition to these related topics, this research was limited in reference to the yeshiva study program—the Talmudic approaches that several of the yeshiva heads delineated, and the types of Musar methods that distinguished the spiritual supervisors. This broad topic that has been barely researched up until now is worthy of separate studies. In this book, only outward expressions of these approaches and methods are mentioned when they have a direct connection to the material under study.

This book consists of three sections:

- The first section (chapters 1–2) traces the reestablishment of the yeshiva world after the First World War. The social and economic conditions in Lithuania and Poland, which had just received their independence, presented the yeshivas with complex challenges. Despite the difficulties that faced them, they succeeded in rehabilitating and establishing themselves, most of them in their original locations. As if not satisfied by that which already existed, the yeshiva world chose to expand to new areas, whether among the Hasidim of Poland or in the Land of Israel. Moreover, its methods were copied by Hasidic Lithuanian circles according to a format similar to that of the traditional Lithuanian yeshiva.
- The second section (chapters 3–6) offers an in-depth observation into the interwar yeshiva world from an economic, organizational, educational, and human standpoint. Even though each of these aspects presents an independent measure, often mutual influences can be found, and interdependency between them is evident. The proper examination of these aspects is therefore similar to observing different components of one common picture, and this is what created the special character of the yeshiva world in the decades between the two cataclysmic world wars.
- The third section (chapters 7–8) deals with the period beginning with the outbreak of the Second World War and ends with the start of the extermination of the Jews in Lithuania. In the course of this period, the yeshiva world experienced a very rapid succession of events. The occupation of Poland and the political changes led to the flight of most of the yeshivas from the former Polish territories to Vilna. Within a short time, they succeeded in reorganizing themselves in Lithuania, and after its Soviet takeover, they and their local counterparts continued their attempts at survival there while trying to leave

that country. The fate of most of these yeshivas was sealed for the worst with the beginning of Nazi German bombing over Lithuania.

The first version of this work, published in Hebrew by the academic publishing house of the Zalman Shazar Center in Jerusalem in 2014, encompassed the world of Lithuanian yeshivas in the years before the First World War until the outbreak of the Second World War. The events that occurred in the yeshivas in the war years 1939–1941 were not presented; thus the picture of the Lithuanian yeshiva world was incomplete because the link between the old yeshiva society and the yeshiva world that was miraculously rehabilitated before our very eyes in its new homes is missing. This book has filled the gap, and an entire section has been added that shows the fascinating transformations—amazing by any standard—that took place in the yeshivas from the beginning of the Second World War. The chapters in this section show the fate of that old yeshiva world, the greater part of which was cruelly liquidated by the Germans and Lithuanians; only a small fragment survived in order to continue the wondrous tradition of Torah study.

Throughout this work, the transliteration of Hebrew terms has been according to the Sephardic pronunciation commonly used in Israel and in academic circles elsewhere rather than the Ashkenazi pronunciation used in the yeshiva world described in this book and the Haredi world today (e.g., *beit-midrash* rather than *beis-medresh*). This was done as a matter of academic convention rather than an assertion that one is somehow more "correct" than the other. The spelling of names of geographic locations in Eastern Europe has been mostly according to the common local Jewish pronunciation of the time.[38]

I hope that the readers, whether members of the academic community, general readers, or those who feel a connection to the yeshiva world, will hear the authentic voice of the subjects of this book speak to them from its pages.

NOTES

1. Schmukler, *Toledot*, 33 (from Hebrew; the quotes in this book are translations from Hebrew, unless otherwise stated).

2. See *Tevuna* 4 (1941): 33–34; Stampfer, *Lithuanian*, 2–3, 27–28, 33–34; Etkes, *The Gaon*, 168–71, 202–6; Zalkin, "Ir," 135, 138–42.

3. Stone, *The Polish-Lithuanian State*, 62–63; Samsonowicz, "Polish Politics," 53; Bideleux and Jeffries, *A History*, 122, 126. Regarding the time of the establishment of the council, even before the Union of Lublin, see Haylperin, "Reshito," 55, 57. On the tasks of the council, see Spector, "Va'ad," 127–35.

4. Kloizner, "Toledot," 38–40, 46, 55–57; Dubnov, *Pinkas*, 126.

5. For example, Slouschz, "Toledot," 40; Trunk, *Poiln*, 129–30.

6. *Pirkei Avot* 4:14.

7. Zalkin, "Ir," 135, 139; Pipes, "Catherine," 17–18; Scott, *The Emergence*, 181–82. See also Murphy, *From Citizens*, 23, 127, 147, 152, 231. For the number of the Grand Duchy Jews in the 1764 census, see Mahler, *Toledot*, 231–33.

8. Etkes, *The Gaon*, 211–15; Stampfer, *Lithuanian*, 34–36, 45–47.

9. Stampfer, *Families*, 216–18; Zalkin, "Ir," 142–44.

10. Deinard, *Zichronot*, 34–37, 39.

11. E.g., Hurwitz, *Zichronot*, 36–41. See Stampfer, *Lithuanian*, 5–6; Slutsky, *HaItonut… haTesha-Esreh*, 26; Mazeh, *Zichronot*, 53–55.

12. For example, the yeshivas Knesset-Yisrael of Slabodka (Tikochinski, *Lamdanut*, 23–24, 59), Zvhil (Leoni, *Korets*, 277), and Radin (Poupko, *Michtavei*, 34, 52).

13. Etkes, *Rabbi Israel*, 135–52, 174. Rabbi Lipkin was often known by the sobriquet "Salanter" because he settled and studied in Salant, Kovna Province.

14. Bacon, *The Politics*, 22–32; Stampfer, *Lithuanian*, 8–9, 333–34; Salmon, *Do Not Provoke*, 85–97, 281–306; Salmon, "Reshit"; Klibansky, "Lama," 20–40. See also Samet, *HeḤadash*, 33–44; Etkes, *Rabbi Israel*, 193–94, 261–68; Zalkin, "Ortodoxei."

15. Klibansky, *KeTzur*, 47, 51, 66; Salmon, "Reshit," 164–65. Rabbi Reines was forced to close his yeshiva two years later. Moreover, the relative success enjoyed by the Musar movement in the yeshiva world was the subject of sharp debate among the rabbis in the Lithuanian cultural space in 1897; it focused upon the issue of whether it was proper to integrate a new area of study alongside traditional Talmud study, however important it may be. Regarding this Musar controversy, see Katz, *Pulmus*, and briefly in chapter 4, near note 3.

16. For example, Assaf, "Shenot," 42; Shulman, "HaRuaḥ," 135. Cf. *HaNe'eman* 2 (1928–1929): 3–5. See Frankel, *Crisis*, 58–62; Ascher, "Interpreting 1905," 27–28; Ettinger, *Bein Polin*, 324.

17. For example, Shulman, "HaRuaḥ," 144, 147; Unterman, "Torah," 13. Cf. Nissenboim, *Alei Ḥeldi*, 45, regarding the yeshivas in the nineteenth century.

18. See Slutsky, *HaItonut… haEsrim*, 240. Examples of supracommunity yeshivas that were established in the first decade of the twentieth century can be found in the towns of Shadeve (Baksht, *Lev*, 13), Lida (Salmon, *Do Not Provoke*, 300–301), and Stutchin (Ḥasman, *HaOr*, "From His Biography"). Cf. Zalkin, "Ir," 159–60.

19. Klibansky, *KeTzur*, 73. For yeshivas that expanded their facilities, see, e.g., Stutchin (Ḥasman, *HaOr*, "From His Biography"), Ponevezh (Rivkind, "Yeshivat," 2), Radin (Yoshor, *The Chafetz Chaim*, 347). The doubled number of talmidim in yeshivas that was accepted in the yeshiva world at the beginning of the twentieth century is stereotypical and exaggerated (see *Sinai* 91 [1982]: 173; Weinberg, "Die Jeschiwoth," 118; Helmreich, *The World*, 14).

20. Among the yeshivas that closed were Stutchin (Vilna Province), Shadeve (Kovna Province), and Braynsk (Grodno Province). For a list of all the yeshivas that were closed, compare table I (p. 74) to table II (p. 118) in Klibansky, *KeTzur*. Regarding the dire situation in the Slutsk Yeshiva, for example, see Meltzer, *BeDerech*, 108–9.

21. Among them the Ponevezh Yeshiva (Mark, *Gedolim*, 133). Approximately 120,000 of the expelled Jews were from Kovna Province (Zagranitchniy Komitet Bunda, *Doklad*, 39). A month earlier, Jews were also expelled from many towns of Suvalk Province, Poland. For the background and the reasons for the mass Jewish expulsion from the northwestern front, see, e.g., Lohr, "The Russian Army," 404–11.

22. Matthäus, "German *Judenpolitik*," 156. See Y., "Zichreines," 85–86, and Zolf, *Oyf Fremder Erd*, 161–62, about memoirs of Jewish flight.

23. Among them were, e.g., the yeshivas of Novardok (Nekritz, "Yeshivot," 255) and Lida (Poliachek, "Goral"). See Slutsky, "Diyunei," 43, 56, regarding the opening of the gates of the Russian interior to the Jewish exiles.

24. Among the "newer" yeshivas were Volozhin (Drushkovitz, *Sha'arei*, preface) and Mir (Epstein, "Yeshivat Mir," 98–99). Among the more veteran migrating institutions were, for example, Knesset-Yisrael of Slabodka (Katz, *Tenuat*, III, 73) and Radin (Zariz, "Yeshivat," 192).

25. For a summary of yeshiva moves, see Klibansky, *KeTzur*, 118, table 2. For a contemporary description of the feelings of a student who moved to the Lomzhe Yeshiva in the area under German occupation, see Yoshor, "Epilogue," 256.

26. See, e.g., Rozin, "HaYeshuv," 7; Altshuler, "HaNisayon," 75.

27. Altshuler, *HaYevsektsiya*, 295; Gershuni, *Yahadut beRussia*, 17, 23, 95; Committee, *The Pogroms*, 23, 70, 73, 98; Zuckerman, *Zichreines*, II, 171–73. Regarding the Red and White struggle, see, e.g., Kenez, *Civil War.*

28. Both Slutsk and Zvhil will be discussed later on. About the others, see Klibansky, *KeTzur*, 99–103, 105–9. Six migrant yeshivas survived the horrors of those difficult years, and one, Novardok, even went so far as to divide itself up into several respectable yeshivas.

29. Rabbi Notte-Hirsch Finkel, for example, considered the difficult conditions that his yeshiva, Knesset-Yisrael of Slabodka, underwent in Ukraine as a significant source of its strength (Oshri, "Yeshivat," 152). See also Berlin, *MeVolozin*, II, 166.

30. See Assaf, "Shenot," 43.

31. These expenditures were not limited to rent and food but included clothing and healthcare, and even fees for army exemptions.

32. As previously mentioned, many of the students came from lower middle-class families, and it was therefore likely that the conditions at home were no better than those in their yeshivas.

33. The term *Lithuanian yeshivas* here and later in this book refers to those that preserved the format of the yeshivas of the last decades of the nineteenth century centered in the cultural milieu of Lithuanian Jewry. It is possible to summarize this format as one that was unique in its educational aspect and in its emphasis on *Torah liShma*—Torah study for its own sake—without any formal studies of halachic rulings or professional training for a rabbinical career. The term *Lithuanian* referring to the interwar period is therefore a cultural marker rather than a geopolitical one. The term *Kongresówka* refers to the area within the pre–First World War borders of Poland, which Poles continued to call by this name even after the establishment of the Second Polish Republic. The term *Kresy* (or *Kresy Wschodnie*) refers to the eastern portion of the republic, east of the Curzon Line.

34. Apart from these, three Polish yeshivas or parts of yeshivas arrived at Vilna as well.

35. It is worthy to note the intention of Eitam Henkin to write a comprehensive critical biography of the Ḥafetz-Ḥayim. (This is the name of one of the volumes dealing with the biblical laws of slander and gossip, which Rabbi Yisrael-Meir HaCohen authored.) Alas,

his life was cruelly cut off before he was able to put his plan into action. A book dealing with the jurisprudence of Rabbi Shkop (Vozner, *Ḥashiva Mishpatit*) is not a critical biography of this *rosh-yeshiva*. A study of the Slabodka Yeshiva (Tikochinski, *Lamdanut*) deals with the history of this yeshiva in Lithuania up until 1925 and therefore cannot be considered its complete monograph.

36. In addition, two Lithuanian-type yeshivas were established in Latvia in the 1930s.

37. Regarding research on one of these branches, the Slabodka yeshiva in Hebron and Jerusalem, see Tikochinski, *Lamdanut*. Yeshivas based on the Lithuanian model that were established in Western Europe between the wars include Torat-Emet in Frankfurt and in London by Rabbi Moshe Schnaider, a graduate of Slabodka and Radin yeshivas, and Gateshead in England and Heide in Belgium by graduates of Radin Yeshiva David Dreyen and Rabbi Shraga-Faivel Shapiro, respectively. Yeshivas established in the United States include Ner-Yisrael in Baltimore by Rabbi Ya'akov-Yitzhak Ruderman, a graduate of Slabodka Yeshiva; Rabbeinu Yisrael-Meir HaCohen in Williamsburg, New York, by Rabbi David Leibowitz, a graduate of the Lomzhe, Radin, and Slabodka yeshivas.

38. The geographic locations that are mentioned in the text can be identified in the relevant maps throughout this work.

I

Consolidation and Expansion

The first section of this volume investigates the integration of the Lithuanian yeshivas into the new world that developed after First World War. At the very start of this period, they found a reality quite different from the one they knew before the war: the oppressive and discriminatory policies of the Russian Empire were no more, and instead the yeshivas functioned under the democratic rule of the young, independent states Lithuania and Poland, which granted equal rights to all their citizens.[1] Many of the Jewish inhabitants of these states even hoped to be granted national autonomy by the new regimes. In Lithuania, these hopes were realized in the first years of its existence. The autonomy in this country was based on the obligation of all Jews to affiliate with Jewish communities in the districts where they lived, as well as on the election of local community councils by democratic vote. These councils were given extensive authority to administer Jewish community matters including levying taxes, and their representatives selected a Supreme Council, which coordinated the complex autonomy system. Lithuanian Jewry was also granted a representative in the government, Max Soloveitchik (1883–1957), a minister without portfolio for Jewish affairs. He effectively stood at the head of the national autonomy and worked hard to establish the status of its institutions in the Lithuanian constitution, without great success. In Poland, the fate of autonomy was different, and the hopes of many Jews for its realization were very quickly met with disappointment. In the beginning of 1919, a presidential order established the authority of the Jewish communities in the Kongresówka to deal only with religious matters, and this order was gradually extended to additional regions in Poland. The other powers relating to Jewish affairs were given over to the Ministry of Religion and Public Education.[2]

The reluctant attitude of the Polish authorities toward the aspirations of their Jewish citizens became evident over the course of a few years in neighboring Lithuania as well. This hostile atmosphere was encouraged by the Christian-Democratic bloc that had a small majority in the Lithuanian *Seimas*. The bloc consistently harmed the position of the Jews and exerted a continuous economic stranglehold over them. In this situation, the national autonomy did not hold ground for long. In the beginning of 1924, the office of the Minister for Jewish Affairs was removed from the national government administration, and half a year later the state disbanded the plenary meeting of the Supreme Council. In March 1926 autonomy came to an end; the last of its symbols, the elected community councils, was annulled. About a year later, they were replaced by community councils for religious matters.[3]

Even so, the Jews of Lithuania and Poland could pride themselves with a significant achievement. They had attained cultural autonomy, which continued for the entire interwar period, despite the increasing difficulties heaped upon it by the authorities of these states. Parallel to opening all government educational institutions to Jewish youth, local and international Jewish organizations were permitted to establish there comprehensive educational networks: Orthodox in its various streams, Zionist, and Bundist-Yiddishist. These networks represented a broad ideological spectrum, which was a direct result of the accelerated processes of modernization and secularization among Eastern European Jewry. The yeshivas also played a part in this new cultural and educational fabric, however this time, unlike in the not-so-distant past, they were in an inferior position. Alongside the yeshivas, there were Jewish gymnasia that fulfilled the aspiration of young men to combine a homelike feeling with academic and professional training. In Poland, there were even religious Jewish gymnasia that provided their students with basic knowledge of the Talmud in addition to academic studies. In Lithuania, a gymnasium like this was established under the authorization of the government in Kovna in 1931. The senior yeshivas no longer served as the only Jewish educational frameworks, and among the modernized community, they had lost their status as elite intellectual institutions.[4]

This new reality, which increasingly solidified due to the dominance of a practical approach, was liable to marginalize the yeshivas and make them irrelevant as educational institutions. However, the heads of the yeshivas did not see it this way. They had succeeded in maintaining their yeshivas under very difficult conditions during the First World War through their belief in the absolute value of the Torah study, unlimited by time or place. The new social circumstances—problematic, from their vantage point—did not weaken their determination, especially because the new political and economic situation in Poland and Lithuania was incomparably more favorable in their view than the one that existed during the war. The heads of the yeshivas felt that they could succeed in their life's mission with the help of the older students, who had become strengthened as well through wartime conditions; preserve the study of Torah in the new atmosphere; and perhaps even serve as a barrier to the rapid process of secularization.

The yeshiva heads did not stand alone in the forefront of the struggle for the preservation of Torah study. Increasing politicization of Jewish life in Eastern Europe after the First World War also caused the traditional community in Lithuania and the Kresy districts of Poland to sharpen its positions, and large segments of that population identified with Orthodox political parties or organizations. In broad generalities, it can be stated that half of the Jewish populace still maintained strong ties to tradition, and this was clearly expressed in the elections to community councils that took place in Lithuania and the Polish Kresy districts. As previously mentioned, the representatives of the Jewish community councils in Lithuania elected a Supreme Council, and the party affiliation of its members was meant to reflect the results of the local community elections. At the end of the 1922 elections for this council, the Orthodox *Aḥdus* had 40 percent representation, and 10 percent went to *HaMizraḥi,* an Orthodox Zionist party. In the Polish Kresy, there was a similar configuration, and *Aḥdus,* an Orthodox faction of *Agudat-Yisrael* and HaMizraḥi members as well as nonmembers, garnered half of the votes in the community council elections of 1928. In addition, in several communities factions of Orthodox workers or merchants participated in the elections separately, and they also won positions in elected councils. This large traditional public that voted for the Orthodox factions provided support to the yeshivas and served as their social and economic infrastructure between the two world wars.[5]

In the new era, the distinction between the various streams of Jewish education became clearly delineated in the eyes of the public. Alongside academic studies under Zionist or Yiddishist auspices, and vocational studies created by the Yiddishists, the yeshiva stream was considered unique in terms of intensive religious studies. Its students were often the sons of religious functionaries, for whom studying in yeshiva seemed a natural continuation of the family tradition. Other students were talented young men from traditional homes who had been educated to prefer yeshiva scholarship over the practical studies offered in the gymnasia. But it was not only for ideological reasons that youngsters turned to the yeshivas. A lack of funds among many lower middle-class families prevented their sons from studying in the general Jewish educational institutions. The yeshivas served as a worthy substitute for their academic studies and for educational and social advancement without necessitating an investment of material resources.[6]

Despite all the economic, organizational, and social difficulties, the yeshivas quickly reintegrated into their natural habitat and functioned as they had before the war. However, to say that things returned to routine would unfairly diminish the image of the yeshiva world between the wars. A more careful examination would reveal a shift in its normal pattern of action, which could be considered a miniature revolution. The situation in Poland and Lithuania required a form of contraction of the yeshiva world and its seclusion behind protective walls. This background serves only to highlight the initiatives of individuals and organizations to establish new yeshivas after the First World War. Ostensibly it would be enough to mention the Novardok movement, which established senior yeshivas throughout Poland and set up an extensive system of preparatory yeshivas for younger students around them. However, others also did this and decided to operate in the Hasidic districts of Vohlin, which were empty of yeshivas. Moreover, even the Hasidim who lived in the cultural surroundings of Lithuanian Jewry established their own yeshivas, based on the traditional Lithuanian model in particular. In effect, parallel to the notion that the yeshiva world had become distant from the center of public attention and grown more secluded, a stirring sense of mission sprang up from within it toward new populations.[7]

The first section of this book will present the consolidation and expansion stages of the Lithuanian yeshivas' integration in the new Eastern European states in the interwar period. Sometimes these two stages overlapped in time, and while several yeshivas exerted efforts to settle and become established in their locations, others had already been active in new areas where the very existence of a Lithuanian yeshiva was unknown. To simplify these complex processes, the two stages will be schematically separated. The first chapter will present the consolidation of the yeshivas in their old-new surroundings against the background of the internal and external challenges they faced, examining their response to the complicated conditions that prevailed. The second chapter will focus upon the expansion of the yeshiva world and deal with the major trends in this surprising process.

NOTES

1. In actuality, equality did not prevail in all areas. See Garfunkel, "MeIgra," 31; Hartglass, "Milḥamot," 143.

2. Netzer, *Ma'avak*, 203–7; Gringauz, "Jewish," 225–46; Liekis, *A State*, 81–210. This ministry even took the place of the Religious Council of the Jewish Communities, which was supposed to be established by the presidential order mentioned but was never convened. On the Lithuanians' flexible attitude regarding the status of minorities in Lithuania after the collapse of Germany in the end of 1918, see Zilber, "HaHanhaga," 152–55. The first democratic elections there took place in the second half of 1919.

3. Gringauz, "Jewish," 237–40; *DIdS*, May 22, 1925, May 25, 1925, Jan. 21, 1926. See also *IdL*, Feb. 22, 1924.

4. Evron, *Ḥinuch*, 200–208; order of the Lithuanian Minister of Education (LCSA, 391/2/608; cf. Etzion, "HaZerem," 163); Teitelbaum, "Report"; Eisenstein, *Jewish Schools*; Cohen, "HaḤinuch." Unlike the Jewish gymnasia in Lithuania, which awarded their students with a government matriculation certificate, the Jewish gymnasia in Poland did not receive official authorization to do so; their graduates had permission to be tested by government examination boards (Levinson, *HaTenu'a*, 373; Lipetz, "HaḤinuch," 119).

5. Garfunkel, "HaMa'avak," 55; *DoV*, June 29, 1928, July 6, 1928, July 20, 1928.

6. Regarding the high cost of private gymnasia education, see, e.g., Langleben-Klibansky, *MiYarketei Tzafon*, 35.

7. These new populations were even in countries outside of Eastern Europe; see chapter 2.

1

The Renewal of the Yeshiva World

The First World War struck a heavy economic blow to the lives of the Jewish inhabitants in the northwestern provinces of the Russian Empire. The main victims were the residents of the Kovna Province, most of whom were expelled by the Russian authorities and forced to set out with nothing for an extended exile.[1] The Jews from nearby provinces, out of fear of the cruel retreating Russians and the approaching Germans, uprooted themselves and fled to Russian and Ukrainian territories, abandoning all their property and belongings in their flight. After the war, many of these exiles and refugees returned to their hometowns, forced to invest their efforts into rebuilding their homes, which had been destroyed or plundered, and reestablishing their businesses.[2] The fate of the Jews who did not have to migrate from their homes during the war was not much better. Those who came under German rule lost much of their property as a result of the heavy hand of German occupation. Others who remained under the Russian rule found themselves caught in the Bolshevik state at the end of the war, with no legal way to leave, and whoever decided to escape over the border would leave all their belongings behind.

The Lithuanian yeshivas were no exception, and their assets and properties were also severely harmed by the First World War. Immediately after the war, however, they began to act with vigor to rehabilitate themselves. These efforts in the early years after the war were not all of one cloth. A yeshiva that returned to its natural place and familiar surroundings experienced a process of acclimatization that was different from a yeshiva that was forced to find a new home among strangers, and the experience of a yeshiva that had been exiled and obliged to deal with the renovation of its destroyed building and creation of a support system after its return was not the same as a yeshiva that had retained its set location during the war and continued to function in as regular a fashion as possible under German or Russian rule. In this chapter, examples will be given of three models: yeshivas that returned from exile, yeshivas that remained in place during the war under German rule, and yeshivas whose original and natural premises came under the Bolshevik regime, forcing them to flee from its control.

YESHIVAS THAT RETURNED FROM EXILE

Eleven yeshivas were uprooted from their places in the First World War and went into exile or even into a series of exiles. In Russia and Ukraine, they experienced alternating periods of great want and openness and freedom of thought, as well as harsh treatment and riots. Only six yeshivas survived the horrors of the war, and one of them, Novardok, was able to succeed and subdivide into several impressive yeshivas. At the end of the war, the yeshivas were trapped within the Bolshevik state, which prevented the free movement of its inhabitants outside of its borders.

Many of the confined refugees/exiles hoped to return to their original homes. These aspirations made them a force for instability in the country and spurred the government to get rid of them. On June 30, 1920, Russia signed a repatriation agreement with Lithuania, which permitted the Lithuanian refugees to leave their exile. Like most of the Jewish returnees, the yeshivas made great efforts to return to their former places of residence. Before the war, they had worked hard to make their name and place known among donors from neighboring countries and overseas, and the continued sympathy and vital support of these donors were largely dependent on the preservation of the historical names and symbols of the institutions. Besides, the original buildings, which were considered significant financial assets, still remained and could allow for a convenient continuation of instruction as in the past. Above and beyond these practical considerations, the original locations seemed to the yeshivas to be optimal because they were now in new and liberal states and familiar environments. However, the reality of the situation in the early 1920s was less ideal than it seemed from afar.

Several of the returning yeshivas found Vilna to be a convenient initial gathering point on their way back from exile. What was so special about this city that it attracted yeshivas, even though it suffered frequent transitions between Polish and Russian rule in 1919–20? About two weeks after the signing of the aforementioned repatriation agreement, the Russians liberated Minsk and Vilna from Polish hands. During the same period, on July 12, 1920, Russia signed a peace treaty with Lithuania, according to which Vilna had to be turned over to the Lithuanians a month and a half later. This city thus became a convenient crossing point for the exiles on their way back to Lithuania. However, this ideal situation did not last long. The transfer of Vilna to Lithuania was openly displeasing to Poland, and on October 9, 1920, Polish forces headed by General Lucjan Żeligowski (1865–1947) invaded Vilna and seized it from the Lithuanians. In the end, Poland annexed Vilna and its district, despite the vigorous protests of Lithuania.[3]

These rapid transitions in government in 1920 Vilna were not random; they were a result of the ongoing war between Poland and Russia. In the first half of that year, the Poles were fighting the Russians on their eastern border, and even worked in tandem with local nationalists to successfully attack the Russians in Ukraine. The Russian Army responded with a mighty push into Poland. On its way, it conquered Minsk and Vilna (as noted previously) and succeeded in reaching Warsaw. Only a counteroffensive, known as "the miracle on the Vistula," prevented the annihilation of the young Polish state.[4] At that point, Poland opened with an unrestrained onslaught, which was halted by the onset of a ceasefire on October 12, 1920. The takeover of Vilna by Poland's General Żeligowski, only days before, was an unofficial part of this impressive counteroffensive. The struggle between the two countries ended on March 18, 1921, with the signing of a peace treaty that delineated the official border between them. This brought about the evacuation of Russian forces from border towns and extended Polish rule over them. Vilna would remain in Polish hands until 1939.

The military and political complications mentioned here posed significant difficulties for a number of yeshivas that returned from exile through Vilna—Knesset-Yisrael, Mir, and Knesset Beit-Yitzḥak.[5] The next section will explore the processes that were necessary for these yeshivas to reach their permanent settlement and the complicated situation that confronted them there. The differences in their respective return times and destinations caused each yeshiva to act in a unique manner and sealed a different fate for each in those daunting years.

The Knesset-Yisrael Yeshiva of Slabodka

The Slabodka Yeshiva was founded in 1882 by Rabbi Notte-Hirsch Finkel in the town of Slabodka near Kovna. He instituted the study of Musar there and thus made it unique among the Lithuanian yeshivas of the time. In 1893, he appointed two instructors of the Talmud in the yeshiva, Moshe-Mordechai Epstein and Isser-Zalman Meltzer, brothers-in-law who were graduates of the Volozhin Yeshiva. In 1897, Rabbi Meltzer was sent to establish a yeshiva in Slutsk in the Minsk Province and serve as its head. Rabbi Epstein remained the sole Talmud instructor in Slabodka. That year, a fierce argument broke out among the students of the yeshiva, and sixty or seventy young men who sided with the Musar approach of Rabbi Finkel were forced to leave and establish a new place of study in Slabodka. This school was reorganized along lines of a yeshiva and named Knesset-Yisrael, with Rabbis Finkel and Epstein at its helm. The number of students grew rapidly. In 1900, Rabbi Epstein became the actual head of the yeshiva, while Rabbi Finkel chose to remain behind the scenes and serve only as a Musar supervisor.[6]

When the First World War began, the Jews of Slabodka—where a battle-fortified fortress stood nearby, ready for combat with the German foe from the west—were ordered to leave their homes. General pandemonium broke loose in Slabodka; the town's Jewish inhabitants started to prepare themselves for flight, among them the many students of Knesset-Yisrael. The rosh-yeshiva Rabbi Moshe-Mordechai Epstein chose the city of Minsk as his destination, since it connected with Kovna directly by train, and the homes of a significant group of his hastily departing students were located there and in the vicinity. In this city, he found a proper home for his yeshiva, and the students returned and renewed their activities.[7]

The battlefront in Minsk Province heated up in the summer of 1916. The yeshiva administration decided to divide the school in two, sending one part to the Ukrainian city of Krementchug in Poltava Province. This split lasted until the beginning of 1918, when the Germans made a surprise invasion of the Russian interior, and within a few weeks took over large swathes of territory, including Minsk. The portion of the yeshiva remaining in Minsk abandoned the city, whether before its occupation or during the attack, and joined the group in Krementchug. From that point, the yeshiva functioned as a united institution in Krementchug.

The Bolshevik takeover of Ukraine and the stabilization of their rule there at the end of 1919 and the beginning of 1920 prompted the yeshiva to investigate ways of leaving Krementchug. It quickly became clear that there was no legal way to do so. It was only after the signing of the repatriation agreement with independent Lithuania that about one hundred students were authorized to depart in an organized fashion. The Russian government set aside two special railroad cars going to Vilna for the yeshiva, and the school's staff and students left Krementchug in late summer of 1920.[8]

The yeshiva arrived in Vilna a very short time before the city was conquered by Żeligowski's army, and it returned to Slabodka without delay in September 1920. The yeshiva building in Slabodka was in good repair and fit for use by the returning students, unlike other yeshivas' premises that had been neglected during the war and required large sums for renovations. The returnees were surprised to find in their building a yeshiva that had been established during the German occupation and under its protection, with Rabbis Baruch Hurwitz (1871–1936) and Nisan Yablonsky (1877–1928) and Musar supervisor Rabbi Yeruḥam Levovitz at its head. The level of its students was quite high, and their number was similar to that of the returning yeshiva—about one hundred students in all.[9]

The original administration faced an organizational dilemma as well as a personal one. It was clear that it would be impossible to set aside one yeshiva in favor of another, but the continuing functioning of two yeshivas in separate buildings was out of the question considering the difficult economic circumstances after the war. The practical solution was to unite the two institutions. This step was accompanied by a painful personal price. The united yeshiva could not long bear the double administration. The wartime heads saw clearly that they would have to step aside in favor of the original Slabodka administration—the mashgiaḥ Rabbi Notte-Hirsch Finkel and the rosh-yeshiva Rabbi Moshe-Mordechai Epstein. While new students were attracted by the expanded yeshiva, which by the beginning of the 1921 summer term already numbered 250 students, changes in the administration took place and Rabbis Yablonsky and Levovitz were obliged to leave.[10]

Besides the organizational changes, essential pedagogic modifications in the yeshiva were needed as well. Recently established Jewish educational institutions in independent Lithuania had adopted modern standards. The yeshiva was an anomaly compared to these institutions, since its students of all different ages and levels studied together in one shared hall. The age gaps became even more pronounced when the number of new students significantly increased, among them gifted youngsters who were accepted to the yeshiva despite their age. The yeshiva administration thus saw it essential to redefine its institution. In 1922, the yeshiva-ketana Even-Yisrael for twelve- to sixteen-year-old students was established in Slabodka. A year later, the administration brought about pedagogical and structural change in the yeshiva-gedola itself when it established in the Butchers' Beit-Midrash a *mechinah*—a branch with a preparatory program, Ohr-Yisrael, for seventeen- to nineteen-year-old students. The mechinah was dependent on the budget of the yeshiva-gedola, and outwardly the students of both schools continued to appear together in both official documents and class pictures.[11]

New students were constantly knocking on the doors of the yeshiva—sons of exiles from Lithuania who had recently returned to their homes and penniless young men from Russia. In the 1922 summer term, there were about three hundred students in the yeshiva. This expansion posed a challenge to the yeshiva administration, which was obliged to bear the burden of heavy monthly expenses. The economic crisis in Europe added to this difficult situation, which was felt keenly in Lithuania and influenced local donations to the yeshiva. Rabbi Moshe-Mordechai Epstein had no choice but to set out at the beginning of 1924 for the United States to collect funds for his yeshiva.[12]

The Mir Yeshiva

The Mir Yeshiva was one of the venerable Lithuanian yeshivas. It was founded according to the communal format in the town of Mir in Minsk

Province in 1817, fifteen years after the establishment of the Volozhin Yeshiva. By the middle of the nineteenth century, it was already operating as a supracommunity educational institution. Rabbi Eliyahu-Baruch Kamai (1841–1917), appointed to head the yeshiva in 1899, instituted significant changes in the old method of study and based his lectures on teaching selected *sugyot*—topics in Talmud study—as was the accepted practice in the younger Lithuanian yeshivas. In 1903, he became related by marriage to the Slabodka Yeshiva when his daughter wed Eliezer-Yehudah, the son of the Musar supervisor of Slabodka, Rabbi Notte-Hirsch Finkel. In this way, he opened the doors of the yeshiva to the influence of the Musar movement. Indeed, in 1910, Rabbi Yeruḥam Levovitz was appointed Musar supervisor; he turned Mir into a recognized Musar yeshiva and became a leading and influential personality there.

After the breakout of the First World War and the defeats of the Russian Army on the front in 1915, German forces rapidly advanced eastward. The positioning of the front line west of the town of Mir at the end of the year allowed the yeshiva to remain in place. Only after the intensification of fighting on the front in the summer of 1916, did the yeshiva leave Mir and move to the town of Poltava in Ukraine, with the young Talmud instructor Rabbi Eliezer-Yehudah Finkel and the mashgiaḥ Rabbi Yeruḥam Levovitz at its head. In Poltava, the yeshiva was secluded and isolated. Its rosh-yeshiva Rabbi Eliezer-Yehudah Finkel was solely responsible for its support, and from 1918 led it on his own, after the mashgiaḥ Rabbi Yeruḥam Levovitz temporarily returned to Lithuania and, upon his arrival there, was prevented from going back to his yeshiva.[13]

After a repatriation agreement with independent Lithuania had been signed on June 30, 1920, the Mir Yeshiva began preparations to leave its exile in Poltava. It may be that initially the yeshiva tried to receive an exit permit for all of its students as one group, and if that is what indeed happened, it makes sense to assume that this attempt was unsuccessful, since before the war the yeshiva was located in Minsk Province and not in one of the proper Lithuanian provinces. Some of the young men, natives of the former Kovna Province, individually put their documents in order with the government and tried to leave on their own. But many left Poltava without any permits and wandered on winding roads toward the western borders of Russia and Ukraine, as described in one of the yeshiva's printed appeals: "They walked tens of *versts* on foot, through forests and fields they made their way, for weeks they wandered day and night, their backs broken and soul-weary, in the wilderness of ruined Russia."[14]

Gradually the students began to gather in Vilna. Their yeshiva was unable to return to Mir, since the Russian Army was stationed there at the time. The baḥurim were forced to remain temporarily in place and began their study program under the leadership of Rabbi Eliezer-Yehudah Finkel in the beit-midrash in the suburb of Lukishok. Their rabbi bore the burden of material sustenance for about eighty talmidim, all adults living in rented apartments in the city. An active local council came to his aid and took care of the needs of the yeshiva, but the main and most significant support was received from the American Central Relief.

The yeshiva's stay in a strange and lively city instead of in its own premises in Mir gave it a sense of impermanence. When it became known to its students that their former mashgiaḥ Rabbi Yeruḥam Levovitz was serving as the Musar supervisor in Slabodka, their attraction to him outweighed the commitment to their yeshiva, and many of them decided to join him. Only a few dozen of the youngest talmidim remained in the yeshiva in Vilna. However, the Mir Yeshiva's numbers increased quickly as new students streamed into Vilna at that time from Russia and Ukraine, and in 1921, there were already more than 130 talmidim there.[15]

The road to return to Mir was opened with the signing of the peace treaty between Russia and Poland on March 18, 1921. According to this treaty, Mir was to be under Polish rule, and at the end of summer 1921, the students left Vilna for Mir.[16] When the yeshiva arrived there, it found that it had a way to go before it would be reintegrated into the town. The yeshiva building had come under the control of shifting authorities, which used it for their own needs. Before the yeshiva went into exile, the Russians had already turned it into a hospital for wartime casualties. Subsequently, the ample building turned into a theater, and the new Polish authorities went further and turned it into a stable for horses. Rabbi Finkel's first difficult challenge was to return the building to the yeshiva's ownership, and to that end, a permit from the governor was required. Once he achieved this, it became clear to him that fundamental renovations were needed in order to make it suitable for regular study, and this would require significant funds and time. In the meantime, disorder prevailed. Out of a lack of choice, studies went on in the building in its existing state. The students took their Sabbath meals with the town residents, and several found lodging in the home of the rabbi of Mir, Rabbi Avraham-Hirsch Kamai. Once again, external financial aid, in addition to help in the form of food and clothing from the Vilna branch of the relief organization YEKOPO, made it possible for the yeshiva to become established in the town and return to regular studies.[17]

There was another sensitive issue that faced Rabbi Eliezer-Yehudah Finkel in the administration of the yeshiva. Before the yeshiva's exile, Rabbi Eliyahu-Baruch Kamai, Rabbi Finkel's father-in-law, stood at its helm, and also served as the town rabbi at the same time. He preferred to stay in Mir and not set off to Ukraine with the yeshiva. After his death in 1917, his exiled son Avraham-Hirsch was appointed in his place and came to Mir to assume his new position. It would seem that when the yeshiva returned to its place several years later, he had the right to the position of rosh-yeshiva as well as town rabbi, but Rabbi Avraham-Hirsch Kamai was not the sort of person to make such a demand. It was clear to him that his brother-in-law, Rabbi Finkel, who took care of the yeshiva during its years of exile, suffered along with it, and risked his very life for the good and welfare of its students, deserved that position. But since he had a right to the position of Talmud instructor as his father's heir, Rabbi Kamai did not withdraw from the yeshiva altogether, opting to give comprehensive weekly lectures there. Rabbi Finkel consequently served as head of the yeshiva until its last days in Mir.[18]

When the yeshiva became established in Mir, the studies there fell into a fixed pattern. Its administration even set up a kollel program for married students who received stipends that relied on the yeshiva's funds. At the end of the summer of 1924, there were 10 talmidim in the kollel. The regular student body had grown at that time to 165. All of this required a significant monthly budget at the same time that the yeshiva's income had been reduced by the financial crisis in Poland and the decreased support of the American Central Relief. The material condition of the Mir Yeshiva continued to worsen, and in 1925, the yeshiva fell into a deep deficit. Rabbi Finkel began to feel increasing pressure from the suffering students, and perhaps he even received an ultimatum. He saw no alternative but to sail to the United States to collect money for the yeshiva in order to save it.[19]

The Knesset Beit-Yitzḥak Yeshiva of Slabodka

The mentioned split in the Slabodka Yeshiva in 1897 as a consequence of the argument between the talmidim over the role of Musar caused the rabbi of the town Moshe Danushevsky (1834–1909) and the rabbi of nearby Kovna Hirsch Rabinowitz (1847–1910) to take under their protection those students who opposed Rabbi Finkel's Musar approach. These baḥurim had remained in their place and provided the basis for the new yeshiva, Knesset Beit-Yitzḥak, established for them by Rabbis Danushevsky and Rabinowitz. In 1904, the administration of the yeshiva appointed the rabbi of Hlusk, Baruch-Ber Leibowitz, as its head. Since Musar studies were absent in the yeshiva, Talmudical research was its main focus, and the lectures of its new head became the central weekly event. These in-depth lectures created a reputation for the yeshiva, and talmidim from other Torah-study institutions began to flock to it and fill its hall.

In the panic that took hold of Slabodka when the First World War broke out and an order was issued to leave the town, students from Knesset Beit-Yitzḥak returned to their homes. It is not clear whether Rabbi Baruch-Ber Leibowitz left Slabodka then or if the expulsion order that descended upon the Jews of the Kovna Province in May 1915 forced him to leave. Either way, he set out with his family and a few select students, and after passing through Vilna, they stayed in Minsk. Students who had left his Slabodka Yeshiva and also gone into exile began to gather around him until he was able to reestablish the yeshiva anew in the strange city.

The intensification of fighting at the Minsk Province front in the summer of 1916 caused Knesset Beit-Yitzḥak to drift from town to town in Russia. During this period of wandering, Rabbi Leibowitz's father-in-law, the community rabbi of the *Mitnagdim* (non-Hasidic Jews) of Krementchug, Avraham-Yitzḥak Zimmerman (1840–1917), died. Rabbi Leibowitz received an invitation from the heads of the community to serve as their rabbi. He accepted it, and the members of his yeshiva migrated with him to Krementchug. In this city, the yeshiva operated in a regular fashion. Rabbi Leibowitz even made new appointments: his son-in-law Reuven Grozovsky (1886–1958) was appointed as the Talmud instructor, and his brother-in-law Naftali-Ze'ev Leibowitz was appointed as the Musar supervisor.[20]

After the signing of the repatriation agreement with independent Lithuania, the yeshiva, with its Talmud instructor and mashgiaḥ, set out from Krementchug for Vilna, at that point already under Polish control, reaching it in the beginning of 1921. The inability of the yeshiva to continue on to Slabodka due to the high tension between Lithuania and Poland forced Rabbi Reuven Grozovsky and his students to remain in place for some time. They were ensconced in the Remayle Kloyz, where the city's *Moreh-Tzedek* (authority on Jewish Law) Rabbi Meir Bassin (1877–1931) led a yeshiva for refugee students until that time. The expanded institution numbered eighty-five young men, and Rabbi Grozovsky was appointed as its head.[21]

Rabbi Baruch-Ber Leibowitz himself did not rush to leave his place of exile in Krementchug and join his yeshiva. The local community pressured him not to abandon them and even convinced the members of his household to remain in the city. His father's advanced age also made it difficult to set out on the torturous road from Ukraine to Vilna. Moshe Bernstein, Rabbi Leibowitz's new son-in-law, pressed his father-in-law to rejoin the yeshiva. His efforts bore fruit, and the family set off after Passover 1921. They suffered the hazards of the road, mishaps, and mortal danger until they arrived in Minsk, and from there they traveled to Vilna.[22]

The yeshiva was reunited under the leadership of Rabbi Leibowitz, and he began to deliver his Talmudic lectures in Remayle Kloyz. Only at the end of summer 1921, when the baḥurim from Mir vacated the beit-midrash in the Lukishok suburb, were the Knesset Beit-Yitzḥak talmidim able to establish themselves in this permanent setting. However, the instability had reduced the number of students, and the yeshiva was diminished to a few dozen.

Rabbi Leibowitz was faced with the urgent task of obtaining financial resources to maintain the yeshiva in Vilna. Naturally, the American Central Relief supported the yeshiva, as it did all the yeshivas that had returned from exile, but this was not sufficient. Local relief organizations got together to establish its place in the city: Rabbi Ḥayim-Ozer Grodzensky helped all he could, a special women's committee took care of the yeshiva's needs, and the city's residents contributed generously. The Vilna community even appointed Rabbi Leibowitz as one of the halachic authorities in the city—by virtue of his Torah scholarship, but motivated also by the desire to materially support his yeshiva. This appointment made it clear to everyone that Vilna was the permanent home of the yeshiva. Young refugees from Russia and students from all over Poland enrolled, and in 1924 there were seventy-four talmidim studying there.[23]

The material state of the yeshiva continued to deteriorate. One of the obvious contributing factors was its expansion, but the main cause was its presence in a large and expensive city. The price of rent and food in Vilna was incomparably higher than in the towns of Poland, and this made it very difficult to maintain the yeshiva. Rabbi Leibowitz did not find it necessary at this point to go on a fundraising trip to America, as did his colleagues; however, he did consider moving the yeshiva to a small town where the tranquil atmosphere would be conducive to yeshiva studies. Offers began to reach Rabbi Leibowitz from several towns that wanted him to serve as their rabbi and transfer the yeshiva there. He consulted Rabbi Yisrael-Meir HaCohen, the Ḥafetz-Ḥayim, and accepted his advice to choose the town Kamenitz-Litevsk, near Brisk, as the home for his yeshiva. At the end of summer 1926, after nearly six years in Vilna, Knesset Beit-Yitzḥak took up the wanderer's staff once more and moved to Kamenitz.[24]

The yeshiva made its home in a local beit-midrash and again began the process of becoming integrated into an unknown community. The Ḥafetz-Ḥayim, who had a part in the transfer to this isolated town, expected difficulties and issued a letter asking the rabbis for help. Among other things, he wrote, concerning Rabbi Leibowitz: "Indeed, now, towards his old age, he has designated the town Kamenitz-Litevsk near Brisk as a dwelling place for himself and his yeshiva. I ask all the rabbis, my acquaintances, to draw the holy yeshiva near, and it is known that the reward for supporting Torah is greater than ever before, and even more so today when the holy Torah is much disgraced."[25]

As was to be expected, the move was not at all easy in material terms. In addition to the high cost of the move itself, the initial expenditures of the yeshiva for food were high while its income was negligible. The yeshiva was forced to buy everything on credit based on the optimistic assumption that outside help would cover its debts in the future. The local inhabitants saw this extravagant policy as a bit peculiar, and described it in the following short and critical words: "When they first arrived here, 'the ledger is open and the hand records therein, and the shopkeeper offers credit.'"[26] But outside help was delayed, and the debts increased until they doubled in half a year.

It was not only in the field of economics that the yeshiva needed substantial help. In the move from Vilna to Kamenitz, students dropped out of the yeshiva, among them some of the very best. The administration thus decided to reinforce the institution with senior students from other well-established yeshivas. Yitzḥak Turets (1885–1967), son-in-law of Rabbi Leibowitz, was sent to the Mir Yeshiva, where he had once been one of its best students, to influence several talmidim to come and study in Kamenitz. With the help of Rabbi Eliezer-Yehudah Finkel, he succeeded in convincing nine talented young men to transfer to the regenerating yeshiva for a period of six months to a year. There is seemingly no evidence of the extent of their influence on the yeshiva in Kamenitz, but even without any connection to their studies there, the yeshiva's reputation grew and the number of its students reached 118 by the beginning of the 1927 summer term—an increase of 40 percent in one semester. This expansion put an additional burden on its budget, and the deficit grew. In spring 1928, Rabbi Leibowitz was forced to set off to the United States in order to save his yeshiva from economic collapse.[27]

YESHIVAS THAT REMAINED IN PLACE DURING THE WAR

Six yeshivas were fortunate enough to remain in their original locations in the western provinces of Russia and Poland during the First World War and did not participate in the long wanderings of their counterparts. They suffered and shrank significantly, but they had a definite advantage over those yeshivas that migrated in that they continued to remain in their towns and even in their own buildings, maintaining their connections with their surroundings. When the war ended, they were at a good starting point; they were immediately able to fully enjoy the freedom that the independent states of Lithuania and Poland provided their minorities. The next section will examine two yeshivas that experienced the transition from war to freedom in different ways.

The Slonim Yeshiva

During the period of Tsarist rule, a large educational institution operated in Slonim, in Grodno Province, that included a *Talmud-Torah* (a community school for children and youngsters) and a yeshiva, named Etz-Ḥayim, for older students. The date of the yeshiva's founding is obscure, but it is accepted that this occurred in 1831.[28] Over the years, the roshei-yeshiva were appointed by gaba'im (officials of the institution) who were elected from among the members of the Slonim community. Despite the community affiliation of the yeshiva, its economic support came not only from local residents but also from fundraising campaigns and emissaries.

In the period of the German occupation of Slonim during the First World War, the material circumstances of the yeshiva became greatly reduced, particularly due to its isolation from outside sources of support, and only a few talmidim remained there. After the war, Polish rule was extended to Slonim and its environs. Young men joined the yeshiva, and it began to rehabilitate itself and return to its original position. The rosh-yeshiva, Rabbi Shabtai Yogel, who headed the entire educational institution as well, quickly identified the new situation that faced him. He had to prepare for contingencies wherein it would no longer be possible to maintain the institution through local support or the donations of Russian Jewry, as in the past. Support from Western countries was limited in nature, and his financial exigencies left him with little choice but to separate the branches of the institution organizationally and administratively. The Talmud-Torah, with its seven classes and three hundred students, became an independent institution under community auspices, and the yeshiva, with its three classes for beginners and a *kibbutz* class for advanced students who had already reached the level of independent study, began to stand on its own.[29]

Rabbi Yogel's administrative step caused the yeshiva to part from an archaic pedagogical framework. However, Rabbi Yogel abstained from taking a further step and establishing a yeshiva-ketana separate from the yeshiva-gedola, as other Lithuanian yeshivas did. Even though in practical terms he had done this—the yeshiva classrooms, where students up until the age of eighteen studied, shared a common courtyard with the Talmud-Torah classes, while the kibbutz class was located in a separate beit-midrash—this was only an operational division that was not accompanied by the necessary administrative-economic separation. One can assume that the first division was sufficiently revolutionary in Rabbi

Yogel's eyes and that he was reluctant to further burden the institution's gaba'im with the maintenance of the yeshiva-ketana.

From his letters, it seems that he was not even aware of the substantive divisions between older and younger students made by other yeshivas. He had heard of the establishment of junior yeshivas attached to senior yeshivas, but he considered this to be only an ostensible division for the purpose of receiving greater funding, as was expressed in the sarcastic and witty style of his letter to the director of *Va'ad-HaYeshivot* (The Yeshiva Committee), Yosef Schuw: "I have already pointed out a number of times the injustice done to our yeshiva regarding the rest of the yeshivas, both bigger and smaller, which constantly receive double [funding] from Va'ad-HaYeshivot, namely their set percentage . . . and a small prize of $30 for a yeshiva-ketana, that is to say, their lower classes. The Slonim Yeshiva is the exception, and it has no portion in double payments. Apparently it is so important that in their [Va'ad-HaYeshivot] eyes it is senior (*gedola*) from bottom to top."[30]

In the beginning of 1929, Rabbi Yogel created this ostensible separation in his own yeshiva as well, when he labeled its two lower classes a yeshiva-ketana and (from his standpoint) completed the organizational revolution.

Rabbi Yogel did not stop with organizational changes and decided to reform the yeshiva in other ways. He aspired to adapt its characteristics to those that were customary in the yeshiva world, and to this end introduced Musar-study sessions and even appointed a Musar supervisor—in the beginning, Rabbi Yitzḥak Weinstein and, after him, Rabbi Avraham-Zvi Listovsky. This was a revolutionary step in a yeshiva where, until this point, the Musar talks of its head were considered sufficient.[31]

The Telz Yeshiva

The Telz Yeshiva was founded according to the communal format in the town of Telz, Kovna Province, in 1881. This yeshiva's character was changed in 1883 when the new rabbi of Telz, Eliezer Gordon, was appointed as its head; by virtue of his energetic personality, he was able to make a reputation for the school in the Pale of Settlement. His student and son-in-law, the *avrech* (married student) Rabbi Yosef-Leib Bloch, arrived after him in Telz and joined the rabbinic faculty of the yeshiva. Its talmidim were divided by age and knowledge into classes—a rare arrangement at that time in yeshivas, where older students and talented bar-mitzvah boys studied together.

The yeshiva was known for the periodic revolts of its students, most of which were a reaction to the attempt to include Musar studies in the curriculum. These rebellions led to the resignation of its rabbinic faculty in 1902–1903, and even to the yeshiva's extended closure in 1905. After Rabbi Gordon's death in 1910, Rabbi Yosef-Leib Bloch took his place as rabbi of Telz and head of the yeshiva, where more than 220 students studied at that time.

When the First World War broke out, many students left the yeshiva and returned home, similarly to what occurred in other yeshivas. Fortunately, Telz had been occupied by the German forces before the exile of the Jews from Kovna Province occurred, and the yeshiva could stay in place during the German occupation. However, only older talmidim remained and continued to study under their head, Rabbi Bloch, and with the Talmud instructor Rabbi Ḥayim Rabinowitz (1860–1930). Over the course of the war years, the yeshiva became somewhat restored as both veteran and new students joined it once more.[32]

The new independent state that Lithuania had become did not immediately find its expression in the yeshiva, and its rabbis continued to teach their regular classes to a limited student body. The seats in the yeshiva slowly filled, and this trend grew with the return of the Lithuanian exiles to their homes. Rabbi Bloch already saw the need of an additional Talmud instructor for the yeshiva in 1921, and he appointed his son Avraham-Yitzḥak to this position.[33]

A few years before, during the German occupation, young men began to knock on the doors of the yeshiva even if they were as yet unqualified to study there and required preparatory classes. When the number of these students increased, an organized mechinah, preparatory program, was set up for them, and the avrech Mordechai Katz (1894–1964), the young son-in-law of Rabbi Bloch, was chosen as its principal. As years passed, there were four classes, and the exceptional students in the mechinah's upper class reached the status of "auditing students," meaning that they attended the yeshiva to hear lectures.[34]

This expansion of the yeshiva and its organization into two separate institutions, according to pedagogic norms that had become common in Lithuania, were not, as was mentioned, the sole province of the Telz Yeshiva. Nevertheless, there was a revolutionary novelty in that yeshiva—a set program of secular studies in its mechinah during the evening hours. Before the First World War, the Lida Yeshiva in Vilna Province was unique among Lithuanian yeshivas in its offering general studies. Because of these studies, the Orthodox circles of that time leveled harsh criticism at the yeshiva and particularly at its head, Rabbi Yitzḥak-Ya'akov Reines. But it was Rabbi Yosef-Leib Bloch himself, who was even referred to as "one of the greatest and most zealous rabbis of Lithuania," who broke the "ban" of the yeshiva world on general studies and introduced them into his yeshiva preparatory program. It is not surprising that this step was accompanied by not a few critical remarks.[35]

Rabbi Bloch did not focus solely on his own yeshiva. He saw this higher Talmudic institution as a beachhead for more comprehensive educational activity. At the time of the German occupation in Telz, Rabbi Bloch was already involved in educational matters that were outside the yeshiva's parameters. In its first year, the new military government made attendance for Jews compulsory in elementary schools that it had set up in many towns, among them Telz. In response, Rabbi Bloch decided to establish in the town two modern Torah schools for boys that fulfilled the pedagogic requirements of the authorities. This was the first link in an extensive chain of educational institutions that were established in Telz after the war and were closely attached to the yeshiva, either through its administration or the involvement of its students.[36]

In 1920, the two aforementioned schools were consolidated into one institution, Beit-haḤinuch, which provided an education to boys from traditionally observant families. In that same year, a similar school for girls opened in Telz. Among the founders were members of Rabbi Bloch's household, and several of the teachers were students of the yeshiva. At the end of 1920, a gymnasium for girls was established in Telz as part of the Yavneh religious educational network, also under Rabbi Bloch's influence. This singular gymnasium, which was meant to be a continuation of the girls' elementary school, had a religious atmosphere and the language of instruction was Hebrew. After a short transitional period, Rabbi Bloch appointed the religious pedagogue Yitzḥak-Raphael Holtzberg (1885–1981), recently returned to Lithuania from exile in Russia, as principal. Rabbi Bloch did not hesitate to include teachers from among his yeshiva students in the faculty of the new high school for girls. Establishing this pioneering institution was not a conventional step in the Orthodox community and raised questions in the minds of several rabbis. However, Rabbi Bloch was not dissuaded from carrying out his innovations.

The autonomy enjoyed by Lithuanian Jews allowed traditional parents to demand the establishment of schools of the Yavneh network in their towns from the authorities. The Ministry of Education usually consented to the parents' demands on the condition that appropriate teachers were available. Hence, training religious teachers for the network's schools in Lithuania was a primary concern for the Yavneh Center, and in 1921 a teachers' seminary was established in Kovna. The religious atmosphere there was weak, and the center's members saw a need to strengthen it. They turned to Rabbi Yosef-Leib Bloch for assistance, and he agreed to accept the seminary under his sponsorship. He appointed Yitzḥak-Raphael Holtzberg, mentioned earlier, as director, and toward the end of 1923, the seminary moved to Telz.[37]

In this institution for training teachers, which was unique in Lithuania, there were four classes corresponding to the upper classes in the gymnasia, and attached to it was a preparatory program for students, mostly those who had studied in yeshiva. The yeshiva atmosphere of Telz pervaded the seminary, so Talmud study was instituted in the morning hours, taught by the rabbi and spiritual director of the seminary Yitzḥak-Eliezer Hirschowitz (1870–1941), a former rosh-yeshiva and brother-in-law to Rabbi Bloch. In its earliest stage, the seminary was a sort of haven for yeshiva students whose rabbi did not consider them to be exceptional scholars and feared that they would lose their way if they left the yeshiva. However over time, the seminary was seen as an effective means for disseminating the yeshiva ideology among the graduates of the Yavneh school system, and it was understood that this task required the best of the yeshiva's talmidim. Indeed, most of the students in the teachers' seminary were graduates of the Telz Yeshiva who saw their mission to serve as teachers.[38]

Rabbi Yosef-Leib Bloch's involvement in religious education outside the confines of the yeshiva was a unique phenomenon amongst his colleagues. Moreover, directing students from his yeshiva toward a career in education was unknown in other yeshivas in Poland and Lithuania. It would seem that Rabbi Bloch's activities were rooted in his innovative approach regarding the role of a yeshiva student and his mission.

YESHIVAS THAT FLED THEIR ORIGINAL PLACES

During the First World War, Lithuanian yeshivas moved to Russian and Ukrainian territories, whether willingly or unwillingly. They saw themselves only as temporary guests in their places of exile. When there was danger from the new Bolshevik authorities and it was possible for them to leave, they hurried back to their original towns. In contrast, the western districts of Russia and the Ukraine—which had been part of the Pale of Settlement—served as the home of local yeshivas of the Lithuanian type, some quite long-established, whose students mainly came from the surrounding area. The Bolshevik takeover of the districts where they were located hastened their end. The yeshivas continued their struggle for survival until they were disbanded due to the Soviet authorities' pressure. The heads of three of these yeshivas managed to cross the border into Poland, with or without their talmidim. In the following section, the operation of two of these yeshivas will be examined.[39]

The Slutsk-Kletsk Yeshiva

The rabbi of Slutsk, Minsk Province, Ya'akov-David Vilovsky (known as Ridvaz, 1845–1913), decided to establish a yeshiva and requested the assistance of Rabbi Notte-Hirsch Finkel to carry it out. Rabbi Finkel answered the request, and in 1897 Rabbi Finkel sent fourteen of his students, headed by Rabbi Isser-Zalman Meltzer, to set up a branch of the Slabodka Yeshiva in Slutsk. The group set itself up in a local beit-midrash, and young men began to join the new yeshiva, Etz-Ḥayim. The increase in the number of students over the years required Rabbi Meltzer to appoint a Musar supervisor in 1902. In the following year, Rabbi Meltzer was chosen to serve as the rabbi of Slutsk as well, after Rabbi Vilovsky resigned his rabbinic position.

The yeshiva, where more than two hundred talmidim were studying, was severely damaged when the First World War broke out, and many baḥurim left. Despite this, the yeshiva did not cease functioning throughout the war. The threat to its existence arose only after the war. The 1921 peace treaty between Soviet Russia and Poland placed Slutsk under continued Russian control. The heads of the Etz-Ḥayim yeshiva already knew the terrors of Bolshevik rule from its earlier impermanent periods in that location due to the frequent changes of authority between the Russians and the Poles. It was clear to them that Soviet rule over Slutsk spelled the end of the yeshiva, and they were obliged to act immediately to save it. It was still possible to take advantage of the twilight period, during which the border was open, and quickly transfer the students to Kletsk on the Polish side. The rosh-yeshiva and rabbi of the town, Isser-Zalman Meltzer, did not wish to leave his community on its own under Soviet rule, and he therefore decided to divide the yeshiva in two. His son-in-law Rabbi Aharon Kotler was meant to accompany the senior students to Kletsk, and the younger ones would continue their studies in Slutsk under the leadership of Rabbi Meltzer and the supervision of the mashgiaḥ, Rabbi Asher Sandomirsky.[40]

Groups from Slutsk that were concerned for their future under Soviet rule took advantage of the temporarily open border and quickly crossed over to nearby Kletsk. Rabbi Kotler's group, made up of several dozen students, was part of this tide of immigrants. They made their way on foot owing to their inability to hire carts because the price had spiraled as a result of increased demand. As they neared Kletsk after their lengthy journey, the Jews of the town came out to greet them. The first night, the exhausted baḥurim slept on wooden benches. The community quickly organized to host them, and each family contributed its part in lodging or food, or even both of these. The rabbi of Kletsk, Ḥayim-Shim'on Hernsohn (1866–1940), whose father and predecessor in that position had unsuccessfully attempted in 1897 to bring the branch of the Slabodka Yeshiva to his town rather than to Slutsk, did not want to miss this opportunity. He acted energetically to establish the yeshiva in Kletsk, leading a local campaign to absorb the talmidim, and together with the town notables, he set out to raise funds in the surrounding area.

Rabbi Kotler, who understood that he could not maintain his yeshiva in the long run by depending on the kindness of the residents, decided to change the circumstances of his students' upkeep to the Slutsk model with which they were familiar:

- Lodgings: Because Rabbi Kotler did not yet have money, he promised the community that he would soon pay the students' rent, and they were sent to choose appropriate lodgings in the homes of the local residents.
- Food supply: Rabbi Kotler succeeded in obtaining a large supply of saccharine, and black bread baked by local women was brought to the yeshiva daily. Each talmid received the most basic food—slices of bread and sweetened water. The students continued to have their meals at the tables of the town residents only on the Sabbath.

These scanty meals went on for about two months until the baḥurim began to receive monthly support, whose apparent source was American Jewish funding. At that point, the local food improved, and the young men were able to vary their daily menu.

The border between Soviet Russia and Poland was closed several days after the exodus from Slutsk, and the town was cut off from Kletsk. In Soviet Slutsk, the yeshiva continued to grow even though studies there were clandestine. As was to be expected, local religious institutions and Torah scholars were persecuted by the new authorities. Rabbis Meltzer and Sandomirsky were even arrested and imprisoned for a short time for secretly teaching Torah to their talmidim. The yeshiva students understood that their continued study put them in danger, and a few considered joining the yeshiva in Kletsk. Supervision over the border was still weak, and it was possible to cross it with the help of professional smugglers. These attempts were not always successful, and a rumor spread in the yeshiva that some baḥurim who had tried to cross the border fell into the hands of Polish police and were sentenced to prison and torture. Despite these rumors and fears, over time several students crossed the border into Poland.[41]

Rabbi Meltzer feared additional imprisonment, and close to Purim 1923, he also crossed the border to the town of Niesvizh, Poland. When he arrived in Kletsk, he returned to his former position in the yeshiva, and from that point the Kletsk Yeshiva could be seen as a natural and direct continuation of the original Slutsk Yeshiva. Its recovery could be seen in the number of its pupils, which grew to 156 at the end of the 1924 summer term. It would seem that Rabbi Meltzer's return to the yeshiva attracted many students as well.[42]

The Amtchislav-Kobrin Yeshiva

One of the fourteen Slabodka Yeshiva students who were sent in 1897 to establish the yeshiva in Slutsk was Pesaḥ Pruskin. From 1905 he served as Musar supervisor in this yeshiva. In 1908 his rabbi, Isser-Zalman Meltzer, sent him to renew a local yeshiva in Shklov, Mohilev Province, in the eastern Pale of Settlement. In 1911 he was chosen as rabbi of Amtchislav in the same province, and he established a yeshiva there. During the First World War, the yeshiva continued to function in its original location, with about one hundred students and four Talmud instructors.

With the Bolshevik takeover of Amtchislav, the yeshiva's freedom of operation was curtailed, and it suffered from the rule of the new authorities. For a few years, Rabbi Pruskin bore the Soviet yoke in silence, but he understood that he could not continue to do so for long. He decided to leave Amtchislav, and in 1923 he crossed over the border into Poland. He returned to Kobrin, the town of his birth, in Polesia Province, where he was welcomed with open arms.[43]

Rabbi Pruskin gained a great deal of experience in establishing and running new yeshivas. With untiring energy, he ignored the difficult economic situation in Poland, which was not a good sign for the upkeep of yeshivas, and planned to establish a yeshiva-gedola in Kobrin. He had no talmidim at that time because they had all remained in Amtchislav. Nevertheless, he set up the yeshiva in the local Ḥayei-Adam Synagogue. About a year later, in 1924, a yeshiva-ketana, Tiferet-Yisrael, was also established. In its early years, it was dependent on the budget of the yeshiva-gedola and naturally supplied it with a steady stream of students.

Young men from the Amtchislav Yeshiva succeeded in crossing the border and joined their rabbi. For their material sustenance they were entirely dependent on his new yeshiva, and considerable resources were required in order to support them. A local action-committee was specially organized in order to provide regular assistance to the yeshiva. Its material condition was further eased in 1924 when Rabbi Pruskin, a popular preacher, was chosen by the majority of the Kobrin Jewish community as the new town rabbi, after the death of the previous rabbi, David Greenberg (1850–1924). As a tribute to Rabbi Pruskin, a special committee was formed in order to build his house near the yeshiva. Craftsmen volunteered for this work, and in short time the building was erected. However, the Zionists and the intelligentsia were not keen on the appointment of Rabbi Pruskin. The same week that he was chosen, they presented a rabbinical certificate to the official rabbi certified by the Polish authorities, Michael Shamush (1884–1930). A fierce local argument arose between the supporters from both sides. This went on for many years and had a significant indirect influence on the yeshiva.[44]

In 1924 there were only thirty-six talmidim studying in the Kobrin Yeshiva. The news of its establishment spread rapidly among yeshiva students, and by the summer of 1926, there were already about eighty young men studying there. The difficult material conditions did not prevent its growth, the number of students increased steadily in the following years, and its deficit grew as well. In an attempt to free the yeshiva from its heavy debts, Rabbi Pruskin was forced, like many of his colleagues, to set out for the United States at the end of 1929 on a fundraising campaign.[45]

SUMMARY

The process of the yeshivas leaving their Russian and Ukrainian exile and their subsequent restoration in independent Poland and Lithuania reveal new and unique characteristics of the Lithuanian yeshiva: survival and continuity. These characteristics can also be discerned in the yeshivas that remained in the areas under German occupation; they suffered greatly but completely resumed their activities after the war. These characteristics cannot be attributed to the talents of the heads of the yeshivas alone because one cannot compare an experienced rosh-yeshiva like Moshe-Mordechai Epstein to his counterpart Rabbi Baruch-Ber Leibowitz. Despite his vast Torah scholarship, it is doubtful that Rabbi Leibowitz could have navigated his yeshiva in the stormy waters after the First World War without the assistance of his helpers and senior students. In addition to a yeshiva's fine reputation and the skills of its administration and faculty, there were other factors in its survival and continuation. These involved the nature of its students as well, as will be shown.

Despite these common features shared by the yeshivas that survived the First World War, each returned to routine after the war in its own way. This activity was categorized into several representative models with their own unique qualities. An analysis of each of these models emphasizes a number of differences in the characteristics of the reestablishment of the yeshivas represented in that model—differences that reveal a multishaded and nuanced picture of the first steps of the yeshivas in this new era.

The first model included yeshivas that returned from exile after a lengthy absence and attempted to return to their natural habitat. A comparative examination of the processes that took place in the yeshivas Knesset-Yisrael, Mir, and Knesset Beit-Yitzḥak shows several points worth mentioning:

- All of the three yeshivas expanded in their permanent homes within several years to an extent that did not permit them to continue functioning due to financial issues. It is difficult to explain the opening of their gates to new students during economic downturns. Indeed, this consequently necessitated their heads to travel to the United States in order to alleviate the problem.
- The Slabodka Knesset-Yisrael Yeshiva reverted to its original location, where everything was ready for its return, and did not require any special process of acclimatization. This optimal situation ostensibly provided it a valuable advantage over other yeshivas. However, one outstanding variable proved to be harmful: the yeshiva's student population immediately doubled when it absorbed the local Slabodka talmidim rather than growing incrementally. This sharp increase placed a huge burden on its budget, forcing its rosh-yeshiva to be the pioneer who went to the United States to find a solution to the yeshiva's financial dilemma.
- The lengthy stay of the Slabodka Knesset Beit-Yitzḥak Yeshiva in Ukraine caused the loss of a narrow window of opportunity to return to its original place in Lithuania and the resulting damage to its development for quite a number of years. However, in hindsight, it

may well be this was to the advantage of the two respected Slabodka yeshivas, Knesset-Yisrael and Knesset Beit-Yitzḥak, which would have had difficulty surviving over time in the same suburb of Kovna under the complex economic conditions that prevailed in Lithuania in the 1920s and 1930s.

The second model included those yeshivas that were able to remain in the area of German occupation during the war, such as Slonim and Telz. An examination of their performance shows that both yeshivas benefited from the fact that they remained in situ and were not required to waste valuable resources in reacclimatization. However, a more careful comparison of the two indicates that the Telz Yeshiva derived optimal benefit from this advantage and was able to maximize its religious influence in the town in particular and in Lithuania on the whole. The difference in their conduct emanated principally from the differing personalities of their heads. Two qualities of Rabbi Bloch, rosh-yeshiva of Telz, moved him to adopt his pioneering steps:

- Flexible thinking: When he saw the transformation that had taken place in Jewish education in independent Lithuania, he adjusted his yeshiva to the new circumstances and harnessed it for the task of expanding Torah education outside the yeshiva walls.
- Resoluteness: This quality was already outstanding in his personality in the early years of the Telz Yeshiva, when he insisted in incorporating the Musar method there and maintained his position despite student protests. Even in the postwar period, he was not dissuaded from carrying out his innovative ideas despite the criticism of rabbis in Lithuania.[46]

Rabbi Shabtai Yogel, rosh-yeshiva of Slonim, was not endowed with these qualities. He did not comprehend the developing situation in all of its depth and lacked the determination required to sustain yeshivas in those days. Nevertheless, he succeeded in his calm and usually humorous way to maintain a yeshiva with a stable number of students throughout the interwar period without having to travel all over the United States—an accomplishment that was unparalleled in those difficult years.[47]

The third model consisted of those yeshivas that were not forced to uproot themselves during the war from their natural and comfortable locations in Russia or Ukraine but afterward found themselves under Bolshevik rule. Two of their heads, the rosh-yeshiva of Slutsk and that of Amtchislav, showed similar characteristic behavior. Both stayed as heads of their communities and yeshivas despite the hostility of the Soviet authorities, and only when no choice remained did they flee by themselves from their towns in the same year, 1923. But unlike Rabbi Pruskin, who began building his yeshiva in Kobrin ex nihilo, Rabbi Meltzer stood at the head of a mature yeshiva in Kletsk after he had succeeded in bringing a significant group of his students to that town before the situation became too difficult.

Notwithstanding the differing background circumstances of the establishment of Kletsk and Kobrin yeshivas, they shared a common characteristic in terms of their expansion. However, if their subsequent histories were to be told, they would quickly reveal that whereas the Kletsk Yeshiva went on to become one of the greatest in Poland, the Kobrin Yeshiva suffered a dramatic decrease in the number of its students until it was nearly closed in the early 1930s. With this extreme difference in their respective fates in mind, one should go back and see whether their beginnings could cast light on what happened to them later. Unlike the Kletsk Yeshiva at the start of its path, which appeared to be a nearly perfect copy of the Slutsk Yeshiva with its veteran students, the Kobrin Yeshiva was actually a completely new institution of learning because the refugees from Amtchislav were only a minority among its talmidim. Granted, the nearly total collapse of the Kobrin Yeshiva was due to its dire financial straits as well as the strained relationship between its heads and mashgiaḥ. But to this one must add the absence of a mature and veteran student body like that in Kletsk, which might have preserved the yeshiva in its darkest hours. Indeed, as was already mentioned, among the essential conditions necessary for a yeshiva's survival and continuity, the nature of its students played a most important role.[48]

NOTES

1. For their numbers, see the introduction, note 21.
2. Liekis, *A State,* 115–16.

3. Liekis, *A State*, 158–59; Va'ad HaAretz, *Der Idisher*, 117; Gar, *Azoy*, 11; Lunsky, *MeHagetto*, 60, in footnote. See contemporary writings such as Vigodsky, *In Shturm*, 213–14; Kruk, *Taḥat Diglan*, 402. This chain of events would have extensive historic significance in terms of the relations between the two countries. Lithuania decided to break off diplomatic relations and even mail service with its aggressive neighbor, and the border was sealed for almost two decades.

4. "The miracle on the Vistula" took place on August 16, 1920, when the Poles, led by Marshal Józef Piłsudski (1867–1935), attacked the Russian cavalry division in the outskirts of Warsaw and within a few days succeeded in surrounding the Russian Army, forcing it to retreat quickly from Poland.

5. Some yeshivas did not pass through Vilna. The Radin Yeshiva, for example, was forced to move south toward Baranovitch and in June 1921 returned to its original location in Radin within the borders of Poland (Greiniman, *Ḥafetz Ḥayim*, 12–13; Yoshor, *The Chafetz Chaim*, 410; Samson-Rabinowitz, *A Jubilee*, 57).

6. Klibansky, *KeTzur*, 47–48. For the circumstances regarding the breakout of the argument, see Tikochinski, *Lamdanut*, 36–39.

7. Klibansky, *KeTzur*, 77–78. The deportation order was part of the new policy of the Russian military administration at the front to expel Jewish residents who lived in nearby fortress-towns (Zagranitchniy Komitet Bunda, *Doklad*, 27–28).

8. Klibansky, *KeTzur*, 88, 90–91, 112.

9. Katz, *Toledotai*, 5; Ezrat Torah, *Zikkaron baSefer*, 57; Katz, *Tenuat*, III, 76; *HaDerech*, Tishrei-Shevat 5681 (1920/1): 132–33. At this point, Slabodka was already a suburb of Kovna. Regarding the establishment of the new yeshiva, see Klibansky, *KeTzur*, 107–9.

10. Katz, *Toledotai*, 5; Rozental, *HaZvi*, 281. The unification of the two yeshivas is evidenced by the unusual increase in the number of students in Knesset-Yisrael at the beginning of the summer term of 1921. The unification was not accompanied by an atmosphere of crisis, since both yeshivas had a similar approach to study and Musar. Rabbi Yablonsky emigrated to the United States and became rosh-yeshiva of Beth HaMedrash L'Torah in Chicago (Yablonsky, *Nitzanei Nisan*, preface); Rabbi Levovitz went for a short time to the Mir Yeshiva and then returned to Lithuania and began to serve as the Musar supervisor of the Ponevezh Yeshiva (letter: Finkel to Ḥasman, Dec. 9, 1921 [VHY/371]; *DoV*, June 12, 1936).

11. Oshri, "Yeshivat," 153; Publication "El Aḥeinu B'nei Yisrael" (To our brothers, the Sons of Yisrael), Apr. 12, 1926 (CRC-129/8). See also Riff, *Ner*, 42. Even-Yisrael was founded by Rabbi Moshe Finkel (1883–1925), a Talmud instructor in the yeshiva-gedola and the son of its Musar supervisor. After his death in 1925, the yeshiva was renamed Ohel-Moshe.

12. Kravitz, *Aḥar He'asef*, 573; Rozental, *HaZvi*, 281; *DMZ*, Jan. 31, 1924; Sher, *Beit Yisrael*, 6.

13. "Geschichtlicher Ueberblick," 3; Surasky, *Marbitzei*, II, 66; *DoV*, June 12, 1936; Klibansky, *KeTzur*, 64–66, 87.

14. Finkel, "Kol Kore" (from Yiddish; cf. Shoshkes, *Lender*, 231; Ḥigger, *Sam*, 54. A *verst* is 0.66 miles, or 1 kilometer). See Epstein, "Yeshivat Mir," 99; Sorotzkin, "HaRav R' Yitzḥak Elḥanan," 279.

15. Epstein, "Yeshivat Mir," 99–100; Finkel, "Kol Kore"; Lunsky, *MeHagetto*, 60, in footnote; Ḥigger, *Sam*, 54, 57–58; Zinowitz, "*Mir*," 67. The aid given to the yeshivas by the Central Relief will be discussed in chapter 3.

16. For a discussion of the departure date, see Klibansky, "HaYeshivot," 98n27. The border between Russia and Poland was fixed next to the town of Stoibtz, east of Mir.

17. Epstein, "Yeshivat Mir," 100; Finkel, "Kol Kore"; HaMerkaz haOlami, *Keren*, 8; Blumental, *Mir*, 161; Sorotzkin, "HaRav R' Avraham Zvi," 39. More than two thousand Jews lived in Mir (more than 50 percent of its inhabitants; Blumental, *Mir*, 43). YEKOPO (Jewish Committee for Aiding Victims of War) was a relief committee established at the beginning of the First World War by Jewish community activists in Petrograd (formerly St. Petersburg) for soldiers at the front and their families at home. After the expulsion of Lithuanian Jews, the committee directed its help toward them. At the end of the war, its activities were renewed in Poland in order to help rehabilitate communities that had been damaged during the war (Pevzner, "Yevreiskiy Komittet"; Shabad, "Der Onheib").

18. Epstein, "Yeshivat Mir," 98, 100–101; Sorotzkin, "HaRav R' Avraham Zvi," 39. Regarding the rules of inheritance, see chapter 5.

19. "Geschichtlicher Ueberblick," 4; Epstein, "Yeshivat Mir," 103, 111; letters: Finkel to Grodzensky, Feb. 8, 1925, and Greineman to Va'ad-HaYeshivot, Aug. 31, 1924 (VHY/371); Finkel, "Kol Kore." In comparison, the number of Mir students at the end of 1921 was one hundred (letter: Finkel to Ḥasman, Dec. 9, 1921 [VHY/371]; for a possible reason for this growth, see chapter 6, note 48). Regarding the reduction in support from the Central Relief, see chapter 3.

20. Klibansky, *KeTzur*, 49–50, 77, 79–81, 88; Lichtenstein, *Degel*, 14.

21. Lunsky, *MeHagetto*, 60, in footnote; HaMerkaz haOlami, *Keren*, 20. Rabbi Bassin served as Moreh-Tzedek in the Vilna suburb of Shnipishok until his death.

22. Berenstein, *Hegyonot*, 64, 93–95; Zeidman, "Yeshivat 'Knesset'," 323–24 (Zeidman was mistaken regarding the date). The distance by air between Krementchug and Vilna is 840 kilometers, but the actual route was longer. The elderly father also reached Vilna and died a short time after.

23. Karp, *Sefer*, 13; Ran, *Yerushalayim*, 293. Let it be mentioned that in addition to Knesset Beit-Yitzḥak, the local Remayle Yeshiva was also a heavy burden on the Vilna community.

24. Karp, *Sefer*, 13–14; Edelstein, *Rabbi*, 35–36; letter: Yogel to Schuw, Jul. 17, 1926 (VHY/579).

25. Karp, *Sefer*, 1.

26. Yeshiva reports, May 30, 1927, and Nov. 9, 1926 (VHY/1129). The quote is from letter: Va'ad-HaYeshivot of Kamenitz to Va'ad-HaYeshivot of Vilna, Jan. 16, 1928 (VHY/212; an adage based on *Pirkei Avot* 3:16).

27. Karp, *Sefer*, 14; Edelstein, *Rabbi*, 41; Yeshiva report, May 30, 1927 (VHY/1129); Epstein, "Yeshivat Mir," 104. See also Rabiner, *Maran*, 261. For a discussion of the number of students in the yeshiva, see Klibansky, "HaYeshivot," 104n75.

28. This date appeared in the yeshiva's letterhead in the interwar period. The yeshiva even celebrated its centennial anniversary in 1931 (VHY/579-560). For other dates, see Gotlieb, *Oholei-Shem*, 363; HaMerkaz haOlami, *Keren*, 8; *HaTzoffe*, Feb. 8, 1946.

29. Lichtenstein and Rabinowitz, *Pinkas*, 183, 246; Yeshiva reports, 1926–28 (VHY/1155); Klibansky, *KeTzur*, 61; letter: Yogel to Grodzensky, Mar. 3, 1925 (VHY/579).

30. Letter: Yogel to Schuw, Nov. 16, 1928 (VHY/579). See letter: Yogel to Schuw, Feb. 26, 1926 (VHY/579); Yeshiva report, Dec. 28, 1927 (VHY/1155). Regarding Va'ad-HaYeshivot and its separate allocations to yeshivot-ketanot, see chapter 3.

31. Letters: Yogel to Grodzensky, Feb. 23, 1925, and Yogel to Schuw, Nov. 10, 1929 (VHY/580); Yeshiva reports, Apr. 27, 1926, and Dec. 28, 1927 (VHY/1155); Rozental, *Torah*, 18. See also Gardi, *Pirkei*, I, 24.

32. Klibansky, *KeTzur,* 51–53, 100.

33. Alperowitz, *Telz,* 62; Klibansky, "HaYeshivot," 107n96.

34. Class picture of the mechinah from 1937 (LHA); report of yeshiva lecturers, Apr. 5, 1938 (LCSA, 391/4/518); Gifter, "Yeshivat," 177; *HaNe'eman* 4 (1928): 17; testimony: Karno.

35. Katz, *Tenuat,* V, 41; Barkai, "Naḥalat," 30; *IdL,* Jun. 20, 1924; "The Telz Mechinah—Studies Program," Dec. 20, 1925 (LCSA, 391/4/502). Secular studies were also part of the mechinah of the Grodno Yeshiva, but it would seem that these studies were of a limited nature (Gershuni, *Sha'arei,* "Even a Child Is Known by His Doings" section). The quote is from Yitzḥak-Raphael Holtzberg (Etzion, "HaZerem," 162). Regarding the Lida Yeshiva, see Klibansky, *KeTzur,* 59–60.

36. For a more detailed review of this activity, presented here in brief, see Klibansky, "LeKadesh."

37. *IdL,* Feb. 1, 1924, and Aug. 1, 1924. Gifter is mistaken on this point (Gifter, "Yeshivat," 178). Yavneh was one of three Jewish educational networks that arose in independent Lithuania (see Etzion, "HaZerem"; Zalkin "SheYihye"). This was a modern, non-party-affiliated network that was under Orthodox sponsorship.

38. Etzion, "HaZerem," 162–63; *IdL,* Dec. 14, 1923; Gifter, "Yeshivat," 178; Wischnitzer, "Ḥomer," II, 607. About a year and a half after his nomination, Rabbi Hirschowitz was appointed rabbi of Virbaln in Lithuania, but even afterward members of Rabbi Bloch's family continued to serve in the seminary and preserve its yeshiva atmosphere.

39. The third one, the Zvhil Yeshiva will be dealt with in chapter 2. Regarding the disbanded yeshivas (such as Shklov, Minsk, Mohilev, and Ḥarkov), see Klibansky, "HaYeshivot," 116–19.

40. Klibansky, *KeTzur,* 68, 78–79; Meltzer, *BeDerech,* 101, 108. Kletsk was located about sixty kilometers west of Slutsk. The new border ran along the Lan River near Kletsk.

41. Ḥigger, *Sam,* 50–52, 54; Naḥmani and Ḥinitz, *Pinkas,* 89–90, 111–13; *Kol Ya'akov,* Sep. 15, 1922; Stein, *Pinkas,* 37, 41, 61, 82, 98, 109, 197, 239; Meltzer, *BeDerech,* 89–90, 109, 293; HaMerkaz haOlami, *Keren,* 21.

42. List of students, Sep. 7, 1924 (VHY/227-228); letter: Kotler to Schuw, May 19, 1933 (VHY/227); Meltzer, *BeDerech,* 139, 293.

43. Wischnitzer, "Ḥomer," IV, 744; Klibansky, *KeTzur,* 68–69; Graubart, *Sefer Zikaron,* 135–36. The distance between Kobrin and Amtchislav by air is 530 kilometers!

44. Wischnitzer, "Ḥomer, " IV, 744; Schwartz and Billitzky, *Kobrin,* 135, 151, 259–65; letter: Nenedik to Va'ad-HaYeshivot, Aug. 19, 1924 (VHY/239); Yeshiva-Ketana report, Mar. 1, 1938 (VHY/237).

45. Letters: Matus to Schuw, Jan. 1, 1930 (VHY/238), and Nenedik-Va'ad-HaYeshivot, Aug. 19, 1924 (VHY/239); postcard: Matus to Schuw, May 7, 1926 (VHY/238); Yeshiva reports, May 2, 1926, and Dec. 13, 1929 (VHY/1131); Hed, "Beit Ulpena," 325; Schwartz and Billitzky, *Kobrin,* 246, 259, 261. At the end of 1929, there were 106 talmidim.

46. Druck, *R' Levy,* 35; Warhaftig, *Shalmei.* See also *HaNe'eman* 25 (1930): 3.

47. This is how the mashgiaḥ Rabbi Avraham-Zvi Listovsky described him: "The rosh-yeshiva would always relinquish what was due him, and was among those who were robbed because of his generosity, goodness and honesty" (letter: Listovsky to Va'ad-HaYeshivot, May 20, 1937 [VHY/579]). The "Ḥafetz-Ḥayim" even called him "The sweet Jew" (Gerlitz, *Ḥidushei,* 44n49).

48. Letter: Nenedik to Va'ad-HaYeshivot, Aug. 19, 1924 (VHY/239). See Klibansky, *KeTzur,* 362–63, regarding this relationship.

2

Expansion Trends in the Yeshiva World

The Lithuanian yeshiva world experienced a new sort of reawakening in the interwar period. This reawakening expressed itself in the opening of quite a few new yeshivas in addition to the loose network of veteran yeshivas that were being rebuilt. Were there really so many young men desirous of yeshiva-style learning who could not be accommodated by the existing yeshivas? In the early 1930s, the answer to this question would tend to be positive, and the rosh-yeshiva of Mir, Rabbi Eliezer-Yehudah Finkel, explicitly said this: "If it is necessary to accept all the students of the yeshivot-ketanot to the yeshivot-gedolot, then we must make sure that there are places open for them in the yeshivot-gedolot . . . or establish another yeshiva-gedola." However this was not the reason for the aforementioned reawakening, which began immediately after the First World War.[1]

There was a great change in conditions in the period after the First World War in Eastern Europe in comparison to the situation before the war. It has already been mentioned that the Jewish public in general no longer regarded the yeshivas as prestigious institutions. At the same time, the yeshiva had competitors among the new Jewish educational institutions in Lithuania and Poland, which attracted the youth and promised hope and a better future for their graduates. In this situation, because the yeshivas were institutions that required support, they could not hope for adequate assistance from the Jews in these countries, and rabbis were reluctant to establish yeshivas in their communities. Only certain energetic individuals who were experienced yeshiva administrators dared to take on this challenge. In Lithuania this was Rabbi Yosef-Shlomo Kahaneman, who had already gained experience in setting up yeshivas for young people in Vilna Province before the war. When he was chosen as town rabbi of Ponevezh in 1919, he decided to establish a new yeshiva there, and in only a few years it joined the ranks of the prominent yeshivas of independent Lithuania. In Poland it was Rabbi Aharon Baksht. Before the war, he had administrated a yeshiva in Shadeve in Kovna Province, where he served as rabbi. When the war broke out, his yeshiva was closed, and he was among those who were expelled from the town during the widespread eviction of Jews from that province. A short while after returning from exile, he was appointed rabbi of Suvalk and quickly set up a small yeshiva there. The common denominator between these two initiatives was the time in which they occurred (immediately after the war and before the veteran yeshivas had recovered) and their place (in large communities where the yeshiva founders served as rabbis and where there were no senior yeshivas in the area).[2]

A significant reinforcement to these individual initiatives came in the wake of the return from Russian and Ukrainian exile of the heads of the Novardok yeshivas, who were experienced in setting up and running yeshivas in those countries. They reestablished their Torah institutions in Poland after the war, similar to heads of other veteran yeshivas who did likewise and whose activities were described in the previous chapter. However, in addition to these, they set up a comprehensive network of new yeshivas, including a few yeshivot-gedolot.

It was not only educators who had seniority and experience who were involved in setting up new yeshivas. It is astounding to find among the initiators enthusiastic youngsters lacking in experience who made all the complicated and practical preparations for establishing their yeshivas on their own, and Hasidic Lithuanian *admorim* who chose to take similar steps and initiated the establishment of Lithuanian-style yeshivas for their own communities. A more profound examination of the new yeshivas, presented in Map 2.1, shows that they did not appear in a void. These surprising initiatives developed out of the new and fascinating trends taking place in the Lithuanian yeshiva world.

MAP 2.1.

Deployment of the Lithuanian yeshivas in the 1930s.

THE NOVARDOK YESHIVA MOVEMENT

The Novardok yeshiva network was an inseparable component of the Lithuanian yeshiva world. Nevertheless, the Novardok yeshivas were endowed with some exceptional characteristics. They stood out because they carried out in practice "the lowliness of man" Musar method, which was based on concepts that were novel and unusual in the yeshiva world.[3] The general Jewish populace was also aware of the Novardok yeshivas in particular because they were spread out in an extraordinary manner in Russia and Ukraine during the war years. When these yeshivas were relocated to Poland, the characteristics of their spread were similar. Each one became a large yeshiva center that established and supervised many yeshivas, and yeshivot-ketanot in particular, in the surrounding area.

This vertical hierarchy, not found in the Lithuanian yeshiva world, applied not only to the relationship of the central yeshiva to those under its sponsorship. Each one of these yeshiva centers, even though it functioned independently financially, was also a part of a large organization with its ruling institutions and a binding code for activity. This complex hierarchical organization required contact among its components, and this contact took on unique characteristics: large general meetings that the organization irregularly held permitted the exchange of ideas between yeshiva officials, and an internal journal provided direct connection between the students and served as an optimal tool for uniting them. There is no doubt that the ranked hierarchy in this organization and the types of connectedness within it gave it the appearance in the Lithuanian yeshiva world of a well-developed movement—the Novardok yeshiva movement.[4]

Location of the Centers

In order to appreciate the singular characteristics of the Novardok yeshivas and their modes of deployment in Eastern Europe, one has to investigate their history. Their spiritual father was Rabbi Yosef-Yozel Hurwitz, who for a short time was one of the talmidim of the founder of the Musar movement, Rabbi Yisrael Lipkin, and developed his own unique Musar system. In 1896 Rabbi Hurwitz set up a yeshiva in the town of Novardok in Minsk Province. In the revolutionary period of the early twentieth century, he strengthened the Musar studies in his yeshiva when he adopted the methods of the radical movements that threatened it. In this way, exchanges of Musar ideas between baḥurim in the framework of a Musar-*birzhe* (Musar Stock Exchange), unusual Musar exercises called "actions," and discussions regarding to the personal Musar level of each student during intimate meetings of Musar groups became part of the yeshiva's regular program. These new modalities succeeded in exciting talmidim and even connecting young people from outside to the yeshiva.

Rabbi Hurwitz aspired to spread his Musar approach and sent the most talented of his avrechim to establish yeshivas in South Russia. Each pair stood at the head of one of the new yeshivas, and their goal was to train their young charges to study at the Novardok Yeshiva. An even greater opportunity to realize these aspirations for growth came with the First World War. The collapse of the Russian front and the movement of the German army eastward at the end of the summer of 1915 drove Rabbi Hurwitz to leave Novardok. He settled with the yeshiva in Homel in Mohilev Province and appointed his son-in-law Rabbi Avraham Yoffen as rosh-yeshiva. After the yeshiva was organized in its new place, Rabbi Hurwitz renewed its traditional activities of expansion in the spring of 1916 and sent his son-in-law at the head of a large group of students to the distant city of Rostov-on-Don near the Azov Sea to establish a new yeshiva-gedola. This was the first of a chain of yeshivas established in Russia and Ukraine. They were headed by the disciples of Rabbi Hurwitz, and each had branches for local youngsters. The new yeshivas maintained close contact with Rabbi Hurwitz, who personally supervised them from the main yeshiva in Homel and visited them often. After his death in Kiev at the end of 1919, Rabbi Yoffen, his son-in-law, took on the administration of the network of Novardok yeshivas, and the rest of Rabbi Hurwitz's disciples saw it as their obligation to continue on their rabbi's path.

The Bolshevik takeover of Russia and Ukraine caused increasing pressure on the Lithuanian yeshivas, including those affiliated with Novardok. In 1921, Rabbi Yoffen and several senior students were arrested and held for a month. This arrest hastened the decision of the Novardok leaders to abandon their places of residence with their yeshivas. The Novardok talmidim, most of whom were natives of Russia and Ukraine, were not eligible for exit permits, and in their desire to follow their rabbis, they prepared themselves for a very complicated, dangerous, clandestine escape campaign. The escapes took place over a two-year period, in which five hundred to six hundred baḥurim crossed the border—and were sometimes arrested and taken back and tried to cross once more.[5]

The Novardok roshei-yeshiva who arrived in Poland decided to preserve the separate yeshiva framework that had existed in Russia and Ukraine and to ensure administrative and social continuity after the move. Even more, it was clear to them that due to limitations of funds and space, they would not be able to establish a united yeshiva for the many Novardok students.[6] But a number of additional factors stood behind this decision:

- Personal reasons: The close disciples of Rabbi Hurwitz, who all had unique personalities, were committed to continuing to run their yeshivas in Poland as well and to passing down the teachings of

Novardok to their students, just as they had received these teachings from their rabbi, in the way that seemed the most authentic to them.

- Ideological reasons: The expansive character of Novardok's activity required the establishment of a network in Poland, which would make the tradition of spreading out possible in that country as well. In this network, the Novardok yeshivas were assigned the role of separate organizational centers, each of which was supposed to spread out over vast geographic areas.

Indeed, over time Rabbi Hurwitz's disciples established five central yeshivas, and one was even located outside of Poland. The first two were set up in 1921, one in Mezritch by Rabbi David Bliacher, who had formerly served as rosh-yeshiva in Kiev, and one in Bialystok by Rabbi Avraham Yoffen, who formerly headed the yeshiva of Homel. One year later, Rabbi Avraham Zelmans, who had served as rosh-yeshiva in Rostov-on-Don during the war, established a central yeshiva in Warsaw. These three were considered the main centers of Novardok, and all the general meetings of the movement met exclusively in these institutions during the interwar years. In 1925 an additional yeshiva-gedola in Ivye, whose rosh-yeshiva Rabbi Shmuel Weintraub had headed the Berditchev Yeshiva in Kiev Province during the war, was designated as central. This designation accompanied the yeshiva during its many moves until it reached its final destination, when it settled in Pinsk in the winter of 1927–1928.[7]

It is interesting to note that none of centers attempted to locate in the town of Novardok, the cradle of Rabbi Hurwitz's yeshivas, a place whose nostalgic name had a special value. Only in 1928 did Rabbi David Budnick (1893–1941), who had been the rosh-yeshiva in Zhitomir, Vohlin Province, during the war, establish a central yeshiva in Novardok. His efforts were not successful, and the new yeshiva remained limited and without prospects of expanding. In the early 1930s, he set up a yeshiva in Dvinsk, Latvia, and this proved to be a central yeshiva, the fifth and last of the movement.[8]

An examination of the location of the Novardok centers, especially the locations of the three first centers Mezritch, Bialystok, and Warsaw, which remained unchanged throughout the years, invites the question as to whether there was a plan involved in their selection. These locations were significant in that they were all situated near the borders of the Kongresówka and even inside those borders. This area was nearly empty of other yeshivas. The heads of the Novardok centers wanted to completely change this situation in their conviction that the influence of their yeshivas on their surroundings would create that change. The final picture of the centers would tend to support this. They were spread over a geographic area that had been very sparse in terms of traditional Lithuanian yeshivas, and each one dominated a large region. Spreading out in this area allowed the Novardok movement to exert optimal influence from Latvia in the north to Galicia in the south. Absent from this vast area were the northern Kresy region and the territories of independent Lithuania, where most of the other Lithuanian yeshivas were located.[9]

These centers were set up in communities that were not used to the special character of Novardok students. However, groups within the communities soon learned to value and appreciate them. The following is a description of the "reception" for the young men of the Bialystok yeshiva: "At first the town regarded them with distrust because of their extreme religious conduct and their odd appearance. But in the end they won the affection of the Orthodox residents thanks to their honest behavior, their virtue and seriousness, and also because that in the course of time they adjusted themselves somewhat to the comportment customary in Poland."[10] In general, the centers experienced similar difficulties in becoming absorbed in the local landscape that the other Lithuanian yeshivas did, as described in the first chapter. Only the yeshiva of Rabbi Shmuel Weintraub, which was the last to arrive from the Ukraine, suffered a long period of wandering and tribulations before it settled in its permanent home.[11]

The Center and Its Branches

One of the outstanding characteristics of the Novardok yeshivas, expansion, was expressed in the interwar years by their efforts to add as many young men to their ranks as possible in the areas where they were located. Rabbi Yosef-Yozel Hurwitz had already acted in this way, especially in Russia and Ukraine during the First World War. His rebuke from that time to the mashgiaḥ of the Mir Yeshiva, Rabbi Yeruḥam Levovitz—that he did not do enough to increase the number of new yeshivas during the same period that Novardok had established forty—was symbolic. Rabbi Levovitz's apologetic reply that he was still obliged to work hard at caring for his single yeshiva emphasizes the unique approach of Rabbi Hurwitz to branching out.[12]

His disciples understandably continued in his footsteps, and the intentional division of their centers throughout Russia and Ukraine served only to increase the proliferation of Novardok. When they succeeded in fleeing the Bolshevik state and settled in Poland, a large arena of activity opened before them once more. In 1924 the Novardok bulletin *Ohr HaMusar* came out with a direct plea to return to the long-standing tradition:

> Now the time has come to be strong and stand in the breach, to build and set up yeshivas to raise up the glory of Torah and *yir'ah* [fear of Heaven] in Israel's dispersion. If in the cities of Russia and the Ukraine—the place of evil and persecution of our holy religion—the holy Torah protected those who studied it and saved young people from dire destruction, Heaven forfend, even more so in our country [Poland] where we have the choice and possibility of acting to teach Torah and yir'ah without interference, the obligation is now to increase our vigor and might in the teaching of Torah and saving the youth who are trapped in the deadly snare of the free-thinkers, may the Merciful One save us.[13]

These words touched a raw nerve in Novardok. In the winter of 1924, there were only six Novardok yeshivot-gedolot in all of Poland (among them three central yeshivas) and seven yeshivot-ketanot for younger students. The branching out of the centers was completely indiscernible, seemingly due to unpreparedness, either from a human or material standpoint. Indeed, in the general meetings of 1924, the task of setting up both yeshivot-gedolot and yeshivot-ketanot branches was assigned to each of the centers in its own vicinity. These decisions were enough to spur on the centers. By the winter of 1925, another twelve Novardok yeshivas appeared, three established by each of the Mezritch and Bialystok Central Yeshivas, two by the Warsaw Center, and four set up by the Ivye Center that had managed to move to Volkovisk. This rapid expansion had an effect on circles within the Polish Kongresówka, and in that same year they began to demand the establishment of similar yeshivot-ketanot in their towns despite the dire economic crisis in Poland. Naturally, it was impossible to continue at a similar growth rate in the following years because the centers were obligated to maintain the branches they had opened until that point. Nevertheless their determination to expand and branch out did not flag. In another three years there were thirty Novardok yeshivas, and by 1937 there were sixty![14]

This was the formula for the expansion of the centers: Each of them was required to take care of setting up an attractive Torah infrastructure in its surrounding geographic area. Every six months, during the intermediate days of the festivals of Pesaḥ and Sukkot, senior students were selected, and their task was to set up branches in the towns in that area and invest in their establishment for a period of several months. Each one of these "roshei-yeshiva" was joined by two or three younger talmidim, and the team served as a local nucleus from which a new yeshiva-ketana was to grow.

The selected roshei-yeshiva, filled with a sense of the Novardok mission, had already gained experience in pedagogy and influencing people, usually from serving as heads of Musar groups in their yeshivas, and therefore they were qualified to fulfill the responsibilities assigned to them. The following tasks were in the list of activities of a rosh-yeshiva of this sort:

- Gathering local young people and studying with them in the beit-midrash as a means of creating the fact of a new yeshiva being established.
- Giving a *derasha* (address) in the beit-midrash to let the townspeople know that a yeshiva had been established.
- Going from house to house to collect food for the yeshiva and attempting to find regular donors who would help in its continued activities.
- Arranging sleeping places for talmidim in the women's section of the synagogue or in vacant houses.

After this initial stage, the rosh-yeshiva continued to run the branch under his charge while maintaining constant contact with the directors in the center. Occasionally he would even send the most exceptional students for a limited stay in the center to spiritually strengthen them.

The establishment of a branch required significant financial outlay. In addition to his lectures, the rosh-yeshiva was obliged to constantly raise funds and even visit neighboring towns for that purpose. Many times the financial support of the center and the contributions collected were not sufficient to maintain the new yeshiva. However, the lack of funds did not prevent the heads of the centers from continuing their efforts to expand, which was considered to be a basic principle of the Novardok movement. Even more so, the establishment of a branch without financial backing was considered training for the "virtue of trust," a virtue that also had a significant place in Novardok teachings both in theory and in practice.[15]

Even though the centers fulfilled their mission to expand and spread out with great determination, their methods were insufficiently organized and had a number of shortcomings:[16]

A) Between the Centers
- There was no comprehensive geographic plan for the establishment of new yeshivas. In some areas there were many yeshivas, but others lacked even one.
- The area of influence for each center was not clearly defined. For example, in 1925 in the Lomzhe area in the Bialystok district, there were several branches of the Bialystok Center and one branch of the Warsaw Center.

B) Within the Centers
- Every center's director was required to devote basic attention to each of his branches. As the branches multiplied, this task became burdensome and was added to the rest of his concerns, of which the principal one was the material survival of his yeshiva.
- The need to set up a new yeshiva every six months forced the centers to scatter the best of their human resources and budget much-needed funding for these activities. At times this led to the neglect of established branches and a lack of sufficient support for them in staff and funding.
- Some senior students were not overly fond of the task of setting up new yeshivas, and they preferred concentrating on their own intellectual and spiritual growth over dedicating their time to serving the community. At the end of the minimum period of time demanded of them, they returned to the centers and passed on the administration of the new yeshiva to their colleagues. It

is obvious that these frequent changes often harmed the new yeshivas.

- Even the younger talmidim who were sent to form the nucleus and strengthen the new yeshivas were not eager to remain in far-flung communities, away from their friends and studies in the center. Their aspiration was to return as soon as they could, and there were baḥurim who did this before their appointed time and without authorization from the administration.

These shortcomings were not invisible to the heads of the centers, and they were discussed in quite a few of the Novardok movement meetings. It was possible to remedy the flaws that existed between the centers through basic decisions made by the heads of the movement. But it was more difficult to ameliorate the shortcomings within the centers. Attempts were made to improve the connection between the centers and their branches through decisions such as appointing a special "secretary" in the center who would serve as a personal liaison with each branch, visits by the director of the center in the branches once a semester, "regional assemblies" with representatives of the center and its branches, and even special committees for the administration of the yeshivot-ketanot. However, because only senior students were required to head the branches, each center was limited in the number of branches it could establish and maintain over time. Considering the lack of enthusiasm of some of the senior baḥurim for these arduous tasks, which did not always fit their talents and aspirations, it is not surprising that several yeshivot-ketanot closed after a few years. By the early 1930s, laxity had even eaten away at the efforts of establishing new yeshivas in place of those that had ceased to exist, and in 1933 it was decided to "strengthen the spirit of building new yeshivas."[17]

It was not only the internal laxity that harmed these activities of community service. The Novardok emissaries sometimes felt that the atmosphere was not encouraging, as described by Rabbi Avraham Yoffen in an article from 1937: "The old-time *ḥeder,* where Jewish children were educated in Bible and Talmud and the desire to go to yeshiva, has been forgotten, and in its place are irreligious schools, where there is not only neither Bible nor Mishna [Oral Torah], but they fill him [the child] with wrong opinions and freethinking ideas, and he runs away from the yeshiva like one who runs from fire. This is why the rabbis of the 'Beit-Yosef' yeshivas have taken upon themselves the obligation of self-sacrifice for establishing yeshivas."[18] In the Bialystok area and other places, there were towns where parents had ceased sending their sons to yeshivot-ketanot, and the schools dwindled. A turning point occurred with the founding of the "Committee to Spread Torah," which took upon itself to send emissaries at the beginning of each semester to the towns. Filled with a sense of mission, the young men stirred both the parents and their sons and succeeded in recruiting dozens of boys for the yeshivot-ketanot, thus leading to the establishment of new yeshivas.[19]

From Network to Movement

Conditions during the First World War hindered regular contact among the Novardok senior yeshivas that were scattered over Russia and Ukraine. In order to raise common issues for discussion, Rabbi Yosef-Yozel Hurwitz would convene the directors twice yearly for a general meeting, and these assemblies' directives were binding on all Novardok students. Six meetings were held in the period of exile, and these turned the Novardok yeshivas into a united network.[20]

In the interwar period, communication between the centers became easier. The most efficient and direct means to create an atmosphere of connectedness was to continue to hold multiparticipant general meetings, where it was possible to discuss the problems that were on the agenda of several yeshivas or the entire network. The first meetings were convened at relatively short intervals of approximately half a year, as took place during the exile. This was because the initial problems in the unfamiliar new locations were still too complex to be best solved at the level of the center's director. The first general meeting was held in Warsaw in the summer of 1923 with the participation of approximately fifty directors and representatives of the most senior Musar groups of yeshivas. The second and third general meetings were held in Bialystok and Warsaw in 1924, and the fourth took place in Mezritch in the winter of 1925. The decision taken in the fourth meeting to schedule the general meetings once a year indicates the beginning of the institutionalization of the Novardok network after it had solved the urgent problems which had troubled it in its early stages.[21]

Indeed, the fifth general meeting was convened in Bialystok in the summer of 1926. In its deliberations, fundamental adjustments relating to the Novardok worldview and the purpose of its organization were examined. Its significance was expressed by a number of decisions that were made:

- Establishing a temporary transfer of selected students from one center to another in order to strengthen the feeling of Novardok unity.
- Establishing a kollel for yeshiva directors for a limited period of time, so they could work on their own personal spiritual and intellectual growth.
- Establishing a joint yeshiva for all the centers in a new location.

These decisions clearly indicate that the fifth general meeting was an important turning point—the transformation of a network of yeshivas to a united Novardok movement.[22]

As the movement became more established, the necessity for frequent general meetings decreased. At the eighth meeting in Bialystok in the winter of 1933, it was decided to further lengthen the period between meetings to two years. The ninth general meeting took place in Mezritch in the winter of 1935, and the tenth, the "Jubilee Meeting," which was also the last, was convened in Bialystok at the end of the winter of 1937. These general meetings dealt with administrational matters and the organization of ongoing activities, but they also related to Musar issues that affected all the yeshivas and to strengthening the bond among their students.[23]

The movement's journal was also an important implement for encouraging intercenter unity. Rabbi Hurwitz had already spoken in favor of publishing periodicals, and he saw in them a useful means for linking the Novardok network's students. His disciples took this task upon themselves, and a new Novardok journal, *Ohr HaMusar* [*The Light of Musar*] was published in 1923. Due to a lack of financial means, the periodical was printed by hectograph in seven issues in its first year, but by the winter of 1924 the journal appeared in regular print. The periodical included articles by the leaders of the Musar movement that had not been previously published, Musar talks of the heads of the Novardok yeshivas, and movement news such as summaries of the general meetings and its achievements in the field of expansion. The periodical's purpose was defined as being "a means of expression and bringing together all those who truly seek God, to increase the possibility, even in this age, to remain in a state of true wholeness."[24]

This journal served as a modern and efficient means of providing periodic updates to the Novardok yeshivas and creating a feeling of belonging to a unified movement among the students. The plan to make it into a quarterly never succeeded. Due to lack of funds, it was published once a year until 1928 and then began a long hiatus that was explained by the need to devote funds to the establishment of a Novardok yeshiva in the Land of Israel. A new publication came out in 1931 in Tel-Aviv. From that point, just two more editions of *Ohr HaMusar* were published (in Tel-Aviv as well), and this infrequency was again justified by the tribulations of constructing the new Eretz-Yisrael yeshivas of the Novardok movement and a lack of funds.

The lengthy stretches of time between editions of *Ohr HaMusar* stimulated the centers to issue their own internal publications using their own money. The yeshiva-gedola in Ostrovtsa went even further and at the initiative of Rabbi Yitzḥak Waldschein (1896–1941), its activist spiritual mashgiaḥ, began to publish a printed monthly called *Ḥayei HaMusar* [*Musar Life*], which came out between 1935 and 1937. Its successor, *El HaMevakesh* [*To the Seeker*], was also printed and appeared in 1938–1939. These two periodicals represented the movement as a whole and served during the second half of the 1930s as a substitute for *Ohr HaMusar* and as a means for uniting all the students of the Novardok movement.[25]

"CAN THE TWO WALK TOGETHER?" HASIDIM AND THE LITHUANIAN YESHIVAS

One of the most interesting phenomena is the attitude of Hasidim toward yeshivas in general and toward Lithuanian yeshivas in particular. This section does not relate to Hasidim who saw their affiliation with Hasidism as largely symbolic, but rather to descendants of Hasidic families who continued in the path of their forefathers, lived in Hasidic communities, and ardently followed their leaders. Their attitude toward yeshivas becomes clear upon examining the situation at the end of the nineteenth century and the beginning of the twentieth. The Hasidic batei-midrash and *shtieblach* in Poland and the Pale of Settlement were filled with young men who studied throughout the day outside any institutional framework, similar to the study kibbutzim, which were part of the cultural milieu of Lithuanian Jewry some decades earlier. Hasidic parents saw no need for an alternative solution because they could easily supervise their sons who remained close to home. But even parents who preferred a yeshiva framework were concerned about sending their sons to a Lithuanian yeshiva because of the "enlightened" practices, in their opinion, that were common there. This is how a Hasidic youth, Yitzḥak Gerstenkorn, described the background to his father's concerns as he weighed sending his son to a Lithuanian yeshiva:

> The dress of a Torah student in Poland was necessarily traditional Jewish dress: a long *capoteh* with a sash, and long side curls, and he would not trim even one hair of his beard. Another rule observed in Poland was that an unmarried young man could not achieve completeness in Torah knowledge, no matter how talented he may be, since true knowledge of Torah cannot be acquired except by one who studies it in purity. Therefore fathers would try to marry off their sons in their youth, and they would seek out a match that came with "provisions," so that the son would be supported by his father-in-law for at least three to five years after the marriage, in order to make it possible for him to achieve completeness in Torah knowledge and its teachings. This was not the viewpoint of the Lithuanian spiritual leaders on this topic. In Lithuania a twenty year old was considered to be but a youth who had not achieved maturity, and he was not highly regarded in the yeshiva. An exception to this rule were only the celebrated *illuyim* [prodigies]; those of ordinary talents did not receive any recognition in the yeshiva until they reached the age of twenty-five, and a young man who was older than thirty was not considered unacceptable. . . . The outer clothing of the yeshiva students, even the most pious among them, the Musar Yeshiva students, was European: their jackets were short and they did not grow their beards.[26]

The yeshiva alternatives for Hasidim in their areas of residence were few and sectorial because admorim designated them for their own communities. The impetus for establishing many of them, besides teaching young Hasidim, was the growing concern about outside influences. Yeshivas within Hasidic courts provided a closer means of supervision and an insular and protective environment.[27]

The First World War and the subsequent years brought dramatic changes to the Jewish street—on the one hand the increasing ruin of livelihoods, and on the other hand the spread of secularism together with the growth of radical Jewish movements. The lack of basic sustenance made it difficult for the Hasidim to remain within the bounds of the shtiebl; they began to be swept up in the practical atmosphere that sought a way out of the dire economic conditions. Without protective walls, Hasidic youth were exposed to outside influences, and it is no wonder that they yearned after promises of a better future in the bosom of Zionist or socialist movements.

In those years, the joint efforts of Eastern and Central European Orthodox circles in Agudat Yisrael brought consonance between worlds that had formerly been distant from each other. The perception of commonality and external threats encouraged meetings and discussion between the leaders of Lithuanian Orthodoxy who dominated the yeshiva world and the Hasidim of Poland, most of whom were Hasidim of the largest and most influential Gur dynasty. These Hasidim believed that most of Hasidic youth who were faithful to tradition would continue to study in the old frameworks, but they also found that the yeshivas led by the prominent Lithuanian Jews with whom they met were likely to provide a supportive Torah environment and an even better buffer against the threats of the outside world.[28]

The traditional Lithuanian yeshivas were not the only alternative. Some Hasidim looked to other solutions such as setting up Hasidic yeshivas in the Lithuanian style and establishing Hasidic-style yeshivas, which were mostly attached to Hasidic courts. In the next section, the first two alternatives that have a direct connection with the Lithuanian yeshivas will be presented.[29]

Hasidim in Lithuanian Yeshivas

Hasidic young men studied in Lithuanian yeshivas not only after the end of the First World War. Years before, sons from Hasidic families frequently studied in several yeshivas that had gained their parents' trust. One of these was the Lomzhe Yeshiva. Its founder, Rabbi Eliezer Shulevitz, who was a disciple of the originator of the Musar movement, Rabbi Yisrael Lipkin, set up the yeshiva in 1883 on the edge of Poland in order to transmit Torah and Musar to the local Jewish residents. In his hope of attracting the sons of Hasidim to his yeshiva, he allowed them to maintain their customs and dress, and many of them joined the yeshiva. The Slonim Yeshiva, located in the Pale of Settlement, also enjoyed the esteem of Hasidic circles, and their young people were granted a sort of internal autonomy in the yeshiva.[30] However, a significant change in the attitude of Hasidim toward the Lithuanian yeshivas could be seen only after the establishment of that sort of Torah-study institutions in the area where Hasidim predominantly lived, that is, in central Poland and in Vohlin Province in the Pale of Settlement.

In Central Poland

Several yeshivas were established throughout Poland that were designated as preparatory programs for more advanced Talmudic learning in the renowned Lithuanian yeshivas. An outstanding example was Torat-Ḥesed in Lodz, which was founded by a local patron, Sender Diskin (1856–1929), in 1908. Its head and Talmud instructors were graduates of Knesset-Yisrael of Slabodka. In order to attract local young men from Hasidic families, the administration decided to make compulsory the observance of Polish Hasidic customs such as the prayer rite and outer appearance. This was the dress code in the regulations at the end of 1909: "The yeshiva faculty and students will wear long garments and sashes, such as worn by the Hasidim of Poland, namely, without a fedora, ironed collars and cuff links. If one of the faculty members directs his home not in accordance with the custom of Poland, he will leave his position, and will have no claims or demands to remain [in his position]."[31] This was a stringent requirement for the members of the yeshiva faculty, who came from the cultural environment of Lithuanian Jewry, but thanks to these rules the yeshiva succeeded in being absorbed into the Hasidic surroundings. One of the Talmud instructors described it in this way: "Young men, sons of Hasidim, whose faces shine with the grace of innocence and profound faith, and whose eyes reflect great intelligence mixed with the pleasantness and gentleness of a Hasidic Jew, these young people are tangled in the thicket of logic and understanding [characteristic] of Lithuanian scholars and masterminds, as though this were a branch of a Lithuanian yeshiva. How good and proper is this joining of the Hasidic fire of emotion with the waters of knowledge and logic in the tent of Torah."[32] Another yeshiva that functioned before the First World War in the heart of Hasidic Poland was "Rabbi Itche's Yeshiva," a yeshiva-ketana in Warsaw directed by Rabbi Yitzḥak (Itche) Grodzensky. Most of its pupils were the sons of Lithuanian Jews who had settled in the city, but local Hasidim studied there as well.[33]

These preparatory yeshivas were greenhouses for the sons of Hasidim, who eventually found their place in the prominent Lithuanian yeshivas as well. Indeed, after the First World War, a significant number of the graduates of Torat-Ḥesed of Lodz studied in the Mir Yeshiva. The popular and sought-after yeshivas among Hasidic circles of the Kongresówka in the interwar period were Ohel-Torah of Baranovitch, Radin, whose founder, the Ḥafetz-Ḥayim, was admired by the Hasidim, and the Novardok Beit-Yosef, whose dedicated students were well-known thanks to their presence all over Poland.[34]

In Vohlin

Similar to Hasidic Poland, Vohlin Province in the Pale of Settlement was not replete with yeshivas in the nineteenth century, and Talmudic studies were concentrated in batei-midrash and Hasidic shtieblach. The tendency of Vohlin scholars toward halachic rulings rather than the yeshiva style of textual analysis lowered their stature in the eyes of Lithuanian Talmud students. On their part, the people of Vohlin took a negative view of the Lithuanian yeshivas: "They already had a bias against the yeshivas and all the scholars of Lithuania, and their cry was very great regarding study not for its own sake [i.e., for ulterior motives] in the yeshivas, better that it should never have been created than created. At the same time that the Hasidim were crying out about study not for its own sake in the yeshiva, a cry could be heard from the Left about study for its own sake in the yeshiva, for what profit was there that yeshiva students should die [i.e. sacrifice themselves] in the tents of Torah."[35] As is hinted here, the *Haskalah* worldview had penetrated Vohlin just as it had the cultural space of Lithuanian Jewry, and its influence on Vohlin's Torah world increased in strength. The local Hasidic population began to recognize the capability of the yeshivas to serve as a shield against this "attack" on religious life and therefore was more willing to accept them. Indeed, there were a few early attempts of Lithuanian scholars to set up institutions of Talmud learning in Vohlin in the 1880s and 1890s. But these efforts only accomplished the establishment of a few yeshivot-ketanot that left no lasting impression in this geographical area. The first significant program was the initiative of a graduate of the Volozhin Yeshiva, Rabbi Yoel Shorin. He saw the Ohr-Torah Yeshiva that he founded in Berezhnitsa in 1897 and transferred it to Zvhil two years later as an influential focal point for restoring the spirit of Torah to Vohlin.[36]

Rabbi Shorin grew up among Lubavitch Hasidim in Poltava and was well acquainted with the Hasidic mentality. Therefore he chose to preserve in his yeshiva, at least symbolically, the Vohlin style of study and included in its daily program learning of halachic rulings, unlike the accepted course of study in Lithuanian yeshivas. Local Hasidic groups appreciated his program and chose to send their sons to the Zvhil Yeshiva. In due time the yeshiva expanded and constructed an impressive building, along with a courtyard and large garden. This growth was halted by the vicissitudes of the First World War. Whereas the yeshiva continued to carry on undisturbed during the fighting, when the Bolsheviks took over Ukrainian Vohlin, Zvhil also felt a severe change. The new authorities began to make trouble for the yeshiva and prevented its regular functioning. Rabbi Shorin understood that it could continue to exist only outside Red Ukraine. He chose the nearby border town of Korets and took his yeshiva to refuge there.[37]

Moving the yeshiva from Zvhil was not just a change of location. The relocation from its natural habitat in Ukrainian Vohlin to the new state of Poland had a far-reaching significance for the yeshiva, and extensive corrective activity was required:

- Creating public relations in its new location after having lost its traditional community, which knew the yeshiva and sent their sons to study there.
- Seeking alternative sources of funding in Poland and elsewhere after the yeshiva was disconnected from its funding sources in Ukraine and Russia.
- Obtaining new premises for the yeshiva.
- Addressing the needs of the students from Ukraine who had lost contact with their families, as well as arranging their costly residence permits in Poland.

At the same time that new and complicated challenges were facing the yeshiva, a change had occurred in its administration: Rabbi Baruch-Mordechai Riz, Rabbi Shorin's son-in-law, began to serve as acting rosh-yeshiva. From that point, Rabbi Yoel Shorin concentrated on supervising the study of the talmidim and testing their knowledge each week. Despite the administrational change, Rabbi Shorin continued to have the Sabbath meals with his students and sat at the head of the table, with his son-in-law at his side. A while later, Rabbi Shorin fell ill with a malignant illness. He was operated upon unsuccessfully in Berlin and died in Warsaw in 1927.[38]

The new period thus brought significant changes to the yeshiva, but they primarily affected its outer characteristics, geographic and personal. Were there changes in its inner aspects as well—its organizational or educational structure? Both preservation and change were part of the Korets Yeshiva's milieu in the interwar period. Even in its new location in Poland, it stood out among the Lithuanian counterparts with its emphasis on halachic ruling. In addition to the usual sessions dedicated to Talmud, *Oraḥ-Ḥayim* and probably other sections of the *Shulḥan-Aruch* were part of its curriculum—a direct result of the yeshiva's settling in the heart of a manifestly Hasidic area. In an attempt to assimilate into this environment, the yeshiva apparently even adopted the Hasidic rite of prayer but did not show any obvious signs of accepting Hasidism. Moreover, the yeshiva adapted itself to its Lithuanian counterparts by studying Musar even though its founder, a graduate of Volozhin, was not accustomed to this. The addition of a new area of study to the yeshiva's curriculum was not merely an outward gesture but permeated its entire program, and to this end a Musar-mashgiaḥ was appointed: Rabbi Pesaḥ Plotnick.[39]

The total student body of the yeshiva gradually increased from the middle of the 1920s and by the end of the decade reached 150. The adults, the talmidim of the kibbutz classes—the small-kibbutz and the main-kibbutz—are especially interesting. Their number at that period of time increased from forty to fifty-five and included ordained rabbis as well. For reasons not clearly stated in the sources, there were changes in the size of the yeshiva in the 1930s, and the number of students in the kibbutz classes decreased to thirty-five. These changes are almost surely a result of the opening of a branch of Ohr-Torah in Rovne by Rabbi Yosef "Zvhiller," the son of Rabbi Yoel Shorin. One of the local residents donated a large new building to this new institution, and talmidim from the Korets Yeshiva chose to study there.[40]

From this mention of the Korets Yeshiva's kibbutz classes, one can conclude that the yeshiva did not change its old multiage structure. Indeed, the students studied in four preliminary classes and two kibbutz classes. Later, one shall see that the other yeshivas that were established in Vohlin afterward had a similar structure. Why did these yeshivas not divide into two, a yeshiva-ketana and a yeshiva-gedola, like most of the Lithuanian yeshivas? The previous chapter showed that a number of Lithuanian yeshivas did this to receive additional funding that was distributed by the Vilna Va'ad-HaYeshivot (The Yeshiva Committee) to yeshivot-ketanot.[41] However, the Vohlin yeshivas were not included in the general list of institutions served by the Va'ad. Similar to the yeshivot-ketanot, Vohlin yeshivas received separate funding, which the Va'ad provided each according to its size. Refraining from dividing these yeshivas meant both greater funding and savings in terms of administration and building costs.

Zvhil-Korets was the first yeshiva-gedola in Vohlin. In its footsteps, other Lithuanian yeshivas were founded in the interwar period in this Hasidic area, one of which was in Ostroh. Several factors were involved in its establishment:

- The initiative of a graduate of the Mir Yeshiva, Leib Weiss, to establish a yeshiva in Ostroh where he lived.
- The desire of the Ḥafetz-Ḥayim and Rabbi Ḥayim-Ozer Grodzensky to renew the local yeshiva of Rabbi Shmuel-Eliezer HaLevy Idels (known as *Maharsha*; 1555–1631) on the three hundredth anniversary of his death.
- The success of the Korets Yeshiva, which served as a proven precedent for the possibility of the integration of Lithuanian yeshivas in the Vohlin community.

In order to help Weiss in his task, scholars who had attended Lithuanian yeshivas arrived in Ostroh, and in 1931 the Maharsha Yeshiva was founded. Rabbi Yosef "Kossover" Berkovitz, a graduate of the Mir Yeshiva, was appointed as its head. In this yeshiva as well, similar to Korets, there were students from a wide range of ages, including adults. In 1938 there were about one hundred talmidim aged fourteen to twenty-four. It appears that the number of students in the kibbutz class was forty.

Despite the yeshiva's short existence, the members of the administration succeeded in creating a strong sense of solidarity among the talmidim. This stood the yeshiva in good stead when, during the dark days at the end of 1939, it was one of the few Vohlin yeshivas that escaped to Vilna, where it continued to function.[42]

Two other Lithuanian yeshivot-gedolot established in Vohlin had a Novardok style, and they also were structured for multiple ages. The first was the Ohr-Torah Yeshiva, which was originally established in Kovel and was relocated to Ludmir around 1923. By the end of the 1920s, it was a notable yeshiva with 185 students, divided into five to six classes and a kibbutz class. In those years, thirty to fifty talmidim aged twenty and younger studied in this kibbutz class, and there were also students from Ukraine and Russia who were older—up to the age of twenty-four.[43]

The second yeshiva was set up in Lutsk by the initiative of Rabbi Avraham Yoffen. He appointed Rabbi Moshe Reiss as its head, because the latter had rich experience in establishing Novardok yeshivas. Already in 1922, Rabbi Reiss had founded a yeshiva-gedola in Pinsk, Polesia Province, and he directed it for five years. In 1927 he moved the yeshiva to Tchechanovitz, near Bialystok. At that time, eighty students between the ages of fifteen and twenty-three studied there. A year later, he was invited to Lutsk and relocated his yeshiva in that town with its framework of two classes and a kibbutz class. He was accompanied by quite a few of his students, and several young men from the central Bialystok Yeshiva joined him to strengthen the ranks. Throughout the years that the yeshiva existed, seventy to ninety talmidim studied there, and the baḥurim in its kibbutz class were as old as twenty-five or twenty-six. Similar to the Ostroh Yeshiva, in 1939 Rabbi Reiss succeeded in escaping to Vilna with a few of his yeshiva students.[44]

The Zvhil-Korets yeshiva was thus a pioneer in the revolution that the Lithuanian yeshiva world brought about in Vohlin—a revolution that expressed itself in the 1930s by five yeshivas with a multiage structure and a respectable chain of yeshivot-ketanot in this Hasidic area. There is no doubt that this was an outstanding sign of the change of attitude regarding Lithuanian yeshivas that took place among the Jews of Vohlin.

Hasidim in Hasidic Yeshivas of the Lithuanian Type

Before founding Ḥachmei-Lublin Yeshiva, its founder, Rabbi Meir Shapiro (1887–1933), visited the Lithuanian yeshivas of Radin, Mir, and Baranovitch; was impressed by them; and even planned to appoint a Talmud lecturer in his yeshiva from among their graduates.[45] Admorim in Poland had also appointed a few graduates of Lithuanian yeshivas to similar positions. But the more fascinating phenomenon in the contact between Hasidim and *Mitnagdim* is the establishment of Hasidic yeshivas in a style that was clearly Lithuanian in the traditional geographic territory of Lithuanian yeshivas. They were few, and they were under the sponsorship of Lithuanian Hasidic courts: Torat-Ḥesed in Baranovitch of the Rebbe of Slonim, and two yeshivas in the Polesia Province, the Luninets Yeshiva of the Rebbe of Karlin and the Stolin Yeshiva of the local rebbe. At the head of each of these Torah-study institutions stood a graduate of a Lithuanian yeshiva who instructed his talmidim, sons of Hasidim, in the spirit of the Torah learning he had imbibed in his youth. The principle unique characteristics of two of these yeshivas will be presented here.

Torat-Ḥesed Yeshiva in Baranovitch

The death of the Rebbe of Slonim, Shmuel Weinberg (1850–1916), in 1916 led to the division of the Hasidic court of Slonim between his two sons during the war. Avraham (1884–1933), the younger son, began to preside over his new Hasidic court in Bialystok, and two years later he moved it to Baranovitch. During the German occupation, the Novardok yeshiva Ohel-Torah, modest in its size, was located in this town. Rebbe Avraham Weinberg initiated the establishment of a new yeshiva adjacent to it, Torat-Ḥesed, for his court's youngsters, and he appointed as its head Rabbi Yosef "Meitcheter" Mordcovsky. As the yeshiva developed, its directors decided to adopt similar practices to those accepted in Lithuanian yeshivas in the area, and to that end they looked for the appropriate rosh-yeshiva. Rabbi Avraham-Shmuel Hirschowitz, known in the Lithuanian yeshiva world as the "illuy from Talsen," was chosen for the position. He succeeded in the task to which he was appointed and raised the standard of learning in his Hasidic yeshiva to a high level, one that paralleled a Lithuanian yeshiva. However, Musar-study sessions were not held there, and it may well be that in addition to the regular Talmud curriculum, Hasidic writings were also studied in the yeshiva.[46]

With the establishment of Va'ad-HaYeshivot in 1924, Torat-Ḥesed was included in the list of yeshivot-gedolot receiving support and obtained regular funding from the Va'ad. In 1926 there were five classes and a kibbutz class, with a student body of 136 boys and young men aged twelve to twenty-two. The students of the four lower classes studied in the yeshiva building, and the older talmidim studied in a local beit-midrash. Material constraints and the special allocations that the Va'ad provided to yeshivot-ketanot eventually motivated the administrators at the end of the summer of 1926 to formally and fiscally separate the younger students from the older ones. The four lower classes were designated as a yeshiva-ketana, and the fifth and kibbutz class belonged to the yeshiva-gedola from that point on. Both yeshivas bore the name Torat-Ḥesed. Rabbi Hirschowitz continued to serve as the head of the yeshiva-gedola and gave regular lectures to the older class as well as to the kibbutz class.

The yeshiva-gedola was relatively small, with sixty to seventy students, most of them in the kibbutz class and originating from outside of Baranovitch and even from the cities of Warsaw, Lodz, and Bialystok. The yeshiva gained two avrechim, married students receiving a stipend, and in 1928 their number grew to five. Over the years the yeshiva grew a bit, and in 1937 there were more than seventy students in the kibbutz class.[47]

Torat-Ḥesed never developed into a very large yeshiva, but among its graduates were exceptional students, some of whom were appointed to serve as roshei-yeshiva in yeshivot-ketanot. A few even studied in the Brisk Kibbutz of Rabbi Yitzḥak-Ze'ev Soloveitchik, a kibbutz of select students that will be discussed later.[48]

The Stolin Yeshiva

After the death of the Rebbe of Karlin, Rabbi Yisrael Perlov of Stolin, known as the *Yanuka* (infant; 1868–1921), his fourth son, Moshe (1895–1942), succeeded him. One year later the new rebbe founded a local Talmud-Torah in Stolin and afterward a yeshiva-ketana, Ohel-Moshe, in order to attract the graduates of the Talmud-Torah. Even though the yeshiva had administrators and directors, all of its outward running was in the hands of the rebbe. He appointed Rabbi Ya'akov-Sender Greenberg, a graduate of Lithuanian yeshivas, as its head, and later Rabbi Elḥanan Solovey from Baranovitch, also a graduate of those same yeshivas.

In 1926, fifty-five talmidim aged twelve to eighteen studied in five classes, and most of them were from Stolin and the surrounding area. In 1927 only about thirty students remained in two classes. It is not clear why this yeshiva-ketana diminished in a brief period of time. It may have been closed at the end of 1929, and in any case its decline caused Rabbi Solovey to leave.[49]

In the beginning of the 1930s, the yeshiva was rehabilitated and received a new appearance and a new name: Beit-Yisrael. A graduate of a Lithuanian yeshiva stood at its head once more: Rabbi Shlomo Halevy "Krementchuger" Slavin. This was not the same yeshiva-ketana that had existed in the past. It had four classes for younger talmidim and small-kibbutz and large-kibbutz classes, and in 1931 there were seventy-five students. The number of its talmidim increased, and in 1936 there were 107 students aged fourteen to twenty-six, including a few from Warsaw, Lodz, Brody, and even Russia. In its new arrangement, this yeshiva earned itself a more prominent position among the Lithuanian yeshivas, and it could indeed be proud of its studies that were on par with a yeshiva-gedola even though it was still listed as a yeshiva-ketana in the books of Va'ad-HaYeshivot.[50]

In the summer of 1938, the yeshiva was enlarged when a special building was constructed for it in place of the local beit-midrash that it had occupied for years. Rabbis from the surrounding area, including the Musar-mashgiaḥ of the Kletsk Yeshiva, Rabbi Yosef-Leib Nenedik, participated in the building's dedication ceremony.[51]

The number of students in the Stolin Yeshiva did not change further until the end of the 1930s. Its expansion was expressed in other areas. It was involved in an atypical chain of actions compared to most of the Lithuanian yeshivas, and similar to the Novardok yeshivas, it established three branches in Poland in those years: in Pohost-Zahorodny in Polesia Province and in Kostopl and Horodok in Vohlin Province. Another branch was established in Tel-Aviv while Rebbe Moshe Perlov was visiting the Land of Israel in the summer of 1937, and Rabbi Asher Sandomirsky, who had a respected past in the Slutsk Yeshiva, was appointed as its head.[52]

ESTABLISHING YESHIVA BRANCHES IN THE LAND OF ISRAEL

The founding of the branch of the Stolin Yeshiva in Tel-Aviv did not occur ex nihilo. This was congruent with a new phenomenon in the interwar Lithuanian yeshiva world: establishing branches in the Land of Israel. Many circles in the Jewish community regarded *aliyah* to Eretz-Yisrael in that period in Zionist political terms, and the participation of yeshivas in aliyah was considered out of the ordinary. In general, the Jewish educational institutions in Lithuania and Poland were attached to organizations with a political identity: Tarbut, Yavneh, CISZO, Kultur-Ligge, and others. In contrast, the official position of the yeshivas was nonpolitical because they depended on all sectors of the Jewish community for material support.

However, it was difficult to ignore the activities of their heads in Agudat Yisrael. The roshei-yeshiva of Slabodka, Telz, Ponevezh, and Kletsk participated in the first world convention of that organization in 1923, and the activists of the organization were outstanding yeshiva personalities, among them Rabbis Aharon Kotler, Elḥanan Wasserman, Shabtai Yogel, and Reuven Grozovsky. There was good reason for the Jewish public to see the yeshivas as bastions of the Agudah, as is illustrated by a quote from the Kovna newspaper *Di Idishe Shtime* in 1928: "The Slabodka Yeshiva, dear to all religious Jews, gives the impression of a clearly Agudah party institution, participating in all the elections on the side of Agudah and in general is considered its stronghold."[53] Moreover, talmidim were even sometimes persecuted for their declared support of other parties. This unofficial affinity of the yeshivas toward the non-Zionist Agudah was liable to discourage them from aliyah to the Land of Israel. So wrote Zeraḥ Warhaftig (1906–2002) regarding his impression of the attitude of the heads of the yeshiva world: "In my many conversations with Rabbi Aharon Kotler, as well as with Rabbi Ḥayim-Ozer Grodzensky at the time, I occasionally got the impression that they saw Torah study and the love of Torah as the sum total of everything, and they were jealous of the love of Zion and Jerusalem, as though it vied for the heart of the Jewish people, and as though one love impinged on the other."[54] Despite this unbalanced "competition," several roshei-yeshiva launched an unanticipated project to open branches in the Land of Israel. Had "the love of Zion and Jerusalem" overcome in their considerations?

The heads of Lithuanian yeshivas held a broad range of worldviews regarding aliyah to the Land of Israel. These attitudes were not always identical to what was actually carried out. Only in the case of Knesset-Yisrael of Slabodka was there a consistent congruence between the principled views of its heads and their desire to fulfill them, and it is not surprising that this yeshiva was the first in settling the Land of Israel. Even though their aliyah did not begin at their own initiative but rather because of the necessity to avoid the drafting of talmidim into the Lithuanian army, it is clear that the choice of the Land of Israel was well anchored in their worldview and aspirations.[55]

The Eretz-Yisrael branch of Slabodka was opened in 1924. A short time later, the heads of the Lomzhe Yeshiva began to make practical preparations toward aliyah, also due to the requirement to serve in the Polish army. They had a similar viewpoint: the rosh-yeshiva Rabbi Eliezer Shulevitz was the first to act and decided to make aliyah on his own to the Land of Israel in 1923. I have not found a proven connection between his aliyah and the opening of a branch of his yeshiva in the Land of Israel by his son-in-law Rabbi Yeḥiel-Mordechai Gordon, but it is reasonable to assume that Rabbi Shulevitz influenced this courageous decision.[56]

This activity that took place relating to the establishment of branches in Eretz-Yisrael did not go unseen by the other yeshivas, but very few were influenced by these processes. The duty of military service was cancelled in Lithuania, and therefore aliyah was not necessary for its other yeshivas. However, even the yeshivas of Poland, where military conscription was in force up until the Second World War, did not rush to imitate Lomzhe. Only in the Volozhin Yeshiva and the Novardok movement were voices heard regarding the establishment of yeshivas in the Land of Israel starting in 1925. In the case of Novardok, these ideas percolated for several years, and two Novardok yeshivas were opened in the Land of Israel. In the following section, the processes of setting up the aforementioned branches is presented.[57]

The Slabodka Branch

Slabodka was the pioneer of the Lithuanian yeshiva world in establishing a branch in the Land of Israel. The chain of events concerning this aliyah began as a complete surprise at the time that the rosh-yeshiva, Rabbi Moshe-Mordechai Epstein, was starting off on a lengthy fundraising tour of the United States on behalf of his yeshiva. In January 1924, military deferment, which had up until then been granted to yeshiva students in Lithuania, was suddenly cancelled, and dozens who were of the proper age were required to report to the draft boards. The yeshiva's mashgiaḥ, Rabbi Notte-Hirsch Finkel, began to act vigorously for the cancellation of the decree. He directed his senior student, the avrech Yeḥezkel Sarna, to act in concert with local Jewish community activists and even to participate in lobbying delegations to the leaders of the Lithuanian government regarding this issue. The public pressure succeeded, and the conscription of yeshiva students was raised for government debate. The government made it clear that in the background of the cancellation of military deferment stood the absence of a general studies curriculum in the yeshivas, and it stated that it would not be proper to recognize the former privilege of military deferment until such a curriculum was approved.[58]

This decree affected all the yeshivas in Lithuania. Slabodka was the most vulnerable because its students were older than their counterparts in other yeshivas, and some of the talmidim who did not want to be drafted were forced to cross the border into Poland. Ostensibly, it would have been possible to find creative solutions to the problem that faced the yeshiva—for example, the possibility of acting in the same way as the Telz Yeshiva, which applied to the authorities to grant a deferment for its students based on the claim that its preparatory program included organized secular studies. However Rabbi Finkel did not agree to take a similar step: to include general studies in the Even-Yisrael Yeshiva-ketana, and to formally annex it to his institution. If this was the situation regarding the yeshiva-ketana, he was certainly unwilling to consider even a hair's breadth of change in the traditional curriculum of the yeshiva-gedola or its Ohr-Yisrael mechinah, even when the cost of refusing the government's demands was completely clear to him.[59]

As mentioned earlier, the rosh-yeshiva Rabbi Epstein had just then arrived in the United States. As an active and decisive figure in Slabodka, as well as a significant one in Lithuanian Orthodoxy, his absence was keenly felt at a time when important decisions had to be made regarding the military draft. He received current reports from the yeshiva administration, and five years later he described the events as he saw them while visiting the United States:

> Then came to me the not-good news from the holy Slabodka Yeshiva that a decree had been issued that would destroy it, God forbid, and that definitely, if we do not change the spirit of Torah learning in it—it [the yeshiva] cannot stand. Thus, there is no other counsel unless we look for another location. And the light of our eyes . . . Rabbi Nattan Zvi Finkel, may the memory of the righteous and holy be for a blessing, the pillar of the yeshiva, turned to me with this information and asked my opinion, and I answered that in my opinion, it is necessary to establish a yeshiva in the Holy Land, and that there is hope that our generous brothers in America will support this sublime project that concerns all of the holy nation and the matter of settling the Land of Israel, which is dear to all of Israel.[60]

Rabbi Epstein found the right moment to fulfill his old vision that he had formulated during the years of the exile to Ukraine during the First World War: to move the Knesset-Yisrael Yeshiva, or part of it, to the Land of Israel to influence the society being built there, which was in danger of spiritual collapse. Up until this point, obstacles stood in the way of fulfillment: at first he did not receive an exit permit from Bolshevik Ukraine to the Land of Israel, and after he succeeded in reaching Slabodka, he was obliged to stabilize the dire financial condition of the yeshiva that was being rebuilt. While he was in the United States, in one instant the proper timing came into being, according to his outlook—an immediate necessity to move part of the yeshiva to Eretz-Yisrael on one hand and the opportunity for an economic solution to carry out this idea on the other hand. He no longer needed amorphous ideological explanations to convince the American supporters about the importance of bringing the yeshiva to the Holy Land in order to influence the state in the making. This time the transfer to the Land of Israel was a vital need for preserving the yeshiva, and Americans understood this language well.[61]

It was mentioned before that some of the talmidim found an immediate solution—crossing the border into Poland—and there might have been a chance for the heads of the Slabodka Yeshiva to find a refuge in neighboring countries for the whole yeshiva in the same way until the Lithuanian authorities relented. In their instinctive decision to implement the solution in the Land of Israel, they expressed Rabbi Epstein's strong aspirations, concurring with those of Rabbi Finkel.[62]

After the decision to make the move had been accepted by the yeshiva's administration and worked out in detail, its fulfillment was carried out in two stages.[63]

- Yeḥezkel Sarna was sent in May 1924 to Eretz-Yisrael in order to examine the *Yishuv* (pre-State Jewish community) and search for an appropriate location for the yeshiva.
- The chief rabbinate of the Land of Israel was pressed into action in order to obtain approval and help from the British mandatory authorities for the idea of the yeshiva's aliyah.

Hebron was chosen as the future home of the yeshiva. Besides its holiness, Hebron was a quiet and pleasant place for studies, far away from the bustle of the city, and its atmosphere recalled the Slabodka suburb. Rabbi Finkel's original idea had been to establish a small yeshiva particularly in Jerusalem, but the hubbub of its streets and the echoes of internal dissension there were not suited for study. Moreover, the modern image of the Slabodka student did not fit the archaic customs of the Old Yishuv and was liable to arouse opposition and dispute.[64]

When the future location had been decided upon with the agreement of the yeshiva administration, Rabbi Epstein made an announcement at a special convocation held in New York. A local committee was formed for the fulfillment of the decision, and well-known American donors were chosen to head it; twenty thousand dollars was raised to finance the transfer of young men from Slabodka to Hebron. At the same time that the necessary funds were obtained, the British mandatory authorities issued a permit for the yeshiva students' aliyah, and with the intervention of the president of the religious Zionist organization HaMizraḥi, Meir Berlin

(Bar-Ilan; 1880–1949), who was in Eretz-Yisrael at the time, the British agreed to allocate one hundred immigration certificates for the move.[65]

Yeḥezkel Sarna was appointed as head and director of the new Hebron branch. In advance of the High Holy Days in 1924, the first ten talmidim arrived. In the winter of 1924–1925, many more students came. After them, the Talmud instructor Rabbi Moshe Finkel arrived at the head of a group of Slabodka students who continued to fill the quota of certificates that had been allocated. Yitzḥak Hutner expressed some of the excitement about the aliyah of the students that he felt in 1925 when he wrote some ten years later, "I remember how much lyric poetry was within me and around me concerning the matter of my preparations to move to the Land of Israel the first time. All the notes that I wrote for myself and letters to friends at the time are only a great expression of this lyric poetry."[66]

Rabbi Epstein, who returned to Slabodka from the United States at the end of 1924, hastened to set off for Hebron and remained at the new branch until the end of the summer of 1925. Even the founder of the Slabodka Yeshiva, Rabbi Notte-Hirsch Finkel, arrived at that time to Hebron and settled there.[67]

Did the administration really intend to transfer the entire yeshiva to Eretz-Yisrael in stages, or was this a plan to start an extension only for older students who were subject to military conscription? At the end of 1924, the idea was to bring most of the students to the Land of Israel and leave a small group of younger students in Slabodka who would be the basis for the renewed development of the local yeshiva. However, in the end the administration was not required to carry out the plan in its entirety. In 1925 the conscription decree was rescinded, and it was again possible to continue studies in Slabodka without fear of drafting senior students. Rabbi Epstein wrote, "Then we saw with our own eyes that the decree came about only so that another holy yeshiva might be established in the Holy Land, a central yeshiva for all of our brethren, because it is God's will and dear to Him a holy yeshiva that spreads Torah to all Israel in our Holy Land, for there is no Torah like the Torah of Eretz-Yisrael."[68] The establishment of the Slabodka branch in Hebron made an impression on world Jewry. It also influenced the decisions of the heads of other yeshivas to open branches in the Land of Israel.[69]

The Lomzhe Branch

The yeshiva that was influenced more than others from the aliyah of Knesset-Yisrael of Slabodka was the Lomzhe Yeshiva. Like Slabodka, that yeshiva had experienced troubles during the First World War. The retreat of the Russian army eastward after the collapse of the front in the spring of 1915 spurred the local yeshiva to join the withdrawing forces in their move to the east. In June 1915 the yeshiva took the step of splitting up. Its head, Rabbi Eliezer Shulevitz, and his son-in-law Rabbi Yehoshua-Zelig Ruch went to Ukraine with most of the talmidim. The younger students were taken by the Talmud instructor Rabbi Yeḥiel-Mordechai Gordon, the senior son-in-law of the rosh-yeshiva, to the not-distant town of Semiatitch, and in August 1915 they returned to the yeshiva's building in Lomzhe after the town had been captured by the Germans.[70]

After the war, the Lomzhe Yeshiva reunited. In 1923 its rosh-yeshiva, Rabbi Shulevitz, decided on aliyah to the Land of Israel, and he left the Lomzhe institution in the hands of his sons-in-law, Rabbis Gordon and Ruch. They deliberated a long time about the issue of conscription to the Polish army faced by their students, and they found a fitting solution in what had been done by the Slabodka Yeshiva. Perhaps their father-in-law encouraged them to take a similar step. In any case, his presence in Eretz-Yisrael would facilitate the implementation of the idea of opening a branch there.[71]

As the plan began to take shape, there was a need to first choose an appropriate location for the branch. Eretz-Yisrael community activists joined the effort to carry out the plan, and in the end a revolutionary decision was made regarding the place: in the New Yishuv, in the veteran colony of Petaḥ-Tikva. Years later, it was written about this decision, "Was there not some sort of forethought, even a totally unconscious one? Perhaps there was a clear purpose to establish a place of Torah in the New-Yishuv—something similar to the establishment of the yeshiva in Lomzhe in particular!"[72]

A special parcel of land was designated for building the branch. At the end of 1924, the placing of the cornerstone was celebrated, and a respectable sum of money was collected for the building. Construction began in spring 1925, and this event was also properly celebrated. In 1926 Rabbi Gordon traveled to the United States in order to build an economic infrastructure for the new branch. Among his achievements, a generous commitment from Pesia Miller-Feigin of Philadelphia to donate two hundred dollars each month stood out—a sum that was sufficient for the ongoing support of ten young men.[73]

In the beginning of the summer term of 1926, the Lomzhe Yeshiva received permission from the British authorities to bring some of the students to the Land of Israel. A group of forty young men laid the foundation for the new extension, and the Musar-mashgiaḥ, Rabbi Eliyahu Dushnitzer (1876–1949), was appointed as its head. In the following years, another few students from Lomzhe received certificates for aliyah to the Land of Israel to study in the branch in Petaḥ-Tikva.[74]

The Novardok Movement Branches

At the end of the 1920s, the head of the Jaffa–Tel-Aviv rabbinical court, Rabbi Yosef-Zvi HaLevi (1874–1960), contacted the directors of the Novardok movement in Poland with a request to help strengthen the Ohr-Zore'aḥ Yeshiva that stood on the border of Jaffa as well as to provide a proper Novardok director for the school. He received a positive answer to his appeal.[75]

Two factors contributed to the willingness of the head of the movement, Rabbi Avraham Yoffen, to accept this challenge: following the previous success of Slabodka and Lomzhe Yeshivas, and implementation of Novardok's policy of expansion in Eretz-Yisrael. The location of the yeshiva that was to serve as the vanguard for the movement's future activities fit in well with the Novardok goal of spreading out: close to the center of the New-Yishuv. Unlike the quiet colony of Petaḥ-Tikva, where the Lomzhe Yeshiva chose to open its branch, Novardok meant to penetrate the heart of one of the busiest spots in the Land of Israel at the time and influence in its own way the weak Torah and spiritual atmosphere of the first Hebrew city.

Tel-Aviv was not Novardok's only destination. The movement hoped to spread out its influence in future years throughout all the Jewish colonies. This desire even appeared explicitly in its journal *Ohr HaMusar* in 1931:

"Only by spreading Torah and fear [of Heaven] in the colonies is there any hope of saving the youth from spiritual destruction, God save us, and restoring the crown of Torah as of old with the help of the One who dwells in Zion."[76]

Rabbi Yoffen arrived in the Land of Israel in the winter of 1929 with veteran member of the movement Hillel Vitkind in order to examine the conditions in the Ohr-Zore'aḥ Yeshiva and the possibility of strengthening it and expanding it as a Novardok yeshiva. Another two years passed until the idea was carried out, and only at the end of 1930 did the first group of Novardok students appear in Jaffa.[77]

Due to the limited allocation of certificates to his Torah institution, Rabbi Vitkind, who had begun to serve as the director of the renewed yeshiva, found it difficult to bring more young men who were interested in studying there. This situation led the directors of the Novardok movement to make efforts in the early 1930s to receive a larger share of certificates, either by appealing to rabbis and public figures in Poland and other countries or by receiving help from the heads of Jewish organizations in England. In the meantime, Rabbi Vitkind's yeshiva was not idle, and in 1932 it moved to central Tel-Aviv. A short time later, another Novardok yeshiva was opened in Eretz-Yisrael by the head of the Mezritch Yeshiva, Rabbi David Bliacher, and this time in the young colony of Bnei-Brak, which up until then had no yeshivas.[78]

The attempts of the Novardok movement to obtain permits finally bore fruit, and it received quite a large number of certificates. The lists of young men recommended by their roshei-yeshiva to go the Land of Israel, as well as their traveling expenses and other essential arrangements, were handled by the offices of the central Novardok yeshiva in Warsaw. In the winter of 1933, the first groups of talmidim arrived in Eretz-Yisrael using the quota of certificates that were obtained, and they were divided up between the two Novardok yeshivas.[79]

The directors of these yeshivas were in need of Talmud instructors for their growing institutions. Rabbi Aharon Weinstein, who had lectured in Talmud in the Mezritch Yeshiva, was selected by the Tel-Aviv Yeshiva, and the yeshiva in Bnei-Brak invited Rabbi Ya'akov-Yisrael Kanyevsky (1899–1985), who had served as Talmud instructor in Pinsk, to teach there. Thus two yeshivas of the Novardok style began to operate in the Land of Israel, both in the heart of the New-Yishuv. The appointment of a lecturer from Mezritch in the Tel-Aviv Yeshiva (established by the head of the Bialystok Yeshiva) and a lecturer from Pinsk who had studied in Bialystok in the past, in the Bnei-Brak Yeshiva (founded by the rosh-yeshiva of Mezritch), proves that they were not meant to be extensions of their particular founding yeshivas but to serve all the Novardok talmidim who were expected to come from Poland on aliyah to the Land of Israel. The movement's characteristic spirit of joining together was hereby expressed in Eretz-Yisrael as well. Moreover, the Novardok hierarchy began to emerge also there: the Tel-Aviv Yeshiva became a center and opened branches in Haifa, Hadera, Reḥovot, and in 1937 even Jerusalem.[80]

SUMMARY

Despite the obstacle course that the yeshivas were forced to navigate on their way to recovery after the long period of war, most succeeded in getting back to the routine they were accustomed to before the First World War. However, not long after this, economic burdens began to weigh on them, whether because of the increase in the number of students or due to the decrease in donor support. At the same time that the roshei-yeshiva were struggling with material problems and exhausting fundraising in their own country or overseas in order to save the schools from collapse, new trends of expansion began in the Lithuanian yeshiva world. An examination of these various projects shows that new schools were established only partly because of a lack of yeshivas in certain geographic areas. Movements or groups had ideological interests that did not always take nearby yeshivas into consideration. The most extreme example is one where a Hasidic-Lithuanian yeshiva was set up in the vicinity of another Lithuanian yeshiva in the same town, Baranovitch. Notwithstanding, there is no doubt that these new trends brought about the growth of the Lithuanian yeshiva world in Eastern Europe as well as in Eretz-Yisrael.

The Novardok expansion project was the most impressive because of its scope. During the First World War, the mother yeshiva acted to open many new branches throughout Russia and Ukraine, and the Novardok movement intensified these efforts in Poland and Latvia in the interwar period. In its new network of Torah-study institutions, Novardok opened prominent yeshivot-gedolot as well as numerous yeshivot-ketanot that were established by veteran students. The list of yeshivot-ketanot indicates their impressive spread not only in the area of Lithuanian Jewish culture but also in towns in the heart of Latvia, the Kongresówka, and Galicia. They were established not just in small towns where it was easier to obtain the help of the local rabbi and townspeople but also in the important communities of Lodz, Shedlets, Biale, Kelts, Radom, and others. Prima facie it would seem that the Novardok movement was prone to "wholesale manufacture" of yeshivot-ketanot without considering the outcome of its actions. However, the numbers, which are incomparable among the yeshivot-ketanot established by the graduates of the other Lithuanian yeshivas, show the success of the system of expansion carried out by this movement in its two decades of activity in Eastern Europe, despite financial difficulties within and the discouraging attitude without.[81]

The most surprising among all the expansion projects was the establishment of yeshivas built on the Lithuanian model in the midst of concentrated Hasidic areas. An analysis of their characteristics shows that their kibbutz classes remained relatively limited in size and did not succeed in keeping up with the growth trend in the Lithuanian yeshiva world. This phenomenon can be observed both in the Vohlin yeshivas as well as in the Hasidic-Lithuanian yeshivas.[82]

After the First World War, there was only one yeshiva, the Korets Yeshiva, in the Vohlin district, but very quickly new yeshivot-gedolot were founded there, and even a string of yeshivot-ketanot. It was the graduates of Lithuanian yeshivas who initiated their establishment because of the importance these scholars assigned to spreading Torah learning among the local Jews. Did Rabbi Yoel Shorin, the Korets rosh-yeshiva, succeed in breaking the barriers in the community's approach regarding yeshivas in general and Lithuanian yeshivas in particular? The remarks of an emissary of the Lubavitch Rebbe, Yosef-Yitzḥak Schneersohn (1880–1950), who arrived in Vohlin in 1931 to see whether it was possible to establish a yeshiva in the spirit of the Lubavitch Tomchei-Temimim there, are interesting: "When I came to Kovel, I had to explain that a yeshiva was essential [there], and after all that, they were very cold. But here [in Ludmir] everyone is in agreement that a yeshiva is necessary and that it is good as well, and there is no need to speak about this, and it is possible that this is because there is a [Novardok] yeshiva here."[83] It can be seen from his words that there was a change in attitude on the part of the Jews who lived in the vicinity of yeshivas, as in Ludmir. Actually, the very fact that the yeshivas were accepted in their specific locations was the first sign that change was possible in the attitude of the Vohlin Hasidic population, which was not yet entirely comfortable with the concept of yeshivas, and its sons did not number among their students.

The situation of the Hasidic-Lithuanian yeshivas was even more complicated. They were intended from the start for a limited group, the sons of Hasidim, and their special character distinguished them in their organizational and administrative aspects from their Lithuanian counterparts. The Lithuanian yeshivas were usually under the ownership of their roshei-yeshiva, who passed them down to their sons or sons-in-law. In contrast, the Hasidic yeshivas were under the responsibility of the admorim, and they appointed "hired" officials as their heads. Even so, this fact was not reflected in the positions of Rabbi Avraham-Shmuel Hirschowitz in Torat-Ḥesed of Baranovitch and Rabbi Shlomo Slavin of the renewed yeshiva in Stolin. They saw themselves as roshei-yeshiva and served in that position as long as the yeshivas were in existence.[84] Moreover, their dominance succeeded in putting into effect the Lithuanian method of study, which they had accepted from their inception. These yeshivas were therefore similar to Lithuanian yeshivas, and the characteristically Hasidic format of study (as was common in the Lubavitch Tomchei-Temimim yeshivas) was not discernible there. It is not surprising that with no significant differences in study format, their natural candidates preferred to study in the more traditional and well-known Lithuanian yeshivas, even if this meant giving up the "homelike atmosphere." Thus the number of students in each of the kibbutz classes in the Hasidic yeshivas remained limited.

The flocking of Hasidic young men to the Lithuanian yeshivas had its price. Many of these sons of Hasidic families ceased to ascribe importance to their background, as can be seen in the testimony of a visitor to the Lithuanian yeshiva of Kamenitz, close to the Hasidic Kongresówka:

> In the yeshiva here there is a large number who are from Hasidic background, but besides the Slonim Hasidim, of whom there are in the yeshiva some with beards, and in general they are more God-fearing and also pious . . . [others] are very cold regarding Hasidism and they have no faith

> in their admorim. They ask how it will help them to go to the admor and grab *shirayyim* ["leftlovers"]. And the way [of Hasidism] they also say what [good] is it. Therefore they say that the way of Musar is better, and they also go without a beard.[85]

The sons of Hasidim who were accepted into this yeshiva, which is exemplary of the other Lithuanian yeshivas, adopted a scornful attitude toward the most basic customs observed in their parents' homes, and they preferred to take on the "local custom" whether in terms of appearance or "fear of Heaven."[86]

In contrast, not a few young Hasidic men who went to study in Lithuanian yeshivas reached high levels; their background did not stand in the way. One of the outstanding ones was Rabbi Yehoshua-Zelig Ruch, an excellent student in Knesset-Yisrael of Slabodka and scion of a Lubavitch family from Rakishok in Kovna Province. He was chosen to be the son-in-law of Rabbi Eliezer Shulevitz and served as Talmud instructor in the Lomzhe Yeshiva, and for many years in the interwar period, he was its head in practice. Another example was Rabbi Pesaḥ Pruskin, a talmid of Slabodka and a descendant of the founder of the Hasidic court of Kobrin, Rebbe Moshe Polier (1784–1858); Rabbi Pruskin headed several Lithuanian yeshivas, the last of which was in Kobrin. However, it would seem that the most picturesque example is Rabbi Hirsch Glickson, the son of a Hasidic layman in Warsaw, who was chosen to be the son-in-law of Rabbi Ḥayim Soloveitchik. He was well versed in his father-in-law's teachings, and at the end of the First World War, he was chosen as rosh-yeshiva of the Lithuanian Torat-Ḥayim in Warsaw. He continued to head this yeshiva until the Holocaust.[87]

The Lithuanian yeshiva world was not limited to the Eastern European countries, and it had significant representation in Eretz-Yisrael as well. The beginning of this revolutionary process did not come out of the trend of the yeshiva world to expand that took place between the two world wars. An examination of the history of the branches of Slabodka and Lomzhe in the Land of Israel reveals that the duty to serve in the military in Lithuania and Poland, respectively, motivated their founding. However, it would not be correct to link the Novardok branches with the issue of conscription; the movement's approach toward expansion lies at the foundation of their establishment.[88] Despite these contrasts, all of the incidents of the aliyah of yeshivas have a common element that resulted from the vicissitudes of the period: the yeshivas were prevented from establishing branches without a significant allocation of immigration certificates for their students. When these quotas were not available, the yeshivas were obliged to involve outside institutions and individuals in petitioning the British authorities and convincing them of the value of opening branches in the Land of Israel. The establishment of these branches had unforeseen historic importance because it opened the path to setting up Lithuanian yeshivas outside their natural geographic space. Thus was set into place the cornerstone of the Lithuanian yeshiva world that would arise anew after the Holocaust.

NOTES

1. Letter: Finkel to Schuw, April 24, 1930 (VHY/371).

2. See Klibansky, *KeTzur*, 53–54, 82; Katz, *Tenuat*, V, 116–17; Shadeve council minutes, Nov. 27, 1921 (LJC/1207); Klibansky, "HaYeshivot," 83n176.

3. Regarding this method and its implementation, see chapter 4.

4. About the extensive journalism and its influence on the students of Novardok, see Klibansky, "Hitagdut."

5. Klibansky, *KeTzur*, 66–67, 95–99, 113–15; Henkin, *Ta'aroch*, 139–57.

6. Fishman, "The Musar Movement," 254.

7. *Ohr HaMusar* 8 (1924): 52; *Ohr HaMusar* 9 (1925): 43; *Ohr HaMusar* 13 (1928): 49; Weintraub, *BeSufa*, 93; Herschberg, *Pinkes*, 336; Nekritz, "Yeshivot," 275; Bruk, *Gevilei*, 37–38.

8. *Ohr HaMusar* 14 (1931): 47; testimony: Margalit; Klibansky, "HaYeshivot," 127n10.

9. This analysis ignores the central yeshiva in Ivye, which originally was set up in Kovel in Vohlin Province, but moved from place to place due to various constraints. Likewise, the attempt to set up a central yeshiva in the town of Novardok, which was near well-known Lithuanian yeshivas, was due to nostalgia and the potential for influence that was linked to the name of the town. Regarding the absence of the Novardok movement in Lithuania, see *Ohr HaMusar* 16 (1938): 39.

10. Herschberg, *Pinkes*, 336 (from Yiddish).

11. For a detailed description of the wanderings of the yeshiva, see Weintraub, *BeSufa*.

12. Hurwitz, *Madregat haAdam beTikun haMiddot*, 57; Levovitz, *Da'at*, 257. For a literary echo of this debate over fundamentals, see Ben-Artzi, "Bein Yotzer," 25.

13. *Ohr HaMusar* 8 (1924): 54.

14. *Ohr HaMusar* 8 (1924): 52–54; *Ohr HaMusar* 9 (1925): 42–43; *Ohr HaMusar* 10 (1925): 65; *Ohr HaMusar* 12 (1927): 49; *Ohr HaMusar* 13 (1928): 47; HaHitagdut, *Ḥoveret*, "Az Nidberu." The number of yeshivas in 1937 includes Novardok Torah institutions in Latvia, the Land of Israel, and England.

15. *Ohr HaMusar* 10 (1925): 63; Weintraub, *BeSufa*, 210; Berman, *Siḥot*, 108–9; testimony: Ben-Artzi. Regarding the Musar groups and the "virtue of trust," see chapter 4.

16. *Ohr HaMusar* 8 (1924): 53; *Ohr HaMusar* 9 (1925): 43; *Ohr HaMusar* 10 (1925): 63; *Ohr HaMusar* 11 (1926): 90; testimony: Ben-Artzi. See also Desler, *Shenot*, I, 480–81; Levin, *Zichron*, 28.

17. *Ohr HaMusar* 10 (1925): 63; *Ohr HaMusar* 15 (1933): 40–44. Also see Berman, *Siḥot*, 111.

18. HaHitagdut, *Ḥoveret*, "Az Nidberu." "Beit-Yosef" was the name of the Novardok yeshivas after the death of Rabbi Yosef-Yozel Hurwitz.

19. HaHitagdut, *Ḥoveret*, "Harbatzat HaTorah"; the logo of the letters of Yehudah-Leib Kogan to the members of his family at the end of the 1930s (YLKA).

20. *Ohr HaMusar* 15 (1933): 39. See also Hurwitz, *Madregat haAdam beTikun haMiddot*, at the end of the pamphlet.

21. *Ohr HaMusar* 8 (1924): 53; *Ohr HaMusar* 9 (1925): 42; *Ohr HaMusar* 10 (1925): 62.

22. *Ohr HaMusar* 11 (1926): 90. Fishman mentioned more general signs of the transformation of Novardok from a network to a unified movement (Fishman, "The Musar Movement," 254–56).

23. *Ohr HaMusar* 15 (1933): 43; *HaBote'aḥ* 10, no. 54 (1935): 4; *Di Voch*, Mar. 22, 1935; HaHitagdut, *Ḥoveret*, announcement at the end of the booklet. See also Bruk, *Gevilei*, photos at the end of the volume.

24. *Ohr HaMusar* 8 (1924): 3. A hectograph is a copying machine.

25. *Ohr HaMusar* 9 (1925): 3; *Ohr HaMusar* 14 (1931): 48; *Ohr HaMusar* 16 (1938): 1. Indeed, the internal periodicals attempted to publicize movement news as well (Klibansky, "'Hitagdut'," 120–21). Regarding the establishment of Novardok yeshivas in Eretz Yisrael, see later in this chapter.

26. Gerstenkorn, *Zichronotai*, 23. See also *Digleinu* 79 (1954): 2; Elberg, *Varsha*, 159–60, 220; Zemba, "Shtiblach," 367. An essential difference between the Lithuanian beit-midrash and the Hasidic one was the custom of Lithuanian youth to leave their homes to study Torah in a kibbutz, usually in a faraway beit-midrash, whereas the Hasidic young men remained in a beit-midrash close to home and under their parents' watchful eyes. Capoteh is a traditional frock coat, usually made of black silk or wool.

27. For a list of these yeshivas, see Stampfer, *Families*, 256–60.

28. Elberg, *Varsha*, 80, 220–21, 227, 232–33; Krone, *Morai*, 92. For the unique attitude of the Lubavitch Rebbe toward Lithuanian yeshivas, see Klibansky, "HaYeshivot," 147–49.

29. Regarding the third alternative, see Stampfer, *Families*, 260–74.

30. *HaTzoffe*, Feb. 8, 1946; Levinsky, "Pirkei," 52. For the history of the Lomzhe Yeshiva, see Klibansky, *KeTzur*, 70–71.

31. Gelbart, *Di Groise Yeshive*, 25, regulation 9. Regarding this yeshiva, see Klibansky, *KeTzur*, 72.

32. Gelbart, *Di Groise Yeshive*, 62. See also page 20.

33. Zeidman, *Ishim*, 2.

34. Gelbart, *Di Groise Yeshive*, 49, 75; Landoi, *Yeshivot*, 38; Trop, *Ḥidushei*, 8n21. Regarding background of the Radin and Baranovitch yeshivas, see Klibansky, *KeTzur*, 58–59, 67, respectively.

35. Shapira, *Igrot*, 151. See Fichman, *Bialik*, 81; *Nettiva*, Aug. 27, 1936; Zinowitz, *Ishim*, 441. Cf. chapter 4, note 6.

36. Shapira, *Igrot*, 151. See Klibansky, "HaYeshivot," 149n167. Zvhil lies about 120 kilometers southeast of Berezhnitsa.

37. Shapira, *Igrot*, 151–52. See also Klibansky, "HaYeshivot," 150n171. Korets is located about thirty kilometers west of Zvhil.

38. Leoni, *Korets*, 122–23, 125, 278–79; Shapira, *Igrot*, 152–53; *Hatzefira*, Aug. 10, 1927; Yeshiva reports, May, 17, 1926 (VHY/1132), and June, 25, 1930 (VHY/258); letter: Riz to Va'ad-HaYeshivot, Jan. 4, 1928 (VHY/258).

39. Postcards: Plotnick to Va'ad-HaYeshivot, Mar. 13, 1930, Yisrael to Va'ad-HaYeshivot, Jun. 8, 1928, and Riz to Va'ad-HaYeshivot, Jun. 4, 1928 (VHY/258); Yeshiva reports, 1926–1931 (VHY/258), and 1936 (VHY/1132). Oraḥ-Ḥayim is the section of the Shulḥan-Aruch (the Code of Jewish Law), dealing with laws relating to day-to-day observance.

40. Yeshiva reports, 1926–1931 (VHY/258), 1936 (VHY/1132), and 1938/1939 (MWP/Rovne); *DoV*, Mar. 1, 1934; letter: Sorin to Va'ad-HaYeshivot, Apr. 6, 1936 (VHY/258); Leoni, *Korets*, 125.

41. See chapter 1, by note 30. *Multiage* in this work refers to an institution that serves students of different age groups, that is, both yeshiva-gedola and yeshiva-ketana together.

42. Yeshiva report, 1938/1939 (MWP/Ostroh); Ayalon-Baranik, *Pinkas*, 100; Berkovitz, *Ḥelkat Yosef*, prefaces; Va'ad-Hatzala, *Ḥurbn*, 148. See also Zinowitz, *Ishim*, 445.

43. Yeshiva reports, 1928–1930, and students' list, 1930 (VHY/713); letter: Maggid to Va'ad-HaYeshivot, Jun. 2, 1937 (VHY/713); Bruk, *Gevilei*, 181; *Ohr HaMusar* 8 (1924): 54. See also Levin, *Zichron*, 8, 13. The founder and the rosh-yeshiva was Rabbi Shraga-Ze'ev "Varzhaner" Maggid.

44. Reports of the Lutsk Yeshiva, 1929–1930, 1936 (VHY/1139), and Ciechanowiec Yeshiva, 1927–1928 (VHY/1120); Bruk, *Gevilei*, 170, 203; Va'ad-Hatzala, *Ḥurbn*, 148. See also Klibansky, "HaYeshivot," 154n199.

45. Zeidman, "Yeshivat Ḥachmei Lublin," 406; *DIdV* 290 (1990): 51–54; *HaTzoffe*, Aug. 6, 1957; Mandelboim, *Yeshivat*, II, 419–30.

46. Klibansky, "HaYeshivot," 144n128; Nadler, "HaSinteza," 409; Lichtenstein and Rabinowitz, *Pinkas*, 243; Ayalon, *Sefer-Zikaron*, 94–95; Stein, *Baranovitch*, 269–70; Berezovsky, *Zikaron Kadosh*, 84–85, 89; Yeshiva report, winter 1926/1927 (VHY/1114).

47. List of allocations, Jan. 13, 1932 (VHY/1106); Yeshiva reports 1926–1928 (VHY/1114); Shalitt, *Oif di Ḥurves*, 699.

48. Letter: Hirschowitz to Va'ad-HaYeshivot, May 9, 1937 (VHY/13). For more about the Brisk Kibbutz, see chapter 4.

49. Yeshiva reports, 1926–1927, and letter: Zingerman to Va'ad-HaYeshivot, Oct. 29, 1926 (VHY/1157); postcards: Gutman to Va'ad-HaYeshivot, Oct. 2, 1929, and Sep. 21, 1930 (VHY/10); Yisraeli, *Beit Karlin*, 335–36; Ayalon, *Sefer-Zikaron*, 106–7.

50. Yeshiva report, summer 1936 (VHY/1157); the list of yeshivot-ketanot, 1931 (VHY/1107). For Rabbi Slavin's Torah novellae, see *Knesset Yisrael* [Slabodka] 14 (1939), 22 (1939), and 26 (1940).

51. "Kol Koreh leEzra!" [A Call for Help!], May 15, 1938 (CRC-227/22). See also Levi, "HaRav," 94 (he wasn't exact).

52. Letters to Central Relief, Feb. 9, 1938, and Jul. 19, 1937 (CRC-227/22); "Kol Koreh leEzra!" May 15, 1938 (CRC-227/22); the list of yeshivot-ketanot, winter 1938/1939 (VHY/1107).

53. *DIdS*, May 1, 1928 (from Yiddish). For other yeshivas, see Herschberg, *Pinkes*, 336; Yakobzohn, *Zichronot*, 119; *HaTor* 6, no. 40–41 (1926): 25. See also *IdL*, Aug. 10, 1923; Levin, *Toledot*, 3; Parush, *Sharsheret*, III, 324; Surasky, *Ohr*, II, 119–26; Lichtenstein and Rabinowitz, *Pinkas*, 131–32; Zeidman, "Yeshivat 'Knesset'," 324.

54. Warhaftig, *Palit*, 223. See Klibansky, "HaYeshivot," 156n215.

55. Cf. Barkai, "Naḥalat," 18–19. In Lithuania, young men were drafted within two months of the cancellation of military deferments for yeshiva students (*IdL*, Jun. 20, 1924).

56. Sasson, *Naḥalat*, 475.

57. Shapira, *Igrot* (1990 reprint), 275–76; *Ohr HaMusar* 9 (1925): 43. Regarding the fate of these ideas in Volozhin, see Klibansky, *KeTzur*, 195.

58. *DIdS*, Feb., 1, 1924, and Feb. 10, 1924; *IdL*, Feb. 8, 1924, and Jun. 20, 1924. See also Oshri, "Yeshivat," 157 (he wasn't exact); Katz, *Toledotai*, 6; Katz, "Maran," 148; Grossman, *Ki Im*, 33 (with several errors there). Concerning Rabbi Epstein's trip, see chapter 1, by note 12.

59. Even-Yisrael was the parallel institution to Telz's preparatory program. According to Barkai, the Slabodka administration opposed the adoption of a secular curriculum even in the Telz mechinah (Barkai, "Naḥalat," 30). See Katz, "Maran," 148; Tikochinski, *Lamdanut*, 201–3; *Tevunah* 81 (1947): 143; Oshri, "Yeshivat," 157–58; Kravitz, *Aḥar He'asef*, 561.

60. Epstein, *Levush*, II, 5.

61. Rozental, *HaZvi*, 280–81; Friedland, "HaGaon," 7; Oshri, "Yeshivat," 157. Cf. Tikochinski, *Lamdanut*, 199–200.

62. Grossman, *Ki Im*, 33; Riff, *Ner*, 73; Kravitz, *Aḥar He'asef*, 565–66. Cf. Tikochinski, *Lamdanut*, 200–201.

63. Katz, "Maran," 148; Sarna, Transcription; *Sha'arei Tziyon* 4, no. 10–11 (1924): 16 (2); Epstein, *Levush*, II, 5.

64. Tikochinski, *Lamdanut*, 215–16; Katz, "Maran," 148; *Hed haAm* 1, no. 25 (1924): 4; letter: Slonim to Epstein, May 27, 1924 (DSA); Epstein, *Levush*, II, 5. See also Margaliot, *Amudei*, 7, 24; Friedman, *Ḥevra*, 140–142; Edelstein, "Keitzad," 104; *Hed Litta* 17 (1924): 2; *Kol Ya'akov*, Oct. 6, 1922.

65. *Jewish Chronicle*, Aug. 8, 1924; *Sha'arei Tziyon* 4, no. 12–13 (1924): 15 (2); Edelstein, "Keitzad," 103–4; Sarna, *Daliyot*, 310–11; Sarna, Transcription; Katz, *Toledotai*, 6; Epstein, *Levush*, II, 5.

66. Tau, *Sefer*, 10. For Hutner, see chapter 6, by note 80. See also Epstein, *Levush*, II, 5; Katz, *Toledotai*, 6; Katz, "Maran," 149; *Hed haAm* 2, no. 8 (1924): 6; *IdL*, Feb. 22, 1925; Berenstein, *Yeshivat*, 1285; Hutner, *Paḥad*, 179; Sarna, Transcription. Cf. letter: Grodzensky to Finkel, Jul. 31, 1925 (SEA).

67. Tau, *Sefer*, 11; *Hed haAm* 2, no. 37 (1925): 6; *HaNe'eman* 3 (1928): 7. Rabbi Epstein returned to Slabodka on December 1, 1924 (*IdL*, Dec. 8, 1924) and set off for Hebron on February 15, 1925 (*IdL*, Feb. 22, 1925). Regarding his arrival in Jerusalem on February 25, 1925, and his trip to Hebron the next day, see *Sha'arei Tziyon* 5, no. 5–7 (1925): 19 (1)–19 (2) and *Hed haAm* 2, no. 22 (1925): 6.

68. Epstein, *Levush*, II, 5. See also *IdL*, Dec. 8, 1924; Sarna, *Daliyot*, 311.

69. Sarna, *Daliyot*, 309–10.

70. Klibansky, *KeTzur*, 84.

71. Levinsky, *Sefer*, 130; Zinowitz, *"Mir,"* 118; Katz, *Tenuat*, II, 347; Sasson, *Naḥalat*, 475; Rosenstein, *Ahavat*, 299; Lomzhe Yeshiva, *Keren*, 3, 14; Rand, *Toledot*, 16. Cf. Yoshor, "Nasich," 9.

72. Krone, *Ishim*, 20. See also Levinsky, *Sefer*, 130, 226–27; Katz, *Tenuat*, II, 347; Yoshor, "Nasich," 9; Yadler, *BeTuv*, 332; *Hed haAm* 2, no. 8 (1924): 6. As mentioned in the previous section, the Lomzhe Yeshiva was set up on the edge of Poland in order to transmit Torah and Musar to the local Jewish residents.

73. Levinsky, *Sefer*, 130; Katz, *Tenuat*, II, 347; *Hed haAm* 2, no. 8 (1924): 6; *Hed haAm* 2, no. 11 (1924): 7; *Hed haAm* 2, no. 28 (1925): 7; *Sha'arei Tziyon* 5, no. 3–4 (1924/1925): 16 (2).

74. Letter: Ruch to Va'ad-HaYeshivot, May 3, 1926 (VHY/1136); *DIdS*, Apr. 21, 1926; Levinsky, *Sefer*, 130; Katz, *Tenuat*, II, 347; Yoshor, "Nasich," 9; Rabinowitz, "Yeshivat," 219; Lomzhe Yeshiva, *Keren*, 4, 14. See also Samson-Rabinowitz, *A Jubilee*, 125.

75. *Ohr HaMusar* 14 (1931): 34, 46; Schechter, *Zichronot*, 36, 41; Domb, "Pirkei," 14; *HaHed* 4, no. 1 (1928): 8.

76. *Ohr HaMusar* 14 (1931): 47.

77. Ibid., 46; Frank, *Esah*, 46; *HaYeshiva* [Satmar] 1, no. 4 (1929): 44; Hurwitz, *Madregat haAdam*, 4. See also Parush, *Sharsheret*, VI, 211; *Tevunah* 78 (1947): 107.

78. *Ohr HaMusar* 15 (1933): 37–38; Billadi, "Toledot," 101, 113; Kanyevsky, *Toledot*, 75; *Sha'arei Tziyon* 12, no. 7–9 (1932): 30. See also Bergman, *Orḥot*, 23; Frank, *Esah*, 52. Rabbi Bliacher received help from Ze'ev Shtchigel in establishing the yeshiva.

79. *Ohr HaMusar* 15 (1933): 38; Billadi, "Toledot," 103. Cf. Parush, *Sharsheret*, VI, 211. See *DoV*, Mar. 16, 1934.

80. *Ohr HaMusar* 16 (1938): 62; Weintraub, *BeSufa*, 217; Kanyevsky, *Toledot*, 76.

81. Even though some of the yeshivot-ketanot were short-lived, by the end of the 1930s, four thousand Novardok students studied in eighty-five yeshivot-ketanot in Poland and Latvia (Nekritz, "Yeshivot," 267–69, 277. For an examination of this number of students and its validation, see Klibansky, "HaYeshivot," 132n44). Regarding Novardok yeshivas in Galicia, see Weintraub, *BeSufa*, 211; Vunder, "HaYeshivot," 100.

82. The growth trend will be presented in detail in chapter 6.

83. Levin, *Zichron*, 17.

84. This cannot be said about the Luninets Yeshiva, which was not mentioned in this chapter; from the time of its founding in 1930, three talented roshei-yeshiva served there. However, in terms of its characteristics, it was quite similar to the renewed Stolin Yeshiva. The ownership of Lithuanian yeshivas will be dealt with in chapter 5.

85. Levin, *Zichron*, 33. There is a Hasidic custom for the admor to taste food and distribute the rest, shirayyim, among his Hasidim who eagerly take it, believing it is blessed.

86. See Ben-Artzi, "Te'unat," 13; Ben-Artzi, *Shivti*, 114; Zilberg "Kat," I. On essential differences between the Musar approach and Hasidism, see Etkes, *Rabbi Israel*, 320–22.

87. Elberg, *Varsha*, 169–71; Zinowitz, *Ishim*, 437.

88. Unlike Slabodka and Lomzhe, the Novardok branches were set up only as organizational frameworks and drew students from all the yeshivas of the movement.

II

Aspects of the Yeshiva World

This section is the heart of the book and deals with the characteristics of the Lithuanian yeshiva world during the period between the two world wars. Despite the apparent isolation of the yeshivas and their relegation the margins of public interest, they were exposed to profound developments that took place after the First World War among Eastern European Jewry in particular and the Jews of the world in general. This exposure will be examined regarding its various aspects and significances throughout those years in four chapters:

- Economy: In most of the years of their existence during the interwar period, the yeshivas were forced to deal with growing financial deficits. Their roshei-yeshiva hoped to find a solution through generous allocations from foundations and lengthy fundraising trips. This chapter reveals the material conditions in the yeshivas by focusing on the enlistment of the prominent aid organizations to their help and on the organizational steps taken in the Kresy region of Poland to assist the yeshivas there.
- Studies: Outwardly, no substantial changes took place in the yeshivas' curriculum after the First World War. The core material studied was in-depth Talmudic research and, alongside this, involvement with Musar studies. Nevertheless, changes took place in these two aspects of yeshiva learning—changes that will be discussed in this chapter.

- Leadership: In the interwar period, the Lithuanian yeshiva was directed by two educators: the rosh-yeshiva and the Musar-mashgiaḥ. Each one had his own responsibility related to a defined aspect of yeshiva life. This chapter discusses the choice of these two educational figures and investigates their position and the dimensions of their influence in the yeshiva.
- Students: In the years between the wars, significant changes took place in the characteristics of the talmidim of the yeshivas. Their measurable parameters—number, age, and background—will serve to analyze these changes and the effect of the outside world on the yeshivas in this chapter.

3

Economy

The First World War brought about change in the spread of the Lithuanian yeshivas. Even though the great majority of yeshivas returned to their original places or remained in them during the war years, they were no longer under the rule of one country, namely Tsarist Russia, as they had been in the past. In the geopolitical partitions that took place after the war, most of the yeshivas could be found in two democratic states: Lithuania and Poland. The new extensive Jewish educational institutions in both of those countries were supported by tuition and sometimes even government funding. The Lithuanian yeshivas did not have access to similar budget sources, so they were forced to depend on the financial help of Jews in their own country and overseas.[1]

This economic dependence was not new. From the time that the supra-community yeshivas were founded, their directors were forced to wander among the towns of the Pale of Settlement, and even those of the Russian interior and Poland, to seek support. The increased needs pushed them to set up networks of paid emissaries. These networks were deployed throughout Tsarist Russia and the Central European countries to collect donations and distribute charity boxes there. After the war, these traditional methods of collecting donations needed to be updated due to the political, economic, and social changes that had taken place among Eastern European Jewry in that era:[2]

- Isolation from the outside world of Russian Jewry, which had been a significant source of funding for Lithuanian yeshivas up until the Bolshevik Revolution
- Impoverishment of the Jews of Lithuania and Poland, who had lost many of their assets in the ravages of the war, and who after it continued to be stressed because of economic crises and the policy of discrimination of the new authorities there
- Marginalization of the yeshivas in the Jewish community because of the wide processes of secularization
- Attribution of political identity to the yeshivas, even though they were formally nonparty institutions, due to the sharply defined political affiliation among the Jewish public

The shortage that resulted from the dearth of local help to the yeshivas in Poland and Lithuania was made up by organized aid from abroad, from German Jewry in the 1920s, and from the Jews of London in the second half of the 1930s.[3] However, the most significant aid to the yeshivas came from a source that had previously been untapped: American Jewry. This community had already organized during the First World War to aid its downtrodden brethren in Eastern Europe, many of whom had become refugees. The Orthodox set up large aid committees that supported refugee rabbis and yeshivas. When the war ended, the committees continued in their volunteer work as the yeshivas returned to their places and needed of increased support. However, as time passed the needs of the yeshivas grew while the organized Jewish American aid lessened.

This new reality no longer allowed the yeshivas to rely solely on generous donations from America; they also had to turn to the local Jews who had not even supplied all the yeshivas' needs in "the good times." Within the borders of the Polish Republic, there were about twenty Lithuanian yeshivot-gedolot, most of them in the eastern Kresy region. The intentional policy of the Polish authorities caused the rapid economic decline of the country's Jews. Under these circumstances, the independent collection of funds by the many yeshivas in the limited geographic area of the Kresy would have failed and harmed each one of them.[4] The Orthodox leaders in the eastern provincial region, among them several yeshiva heads, made the effort to search together for a solution to this difficult problem. The resolution that was finally found was revolutionary in its centralization of authority in a new organization after taking away the authority that was traditionally in the hands of the roshei-yeshiva, as well as a comprehensive consolidation of Orthodoxy that was previously unheard of in Eastern Europe.

The situation in independent Lithuania was less complicated. Four yeshivot-gedolot existed there. From 1919 there was an active Rabbis' Association in the country, but this could not steer the local economic activities of these yeshivas, which were the glory of Torah Judaism in Lithuania. Every now and then, they received declarations of support from the Rabbis' Association or from the rabbis of Lithuania in general, but the main burden fell on their directors.[5] It would seem that these directors even preferred independent action, either because they relied on their institution's fine reputation or because they had faith in their personal ability to convince the Orthodox public in Lithuania or abroad to open wide their pockets. Because of this, during the interwar period, there was no change in the yeshivas' organizational structure in Lithuania compared to the era before the First World War. Each of these Talmudic institutions continued to act independently in an attempt to survive without any effort to concentrate their activities under one roof.

Modest assistance and philanthropic organizations in America and Central Europe, and even South Africa, joined those larger local and overseas organizations that attempted (with no proven success) to provide a solution to the chronic deficits in the yeshiva budgets. Each of these helped at times to overcome the critical financial situation that often characterized the yeshivas. This outside support was not ex nihilo. An almost necessary condition for its existence and wide scope was the ongoing and costly activity of the roshei-yeshiva, which was intended to publicize their institutions' reputation among Diaspora Jewry and to cultivate relationships with all the various philanthropic organizations. Indeed, one of the most exhausting activities of the yeshiva heads was to keep in constant close contact with all the donors in order to encourage them to continue giving and soliciting donations from others. It is no wonder that the "financial" letters are the lion's portion of the Lithuanian yeshivas' archival materials. They testify to the nature of the support organizations and the extent of their assistance and contribution to the yeshivas' upkeep. A deeper look at the system of support of several of these organizations can show the actual material circumstances of the yeshivas in the interwar period.

ON THEIR OWN INITIATIVE

The economic and social changes that took place in Jewish society in Poland and Lithuania did not improve the condition of the yeshivas in those countries. A clear indication of the hopelessness of relying on local help can be found in the few community yeshivas that survived the First World War. The Remayle Yeshiva in Vilna, which had derived significant income from local contributions in the past, lost this source of funding after the war due to the community's destitution. The yeshiva, in its dire straits, turned to the religion department of the community council with a request to supplement the yeshiva's budget and make it possible to pay its instructors' salaries. In 1929 the yeshiva again asked help from the new community council in Vilna, this time for considerable monthly support that was essential for its existence. The Brisk Yeshiva, which still retained some semblance of community affiliation, did not derive a great deal of benefit from local contributors. Even before the war, the yeshiva had relied on help from the outside, and the support of the city's Jews was not needed. Those who had recovered economically after the war had become used to not supporting the yeshiva; their entire contribution was not sufficient to cover the yeshiva's expenditures for two days a month. The Slonim Yeshiva, which had separated from the local Talmud-Torah as previously mentioned, was not dependent on local residents. As in the case of other yeshivas, Slonim benefited from the assistance of Jewish American aid committees, as well as from the support of Jews who had emigrated from Slonim to the United States, and the revenue from real estate donated by Jews from Slonim. However, these sources of income ceased fulfilling its needs, and from 1925 the erosion of its established position was evident.[6]

What did the community yeshivas do to escape their predicament? When all the funding sources of the Remayle Yeshiva, among them emigrants from Vilna in the United States, dried up, it was necessary to send rabbinical emissaries overseas to raise funds. This can be seen in the words of its patron, Rabbi Ḥayim-Ozer Grodzensky: "The Remayle Yeshiva of our community is in danger of closing, Heaven forbid. Up until now, I have tried with all my strength not to send emissaries, only the Joint [Distribution Committee] and help from our city [maintained it]. But since the help from the Joint ceased and poverty has grown enormously in our city, its entire existence is a daily miracle."[7] Indeed, most of the Lithuanian yeshivas began to pin their hopes on rabbinical emissaries to raise funds. These representatives had to be acquainted with the communities that they visited on behalf of the yeshivas, and they have needed the ability to speak publicly and convince their audiences to donate. Most acted out of personal motivation, and fundraising was a means of earning a livelihood and supporting their families. It was to be expected that not all of them brought real benefit to those who sent them. Rabbi Aharon Kotler complained in 1925, "From the emissaries we have nearly nothing from the field now. Up until now we have received only $220 from all of them together (including from America), while we spend $300 for bread alone each month."[8] This situation of the Kletsk Yeshiva did not change in subsequent years. The Radin Yeshiva's emissary in England was unsuccessful in his mission; the total income from his fundraising came to less than half a single month's expense for the yeshiva. The Grodno Yeshiva also suffered disappointment from its agent in the United States in the 1920s, when he brought it no benefit at all. In contrast, the Slonim Yeshiva was quite satisfied with the performance of several of its overseas emissaries.[9]

However, the assistance from the emissaries could not be measured only in terms of the amount of money that slowly trickled into the yeshivas. The publicity and awareness of the yeshivas' existence and the recognition of their unique qualities and financial problems among their target audience were incomparably more important. This sort of exposure was expected to provide long-term benefit to the yeshivas.

It was clear that the emissaries alone could not change the financial balance of the yeshivas, which suffered from a profound deficit. Significant change could be accomplished only by their roshei-yeshiva, whose name and reputation attracted an audience of potential donors. Many were forced to leave their students and set off to wander in foreign countries. A few of them saw a need to remain overseas for months or even years. Rabbi Baruch-Ber Leibowitz, for example, spent more than a year and a half in the United States in 1928–1929, and Rabbi Moshe-Mordechai Epstein was in the United States for two and a half years in 1924–1927.

Rabbi Yeḥiel-Mordechai Gordon went even further when he set out for the United States in 1933 from his yeshiva in Lomzhe and never returned. As was previously mentioned, Rabbis Epstein and Gordon established branches of their yeshivas in Eretz-Yisrael, and their fundraising voyages were meant to provide for two yeshivas at the same time.

The worldwide economic crisis forced the yeshiva heads or their representatives to go abroad at the same time in order to save their institutions. In 1929 Rabbis Reuven Katz (1880–1963), in the service of the Radin Yeshiva, Shim'on Shkop of Grodno; Baruch-Ber Leibowitz from Kamenitz; Baruch Hurwitz of Slabodka; Yosef-Shlomo Kahaneman from Ponevezh; and Pesaḥ Pruskin of Kobrin were all in the United States. Roshei-yeshiva did not receive previous training in such public relations. Thus, the fundraising sermons of Rabbi Baruch-Ber Leibowitz, which were delivered in local synagogues in the United States several times a week, became publicity for all of the suffering yeshivas, and his son-in-law Rabbi Reuven Grozovsky was obliged to go up to the lectern at the end of each sermon and make clear to the listeners the specific purpose of the speech. However, there were roshei-yeshiva who not only had the gift of public speaking but also had the needed talent of marketing. One of the most outstanding was Rabbi Yosef-Shlomo Kahaneman, who was aware of this advantage and knew how to utilize it well. It would seem that he exceeded all of his counterparts in the number of overseas fundraising trips he took, and he even reached as far as the Lithuanian Jewish communities that had settled in South Africa.[10]

Did the exhausting journeys of the roshei-yeshiva bring any concrete benefit to their institutions? An examination of the yeshivas' budgets indicates that there was a considerable improvement in their situation and that their deficits appreciably decreased. Rabbi Leibowitz was successful in raising thirty-five thousand dollars in his aforementioned trip to the United States, an amount that was able to cancel the Kamenitz Yeshiva's heavy debts. Rabbi Gordon collected sixty thousand dollars in the many years he spent in the United States, and he paid back 75 percent of the Lomzhe Yeshiva's debts. As a result of his fundraising trip to the United States, Rabbi Pesaḥ Pruskin was successful in reducing the Kobrin Yeshiva's deficit from $6,000 to $2,500 in one year despite being in the midst of America's Great Depression.[11]

These fundraising trips and others like them served to ameliorate the yeshivas' material difficulties, but substantial yearly expenditures continued to swell their deficits. Most of the yeshiva heads were unable to go on overseas fundraising trips year after year. A successful solution was in establishing a beachhead in the United States. Many yeshivas opened their own offices there in the 1920s. These offices could organize the local fundraising campaigns, coordinate the efforts of the emissaries, and forge connections with the local aid organizations and federations. Some yeshivas went even further and set up special aid committees in the United States, or they encouraged activists there to establish them. Thus was founded the Association of Slabodka Alumni in America, which set out to construct a new building for the mother yeshiva. Alongside the office of the Mir Yeshiva, ladies' auxiliaries were founded, and they acted to obtain resources for that Talmudic institution. Another women's organization was established in New York for the Kamenitz Yeshiva at the initiative of the son-in-law of its head, Yitzḥak Turets, during his visit there in 1935.[12]

There were two yeshivas that lacked offices that could handle their interests in the United States: Volozhin and Kobrin. It is not surprising that the heads of Kobrin were perplexed and bewildered when it came to approaching the overseas aid organizations. They had no idea how to do this, as was apparent from a 1939 letter written by the yeshiva's Talmud instructor, Rabbi Shlomo Matus, to the treasurer of Va'ad-HaYeshivot:

> All the doors to sources of support and help are locked before us, we do not have the address of any council or aid organization. The little help that we had from individuals has decreased until it has nearly ceased altogether. . . . We have heard that there are federations in Cleveland, in Michigan, in Cincinnati, in Indianapolis, in St. Louis and other aid committees in the big and small cities, but we do not know their addresses. . . . We have also heard that there are various federations in England to help the yeshivas that we do not know about at all. Please tell us about them and give us some good advice.[13]

Such a total lack of connection with the funding sources from which the other yeshivas benefited was a great detriment to the Kobrin Yeshiva, as was mentioned at the end of the first chapter.

ORGANIZED FOREIGN AID

On September 28, 1914, after the outbreak of the First World War, the Union of Orthodox Jewish Congregations of America established an aid organization for the suffering Jews of Eastern Europe. When the Union of Orthodox Rabbis and other groups joined these efforts in early October, this became the Central Committee for the Relief of Jews Suffering through the War, or for short Central Relief. In the beginning, non-Orthodox institutions joined its activities. However, ideological differences caused the liberal groups to set up a separate organization: the American Jewish Relief Committee. These two organizations acted to obtain contributions from their communities for the Jews of Eastern Europe. In order to coordinate the distribution of the money they collected, on November 27, 1914, the two organizations' representatives decided to join together in an umbrella organization: the Joint Distribution Committee of American Funds for the Relief of Jewish War Sufferers, or in short, the Joint or JDC. The JDC's mode of operation was influenced by the eastward movement of the German-Russian battlefront and the German military's growing conquest of large territories. That organization chose to work together on a temporary basis with the Berlin-based *Hilfsverein der deutschen Juden* and the Vienna branch of the *Alliance Israélite Universelle* to make financial contact possible through them with the Jewish population in occupied German territories.[14]

The goals of the Central Relief's aid were quite general. On August 25, 1915, the Union of Orthodox Rabbis of America decided to set up an adjunct organization, *Ezrat-Torah,* headed by Rabbi Yisrael Rosenberg (1875–1956), with a more focused goal: support for rabbis and religious functionaries who were suffering, as well as Torah educational institutions in Eastern Europe, such as the yeshivas. The funding was meant to come from a narrow sector of American rabbis and religious functionaries, with the aim of not harming the general fundraising campaigns of the Central Relief. It was obviously inadequate. Pressure from the religious Zionist HaMizraḥi, which had joined the activities of Ezrat-Torah, and the Union of Orthodox Rabbis led the Central Relief to fund this organization as well from its budget, and the money was distributed among the beneficiaries through ten rabbis from Europe. Indeed, the yeshivas benefited from the limited support of Ezrat-Torah during the war and, in the year afterward, from aid that was somewhat increased. But when the funding from Central Relief to Ezrat-Torah decreased, the latter organization ceased its support of yeshivas and solely concentrated on aid to rabbis.[15]

After the war, Central Relief examined its goals and the necessity of its existence. In 1920, it decided not to continue its involvement in providing for the material needs of the Jews of Eastern Europe. Rather, it focused on maintaining their religious and cultural identity. When the yeshivas returned from their exile, the Central Relief was the group that financially helped them to rehabilitate and return to regular activity. In 1921 its considerable contribution to each yeshiva began to shrink because the funds were distributed to an increasing number of yeshivas returning from Russia and Ukraine. However, this was not the only reason for reduced financial aid. At the end of that year, far-reaching modifications took place in its support of yeshivas after the JDC made some organizational changes.

After the war was over, the members of the Joint realized that the Jews of Lithuania and Poland saw existential meaning in the establishment of educational institutions for their children, and often even at the expense of funds provided for their physical well-being. On the basis of these findings, the JDC executive decided to change the goal of the organization and serve not only as a passive conduit for support but also as an active agency. In December 1921, it set up a Committee on Cultural Affairs for Jewish education with the aim of allocating this committee a fixed portion of the funds that were collected. Dr. Cyrus Adler (1863–1940) was chosen to head the committee, and each of its six members, representatives of the various groups in the Joint, was responsible for a designated field in Jewish education.

The representatives of Central Relief on the committee, Meir Berlin and Peter Wiernik (1865–1936), chose to be involved chiefly in aid to the yeshivas and other Torah institutions. To their dismay, the portion of funding that their organization provided on an ongoing basis to the JDC was in danger. At the beginning of the war, the purpose for the founding of the Central Relief was defined as aiding the suffering Jews of Eastern Europe. After the war was over, the continuation of its activities could no longer be taken for granted. In order to direct its programs in a new direction—maintaining religious life and Jewish tradition in Poland and Lithuania—it was necessary to go out and convince the Jewish multitudes that this was essential and deserved their ongoing support. The Central Relief committee asked well-known rabbinic figures to join its appearances before the American public and present the condition of the yeshivas in their countries themselves, without any intermediary, but this request was not accepted. On January 7, 1923, the Central Relief held a conference where it described its updated goals, but these attempts at renewal were unsuccessful. Toward the end of that year, its financial status severely weakened, and the Joint's funding of the yeshivas was delayed and perhaps even ceased. This situation, as well as the economic crisis in Europe that continually grew worse, put the yeshivas in a position of serious economic decline that endangered their very existence.[16]

In order to bring change to its own situation and that of the yeshivas, the Central Relief decided to take steps that were more creative and emphatic. It wished to create a large and set fund, *Keren-HaTorah,* that was meant to serve as an economic basis for the yeshivas' existence in Eretz-Yisrael, Lithuania, and Poland. Its budget would have to come from a million-dollar campaign. In order to achieve such an ambitious goal, appropriate high-profile figures were needed to attract the American Jewish public and convince them to contribute to this important cause.

The Central Relief planned to have five prominent rabbinic figures head the campaign: Avraham-Yitzḥak Kook, Meir-Simḥa HaCohen of Dvinsk (1843–1926), Yeḥezkel Libshitz of Kalish (1862–1932), Ḥayim-Ozer Grodzensky, and the Ḥafetz-Ḥayim. However, the Eastern European rabbinic personalities were unable to make the long journey to the United States due to their advanced age. At a meeting of the roshei-yeshiva of the Kresy at the end of 1923, it was decided to suggest Rabbi Shim'on Shkop of Grodno and Rabbi Isser-Zalman Meltzer of Kletsk in their places, but things developed differently. Rabbi Kook, the chief rabbi of the Land of Israel, did participate in the rabbinic mission, but none of the representatives from Poland arrived at all. Rabbis Avraham-Duber Shapiro of Kovna and Moshe-Mordechai Epstein (who at that time was in the United States to raise funds for his yeshiva, Knesset-Yisrael of Slabodka) did join the mission. In addition to the numerous appearances of the mission in 1924, on September 9 it participated in a conference to mark the tenth anniversary of the Central Relief. At that festive gathering it was decided to extend the organization's existence for at least three years.[17]

Had the Central Relief succeeded this time? It appears that it had not realized its goal, and the drive yielded only three to four hundred thousand dollars. Rabbi Avraham-Duber Shapiro wrote in disappointment to Rabbi Avraham-Yitzḥak Kook about these results of combined efforts over the eight months they stayed in the United States: "I regret the tremendous work we put into the Relief Committee, and it has brought us shame. They didn't send a penny the entire winter."[18]

Despite these paltry results, the Central Relief had penetrated into the consciousness of the Jewish masses and established itself among them. Actually, in the following years it obtained significant contributions from them, and these provided the yeshivas an important and reliable source of support.

As time passed, there were ups and downs in the assistance of the Central Relief for the Lithuanian yeshivas. As early as the last months of 1927, there were rumors of an end to its support, and it ceased entirely at the end of the 1920s. To discuss this painful issue, representatives of the yeshivas met with the directors of the JDC in Zurich in the summer of 1929. These directors offered surprising solutions, such as reducing the number of the yeshivas and introducing vocational studies in them. In response, it was decided to send a detailed memorandum to the Joint, signed by all the roshei-yeshiva, with an explanation of the importance of the yeshivas in their traditional framework. It is interesting to note the remarks of the mashgiaḥ of the Kamenitz Yeshiva, Rabbi Naftali-Ze'ev Leibowitz, which reflected the basic views of his colleagues: "It seems as though we must explain to them according to their distorted opinion that we need at least this number [of yeshivas] and more in order to supply rabbis and ritual slaughterers—which is a need of the entire Jewish people, and due to this it is impossible to reduce the number. And not to teach them a craft, as this is the opposite of what is desirable or necessary, because they [members of the Joint] understand nothing except the practicality of making a living."[19] At the beginning of the 1930s, the ability of the Central Relief to help the yeshivas was further impaired by the economic depression in the United States. A conference of rabbis and roshei-yeshiva was convened in Vilna at the end of 1932 regarding the dire situation of the yeshivas in all countries. A grave state of affairs was described: "[The yeshivas] are at a crisis point and in danger of closing, Heaven forefend. The roshei-yeshiva and tens of thousands of talmidim are exhausted from bearing the terrible burden of poverty, since due to the international crisis the income from the emissaries has dwindled and the assistance of the Joint and the Central-Relief has ceased altogether."[20]

This conference implored the Union of Orthodox Rabbis of America to exert influence on the Central Relief to renew its activity, despite the serious economic situation in the United States. It also made concrete recommendations regarding the creation of new sources of funding, including taxing Passover matzah and kosher slaughter, or a fixed annual allocation from local federations to maintain the yeshivas.[21]

Later in the 1930s, the Central Relief was more successful in its activities. Well-ordered records of most of the yeshivas from 1938 show the proportional contribution of the JDC and Central Relief to the yeshivas' budgets. These records indicate that in that year, the organizations provided only 4 percent of the yeshivas' income. This tiny portion does not include other subsidies provided by the Joint over the years intended for clothing and vacations for the talmidim, building renovation, and assistance to students from Germany and other purposes.[22] Nevertheless, these modest allocations seem disproportionate to the emergency meetings, pressures, letters, and telegrams of the roshei-yeshiva to the Central Relief and the JDC. This somewhat surprising treatment can also be discerned in that of another large aid organization that will be described forthwith, which provided a portion of the yeshivas' funds that was not much greater.

VA'AD-HAYESHIVOT

The four senior yeshivas located in Lithuania succeeded in maintaining themselves through the contributions of the country's Jews and overseas support. In contrast, the yeshivas scattered across the Kresy provinces of the Polish Republic found this difficult due to their large number. In order to make possible the survival of twenty yeshivas in the limited geographic area, the heads of Orthodoxy in the Kresy worked hard and found a creative solution in the establishment of an economic body, Va'ad-HaYeshivot (The Yeshiva Committee). The committee's uniqueness was the concentration of efforts in a framework that was common to all the yeshivas. This was not a completely new idea in the area of Lithuanian Jewish culture because centralized collection of funds already existed there in the nineteenth century.[23] However, the new committee had some innovative characteristics that were previously unfamiliar. This was quite an ambitious arrangement that was intended to create a fixed system of fundraising that would almost obligate the members of all the Jewish communities in the Kresy region to contribute to the yeshivas. This broad geographical and organizational scope for fundraising was not attainable for the yeshivas through separate activity.

The Shekel Donation

The idea of establishing Va'ad-HaYeshivot, which offered a response to the material difficulties of the Lithuanian yeshivas in Poland, was not merely a technical and economic solution. The idea arose as a reaction to a grave sense of crisis in the early 1920s among the leaders of Orthodoxy in the Kresy. In this region, rapid spiritual and cultural change had occurred, and a pronouncedly secular atmosphere had increasingly taken the place of Jewish tradition. One of Orthodoxy's leaders, the Ḥafetz-Ḥayim, who had managed to see during his long life every stage of the spread of modernism and secularism from their initial stages, provided a wide-ranging view of the situation in each of the Kresy towns: "When a person imagines how his town appeared several decades ago, he will be forced to wonder how the study of Torah has diminished in such a short time. Vilna, for example. How much time has passed since Vilna was a city filled with scholars and scribes? And today? Today there are only a few Torah-students. And it is the same everywhere."[24] The result of this situation was formulated in one of his speeches in piercing tones: "In those towns where Torah study has ceased and where there is no yeshiva, all Judaism has been destroyed."[25] Indeed, most of the towns did not have a yeshiva or even a yeshiva-ketana for the local young people. This was due to either the difficulty in maintaining one or the lack of consciousness of the necessity of such an institution. Even the yeshivas that existed, the last bastion of Torah learning, stood on the edge of collapse. Their situation was described by three of the senior roshei-yeshiva in 1924:

> The condition of all of the yeshivas is terrible and quite well-known. Expenses, due to high prices, have greatly increased. Income has ceased. The emissaries are considered as nothing. Support from America—a

> handful does not bring satiety, and their hands have become weak even from that small amount, and it has nearly ceased altogether, and why are we silent? The ruin of religion, the insult to the Torah [is] in every spot and corner. Nothing is left for us except the yeshivas that are preserved in purity, and they are the foundation for the remnant of maintaining religion and its existence. . . . They all are on the threshold of destruction, Heaven forbid, due to a lack of means.[26]

The leaders of Orthodoxy, who wistfully saw how the yeshivas suffered under the burden of heavy debt, were nearly at a loss in the face of the dire situation. On April 29, 1924, they convened a meeting headed by Rabbi Ḥayim-Ozer Grodzensky in Vilna to discuss possible steps for rescuing the yeshivas from the grave crisis. The venerable Ḥafetz-Ḥayim was the one to raise an ambitious and surprising solution. Its main points were as follows:

- Levying a semiannual donation of a shekel (one dollar) for maintaining the yeshivas from each household in the "Lithuanian" Kresy provinces of Vilna, Novardok, Bialystok, and Polesia
- Rabbis and roshei-yeshiva volunteering to persuade their local and nearby communities to contribute these donations
- Setting up local committees in each town for the purpose of collecting the periodic contributions
- Establishing a central yeshiva committee in Vilna to oversee local committees in particular, and to coordinate the activities for the Lithuanian yeshivas in the Kresy in general

It would seem that the first point is the most revolutionary. The Ḥafetz-Ḥayim envisioned this as he faced the need to save the yeshivas from economic collapse. However, this item's very essence had spiritual aspects that the Ḥafetz-Ḥayim valued over its economic potential: drawing all Jews near—even those who were far from *mitzvot* observance—to the concept of the importance of Torah and the merit accrued to the entire community through the support of Torah learning. Regarding the practicality of this levy, the Ḥafetz-Ḥayim did not consider the economic burden of the donation on each household too onerous despite his being conscious of the poverty in the Kresy region. In one of his speeches, he said, "One shekel every half-year for all of the yeshivas is not a large sum, and whoever has the means and is a wealthy man, should give more." And because this amount was not an obstacle in his eyes, he saw no difficulty in the other points, including the establishment of the many-branched system of Va'ad-HaYeshivot.[27]

The idea of setting up a central committee to deal with the economic needs of the yeshivas was not a new one in the interwar period. The first version of the committee was already formed at the end of 1919, and this was the Aid Committee for Religious Educational Institutions. Its founder, Rabbi Ḥayim-Ozer Grodzensky, had returned that year to Vilna from his exile in Yekaterinoslav and found that the funds from the Joint—which were intended to repair the damage inflicted on East-European Jewry by the war—were insufficiently directed toward the Torah institutions. To change this situation, he convened a meeting of Vilna rabbis and convinced them to set up the committee. This new committee was in touch with Central Relief and, through that organization, obtained funds from Jews in America. Rabbi Leib Ḥasman, the rabbi of Stutchin who had returned from exile, was appointed as its head and for a while was the active force behind it.

The committee was active for a number of years, and it was the first step in providing a solid economic base for the yeshivas in the Vilna region. Here, an opportunity arose to give the committee new life and expand its activities. The principal novel and daring feature of the suggested Va'ad was the permanent commitment of every member of the community to be responsible for the yeshivas in the area of his residence. To be sure, a voluntary system could not coerce Jewish residents to donate to a cause against their will. But the plan assumed that setting up strong local committees, rabbinical campaigns of persuasion, and social pressure would have an effect even on those who were not enthusiastic about helping the yeshivas at the start.

The suggested solution was unanimously accepted and ratified by the Vilna meeting's participants, with the signatures of some forty of the rabbis present. However, opposition came from an unexpected direction: a number of the roshei-yeshiva themselves. They maintained networks of emissaries all over Poland, which brought in regular sums of money each month. Their expected redundancy when the joint committee would be set up aroused the apprehension of these roshei-yeshiva concerning harm to their promised income, which prompted their opposition to the new committee. The Ḥafetz-Ḥayim, who was known for his uncompromising nature regarding issues that were fundamental and important to him, succeeded in convincing the opponents that the idea that he had proposed was correct. From this point, the coast was clear for a speedy implementation of the solution.[28]

Setting up a Fundraising System

The Ḥafetz-Ḥayim knew that the agreement of the roshei-yeshiva and some of the Kresy rabbis was insufficient for the implementation of his plan, and he realized that it was necessary to fulfill two fundamental conditions:

- Total commitment of all the town rabbis in the "Lithuanian" Kresy to the suggested solution
- Choosing individuals of high caliber to operate the organizational system that was exceptional in its dimensions, with its center meant to be in Vilna and its branches in all the "Lithuanian" towns of the Kresy region

In order to fulfill the first condition, a large meeting of rabbis was convened in Vilna on July 8, 1924. In a lengthy address, the Ḥafetz-Ḥayim presented the dire situation in which the yeshivas found themselves and his solution. The meeting ratified the previous decision with the signatures of more than 120 rabbis and roshei-yeshiva, and they committed themselves to participate regularly in the publicity expeditions for the new fundraising campaign.[29]

For the fulfillment of the second condition, it was decided to appoint Rabbi Ḥayim-Ozer Grodzensky as the head of the central Va'ad-HaYeshivot. It was expected that he would ennoble the new yeshiva committee with his respected Torah authority, and his abilities were supposed to make it possible for him to prevail in the complex and sensitive issues pertaining to the organizational system and act vigorously in its favor in Poland and the Jewish world. Rabbi Leib Ḥasman, mentioned earlier, served as acting director for a short interim period until he was replaced by the energetic Yosef Schuw. From then on, Schuw was the moving force in everything that concerned Va'ad-HaYeshivot, and the accomplished treasurer, Aharon Berek, stood at his side. This team was soon involved in all of the yeshivas' needs down to the smallest details, and they showed the ability to optimally deploy the new fundraising system.[30]

Carrying out the initial steps for setting up Va'ad-HaYeshivot made it possible to immediately move on to the second stage: going out to the field and presenting the new rescue program to the Jewish public at large. To this end, public meetings were organized with the participation of rabbis, local activists, and residents in Vilna at the end of July, in Grodno in September, and in Bialystok in December 1924. The frequency in which these meetings were scheduled proves that the heads of the committee were determined to actualize their intentions of quickly setting up the fundraising system. However, their novel approach made its appearance a few months afterward when they decided to expand their influence outside the traditional Jewish Lithuanian area into Hasidic Vohlin. In June 1925, they held a fourth public meeting in Rovne, and in this way they wished to recruit Vohlin Jewry for the idea of the "Shekel Donation." Regarding the results of this meeting, they wrote, "The meeting declared publicly—with the agreement of all the admorim and rabbis of Vohlin, may they live a good long life—to impose the fixed regulation that has already been agreed upon in the Lithuanian area upon the Vohlin region as well, for the support of the yeshivas by donating a shekel every half-year."[31] Despite the broad agreement, this new enactment had many substantial difficulties in Vohlin due to the different way of thinking from that in the "Lithuanian" Kresy areas. But Va'ad-HaYeshivot was not deterred and acted to establish its position in this province as well. The committee's rule thus spread over most of the areas of the eastern Kresy region—the provinces of Vilna, Novardok, Bialystok, Polesia, and Vohlin—and the committee even received the official approval of the Polish authorities. The yeshiva emissaries were forbidden to raise funds privately in these provinces, and the Va'ad was the only authorized body that could do so.[32]

The last and most complex stage involved the practical establishment of the fundraising system in the Kresy region. Its implementation was carried out by pairs of volunteer rabbis who were sent to the towns by

Va'ad-HaYeshivot. These visits had a decisive role in operating the fundraising system and in the successful implementation of the idea of the Shekel Donation in the Kresy, as one can see in the self-deprecating and stinging remarks of Rabbi Shabtai Yogel, who visited the town of Lida twice after the Sukkot Festival in 1924: "I felt a cold wind in the town of Lida, which was already cold, and because of such atmosphere one needed a force that is warmer and stronger than I am, at least the rabbi of Rakov [Avraham Kalmanowitz (1891–1964)], but since I had already come, I gathered my strength and made an effort. . . . One can say now that the subject has become accepted and popular in the town of Lida—the public writes, signs and also gives."[33] After many of the town's residents were convinced of the importance of the Shekel Donation, the ongoing work of the local committee started. Its members were given the responsibility for collecting the required funds according to the regulations and sending the money along with a detailed report to the center in Vilna and, at the end of each year, lists of all the donors. Lists like these from many Kresy towns, which can be found in the Va'ad-HaYeshivot collection in YIVO, show the scope of the new organizational system and the dimensions of the Shekel Donation.[34]

Allocation of Funds

The fundraising network that was supposed to rescue the yeshivas from economic collapse was set up for an indefinite period of time. Every six months the local committees sent the donations to Vilna, the funds were given over to the central committee, and this body was required to distribute them among the Kresy yeshivas. In order to set the criteria for allocation without bias, in August 1924 the committee requested all the yeshivot-gedolot to provide their students' particulars. This data was the main criteria used for preparing an allocation table at the end of that year. This table is missing in Va'ad-HaYeshivot collection; the only one available to me is from early 1932, which is presented in table 3.1.[35]

Is it at all possible to reconstruct from the table the original allocation percentages from 1924? The number of students in many of the yeshivot-gedolot rose in the meantime, whereas other institutions failed and the number of their talmidim either decreased or remained the same. These

Table 3.1. Allocation table, 1932

Yeshiva	Allocation (%)
Mir	13.75
Radin	11
Knesset Beit-Yitzḥak	8
Grodno	8
Kletsk	8
Lomzhe	6.5
Ohel-Torah Baranovitch	6.25
Beit-Yosef Bialystok	5.87
Slonim	4.5
Kobrin	4.5
Remayle (Vilna)	4.25
Volozhin	4
Beit-Yosef Mezritch	3.19
Beit-Yosef Pinsk	3.19
Torat-Ḥesed Baranovitch	3
Brisk	3
Beit-Ulpena Bialystok	3

changes created added (and justified) pressure on the Va'ad to update its original allocation chart. For example, at the end of 1928, the head of the Brisk Yeshiva, Rabbi Moshe Sokolovsky, had hard words that expressed a sharp sense of dispossession due to what he saw as the stealing of "the poor man's lamb" by the other yeshivas:

> They all scream about the distribution that was made five years ago (and at that time as well, our yeshiva was the weakest among them, since I am not a screamer), and from that time until now the situation of the yeshivas has changed completely, and those that were in dire straits and burdened by debts are now sitting at the top of the world with dollars, and their income is several thousand dollars each week, and they have fixed donations of several tens of thousands of dollars per year. Va'ad-HaYeshivot gives to them even now (from the pennies collected in our country) some three of four times the amount given to our yeshiva which has no other income other than from Va'ad-HaYeshivot. Even the little we received from America from one of the people we knew in years past, when the

> roshei-yeshiva began to travel to America themselves, it was decreed that no emissary would be allowed to give speeches for a yeshiva unless he was a well-known authority. Therefore we have nothing from America now. You can imagine how one can maintain a yeshiva, even on the most basic level, as according to the way of the Torah, without any income from America.... Is it possible that the distribution [of funds] should be carried out over six years as it was in the past, at a time when conditions have changed completely and the situation is reversed, and the yeshivas that their heads cannot travel on their own should be closed, Heaven forbid?![36]

Indeed, after unrelenting pressure was applied in 1930 and again in 1937, Va'ad-HaYeshivot appointed a special *beit-din* to deal with the claims. Each rosh-yeshiva was asked to send his demands and reasons for necessary changes in the allocation to his yeshiva to the beit-din. From an inspection of the correspondence, it appears that the changes that were made after the beit-din convened were miniscule. However, reading between the lines shows that the 1930 beit-din did make a number of adjustments. The portion of Radin in 1924 was 14 percent and was decreased to 11 percent in 1930, although it is unclear which yeshiva received the difference. Similarly, the initial portion of the Ohel-Torah Yeshiva of Baranovitch was 6 percent, and in 1930 that institution was granted a small increase of 0.25 percent at the expense of the Mir Yeshiva. It is then possible to conclude that in the original table of 1924, Radin and Mir were at the top of the chart with 14 percent each. There are even sources that state that in the beginning, the Novardok yeshivas received a joint allocation, and only after their appeal did the special beit-din decide to see the three Beit-Yosef Yeshivas in the Kresy region—Bialystok, Mezritch, and Pinsk—as independent entities deserving their own funding allocations. This claim can be verified through their percentages, which in the aforementioned table seem to be a clear result of a later numerical process. However, despite these adjustments, the table from early 1932 may largely reflect the allocation percentages throughout the entire existence of the committee. The sharp changes that occasionally took place in the yeshivas did not exert any real influence on these percentages.[37]

The table gives the impression that the source of the allocations to the yeshivot-gedolot was the total amount of funds that the Va'ad had at its disposal, but this was not the case. The committee's responsibility extended to maintaining the yeshivot-ketanot as well, and after Vohlin Province joined in the Shekel Donation campaign, the yeshivas there also came under the responsibility of the committee. The Vohlin yeshivas were unlike their counterparts in two ways:

- They functioned under the auspices of a local yeshiva committee that received their allocation from the Vilna central committee and dispersed it among them.
- From a fiscal standpoint, they were not divided into yeshivot-gedolot and yeshivot-ketanot, and they received their funding as one, unlike the yeshivas in the other Kresy provinces where there was a total separation between the allocations for the two types of institutions.[38]

The heads of the yeshivot-gedolot never complained about the level of support of the Vohlin committee, however they did demand the reduction of the portion that the yeshivot-ketanot received, as can be seen in the letter of Rabbi Eliezer-Yehudah Finkel from 1930: "In this difficult time for the maintenance of the yeshivot-gedolot, we cannot relinquish any of the portion that they deserve for the sake of the yeshivot-ketanot . . . solutions must be found for the maintenance of the yeshivot-ketanot without harming the yeshivot-gedolot and their assured income, for on this foundation was Va'ad-HaYeshivot established."[39] This pressure did help, and the allocation percentages to the yeshivot-ketanot were reduced time after time in order to provide economic breathing room to the yeshivot-gedolot. However, the burning economic issues of the latter were not solved after this addition to their funding, and in their need, the directors sent countless letters to Va'ad-HaYeshivot about the funding they did not receive on time or allocations that were promised but did not arrive. These attempts to exert pressure apparently show that the funds from the campaign had economic significance for all of the yeshivot-gedolot. Even though I do not have organized data regarding their budgets over the years, the details from 1938 indicate that the average segment of the yeshivas' total income from the Shekel Donation in that year was only 6 percent. Consequently, this fundraising campaign did not solve the yeshivas' financial problems, and moreover it was not essential to their existence. This surprising information calls for an explanation.[40]

Implementation and Its Difficulties

A short time after the founding of Va'ad-HaYeshivot, it was successful in casting its impressive organizational net throughout the Kresy region by setting up local committees. Letters that were sent from the towns show that the local activists were enthusiastic when the Shekel Donation campaign was launched. But the nature of initial enthusiasm is that it soon dissipates. At the same time, the Va'ad was required to maintain the collection system for the entire period of the yeshivas' existence and to operate it unceasingly. To ignite the spark of enthusiasm anew from time to time and maintain the commitment of the public to the fundraising campaign, the committee used two principle ongoing methods: rabbinical persuasion tours and contribution boxes. There were not a few rabbis who were activists possessing the talent of public speaking who saw the fundraising campaign as crucial to the existence of the yeshivas and volunteered to go to the cities and towns and use their powers of persuasion for fundraising. One of these activists, within the limits of his abilities, was the most elderly among them, the Ḥafetz-Ḥayim. These are the words that he spoke before the public meeting in Grodno in September 1924: "It was very difficult for me to travel to this meeting in my old age. If they were to give me one hundred gold coins, or even one hundred mitzvot, *lehavdil* [not to compare the two], I would not have come. But for strengthening the Torah--one should not delay. The Torah is in danger, we are all obligated to save it, and we are all responsible one for another."[41] Indeed, in many letters that were sent to the central Va'ad from the local committees, there were requests for visits of publicists, especially successful and well-known preachers, to remind the local community of its obligation toward Va'ad-HaYeshivot. There was nothing comparable to these visits in importance that could rouse the townspeople to donate and raise funds.[42]

Even though the Ḥafetz-Ḥayim saw the Shekel Donation as a reasonable burden that was not beyond the means of most of Kresy Jewry, paying twice yearly was difficult for the public. To make this easier, an old practice was adopted: charity boxes. Already in the nineteenth century, the yeshiva emissaries had been permitted to place boxes for the yeshivas of Volozhin and Mir next to the traditional boxes of Rabbi Meir Ba'al-HaNes, meant for the assistance of the poor of Eretz-Yisrael. In the twentieth century,

Zionist circles adopted this practice. A few rabbis suggested adding a charity box of Va'ad-HaYeshivot alongside the others, which would be an inseparable part of the Shekel Donation. The advantage was the possibility of dividing up the donation into small sums that could be occasionally put in the box until, without noticing, the required amount was reached. However, Va'ad-HaYeshivot originally hesitated to adopt this suggestion for fear of diminishing contributions for the Holy Land. Only after much deliberation was it decided to accept the opinion of the idea's supporters, as can be understood from the words of the rabbi of Slonim, Yehudah-Leib Fein (1869–1941), in the beginning of 1925: "All the people are shouting [bring] 'boxes.' . . . For now send us one thousand boxes. . . . This should have been done immediately when our suggestion was brought up, but you were afraid because of RMBHN [Rabbi Meir Ba'al-HaNes] box. But they [the Zionists] came and did not ask; they removed [the traditional charity boxes] and placed boxes for the KKL [Jewish National Fund; JNF] and say they are for RMBHN. . . . And who knows which boxes they will yet attach."[43] After making the decision, Va'ad-HaYeshivot started to produce its own collection boxes and distribute them among the local yeshiva committees for placing in the residents' homes. The Va'ad even updated its regulations and obligated the contributors to fulfill their commitment through small daily or weekly payments. The local committees were directed to empty the boxes once a month in order to encourage the masses to donate generously. This system in particular, which was meant to make it easier for the contributors, helped the yeshivas with some sort of monthly income and actually served to save the Shekel Donation campaign.[44]

Nevertheless, the aforementioned steps taken by Va'ad-HaYeshivot were not successful in rousing the public to make fixed contributions over time. The willingness of the rabbis to devote themselves to the campaign lessened in later years. The demand that each rabbi, rosh-yeshiva, or mashgiaḥ set out on a two-week-long journey to convince townspeople to donate, even though it did not seem to be too burdensome at the start, was not easily met over time and became increasingly difficult. It was Va'ad-HaYeshivot that scheduled the rabbis' visits to the towns on the dates that it chose. Very often the rabbis were not able to comply due to limitations pertaining to their own yeshivas, health, or finances. These refusals required the Va'ad to deal with the issue of the visits over and over again, and this was only one of the obstacles to its efforts in deriving benefit from the system.

Another problem, usually more difficult than the previous one, was the commitment of the local yeshiva committees. They began their work by energetically appointing directors and operators, but the difficulties they met in raising funds dampened their enthusiasm. One of the main reasons for these difficulties was the damage done to the exclusive right the committees had enjoyed in collecting funds in their towns. The desperate economic straits of the yeshivas and the inability of the central Va'ad to provide even their minimal needs meant that not only did the yeshivas of the Land of Israel and the Kongresówka send fundraising emissaries to the towns, but the Kresy yeshivas did as well. The frequent appearance of their representatives in the towns and cities created significant confusion in the work of the local yeshiva committees. Demands came from the field for a swift solution to the situation, including that of the rabbi of Braynsk, Yitzḥak-Ze'ev Zuckerman: "Crowds of people shout: if the emissaries of the yeshivas go out on journeys, then the regulation of Va'ad-HaYeshivot is superfluous. This will, without any doubt, ruin the material state of Va'ad-HaYeshivot. Therefore, in my opinion, it would be proper to set up a barrier and correct this distorted situation as soon as possible."[45]

Indeed, the Va'ad came out with warnings again and again to cease the private fundraising campaigns and sent many letters of rebuke to the roshei-yeshiva. But it soon understood that its regulations were no longer possible to follow and decided to make the regulations more flexible and to limit the prohibition to go out on campaigns from the fifteenth of Av [late summer] to Ḥanukah [winter]. This was a relatively short period of time but the most fruitful in the year. The yeshivas tried to keep the new rule, but as the years passed, several yeshivas violated this one as well.[46]

The issue of the emissaries was only a symptom of the constant and ongoing problems of the yeshivas, which the Va'ad had trouble solving. As was mentioned, its allocations were only a small percentage of the yeshivas' budgets, but due to the fact that these funds were available nearly each month, they served to supply daily sustenance and made it possible to pay distressing deficits, repay loans on time, and provide the talmidim with some support. Every delay or decrease in funding immediately created an economic crisis. However, the delays became commonplace, and the amounts that did arrive were only partial. This situation forced the yeshivas that were in economic distress—and most were in that condition in the interwar period—to "nationalize" the funds collected in their towns by the local yeshiva committees while deducting this from the sum due to them from the central committee. This method solved some of their immediate problems and sometimes even gave their roshei-yeshiva incentive to increase their activities on behalf of the local committees. Rabbi Shabtai Yogel, with his sharpened pen, tried to explain the conduct of the directors: "Perhaps they were also right, because to wait until the support from the center finally comes back, 'even though it may tarry,' who knows whether there will be anyone left to support."[47] On the other side the committee members looked on with equanimity at this unofficial method of supporting the yeshiva in their town, or stood helplessly in the face of the justified claims of its directors.

The system of "nationalization" prevented the central Va'ad from improving the material situation of the yeshivas in any real way. The violation of its most basic regulations harmed the body in which they were partners and that could assist them. Often the committee could not supply even emergency aid to a needy yeshiva, as is apparent from the sharp letter of the secretary of the Lomzhe Yeshiva to the director of Va'ad-HaYeshivot:

> Not only was [our request] unfulfilled, but our friend did not consider himself obliged to give any response. We stand amazed—has the central Va'ad-HaYeshivot, which is obligated to be an example to the other organizations whose goal is to support institutions of kindness and education, reached such a level of bureaucracy?! Did our friend think to experiment with us and see if the yeshiva would survive, after I wrote him that if we do not give the grocers what is coming to them by Monday, the kitchen would close? His honor was mistaken if he thought a thought like this, woe to such experiments. With our last ounce of strength we struggled that very day, and praise to G-d for His kindness and goodness, He provided credit and another way out.[48]

The most extreme expression of the desperate situation can be found in the words of the head of the yeshiva-ketana in Kobrin, Rabbi Ḥayim Podorovsky, who also did not receive essential help from Va'ad-HaYeshivot or even a verbal reply to his request: "And there is no voice nor is there an answer. Therefore I have come to ask the respected Torah scholars if there is actually still a Va'ad-HaYeshivot?"[49]

SUMMARY

The yeshivas were institutions with no independent income, and from the time that they were founded, they were totally dependent on the donations of the public in the Pale of Settlement and the Jewish communities outside of it. This material backing was undermined by the political, economic and social changes that took place after the First World War, and the yeshiva world was compelled to turn to the kindness of the Jews of America. The Jewish institutions there responded very positively. When their support began to prove disappointing, the heads of Orthodox Jewry founded Va'ad-HaYeshivot in the Polish Kresy. This chapter presented a very incomplete picture of the undertaking of the Va'ad in the yeshiva world. Moreover, its great influence went beyond its being a centralized organization that was active on behalf of the yeshivas in the Kresy region. Over the years, this committee became a powerful force for carrying out programs of the Orthodox leadership in this outlying area of Poland. The Va'ad dealt with a multiplicity of subjects, beginning with Torah-oriented elementary schools of the Ḥorev network and the religious teachers' seminary in Grodno to serious involvement in the elections for the community councils in the Kresy towns and even in the choice of their rabbis. These matters have not been discussed here, and only a central aspect of the comprehensive and impressive activities of the Va'ad within the boundaries of the yeshiva world has been examined.[50]

The Va'ad was set up to obtain resources to support the yeshivas by an optimal method and to distribute them fairly. This was a big and ambitious step in the history of the Lithuanian yeshiva world. In the beginning of the nineteenth century, when the Volozhin Yeshiva was established, its founder did not look to the generosity of the local Jewish townspeople but rather chose to rely on the support of the entire Jewish community of the Russian Empire for the yeshiva's budget. This supracommunity characteristic of the Volozhin Yeshiva, which was unique compared to the characteristics of the community yeshivas, was copied by the Talmudic institutions established in the nineteenth century and especially at its conclusion. The supracommunity characteristic expanded these yeshivas' economic base. Moreover, it had a substantial influence on other aspects, from the strengthening of the reputation and standing of the rosh-yeshiva among the Jewish public to the significant change in image and sense of self-worth of its talmidim.[51]

The establishment of the Va'ad signaled an additional step in the professionalization of operations in the yeshiva world: no longer individual activity of each yeshiva with its potential donors in the Kresy communities, but the solidified appearance of a central body that was supracommunity and above each individual yeshiva. This new organizational framework prevented the predicable collisions between the activities of the many yeshivas in this limited geographical area, and it was the Va'ad that from then on represented all of them and acted in their name in the economic arena.

But is it sufficient to see the Va'ad as merely a technical instrument for optimization on behalf of the yeshivas in the Kresy region? The novelty of the establishment of the committee, as well as its later activities, show that it was more than a tool. Before and during the First World War, there were discussions regarding assistance for the yeshivas, but the solutions suggested were good for their time and of limited scope. Among other causes, this was due to the limitations imposed by the authorities.[52] Essentially, the establishment of the Va'ad was the first attempt of its kind by Orthodox leaders to mobilize in order to provide a holistic and permanent solution for all the yeshivas in the material sphere, whereas practically speaking there was no precedent for setting up an organizational fundraising system that was so comprehensive and would enlist so many rabbis and community activists in carrying out such a complicated and ongoing task of assisting tens of yeshivas.

Even from a narrower and more internal look into the yeshiva world alone, there was a very surprising novelty in the establishment of the Va'ad. This new aspect expressed itself in the damage done to the ownership of the yeshivas. In the fifth chapter, it will be shown that the yeshivas were mostly the private institutions of their founders who stood at their head. The establishment of the Va'ad took a large chunk out of this traditional and accepted ownership when a portion of the economic responsibility and other basic responsibilities were taken away from the rosh-yeshiva. It is obvious that the agreement of the yeshiva heads to limit their authority and to hand over their control in favor of the Va'ad was not voluntary. The most severe economic restraints forced these painful and unprecedented concessions upon them.[53]

Despite the extensive fundraising network spread by the Va'ad in some 350 communities, it was incapable of fulfilling the wishes of the yeshiva heads. In their distress, the roshei-yeshiva began to break its rules and raise funds independently in areas where the Va'ad was active. These deviations caused the decrease in general income and led to further violations of the rules. But the committee itself was part of this problematic situation. Those who needed its services sometimes felt that the Va'ad was unable to keep up with its tasks. More than anything else, the failure of the Va'ad to answer their letters made them angry. There were yeshiva representatives who reacted to this lack with sarcasm. Rabbi Shraga-Faivel Hindes (1880–1936) of the Grodno Yeshiva wrote, "And you also did not reply to my letter. Apparently you have decided to act like Americans, who are not accustomed to answering letters."[54] But there were those who were needy and whose fate hung on the response of the committee, and they were hurt by the manner in which they were treated, which they perceived as disrespectful and humiliating.[55]

What was the cause of this unusual lack of regard? The size of the staff of the committee's office, five people in the 1930s, was the factor that prevented a proper response, and at times any response at all, to appeals. Moreover, such a limited staff was not able to cope with all the requirements of the extensive activities heaped upon its shoulders, including the important work for the yeshivas, which was the main reason for the establishment of Va'ad-HaYeshivot. This work suffered from administrative difficulties and required a new breath of life from time to time, as defined by Rabbi Aharon Kotler, ostensibly taken from the world of physics: "It is impossible to assume that the matter will run by itself without reinforcement, on the strength of the original force."[56]

Over the years, there were highs and lows in the activities of the Va'ad, but in general its support of the Kresy yeshivas covered only 6 percent of their income—a small segment in proportion to the great and never-ending activity of their directors regarding its allocations. Even the part of the American Central Relief and JDC, which attempted to resuscitate their activities multiple times, though not always with great success, was not more significant, and their support reached only 4 percent of the income of the yeshivot-gedolot. Even so, the yeshivas of Lithuania and Poland were constantly discussing their work as well, and they even credited the Joint with their success in surviving.[57]

It is surprising that the yeshivas' directors exerted so much pressure over the years on these organizations, which can be seen from their multitudinous correspondence, for such piddling sums. In order to understand this, the following is a quote of a somewhat amusing remark of the secretary of the Kletsk Yeshiva about the results of a fly-by-night fundraising campaign in South Africa: "And the African coins? Aren't they also legal tender? And after subtracting the yeshivas not entitled to these coins, our percentage is two times as much, then why is there still no money?"[58] His words show the importance assigned by the yeshivas to every donation and fundraising campaign, no matter what the result. Their financial situation was most severe in the entire period between the wars. They were up to their necks in deficits and debts that sometimes had to be repaid with interest, and they were often threatened with the closing of their kitchens or with ending their supply of basic food items. Even the most meager income gave them room to breathe and repay their loans. Their obsessive concern about the fixed income they usually received from Va'ad-HaYeshivot or Central Relief, or from even more limited sources of assistance, is therefore not surprising.

When the yeshivas learned that their salvation would not come from the institutional organizations, most were clever enough to set up offices in the United States in order to boost their presence in that country and organize a system of emissaries there. At the same time, the roshei-yeshiva, whose role was to educate their talmidim to a high level of Talmud scholarship, were forced to neglect their main task for long periods and set off on fundraising journeys in the Diaspora. Together with the offices' fruitful activities, they succeeded in bringing back significant contributions that supplemented the income from the aforementioned institutional assistance.

But even the varied sources of income did not supply an ultimate solution to the material problems of the yeshivas, and the fixed deficit in their annual budget only increased their debts. This ongoing situation weighed heavily upon the shoulders of the roshei-yeshiva throughout all the inter-war years. Rabbi Mordechai-Yeḥiel Gordon, head of the Lomzhe Yeshiva, gave expression to these difficulties: "The situation is truly beyond human endurance, and I know this myself, because I feel every day that my strength is at an end, may G-d have mercy."[59] Nevertheless, the yeshivas succeeded in surviving many years under great economic pressure, and it would seem that the statement of the Ḥafetz-Ḥayim that "their very existence depends on a miracle" fit their situation.[60]

NOTES

1. Wischnitzer, "Di Banayung," 34. Only two Lithuanian yeshivas charged tuition fees (reports of "Torat-Hayim" Yeshiva of Warsaw, Dec. 22, 1938, and Kelm Yeshiva, Dec. 28, 1938 [MWP]).

2. Appeal, July 1924 (VHY/1217-8); Shulvass, "HaTorah," 33; Zaks, *Michtavim*, 143; Krakovsky, *Arzei*, 103–4.

3. See Klibansky, "HaYeshivot," 195n94, 201–10.

4. Hartglass, "Milḥamot," 142; Berger, "HaMivneh," 205–8; Gelber, "Korot," 126; Teitelbaum, "Report," 8.

5. Declaration of the Rabbis' Association Council (LJC/1394); *DIdS*, Jan. 24, 1930. In the yeshivas' financial reports of 1938, the limited extent of local support stands out, reaching only 30 percent of their total income in most cases (yeshivas reports, 1938–1939 [MWP]; cf. Teitelbaum, "Report," 14, which stated that the yeshivas could raise 10–15 percent in 1926). On the limited power of the Rabbis' Association in Lithuania, see Klibansky, "BeMakom."

6. Lichtenstein and Rabinowitz, *Pinkas*, 245–46; *Hamsilah* 5, no. 4–5 (1940): 13; letters: Yogel to Grodzensky, Feb. 9, 1925 (VHY/579), Yogel to Va'ad-HaYeshivot, Sep. 2, 1925 (VHY/580), Sokolovsky to Va'ad-HaYeshivot, Dec. 26, 1928 (VHY/49), Grodzensy to Fried, 1920, and Grodzensky to Community Council, Jun. 12, 1929 (VHY/699); Remayle Yeshiva report, Dec. 15, 1938 (MWP/Remayle). Regarding the Remayle and Brisk Yeshivas before the war, see Klibansky, *KeTzur*, 57–58, 62.

7. Kossovsky-Shaḥor, *Igrot*, I, 219.

8. Letter: Kotler to Schuw, Jul. 10, 1925 (VHY/229). See also the reports of the Kletsk Yeshiva, Oct. 28, 1926, and Dec. 30, 1927 (VHY/1130).

9. Zaks, *Michtavim*, 140; letters: Hindes to Va'ad-HaYeshivot, Feb. 24, 1930 (VHY/145), Kotler to Grodzensky, Sep. 14, 1925 (VHY/229), and Shabtai Yogel to Berek, Nov. 30, 1936 (VHY/580); postcard: Peretz Yogel to Va'ad-HaYeshivot, Jan. 1930 (VHY/580).

10. Edelstein, *Rabbi*, 114; testimony: Fortman; Nishri, *Me'ir*, IV, 431; Kol, *Eḥad*, 304; letter: Matus to Schuw, Jan. 1, 1930 (VHY/238).

11. Karp, *Sefer*, 15; Yoshor, "Nasich," 11; Lomzhe Yeshiva report, Jan. 19, 1939 (MWP/Lomzhe); Kobrin Yeshiva reports, Dec. 13, 1929, and Dec. 22, 1930 (VHY/1131).

12. Agudat haRabbanim, *Sefer*, 186–94; Epstein, "Yeshivat Mir," 114; Karp, *Sefer*, 54, 56.

13. Letter: Matus to Berek, Dec. 8, 1938 (VHY/238). See also Kobrin Yeshiva report, Dec. 6, 1938 (MWP/Kobrin); Agudat haRabbanim, *Sefer*, 185.

14. Szajkowski, "Concord," 100; Szajkowski, "Jewish Relief," 34–35, 39; Engelman, *Four Years*, 8; Zuckerman, *Zichreines*, II, 118–19. *Hilfsverein* was a German Jewish organization founded in 1901 in Berlin specifically to assist Jewish communities in Eastern Europe that were harmed by riots and war, and it supported the establishment of educational institutions and social welfare organizations there as well. *Alliance* was an international Jewish organization established in 1860 in Paris in order to protect the right of Jews and raise their cultural level.

15. Ezrat Torah, *Luaḥ*, 14–15; Ezrat Torah, *Sefer*, iii–iv, 64, 81; Agudat haRabbanim, *Sefer*, 64–66.

16. Berger, *An Inventory*, 1–3; Grinbaum, *The American Joint*, 4, 6; Kossovsky-Shaḥor, *Igrot*, I, 95–97, 100; Karp, *Sefer*, 13; Epstein, "Yeshivat Mir," 110; letter: Finkel to Ḥasman, Dec. 9, 1921 (VHY/371); Finkelstein and Marx, "Necrology."

17. Berger, *An Inventory*, 3; Hoffman, "Rav Kook's Mission," 80–81; *IdL*, Mar. 7 and 28, 1924; Kossovsky-Shaḥor, *Igrot*, 95–97, 99; Shapira, *Igrot*, 109–10; Yoshor, *The Chafetz Chaim*, 423; *Sha'arei Tziyon* 4, no. 1–2 (1924): 14 (1)–14 (2); Agudat haRabbanim, *Sefer*, 62.

18. Shapira, *Igrot*, 131. See also Berger, *An Inventory*, 3; Hoffman, "Rav Kook's Mission," 86; *DMZ*, Mar. 20, 1924.

19. Letter: Leibowitz to Va'ad-HaYeshivot, Nov. 11, 1929 (VHY/212). See also letters: Va'ad-HaYeshivot to Sokolovsky, Nov. 6, 1929 (VHY/46), Hindes to Schuw, Nov. 7, 1927 (VHY/140), and Morrissey to Grodzensky, Feb. 14, 1929 (AJJDCA/353). For the full memorandum, see letter: Schuw to Warburg, Nov. 7, 1929 (AJJDCA/353).

20. Shapira, *Igrot*, 438. See letters: Adler to Grodzensky, Jan. 7, 1930, and Oct. 7, 1931, Morrissey to Grodzensky, May 5, 1931, and May 4, 1932, and Grodzensky to Berwald, Dec. 5, 1932 (AJJDCA/353).

21. Shapira, *Igrot*, 438–39.

22. Klibansky, "HaYeshivot," 210n129; yeshivas reports, 1938–1939 (MWP). In the 1930s, the Committee on Cultural Affairs allocated 55 percent of its budget to Central Relief purposes (Berger, *An Inventory*, 4). See also Zaks, *Michtavim*, 162.

23. Morgenshtern, *HaShiva*, 50–81; Guttentag, "Eshed," 249–301.

24. Poupko, *Michtavei*, 139 (from Yiddish).

25. Poupko, *Michtavei*, 145. Similarly, see *HaDerech* [Vienna] 6, no. 3 (1924): 13.

26. Manifesto "LeKiyuma shel Torah" [For the Preservation of the Torah], May 21, 1924 (VHY/1209). Similarly, see Poupko, *Michtavei*, 154. See also *HaDerech* [Vienna] 6, no. 2 (1924): 13–14.

27. Poupko, *Michtavei*, 147. See also pages 143–45; *She'arim*, Feb. 15, 1945; Manifesto "LeKiyuma shel Torah," May 21, 1924 (VHY/1209) ; *DoV*, Jun. 22, 1928.

28. *She'arim*, Feb. 15, 1945; Manifesto "LeKiyuma shel Torah," May 21, 1924 (VHY/1209). See also "HaRav R' Elḥanan Wasserman," 88; letters: Finkel to Ḥasman, Dec. 9, 1921 (VHY/371), and Yogel to Va'ad-HaYeshivot, Aug. 18, 1924 (VHY/580).

29. *HaDerech* [Vienna] 6, no. 6 (1924): 14; *She'arim*, Feb. 15, 1945; *DoV*, Jun. 22, 1928.

30. Letters: Matus to Ḥasman, Aug. 24, 1924 (VHY/239), Weinstein to Ḥasman, Sep. 26, 1924, and Yogel to Va'ad-HaYeshivot, Oct. 23, 1924 (VHY/580).

31. Zaks, *Michtavim*, 54. See also page 65; *DoV*, Jun. 22, 1928; *IdL*, Aug. 1, 1924; Poupko, *Michtavei*, 147; Yoshor, *The Chafetz Chaim*, 475.

32. *Statut Stowarzyszenia "Waad Hajszywos"* [Statute of Va'ad-HaYeshivot Association], Mar. 25, 1926 (VHY/1099); letters: Berek to Schuw, Jun. 17, 1925, and Jun. 23, 1925 (VHY/141); Zaks, *Michtavim*, 56.

33. Letters: Yogel to Va'ad-HaYeshivot, Oct. 23, 1924, and Oct. 29, 1924 (VHY/580).

34. Some 350 communities were connected with Va'ad-HaYeshivot (Mohrer, *RG* 25, 3).

35. Table, Jan. 13, 1932 (VHY/1106).

36. Letter: Sokolovsky to Va'ad-HaYeshivot, Dec. 26, 1928 (VHY/49), hinting to the words "this is the way of the Torah: you shall eat bread with salt . . . and live a life of difficulty" (*Pirkei Avot* 6:4).

37. Weintraub, *BeSufa*, 248; letters: Shkop to Schuw, Nov. 1929 (VHY, 373), Levin to Schuw, Jun. 1, 1926, and Radin faculty to Beit-Din, May 9, 1937 (VHY, 511). Cf. Grade, *The Yeshiva*, 278–79.

38. Letter: Petchenik to Va'ad-HaYeshivot, Nov.–Dec. 1927 (VHY/76).

39. Letter: Finkel to Schuw, Apr. 24, 1930 (VHY/371).

40. Yeshivas reports, 1938–1939 (MWP); letter: Kotler to Schuw, Mar. 29, 1929 (VHY/229). See also Shalitt, *Oif di Ḥurves*, 702; Mohrer, *RG* 25, 7.

41. Poupko, *Michtavei*, 146. See Yakobzohn, *Esa*, 317; Grodzensky, *Aḥiezer*, 18; Harkavy, *MeImrei*, 49; Katz, *Sha'ar*, 7; Levi, *Yeshivat*, 11.

42. Letters: Shmoshkovitz to Va'ad-HaYeshivot, Mar. 25, 1929 (VHY/41), and Hindes to Berek, Sep. 3, 1930 (VHY/145).

43. Letter: Fayn to Va'ad-HaYeshivot, Feb. 2, 1925 (VHY/580). See also letter: Yogel to Va'ad-HaYeshivot, Sep. 2, 1925 (VHY/579); Zinowitz, *"Mir,"* 429; Guttentag, "Eshed," 249–301. Regarding KKL (Keren Kayemet LeYisrael) boxes, see Bihm, *HaKeren*, 85.

44. Va'ad HaYeshivot, *Pinkas*, regulation details; letters: Va'ad-HaYeshivot to community organizers, 1928 (VHY/1209), and Eisenberg to Schuw, Feb. 20, 1927 (VHY/14). Cf. *HaNe'eman*, 14 (1929): 14–15.

45. Letter: Zuckerman to Va'ad-HaYeshivot, Aug. 3, 1934 (VHY/43). See letter: Kotler to Schuw, May, 19, 1933 (VHY/227).

46. Letters: Lev to Berek, Aug. 17, 1939 (VHY/43), Kudner to Va'ad-HaYeshivot, Aug. 14, 1936 (VHY/49), and Yogel to Va'ad-HaYeshivot, May, 5, 1938 (VHY/580).

47. Letter: Yogel to Va'ad-HaYeshivot, Oct. 27, 1925 (VHY/580). See Appeal, Jan. 22, 1939 (VHY/1217-8).

48. Letter: Rabinowitz to Berek, Dec. 11, 1933 (VHY/314).

49. Postcard: Podorovsky to Va'ad-HaYeshivot, Apr. 6, 1938 (VHY/239).

50. See letter: Fein to Va'ad-HaYeshivot, Feb. 2, 1925 (VHY/580).

51. See Stampfer, *Lithuanian*, 59, 140–42; Etkes, "Bein Lamdanut," 398–401.

52. See *Sinai* 91 (1982): 170.

53. Besides the economic aspect, the Va'ad determined the acceptance quotas for each yeshiva and selected the relevant yeshivas for the graduates of the yeshivot-ketanot. These revolutionary aspects will be presented in detail in chapter 6.

54. Postcard: Hindes to Berek, Jan. 10, 1927 (VHY/140). See also letter: Hindes to Va'ad-HaYeshivot, Oct. 14, 1935 (VHY/145); Va'ad-HaYeshivot ledger, Dec. 6, 1933 (VHY/786).

55. E.g., postcard: Weinberg to Va'ad-HaYeshivot, May 31, 1929 (VHY/14).

56. Letter: Kotler to Va'ad-HaYeshivot, Dec. 16, 1938 (VHY/230). See also the list of office workers (VHY/1111).

57. Grinbaum, *The American Joint*, 9; *Beit Ya'akov* 68 (1964): 17. See also letter: Shkop to Schuw, Dec. 18, 1925 (VHY/142); postcards: Matus to Schuw, Mar. 19, 1933 (VHY/239), and Podorovsky to Va'ad-HaYeshivot, Oct./Nov. 1936 (VHY/ 237).

58. Postcard: Goder to Va'ad-HaYeshivot, May 8, 1929 (VHY/228).

59. Letter: Gordon to Schuw, Nov. 12, 1931 (VHY/315). Similarly, letter: Leibowitz to Schuw, Oct. 11, 1929 (VHY/212). See also letter: Kotler to Schuw, Jul. 10, 1925 (VHY/229; cf. *HaMelitz*, Apr. 4, 1902).

60. Poupko, *Michtavei*, 114.

4

Studies

One of the most important and fascinating subjects regarding the inner workings of the yeshiva relates to the characteristics of its studies, their curriculum and content. Up until the middle of the nineteenth century, learning other than in-depth Talmud study was unknown in the world of the Lithuanian yeshiva. The first to attempt to introduce a non-Talmudic element into the curriculum was Rabbi Yisrael Lipkin, the originator of the Musar movement. In the mid-1840s, he began his activities among laymen, for whom he set up "Musar houses," intended to serve as places for solitary, profound, and spirited reflection on Musar teachings without fear of ridicule or interference. But it was not sermons on virtue nor Musar exercises for laymen that Rabbi Lipkin realized as the optimal means for spreading his Musar teachings. Rather, to this end he felt a need to concentrate his efforts on young Talmud scholars in particular, at first among the students in the small yeshiva he set up in the Vilna suburb Zaretche, and even more so among the talmidim in the yeshiva he established in the Nevyazher Kloyz in Kovna. His expectation was that they would spread Musar teachings among the Jewish public. However, these yeshivas remained unique at that time and did not serve as a model for imitation by other Talmudic institutions. The esoteric and demanding character of Musar served to distance many from this discipline, and it remained limited to the few who were willing to act according to its teachings and demands.[1]

From the 1840s, the powerful winds of the Enlightenment and pragmatism began to blow and brought about the emptying of many of the study kibbutzim—noninstitutionalized learning groups—and even threatened to create cracks in the yeshiva walls. Nevertheless, the yeshiva world rested on its laurels and felt no need or urgency about updating the curriculum of its institutions. When an attempt to do this was made in the town of Sventchian and its rabbi, Yitzḥak-Ya'akov Reines, integrated basic secular studies into the new yeshiva that he established there in 1882, there was serious opposition among the Eastern European extreme traditionalists to this step, and two years later he was forced to close the yeshiva.[2]

In that same year, 1882, Rabbi Notte-Hirsch Finkel founded the Slabodka Yeshiva, and he too chose to make a change in the traditional curriculum. He imitated the unique tone of the yeshiva that Rabbi Yisrael Lipkin had founded in Kovna, and he included Musar study alongside the Talmud. Although the time formally designated for Musar was very limited, the yeshiva had a new sort of atmosphere and was permeated by self-examination and the search for character defects.

This change, which at the end of the nineteenth century was a great novelty of Rabbi Finkel's, did not arouse loud opposition from without. But when other yeshivas began to go on this new path, a fierce debate opened in the areas of Lithuanian Jewish culture, namely the "Musar Debate" of 1897. The underlying issue was whether it was proper to make changes in the traditional yeshiva educational program and to include other religious subjects in addition to Talmud. Prominent rabbis took sides in the debate, and as opposition spread, it threatened the existence of the Musar yeshivas.

The argument eventually subsided, and the advantage of the Musar approach was vindicated in the 1905 revolutionary period, when some yeshivas nearly collapsed due to the strong influence of the socialist and Zionist movements. These radical movements came out with seductive and rousing slogans about improving society as a whole and Jewish society in particular. In contrast, the Musar movement aspired to an improvement that was more fundamental and simpler, as well as more immediate: improvement of the individual first. The similar concepts from both directions in that revolutionary period, together with the emotional stimuli and the character challenges that were part of the Musar approach, arrested the attraction that the revolutionary movements had for the youth.[3]

The roshei-yeshiva came to the realization at that point that the traditional educational program did not have the strength to stand up to the new winds that blew from outside, and one after another they adopted Rabbi Finkel's Musar system. These Musar studies were not only a rationalistic approach to character improvement but also created a unique atmosphere. The weekly discourses of the new Musar supervisors added a great deal to this setting, and through them they set the Musar tone of the Lithuanian yeshivas.

Parallel to the Musar revolution, a new method of Talmud study began to penetrate the Lithuanian yeshivas: "the way of understanding," based on profound analysis of the Talmudic discussions. The originators of this approach were yeshiva heads in the last decades of the nineteenth century who taught the material in this new and original fashion. Unlike Musar studies, which were to some degree forced upon the students in many yeshivas, the way of understanding was accepted willingly and at times even with enthusiasm by the talented young men. They were captivated by its appeal, and some of them who became roshei-yeshiva in the course of time passed it down to their students. In the years preceding the First World War, the way of understanding had spread to many yeshivas, and each rosh-yeshiva put his own stamp upon it.

Were the Lithuanian yeshivas in the interwar period content with analytic study of Talmud with the addition of Musar atmosphere, and did they view their main purpose as preparing their students to be scholars and to have virtuous characters? Or were they influenced by the practical, goal-oriented atmosphere outside the yeshivas that may have directed talmidim toward professional training and ordination to become rabbis and other religious functionaries? Examining the changes in the yeshivas from the vantage point of Talmud study and Musar can provide an answer to these questions.

TALMUD STUDIES

When young Ḥayim Naḥman Bialik (1873–1934) arrived in the Volozhin Yeshiva in the beginning of the 1890s, he expected to find there the study of the "seven wisdoms" and "seventy languages" together with the Talmud. He found an entirely different situation and remarked in resignation, "I, too, will learn Talmud, Talmud, Talmud."[4] In the interwar period as well, the principal subject in the yeshivas was in-depth Talmud study.

Study for Its Own Sake

The yeshivas located in the cultural space of Lithuanian Jewry had a number of unique and shared characteristics. The most significant among them was the subject matter studied, which was extremely fundamental: the study of a particular Talmudic tractate with its commentaries during the term, without any additional material such as law codes like in the Hungarian yeshivas, or *daf yomi* (a daily page of Talmud) as in the Ḥachmei-Lublin Yeshiva. In addition, instead of navigating the entire "Sea of the Talmud," intensive textual study was limited to certain specific tractates from the orders of Nezikin and Nashim: Bava Kama, Bava Metzia, Bava Batra, Ketuvot, Yevamot, Nedarim, Gittin, and Kiddushin. These tractates offered numerous sugyot that could present valuable intellectual challenges to the student.[5]

Behind this monochrome configuration was a worldview that saw no necessity, or perhaps even no desirability, in studying tractates that contained practical legal material or laws needed by religious functionaries. This was the approach of *Torah liShma*—Torah study that was a value in and of itself. Indeed, many of the sugyot studied in the yeshiva were completely theoretical and had no apparent application in daily life.[6] This study did not especially bother the yeshiva students, as a talmid of the Slabodka Knesset-Yisrael Yeshiva of the years before the First World War, Gedaliah Rogoznitzky, who later became the noted historian Gedaliah Alon (1902–1950), wrote: "'Rabbinical ordination in his pocket,' dreamt about by Bialik's '*Matmid*' in the later years of Volozhin, was not the dream of the student in Slabodka or Radin. . . . An oft-repeated saying in Slabodka was: If you see a student overly involved in studying '*Yoreh-De'ah*' or '*Elu Treifot*' and '*Even-HaEzer*,' and working hard to achieve rabbinical ordination—you can say that he is one of those lacking both talent and [Torah] knowledge in general. . . . The yeshiva itself was not a rabbinical seminary."[7] Despite Alon's explicit statement, one should not conclude that the yeshiva studies were entirely lacking any connection with the future of the talmidim. The preparation that the yeshiva provided, even if it was mainly theoretical, supplied a proper foundation for receiving ordination. When a student was offered a rabbinical position, he was able to go into the nearby beit-midrash and independently complete his applied studies in a few months.[8]

Was the yeshiva curriculum during the interwar period influenced by the pragmatic approach, which was at that time being avidly promoted among the Jewish population? Many young people in Poland and Lithuania received a fine education in the Jewish schools and considered it a means to succeed in the future. Even students who had not completed gymnasia studies were able to find their place in modern industry in the cities and large towns on the basis of their elementary school education. This practical orientation was likely to reflect on the yeshivas and turn them into "rabbinical seminaries," and some did indeed refer to themselves in those terms. However, contemporary sources indicate that the concept of "Torah for its own sake" had not changed at all in the yeshivas. Their students continued to see Torah liShma as the most important value, and growth in Torah scholarship through intensive study was their life's only goal. After his visit to the Mir Yeshiva, the journalist Ḥayim Shoshkes (1891–1964) wrote in 1925, "Honestly speaking, after 6–7 or 10 years, the yeshiva does not prepare its students for anything practical other than the possibility of receiving rabbinical ordination. But the yeshiva baḥurim look at their friends who take a glance into 'Yoreh-De'ah' with a smile. For them it is a sign that they are already thinking about a match or a rabbinical position.... This lack of concern and thought about practical matters or any productive goal in their lives other than warming themselves constantly in the light of Torah is one of the aspects that characterize yeshiva life."[9]

It was a sort of social convention among the students that no other studies had a place in the yeshiva, and no rules or regulations on the part of the administration were required. Moreover, the roshei-yeshiva, Talmud instructors, and Musar-mashgiḥim, who acted according to this principle and studied Torah many hours during the day, served as their models. A description by one of the finest talmidim of Rabbi Naftali Trop in Radin Yeshiva, Rabbi Yitzḥak-Meir Patchiner (Ben-Menaḥem; 1898–1960), shows the value of Torah liShma in his rabbi's eyes:

> Even though during the years of my life I have met and studied with many great Torah scholars, I never saw anyone else who immersed himself and his whole being, talents and genius in the study of Torah like him. . . . And when he would exert himself and succeeded, and the lightning bolt of truth would light up his mind and he would find the words to interpret it, he would jump from inner joy as though Heaven had revealed to him the secrets of the Torah. His enthusiasm knew no bounds and in his zeal he would excite everyone surrounding him, all of his students and those who heard his teachings. He put them all into a different atmosphere, an atmosphere where profound understanding of the Torah prevails, where joy dwells as a result of comprehending the profound reasoning of the Torah.[10]

This sort of comportment of the roshei-yeshiva was a fascinating lesson for their students regarding everything that had to do with the essence of ideal learning. The words of a graduate of the Mir Yeshiva are not surprising: "In a natural way the talmidim made a covenant with Torah and the fear of Heaven with the aspiration towards infinite spiritual ascent, and saw the yeshiva as their permanent home. 'Let me dwell in the House of the Lord all my days'—this was the constant prayer of every talmid."[11]

The concept of Torah liShma was universal in the Lithuanian yeshivas in the interwar period, however there were yeshivas that included some practical halachic studies in their curriculum. Their goal was not to prepare their students to rule on legal matters but to give them a foundation in necessary *halacha* and everyday laws. In the Ponevezh, Ohel-Torah of Baranovitch, Radin, and Korets Yeshivas, halachot from *Oraḥ-Ḥayim* were studied every day after morning prayers. The administrators of Slabodka and Mezritch dedicated an entire winter semester to studying the Talmudical tractate of Shabbat to encourage their students to more punctiliously observe the Sabbath.[12] However, there were exceptions among the Lithuanian yeshivas. In the early 1920s in the Telz Yeshiva, one of the daily *sedarim* of the older students in their third or fourth year was dedicated to study halachic rulings, seemingly because the yeshiva wanted to give them the basic skills in preparation to their going out to the real world. Study of Yoreh-De'ah was customary in the Korets Yeshiva—the only one where the laws of halachic rulings were studied in the 1930's. It is possible to surmise that the fact that it was located in Hasidic Vohlin was the principle reason behind these studies.[13]

In contrast, the Novardok yeshivas opposed studying the formulation of halachic rulings; they even objected to their graduates accepting rabbinic positions. The originator of the Musar movement, Rabbi Yisrael Lipkin, kept his distance from rabbinical positions because he did not seek the financial benefits, honor, and power that went along with them. The Novardok movement followed in his footsteps, but from a nearly reverse motivation: it saw in these positions neither honor nor power, but being subject to the desires of householders and synagogue officials, which would likely lead to flattery and the inability to act independently. This attitude was put to the test when the Karlin community wished to appoint Rabbi Shmuel Weintraub, head of the Novardok Pinsk Yeshiva, as a *dayyan* (rabbinical court judge) in 1930. Due to the dire economic condition of his yeshiva, he felt that this would increase the community's support for the institution and seriously considered the proposal. The fact that he did not immediately reject the offer was enough to set the Novardok movement on fire. The rosh-yeshiva of Mezritch, Rabbi David Bliacher, quickly arrived in Pinsk and demanded that his colleague not deviate from the accepted Novardok path. Rabbi Weintraub did not yield to his pleas and accepted the rabbinic position, occupying it for as long as the yeshiva remained in Pinsk.[14]

Although the general attitude toward studying halachic ruling was not favorable in the yeshivas, a few students included this in their program on their own. Also, those who saw a practical future in the rabbinate in their hometowns abroad or in neighboring Kongresówka invested a great deal of time studying rabbinical rulings to receive ordination before their return home. In the Grodno Yeshiva, qualified students even received permission to study rabbinical decision-making. However, in 1939, for some unknown reason, the administration issued a new regulation: "There is no permission to study Tractate *Ḥullin* or 'Yoreh-De'ah'—even those who previously studied with permission, with no exceptions . . . and anyone who does not act in accord with this aforementioned rule will lose all his rights in the yeshiva."[15]

These exceptional examples reflect on the general rule: in the interwar period, the Torah liShma approach was even intensified in the yeshivas. Their study was based on delving deeply into topics in the orders of

Nezikin and Nashim, and they did not require the students to be overly familiar with other sections of the Talmud. This lack of knowledge was demonstrated, for example, in the poor attendance of talmidim in the classes of Rabbi Avraham-Hirsch Kamai of the Mir Yeshiva. He did not focus only on the topic under study, as was the custom of his brother-in-law Rabbi Eliezer-Yehudah Finkel, but spread out into all the other sections of the Talmud, as described by one of those who attended his lectures: "His classes were artfully crafted of brilliant analysis and amazing comprehensive knowledge, a voyage throughout the length and breadth of the Talmud, with rapid comprehension and sharp insights. In most cases the student audience was not able to follow or keep up with him until the end, and the thread was broken in the middle."[16]

Consequently, Rabbi Finkel found it proper to expand the students' knowledge and include proficiency learning in addition to the traditional in-depth, analytic Talmudic study in his yeshiva. After receiving special funding from America, he proclaimed in the winter term of 1928–1929 a Talmud proficiency competition that would extend for one year. The competitors would be required to be tested on five hundred folio-pages of the Talmud with the basic traditional commentaries, and the promised cash prize was to be fifty dollars (about four hundred zloty). Twenty contestants took part in this ambitious project, which had no parallel in the Lithuanian yeshiva world. Not all of them fulfilled the challenging conditions of this contest, and more than half dropped out in the course of time. The remaining participants were tested by the yeshiva administration at the end of the year, and from that time on they were recognized as the elite of the yeshiva for their proficiency and sharp analysis.

Had this competition really accomplished Rabbi Finkel's goal? It would appear that he saw this as the first stage in a multiyear program in which, at its conclusion, the most serious of the yeshiva students would be proficient in the entire Talmud, and the other talmidim would also increase their studiousness and proficiency. But there was no continuation after the first competition, and perhaps it was the high dropout rate that discouraged the roshei-yeshiva and led to the cessation of the project. However, it would seem that Rabbi Finkel had found another way that was meant to be more successful in raising the academic level of the students in his yeshiva.[17]

"The Way of Understanding"

In the final decades of the nineteenth century, the first shoots of a new method of study appeared in the yeshivas. The way of understanding blazed new and daring paths in Talmudic analysis. This innovative method has been written about extensively. To summarize, it can be said that it was based upon clarifying and identifying the halachic principles in a Talmudic sugya and then refining them to abstracted fundamental concepts and definitions. These abstract foundations were subsequently applied to the conflicting positions of the sages discussing the sugya, and they were also attributed to the *rishonim*, who interpreted the sugya, especially Maimonides, whose legal decisions in the *Mishne Torah* are presented without explanations or sources, and the commentaries on this work.[18]

The way of understanding was unique in its view of the sugya as almost the single source for investigating its concealed elements, and when these elements were discovered, they became useful analytic tools for other Talmudic sugyot. Since this approach did not require the use of a plethora of sources or a comprehensive proficiency in a broad range of Talmudic topics on one hand, and because it offered a scholarly challenge on the other, it provided talented young students with intellectual activity that was equal to delving into philosophies and new social and scientific theories that the modern world offered.

The way of understanding was not the product of a single workshop and was therefore by nature multishaded. Its most prominent exponents were Rabbi Ḥayim Soloveitchik, who was appointed as a Talmud instructor in the Volozhin Yeshiva in 1881, and Rabbi Yitzḥak-Ya'akov Rabinowitz, who served as rosh-yeshiva in Slabodka in the years 1889–1893. During the time they were avrechim, they studied together for a time in Brisk, and it is possible that they influenced each other in their way of learning at that time. Nevertheless, it would seem that the similar method of analysis that both of them adopted came primarily from their individual, independent approaches. In their yeshivas, they taught according to the way of understanding that they developed, and their lectures attracted a large audience. However, they both ceased teaching at about the same time and began to serve in rabbinic positions. Rabbi Soloveitchik was forced to leave Volozhin when the yeshiva closed in 1892, and after he was appointed the town rabbi in Brisk, a small-scale study kibbutz of talented students existed under his supervision. Rabbi Rabinowitz left Slabodka due to a disagreement with the founder of the yeshiva, Rabbi Notte-Hirsch Finkel, and after a short interim as the rabbi of Gorzd, he was appointed as the rabbi of Ponevezh in 1895. In 1911 he set up a small yeshiva in that city, and it remained there for four years until it was forced into exile together with the inhabitants of Kovna Province in the First World War.[19]

In the interwar period, there were no longer any yeshiva students who were familiar with the method of Rabbis Soloveitchik and Rabinowitz directly, without any intermediary. There was no access to this approach because these rabbis' Talmudic novellae were never published. Many of the roshei-yeshiva had been directly exposed to Rabbi Soloveitchik's study method from his years in Volozhin and Brisk, and heads and Talmud instructors of other yeshivas came to know Rabbi Rabinowitz's system from his time in Slabodka and Ponevezh. But most developed independent study methods that deviated from the methods that they had learned from their rabbis, and the original way of understanding became hidden from the eyes of the yeshiva baḥurim of the new era.[20]

The turning point occurred when the new building of the Kletsk Yeshiva was dedicated in 1929. The guest of honor was the former rosh-yeshiva, Rabbi Isser-Zalman Meltzer, who served at that time as the rosh-yeshiva of Etz-Ḥayim in Jerusalem and had arrived especially for the occasion. Roshei-yeshiva, rabbis, the directors of Va'ad-HaYeshivot, and many talmidim were in attendance. Especially prominent students at the gathering were graduates of the yeshivas of Slutsk and Kletsk who were studying in the Mir Yeshiva. Among them was one of the most advanced, Yeḥiel-Michel Feinstein, whose renewed encounter with his former rosh-yeshiva, Rabbi Meltzer, led to discussing Torah matters as well. The rabbi was impressed by his student's progress and advised him to go to Brisk to study Torah from its rabbi, Yitzḥak-Ze'ev Soloveitchik.

Feinsten needed the agreement of Rabbi Eliezer-Yehudah Finkel for this step, and Rabbi Meltzer was willing to arrange this. In the conversation between the two roshei-yeshiva, Rabbi Meltzer lectured his interlocutor about how no benefit was being derived from the exceptional and unique talents of the rabbi of Brisk. The upshot of the conversation was not only Rabbi Finkel's agreement that Feinstein could go to Brisk but also the establishment of a wide-ranging and fixed plan for advanced studies with Rabbi Soloveitchik, to be called "the kibbutz of the Mir Yeshiva in Brisk." According to this plan, the Mir Yeshiva agreed to send groups of advanced students to the Brisk Kibbutz in shifts as well as to continue paying for their maintenance there.

In the winter semester of 1929–1930, the first group of talmidim from Mir, including the most advanced students of the yeshiva, was sent to Brisk. Rabbi Soloveitchik began to give daily classes at his home in the order of *Kodshim* in particular, a section on the Talmud he had mainly studied with his father, Rabbi Ḥayim. The baḥurim in the Brisk Kibbutz became exposed to the original way of understanding created by Rabbi Ḥayim Soloveitchik. They returned to Mir with the Brisk oral tradition and copies of Rabbi Ḥayim's words, and they became very popular in the yeshiva. The influence of the way of understanding of Brisk trickled down to the Mir Yeshiva.

Outstanding students from other yeshivas were soon sent to the Brisk Kibbutz. Young men from Radin who were supported by their yeshiva arrived, as well as select talmidim from Kamenitz and even excellent students from the Hasidic-Lithuanian Torat-Ḥesed Yeshiva of Baranovitch. Exceptional talmidim from the local Brisk Yeshiva, who received increased support from its funds, were also present in the kibbutz. In this fashion, the way of understanding according to the Brisk system spread with great force to the contemporary yeshiva world.[21]

The students of Rabbi Ḥayim of Brisk had been trying to publish his novellae for many years. When Rabbi Eliezer-Yehudah Finkel went to the United States in 1926, he made efforts to obtain funds to publish the book. Rabbi Baruch-Ber Leibowitz, a disciple of Rabbi Ḥayim Soloveitchik, was also a partner in this project, and in 1927 he requested the Central Relief to allocate six hundred dollars to the rabbi of Brisk to enable him to print his father's book. However, it was not until a few years later that the circumstances were ripe, and there was great anticipation in advance of the book's appearance. When it was published in 1936, as expected the book was in high demand in the yeshiva world and in particular among the disciples of the author. Rabbi Leibowitz demonstratively expressed their joy at the dedication of his yeshiva's new building at the end of that year. He strode in front of the dancing talmidim while holding the new book by his rabbi. To sense the excitement and joy of this Torah giant in those moments, it is worthwhile to read the poetic words that he wrote when he turned to the Central Relief in advance of the day of the book's publication.

> Then there will be light and gladness amongst the Jews,
> All the excellent gates of Halacha will be illuminated and opened wide,
> All that is obscure and sealed, and every knotty problem will be unraveled.
> Like a hart that yearns for a flowing stream, so does the soul of a talmid as well as a rabbi, an elder and also a young man,
> Six will cover themselves with one garment to hear the teachings of our rabbi, may his memory protect us.
> For generations, sons born from Israel's source,
> All of them, even infants in their mothers' womb, will open their mouths in song as if by the [Red] Sea,
> As with honey from the rock, they will be completely satiated with the Torah of our rabbi.[22]

The studies in the Brisk Kibbutz revolved around tractates in the order of Kodshim. In this way, this section of the Talmud received increasingly greater attention from advanced students who had already achieved proficiency in the tractates of the orders of Nezikin and Nashim, which had been traditionally studied in yeshivas. The new trend received reinforcement from an entirely different direction: the Ḥafetz-Ḥayim, who had for many years encouraged groups of senior students to study Kodshim in order to properly prepare for the coming of the messiah in good time. In the 1920s, upon feeling the immanence of Redemption, he attempted to influence the heads of yeshivas to set up special, select study groups on Kodshim of their best talmidim. Due to their reservations about his idea, he wrote in 1927 to Rabbi Shim'on Shkop:

> My intention is unique students who have excelled in Talmud study and have gained renown, as well as avrechim who are great Torah scholars; my desire is that they should learn the order of Kodshim as well. . . . And what your Torah eminence wrote, that it is precisely upon those Talmudic orders that roshei-yeshiva usually study they can compose Torah novellae, unlike the order of Kodshim, surprises me. Is it possible that we cannot offer [new] insights also on the order of Kodshim to these exceptional young men, whom we can select eight out of one hundred [students], or perhaps ten at the most?[23]

Despite these attempts at convincing them, the roshei-yeshiva were not enthusiastic about the Ḥafetz-Ḥayim's idea and did not hasten to do as he said. His recommendation was realized in a few years' time when the Brisk Kibbutz was established. This kibbutz exposed its students to the way of understanding according to the original system of Rabbi Ḥayim Soloveitchik, and it initiated studies based exclusively on the order of Kodshim. These two innovations quickly spread throughout the yeshiva world.[24]

Types of Study

The type of study was ostensibly monolithic in the Lithuanian yeshivas: the day was divided into two *sedarim*—morning and afternoon—and in addition a lecture was given by the rosh-yeshiva or Talmud instructor once or sometimes several times a week. Even so, there were different shadings within this picture. In some yeshivas the lecture had a central position, and in others only a few students participated while the others went on with their own Talmudic studies. The lectures of Rabbis Naftali Trop, Shim'on Shkop, and Baruch-Ber Leibowitz—three leading figures in the Lithuanian yeshiva world between the wars—had a common characteristic even though each had his own pedagogic approach. Rabbi Leibowitz dedicated the first lectures of the term to the foundations of the tractate that was being studied in order to properly direct his students in understanding its sugyot, whereas Rabbi Shkop delivered his lectures only after his talmidim had gone over the entire tractate under study in a relatively short time and were already deeply involved in it. Both utilized the educational method of posting source citations before each lecture to enable students to understand the material well. Indeed, their lectures occupied a pivotal position in their yeshivas.[25]

The preparation of these roshei-yeshiva for their lectures is worthy of note. Rabbis Trop and Leibowitz were accustomed to relating their original insights to a select group of advanced students before they delivered their weekly lecture, to ensure that there was no defect in their arguments. Once Rabbi Trop was involved in a particularly complex sugya and traveled all the way from Radin to Vilna to consult with Rabbi Leibowitz, and when he returned, he immediately assembled his students and delivered his lecture with all of its complex points. Rabbi Leibowitz also worked hard on his lectures, and they were carefully arranged with no place left for sudden insights of the moment. If, in the course of the lecture, a student showed one of Rabbi Leibowitz's basic assumptions to be invalid, he did not hesitate to close his books and stop his lecture, just as his teacher Rabbi Ḥayim Soloveitchik was accustomed to do. Indeed, their lectures were masterworks of exactitude in understanding the material, as was well described by Rabbi Shmuel Rozovsky (1913–1979), a talmid of Rabbi Shim'on Shkop in Grodno Yeshiva: "Every word of 'the rabbi' [Shkop], every letter and syllable was considered to be an iron foundation, a clear halacha and the final word. It is possible to argue with one line of reasoning or another, one must delve deeply and understand, but—that was it! That is why there was such great tension when he delivered his lectures in the yeshiva—[the talmidim] were worried about missing even one short syllable."[26] After the lectures had been delivered, the young men continued to discuss the sugya with enthusiasm. During the time when Rabbi Shkop delivered his lectures in his beit-midrash in the Forshtat suburb of Grodno, his talmidim would often volubly argue afterward as they walked to their lunch in the city several kilometers away from the beit-midrash. One remarked, "We were so involved in the subject [of the rabbi's lecture] that we were unaware that we were walking in the street."[27]

The lectures continued to attract interest even in the following days. Select senior students heard a replay of the lecture from Rabbi Shim'on Shkop on Friday evenings. Rabbi Naftali Trop would also repeat his lecture, at the behest of the Ḥafetz-Ḥayim, after the sugya had been further elucidated by means of the questions of the talmidim. When the material had become completely clear and free of any questions, the students were given an opportunity to hear Rabbi Trop's lecture once more after they had delved into it throughout the week.[28]

It wasn't just these famous roshei-yeshiva who made their lectures pivotal in their institutions. Similar characteristics are discernible among some of their counterparts, including Rabbi Pesaḥ Pruskin, who delivered his lectures in Kobrin twice a week. He had a gift for delivery and explanation, and he organized his lectures in such an understandable fashion that many of the local residents also came to listen to them. These lectures were an important event in the yeshiva, and its students reviewed their content and discussed them at length. A similar atmosphere prevailed in Kletsk, even though the daily lectures of Rabbi Aharon Kotler were of a different sort. They were characterized by a unique discernment and profundity, intellectually challenging the listeners. During his lecture, Rabbi Kotler would raise his voice with great fervor, and because of the need for maximum concentration, he allowed no questions or interruptions. At the conclusion of his lecture, one of the outstanding students in the yeshiva, Pesaḥ "Timkovitcher" Hurwitz, would accurately repeat it for the benefit of the younger talmidim.[29]

Usually, many of the yeshiva students would attend these lectures, however only a few would be able to express themselves, particularly the most outstanding among them. In order to involve the rest of the young men in active participation, they would be divided up into smaller study groups, or *ḥaburot*. These groups already existed in some of the yeshivas before the First World War, as described by a graduate of Knesset-Yisrael of Slabodka, Rabbi Yeḥiel-Ya'akov Weinberg (1884–1966): "A large ḥaburah of younger students joined every one of the outstanding talmidim to discuss and debate Torah topics. The older student who headed the group would offer his own novel interpretations or questions on the rosh-yeshiva's lectures, and the younger talmidim would try to refute what he said. Tremendous arguments resulted, and the yeshiva reverberated with the voices of the disputants."[30]

In the interwar period, this practice spread throughout many of the yeshivas. Each ḥaburah was made up of ten talmidim of the same age, with a rosh-ḥaburah at their head, usually one of the more gifted among them. One of the senior students or a Talmud instructor supervised the ḥabura, however it enjoyed relative independence and even scheduled its meetings on its own. The participants took turns preparing Torah novellae to present them to their colleagues. These novel interpretations dealt mainly with the tractate under study, and at the end of the presentation, the participants discussed them in a lively manner. These meetings were also an opportunity to review the lectures of the rosh-yeshiva or Talmud instructor and delve into them more deeply, and to check their comprehension. This is the description of the activities of the ḥaburot in his yeshiva that a student in Telz wrote in his journal in the early 1920s:

> It is very exciting to see how, suddenly, a tumult erupts in the yeshiva, and all the students who were scattered among the yeshiva's benches are running, each to his own ḥaburah . . . the noise and tumult in the yeshiva arise from the arguments of the members who wish to refute the words of the

> speaker, and from the voice of the speaker who justifies his position and defends his original interpretation and ideas. I am also a member of such a ḥaburah, and I speak before them and listen to what others say, which is of great benefit to me.[31]

Indeed, in the interwar period the ḥaburot occupied a significant place in the lives of the talmid in Telz. His activity in the yeshiva circled around his ḥaburah. At most, he was in contact with parallel ḥaburot from the same class, but not more than that. The ḥaburot were divided up between the Talmud instructors, and they delivered lectures to them and sometimes even invited the members of the ḥaburah to their homes. At these meetings, the instructors would pose questions to some of them relating to the sugyot that were being studied in the yeshiva, or they asked others to relate a Torah idea. In this way they would determine the students' knowledge and abilities without any intermediary.[32]

There was no division into classes in most of the yeshivas, and young talmidim studied with ones who were more senior, attending the lectures of their rosh-yeshiva side by side. The ḥaburah was an efficient way of dividing up the baḥurim by age in these yeshivas. Each student could belong to a limited and appropriate group of friends and express himself in the best way possible. Moreover, the ḥaburah also developed important skills in learning and preparation, organizing the material and presenting it in a comprehensible manner to colleagues, and speaking in front of a group. Beyond these basic skills, by delving into the sugyot, each student acquired the ability to think critically and an initial approach to creative thinking and creating original Torah interpretations. Thus the ḥaburah was an advanced tool for motivating students and maximizing the fulfillment of their potential.

MUSAR STUDY

The Musar movement worked its way into two yeshiva circles in the 1880s—the extremely small yeshiva in Kelm, which was founded in 1881 by Rabbi Simḥa-Zissel Broyde, the close disciple of Rabbi Yisrael Lipkin, and a much larger group of students in the Slabodka Yeshiva. Rabbi Notte-Hirsch Finkel gave his yeshiva in Slabodka a pronounced Musar tone, expressed through a "Musar-seder," a half-hour session of solitary Musar study before the evening services, from the classic works of Musar: *Mesilat Yesharim* (*Path of the Just*) by Rabbi Moshe-Ḥayim Luzzatto (1707–1746), *Ḥovot HaLevavot* (*Duties of the Heart*) by Rabbeinu Beḥaye ibn-Pakuda (1050–1120), and others. This study was not characterized by dry, intellectual textual analysis but expressed itself through spirited reading aloud of passages "with burning lips" out of desire to touch the depths of the soul and influence from within the individual's character traits and virtues that were found lacking. Rabbi Finkel, the yeshiva administrator and Musar supervisor, tried to reinforce the influence of this study on his talmidim, and to this purpose he concerned himself with their spiritual state by delivering a number of Musar talks during the week and personally counseling each of them in this area.

For a long time, the Slabodka and Kelm Yeshivas were alone in this method. A new yeshiva was founded in the town of Novardok in 1896, and Musar was a central part of its program. These yeshivas were unique in the world of Torah study and even aroused a fierce debate among prominent rabbis, because material other than the Talmud was being added to their accepted curriculum. However, the dramatic changes that the Jews of Eastern Europe experienced at the end of the nineteenth and especially at the beginning of the twentieth century transformed attitudes in the rabbinic world. Almost due to a lack of any alternative, several roshei-yeshiva were willing to be more flexible and include seemingly esoteric Musar studies in their yeshivas' curriculum as a protective shield against powerful outside influences. The proven benefit that including Musar brought to those yeshivas resulted in its rapid acceptance in others too, even in the Knesset Beit-Yitzḥak Yeshiva.

As mentioned earlier, this yeshiva was founded as an antithesis to the neighboring Musar yeshiva in Slabodka. Moreover, its rosh-yeshiva, Rabbi Baruch-Ber Leibowitz, was a disciple of Rabbi Ḥayim Soloveitchik, who was not a supporter of Musar study. Nevertheless, years later even Rabbi Leibowitz arrived at a similar conclusion regarding the importance of Musar study, and in one of his sermons he said, "Therefore I appeal to each yeshiva student to gather his strength and attend prayers at the yeshiva, to study Musar primarily since it is the beginning of wisdom . . . one must watch over the heart without cessation all the days of one's life, and it is not enough to just be in the yeshiva."[33]

In the interwar period, an element of Musar was added to Talmud study even in the yeshivas that had not absorbed Musar study until then. Besides the inspirational talks given by the Musar supervisors, this was also expressed in Musar-seder and Musar-ḥaburot (peer study groups), which were all intended "to watch over the heart," as described in the words of Rabbi Leibowitz.

Despite the significance of the addition of Musar to the yeshivas between the wars, this only occupied a miniscule portion of the students' daily schedule. Even in the Slabodka Yeshiva, one of the pioneers of the Musar yeshivas, the study of Musar did not have an outstanding place in the curriculum, although it certainly had an influence on the characters and worldview of the yeshiva talmidim. This was not the case in the Kelm and Novardok yeshivas. True, the usual study sessions took place there as in other yeshivas, but the feeling of Musar in those institutions was palpable. The entire experience of the students throughout the hours of the day was infused with this spirit, and they saw their main objective as spiritual and ethical growth.

Musar Sessions

The framework of Musar sessions in the yeshivas remained unchanged between the wars, and a daily Musar-seder continued to take place in the half hour before evening services. It is possible to sense a bit of the atmosphere of such a seder from a description of a visitor, apparently to the Telz Yeshiva:

> Monotone sounds can be heard already from afar . . . they are studying Musar in the yeshiva. Inside: a rare panorama seizes your eye—one mass, figures moving of their own accord. One mass! How many ideas, thoughts, feelings?! Here and there shadows move quietly, the force of thought has moved them from their place. . . . Someone is making an accounting with his Creator. . . . From that far corner of the yeshiva arise isolated tunes of cleaving [to God], heart-breaking and filled with emotion. Here a "German" rumbles a patriotic march, and there the "Englishman" with his rigid tune, made up of half-sounds . . . and in the other corner the "Hungarian" walks with measured steps and his rumbling is a bit more sentimental. From his distant home, from the beautiful views there, he has brought a heart-felt melody that mothers use to put their children to sleep in the moonlight and sing the praises of the beauty of the Blue Danube. . . .

> But the most important place is occupied by our "Litvak" [Lithuanian Jew]. . . . After a full day of dizzying study and intense "intellectual exercise" in the churning sea of the Talmud . . . suddenly his voice breaks and cries out in sadness mixed with a despairing sound: "What is man's duty in the world?" . . . and from a far corner a voice answers: "Only to rejoice in God and enjoy the glory of his Presence."[34]
>
> It is already 9:00. The beadle is already standing by the lectern to knock [signaling the time for evening services has arrived]. . . . Finally, one blow is sounded that is barely heard in the midst of the mighty chorus of voices. One blow, and then another. But this does not disturb the moving mass of people. The cantor is already standing by the lectern, but the mass still continues to move. They do not hear the [opening words of the evening service] "For He is merciful." . . . Then the answer to all inquiries comes down: "Give praise to God Who is to be praised."[35]

Even in the Novardok yeshivas, a Musar-seder took place in this fashion, however an additional similar session was added before afternoon prayers. Only the Kelm Yeshiva was different; the Musar-seder was lengthened to an hour, and there was a five-minute Musar session before the *Musaf* service on the Sabbath as well.[36]

The list of Musar works studied in the seder remained the same during the interwar period. The most common ones and the most desirable to the Musar-mashgiḥim were the classic Musar works *Mesilat Yesharim*, *Ḥovot HaLevavot*, and *Sha'arei Teshuva*. Rarer books were studied as well in some yeshivas, but they were the exception, proving that the best Musar ideas were to be found in the traditional, classic works.[37]

Musar Groups

The mashgiḥim of the yeshivas saw their role as the formation of their students' worldview and its consolidation. This was done through talks, both personal and public, where character improvement and the goals of the yeshiva student were emphasized.[38] One of the supplementary and more effective ways of achieving these objectives was working in groups. Similar to the ḥaburot that were instituted in the yeshivas in the area of study, Musar-ḥaburot were also set up to further the aims of Musar.

The Musar-ḥaburot were not a new idea at all. An early version existed in 1881 in the town of Kelm from the very beginning of the yeshiva there. It can be assumed that this model served as an example to the graduates of

Kelm who became mashgiḥim to the extent that they instituted it in their yeshivas. In Mir in the early 1920s, for example, there were four Musar-ḥaburot that were divided by age. The youngest group was personally directed by the mashgiaḥ and alumnus of Kelm, Rabbi Yeḥezkel Levenstein. In Grodno, the mashgiaḥ Rabbi Shlomo Harkavy, also a graduate of the Kelm Yeshiva, divided up the talmidim into Musar groups based on their age and abilities. He would meet with each group weekly and strengthen its members in Musar and the fear of God. In the Radin Yeshiva, the mashgiaḥ Rabbi Eliezer-Ze'ev Kaplan, a talmid of the Kelm graduate Rabbi Yeruḥam Levovitz, adopted a different method. Each ḥaburah in the yeshiva was made up of students of various ages without regard to their level, with the aim of achieving optimal cohesion.[39]

Even in yeshivas where Musar teachings had not been originally included, the ḥaburot were very effective means for their dissemination. The new mashgiaḥ in Brisk, Rabbi Avraham-Ya'akov Gordon, influenced its outstanding students to set up a Musar-ḥaburah, and this was a benefit to the entire yeshiva. In Telz, it was the students who founded a limited ḥaburah in 1922. When their initiative found favor in the eyes of the administration, its members were requested to expand their influence over the entire yeshiva and set up additional Musar-ḥaburot.[40]

Besides meetings at set times on matters relating to Musar, each ḥaburah adopted a list of rules for itself that included keeping to the prayer and study schedules, paying attention to proper intention and concentration in prayer, attending the talks of the mashgiaḥ, and having a weekly discussion of those talks. The rules even set monetary fines for those who did not keep them.[41]

Parallel to the influence of the learning ḥaburot for the development of study skills of their members, the Musar-ḥaburot motivated their spiritual growth. The combination of the two had a decisive influence on the Torah character development of the yeshiva student.

Musar Practices in the Yeshivas

The study of Musar as a means of character improvement and reforming of personality traits was not the invention of the founder of the Musar movement, Rabbi Yisrael Lipkin, because a variety of Musar books had been published many years before him. Actually, he did not see any need to write extensive compositions in this area; in his view, there were already enough Musar works in existence. The novelty of his approach lay in the way those books were to be studied—a way that made it possible to inculcate Musar into the human personality, and in that manner to deal more effectively with negative character traits and desires. Basing himself on a psychological understanding of the human soul, Rabbi Lipkin considered in-depth study of Musar theory as insufficient. He differentiated between the influence of conscious forces on the individual and the influence of the unconscious forces, rooted deep in the personality. He understood that the ruling element in man's behavior comes from the inclinations of the heart, whereas intellectual knowledge and consciousness are not sufficiently imprinted in his inner personality and so are not strong enough to ensure that he will act according to what he knows and thinks. In order to intensify their influence, intellectual knowledge and consciousness must penetrate his very soul and become part of the subconscious; only then can they overcome natural drives. The way to penetrate the subconscious does not lie in profound investigation and serious research into the study of the fear of God and Musar but through a particular style of learning, and this is what is likely to achieve the desired influence and make its mark on the individual. There are two strata to this type of study:

- Repetition: All intellectual learning makes an impression on the human psyche. Repeated review of the material makes further impressions each time. The aggregate of these impressions is what leads to the creation of a subconscious force.
- Enthusiasm: In order to create a subconscious force of great value, repetition cannot be superficial but requires emotion and enthusiasm. Only a stormy awakening "with burning lips," repeating the emotive words out loud and with a rousing tune, can make the desired impression on the psyche.

Rabbi Lipkin's novel approach expressed itself in defining the optimum (and perhaps only) way to inculcating Musar and the fear of God in the human soul: study of Musar accompanied by frequent repetition and great enthusiasm.[42]

The adoption of this concept in the Lithuanian yeshivas was not carried out in a uniform fashion, and there was a wide variety of approaches to Musar. These approaches were based on the methods crystallized by those individuals who led the dramatic Musar revolution in the yeshivas. It is customary to summarize them thusly: the way of "man's triviality" of Rabbi Simḥa-Zissel Broyde, founder of the Kelm Yeshiva; the way of "man's greatness" of Rabbi Notte-Hirsch Finkel, founder of the Slabodka Yeshiva and its mashgiaḥ; and the way of "man's lowliness" of Rabbi Yosef-Yozel Hurwitz, the father of the Novardok yeshivas.

The Way of Kelm

The Kelm Yeshiva can be considered one of the Lithuanian yeshivas by virtue of its organizational structure as well as in terms of content. Although it also served as a school for avrechim—who did not usually study in yeshivas—these students were a minority among the talmidim there in the interwar period. The yeshiva was outstanding in that it had only fifty students, a limited number compared to other yeshivas. This small number was seemingly due to limited space, but it was more a result of the institution's uniqueness, as one graduate of Kelm explained: "It was a world unto itself that stood apart from other Lithuanian yeshivas."[43] The goal of those yeshivas was to train talmidim according to the ideals of the Torah and to form their religious and ethical personality. The Kelm Yeshiva saw its task "to teach [its students] the art of pedagogy in this field [of Musar] so that [when they complete their studies in the institution they] are capable of going forth to teach and spread the learning they have acquired there."[44] Indeed, the Kelm Yeshiva was intended only for a limited and elite group of graduates of yeshivot-gedolot, who were committed to serving as guides in the study of Musar not only in its intellectual aspects but also in practice.

In order to understand the uniqueness of the Kelm Yeshiva, it is necessary to examine its curriculum. Its sedarim resembled those in the other yeshivas, and the students studied a given Talmudical tractate, as was the custom. A weekly lecture was given on one of the sugyot of the tractate in a side room by Rabbi Daniel Movshovitz (~1885–1941), who stood at the head of the yeshiva. Once or twice during the term, his brother-in-law and director of the institution, Rabbi Gershon Miadnik (1888–1941), would repeat a lecture that he had heard during his studies in Radin from Rabbi Naftali Trop. The somewhat special practice of the Musar sedarim in Kelm has already been mentioned. In addition, after morning services, *Orḥot Ḥayim* by Rabbeinu Asher (known as *Rosh*, 1250–1327) was studied, and those present read verses from the daily chapter. Accordingly, in the yeshiva there were no study sessions that significantly deviated from that which was accepted in the other Lithuanian yeshivas. Moreover, extensive time was not dedicated to outward Musar activities that were meant to lead to personality change and moral edification. Its uniqueness must be sought elsewhere.

It would seem that mental tranquility was the central characteristic of the Kelm Yeshiva. Its founder, Rabbi Simḥa-Zissel Broyde, saw this as a necessary condition for perfecting the character of the individual—whose life was mainly involved in the trivialities of everyday existence—in a moderate, calm, and precise fashion; therefore, Rabbi Broyde made it the central point in his Musar system. The atmosphere of the yeshiva was shaped toward achieving this state of mind:[45]

- Composure: Every action was to be taken only after thinking and planning. The yeshiva was characterized by moderate behavior; rushing and panic were totally absent there.
- Order: Attention was given to clean and neat dress. The study hall was outstanding as well in its order and cleanliness, and to avoid dirtying it, the students left their coats and galoshes in a closet by the entrance.
- Quiet: Students refrained from raising their voices within the school. Even prayers were recited throughout the year in a low voice, almost without any swaying or gestures.
- Exactitude: Students kept to an exact schedule of prayers and sedarim. Time was to be used to maximum advantage, and consequently one should not be surprised that the Musar-seder on Shabbat was five minutes long, because it was possible to derive benefit from even such a short period of time for spiritual growth.

- Concentration: Special emphasis was put on avoiding distractions. Everything that took place in the study hall was required to be continuous and without any interruption, and in that way the effectiveness of study was increased.

In order to get a sense of the atmosphere in the yeshiva, it is sufficient to note that several minutes before the beginning of the morning seder, the study hall was likely to be empty of its students, but when the exact time arrived, everyone was already in his place. During study time, a talmid would not turn to the door to see who had entered, would not look out the window to see what was happening outside, and would not go out of the hall without permission from the gabai. The Kelm Yeshiva was an institution characterized by moderation, order, meticulousness, and especially refraining from any unnecessary action—the very antithesis of the Novardok approach, which is about to be described.[46]

The Way of Novardok

On one end of the Musar scale was Kelm, with the tranquility that ruled it and the outward splendor that it demanded. On the opposite end stood Novardok, with its intense and constant internal war against human drives and neglect of outward appearance. Just like Rabbi Simḥa-Zissel Broyde, Rabbi Yosef-Yozel Hurwitz (the founder of the Novardok system) was a talmid of Rabbi Yisrael Lipkin, albeit for a short time. These two faithful disciples of the father of the Musar movement saw their aim as molding a complete and true individual, and they found that the only way to achieve this goal was through practical Musar action. Rabbi Hurwitz even spent several years in the Kelm Yeshiva and was profoundly influenced by Rabbi Broyde. However, he did not believe in the effectivity of the moderation and restraint that were the very symbol of that institution; he saw a radical system as the proper weapon to use against the powerful temptations that stood in a man's way in the modern world.[47]

Rabbi Hurwitz set up his Musar system based on an approach that allowed no compromises or concessions to the demands of society or earthly living. He was not satisfied with restraining bad personality traits but taught that they must be broken and destroyed; otherwise, their roots would grow back and deceive a person, overcoming his intelligence and consciousness. These traits can only be uprooted through emotion and internal turbulence. When a person reaches a state of heightened feeling, he can transcend his physical desires and break through his internal barriers at once. Only then will he be free to make decisions in a rational fashion, take control over himself, and break his evil desires and character traits. Accordingly, the major thrust of educational effort in Novardok was directed toward "clarifying and repairing character traits" in a heightened state of emotion and inner turmoil, and the daily schedule included "exercises" in uprooting character defects and freeing oneself from them. This Musar activity often took place at the expense of regular Talmud study—an official approach that was sui generis in the Lithuanian yeshivas, including the yeshiva in Kelm.[48]

Beyond organized Musar activities in the Novardok yeshivas, there were not a few talmidim who dedicated significant additional time to Musar matters, and they were referred to as "seekers" and "workers." The seekers were theoreticians of the Novardok Musar teachings who delved deeply into its system and in the investigation of character traits, whereas the workers were men of action who dedicated a greater deal of time to prayer, Musar study, and "exercises" in doing good to others, breaking the will, and so on. Musar matters stood higher on the list of priorities of the talmidim of these two groups than Talmudic scholarship. Naturally, their more studious friends were reluctant to study Talmud with them as learning partners, but the administration accepted the behavior of these groups with understanding and even with sympathy.[49]

An examination of the schedule in the Novardok yeshivas reveals a significant difference compared to the program in their Lithuanian counterparts. There was no difference in the daily learning sedarim and the weekly Talmud lectures, but as previously mentioned, the Novardok yeshivas were unique in adding a Musar-seder before the afternoon prayers and, in a singular activity, the Musar-birzhe (exchange). Imitating the birzhes in the Socialist movement and the Bund of the early twentieth century, the Novardok birzhe was characterized by vocal give and take about Musar subjects and character improvement, and it took place for half an hour between two or three baḥurim. Among them there was usually a senior student, and through their discussions he would examine their spiritual condition and suggest ways of Musar development. Their questions and debates with him while walking vigorously from one side of the study hall to the other would fill them with enthusiasm and spur on their thinking.[50]

These novel ideas were marginal compared to the actions that took place in the Novardok yeshivas on special occasions. This does not refer to the extended period of the month of Elul and the ten days of penitence between Rosh HaShana and Yom Kippur, when Musar study was also expanded in other yeshivas, but throughout the year. In the fourth general meeting of the Novardok network in Mezritch during the winter term of 1925, the following decision was accepted: "To arrange a distinct time period to work on 'refining character traits' at a fixed time in every place, so that all the '*Va'adim*' [sessions] should be united in the same work, and to dedicate specific time [to this], because this causes the participants to work seriously and perpetually even afterwards for many days, similar as regards to the virtue of trust [in God], and through this the work will increase in general and in particular."[51] Up until then, the various aspects of the Novardok system of Musar were based upon fundamental doctrines—"trust [in God] without making efforts," "relinquishing ownership," and more—and the talmidim continually put these principles into practice. The earlier quoted revolutionary decision required the establishment of a new, fixed, and detailed schedule of actions. This calendar, which would be obligatory in all the Novardok yeshivas, concentrated the Musar activities that were to be observed into certain seasons, or periods of time throughout the year. The yearly calendar received a dynamic Musar character of shared examination of particular faults or virtues and their uprooting or inculcation in the souls of the students at each season of the year.[52]

Some of the colorful activity that took place during these periods of time can be seen at the end of the yearly calendar, in "the season of seclusion" after *Purim* until Passover. Unlike the students in other yeshivas who were preparing for the Passover vacation, unusual events could be observed going on in the Novardok yeshivas during that season. The early days of the period were dedicated to "individual seclusion" among the majority of the students. They sat in various batei-midrash and formulated personal goals in advance of the main activity, "ḥaburah seclusion." This was an activity that involved the talmidim going out of their yeshiva with their ḥaburah and studying Torah and Musar with great enthusiasm in batei-midrash in nearby towns and villages. The solitary living had its own regulations, according to which there was only one seder dedicated to Talmud study each day, in order to spend the rest of the time studying Musar. Unnecessary conversation was forbidden in the "seclusion house," as was leaving it, and the duration of meals was limited so as not to waste valuable time. The young men in seclusion were fed by the townspeople, and they also found a place to sleep in the houses of those local residents every night. The last evening, at the end of three weeks, had a special significance because it was intended for the making of "general resolutions." During that evening, talmidim accepted upon themselves the commitment to remain in the Novardok yeshivas for additional years.

This season had a critical influence on the spiritual growth of the young men of Novardok as well as on their future. One of the graduates of the Bialystok Yeshiva wrote, "These days of 'seclusion' always left a powerful and indelible impression on the hearts of the participants in the ḥaburot, a memory of days of joy and elevated spirits."[53]

The centrality of the Musar calendar was prominent in the Novardok yeshivas, but the highlight of Musar action in them was the activity of the Musar-ḥaburot. Like talmidim in many other yeshivas, students in Novardok were divided into Musar groups, approximately ten students in each ḥaburah, according to their age and when they entered the yeshiva. At the head of each group stood an educator—*rosh-haḥaburah* or *rosh-haVa'ad* (session head)—who belonged to a more advanced ḥaburah. The task of this individual was to guide the baḥurim in whom he discerned a tendency toward the way of Musar. Ostensibly these ḥaburot were no different from their counterparts in other yeshivas, and they also investigated Musar concepts and worked on polishing virtues. However, their Musar work was more intense, and practically speaking, the entire life of a Novardok student revolved around his ḥaburah.[54]

Once a week after dinner, a Va'ad was held; it was a session of the members of the ḥaburah with the participation of rosh-haVa'ad. In this meeting, a working plan was decided upon for the Musar activities of the coming week. Shmuel Ben-Artzi described the dynamics of the Va'ad in the Mezritch Yeshiva:

> Sometimes such a Va'ad takes three or four hours instead of the two hours set for it in the schedule. The head of the Va'ad does not stop the conversation as long as there is someone who wants to participate in it. After all, he sees clearly that the ḥaburah is ascending the steps of perfection, and with every additional day spiritual tension increases, and it is necessary to give everyone the opportunity to unburden himself. How and when would this be done if not during the conversation in the Va'ad, which is storming, rising and breaking out from the depths?[55]

On weekdays there were additional meetings of the members of the ḥaburah, during which they examined their achievements or discussed an incident that happened to one of them, analyzed it, and identified the inner forces that it revealed.

The Novardok ḥaburah fulfilled a function similar to that of a study ḥaburah in the other Lithuanian yeshivas. It led to spiritual growth and developed skills and the ability to think in an organized manner and to speak and appear in front of an audience. It also served as a means to increase the enthusiasm of its members, to spur them on to exercises of daring, strengthen them spiritually, and connect them with the movement's approach.[56]

The Way of Slabodka

The two diametrically opposed approaches previously described are the creation of the second generation of the Musar movement. Rabbi Simḥa-Zissel Broyde and Rabbi Yosef-Yozel Hurwitz received the foundations of its teachings or at least absorbed its spirit from the father of the movement himself, Rabbi Yisrael Lipkin. In contrast, the approach to Musar in the Slabodka Yeshiva was articulated by a member of the third generation of the movement, Rabbi Notte-Hirsch Finkel. Even though he was profoundly influenced by his teacher Rabbi Simḥa-Zissel Broyde, over the years he formulated a Musar system of his own. At its base stood the idea that the aspirations of today's man are physical pleasure and fulfillment of his desires. Only deepening his consciousness that he is the very purpose of Creation can lead him to set aside his lowly drives and turn toward elevated spiritual goals. For that reason, Rabbi Finkel repeatedly emphasized in his Musar talks the importance of man and his exalted status, which obligates him in all his actions to strive for spiritual greatness. He sought to imprint in the hearts of his students the faith in their own strength and ability to transcend negative personality traits, as well as aspiration toward reaching a much higher level than they had set for themselves in perfecting their characters and Torah study. Although he did not relinquish the tradition of studying Musar with great emotion, he saw this as only a tool. It was the internal process of realizing one's self-worth and developing high aspirations, which were in his view the principle means of spiritual perfection.[57]

Thus, the Slabodka Musar system set abstract goals for consciousness and aspirations, but unlike in Kelm and Novardok, it did not establish practical means for character improvement. Moreover, even regarding those abstract goals, it did not specify any strategies for carrying them out in practice. This situation did not change after Rabbi Finkel left Slabodka on his way to Hebron and his position as Musar-mashgiaḥ was filled by his disciple, Rabbi Avraham Grodzensky. In Rabbi Grodzensky's Musar talks, he deviated from his rabbi's approach, but this had no significant influence on the practical aspects of the Musar way of Slabodka.[58]

The implementation of the Musar ways of Kelm and Novardok have been presented previously as diametrically opposed, but it would seem that it is possible to see both as having a precise and practical Musar teaching. At the opposite end of the spectrum lies the Slabodka approach, which was vague in its goals and obscure in terms of its practical aspects.

SUMMARY

The significant changes that took place in the field of education among Polish and Lithuanian Jews in the interwar period did not alter the basic outlook of the Lithuanian yeshivas. They continued to advocate Torah liShma—Torah study for its own sake—without any concern for pragmatism. Even when the trend toward practical study was accepted and even obligatory in the view of the Jewish public, the yeshivas refrained from teaching halachic rulings and concentrated on theoretical tractates that lacked concrete application. The study of these tractates was an excellent platform for carrying out the way of understanding that was accepted in most of the Lithuanian yeshivas. The characteristic keeping a distance from halachic rulings through this sort of study became even more pronounced after the "discovery" anew of the system of Rabbi Ḥayim Soloveitchik, the system that became fixed in the consciousness of the yeshiva world as the most faithful representation of the way of understanding. Indeed, only minor discernible changes occurred in the yeshiva curriculum in the years between the wars: many yeshivas introduced the study of practical Halacha, which was aimed at training their students to observe the commandments more carefully; advanced students began to study the order of Kodshim as well, which became accepted and popular as a result of the setting up of the Brisk Kibbutz.

The field of Musar was even more constant. Truly, by the 1920s Musar teachings had become established in the few yeshivas that had not adopted them until then, and thus the Musar revolution that had begun with the founding of the Slabodka yeshiva in 1882 was completed. However, the various Musar sessions established in the yeshivas at the end of the nineteenth century and the beginning of the twentieth century did not change at all during the interwar period. It would seem that the roshei-yeshiva considered this framework, despite its relatively short tradition, the most effective barrier against the penetration of outside influences into their schools. Moreover, after the First World War, the inclusion of Musar studies in the yeshivas nearly ceased to be a subject of debate among the figures of Polish and Lithuanian Orthodoxy, and they too saw it as the proper response at the time to the influences of rapid secularization taking place in the Jewish community.

The principal institutions for teaching practical Musar, Kelm and Novardok, continued their regular activities as in the past. Even the introduction of the Musar calendar in the Novardok yeshivas, which arranged their typical activities at set times of the year, was ostensibly a superficial change that did not create any essential transformation. The description of the Novardok yeshiva by Moshe Zilberg (1900–1975) from the days of the First World War, that "this was perhaps the only place in the world where an entire group got together for character improvement . . . by means of well-known exercises," was still fitting.[59]

This words well describe the Kelm Yeshiva too. There as well, "well-known exercises" were used to create harmony between the study of Musar and real life. Despite the vast difference between the type of activities in Novardok and Kelm, both had the same goal, and their uniqueness among the other Lithuanian yeshivas in the interwar period lay in their attempt to achieve this harmony. In contrast with both of these yeshivas, Slabodka continued its prominence in its abstract aspirations for greatness and its distance from practical activity towards character improvement. However, it would seem that this distance on one hand and the striving for greatness and excellence in learning on the other hand were exactly what contributed to Slabodka's unique success in spreading the ideas of the Musar movement among most of the Lithuanian yeshivas and even to large portions of the Jewish world.[60]

NOTES

1. On Rabbi Lipkin, see Etkes, *Rabbi Israel*; Goldberg, *Israel Salanter*.

2. Salmon, "Reshit."

3. Ovsey, *Ma'amarim*, "HaYeshivot biTekufat haTeḥiya," 51; Fishman, "Musar and Modernity," 42, 46–49; Klibansky, "Lama," 39–40.

4. Fichman, *Bialik*, 80–81.

5. Alon, "Yeshivot," 3; Weinberg, "Die Jeschiwoth," 116; Atlas, "Der Derech," 609–10; Rozental, *HaRav*, 122; Meltzer, *BeDerech*, 38–39; Abraham, "HaYeshivot," 441; Jungreiss, "Yeshivat," 501–3; Mandelboim, *Yeshivat*, I, 322. See also Breuer, *Oholei Torah*, 86–89; Tikochinski, "Darchei," 73–75. Nezikin (damages) is the order that deals with damages and property rights; Nashim (women) is the order that deals with marriage and divorce law.

6. The concept of Torah liShma of Rabbi Ḥayim of Volozhin, emphasized in his work *Nefesh haḤayim*, considered deriving practical halachic conclusions from intensive Talmud study as the ideal, and it was even put into practice in the early years of the Volozhin Yeshiva. By the second half of the nineteenth century, this expression was interpreted in the yeshiva world according to its literal meaning: Torah study without any utilitarian or practical motive (Etkes, "Bein Lamdanut," 390; Gross, "Al Tefisat," 153–59; Stampfer, *Lithuanian*, 42).

7. Alon, "Yeshivot," 3. Cf. Berlin, *MeVolozin*, I, 159–60. Regarding "Rabbinical ordination in the pocket," see Holtzman, *Ḥayim*, 128. Yoreh-De'ah is the section of Shulḥan-Aruch (the Code of Jewish Law), dealing with the laws of Kashrut; Elu Treifot is the laws dealing with prohibited meat; Even-HaEzer is the section of Shulḥan-Aruch dealing with marriage laws.

8. Alon, "Yeshivot," 3.

9. Shoshkes, *Lender*, 231 (from Yiddish). See Klibansky, "HaYeshivot," 261n46; testimony: YBB.

10. Yoshor, *HeḤafetz Ḥayim*, 692. Cf. Schwartzbord, *BaKodesh*, 67.

11. Hertzman, *Nes*, 30. The verse is from Psalm 27:4.

12. Histadrut Talmidei Yeshivat Slabodka, *Kinus*, 14; Ben-Artzi, *Shivti*, 74; Kol, *Eḥad*, 267; Ben-Mordechai, "Metivta," 332; Poupko, *Michtavei*, 174; Korets reports, 1926–1928,

1936 (VHY/1132). Oraḥ-Ḥayim is the section of Shulḥan-Aruch dealing with daily observance.

13. Leoni, *Korets*, 125; Korets reports, 1926–1928, 1936 (VHY, 1132); Barkai, "Naḥalat," 10–11 (cf. *Hamelitz*, Sep. 2, 1902). For Korets, see also chapter 2, by note 39.

14. Valach, *Shmuel*, 54–55; Etkes, *Rabbi Israel*, 73. Karlin is a suburb of Pinsk.

15. Rozental, *Torah*, 314. See also Golan, *HaLaila*, 208–9; Rabiner, *HaRav*, 24. Tractate Ḥullin deals with kosher slaughter.

16. Sorotzkin, "HaRav R' Avraham Zvi," 39. Cf. Epstein, "Yeshivat Mir," 101; Golan, *HaLaila*, 223–24.

17. Epstein, "Yeshivat Mir," 104–5; Vaxman, "HaGaon," 416–18. For a list of those who remained in the competition see Klibansky, "HaYeshivot," 226n32.

18. Zevin, *Ishim*, 48–63; Vilensky, *Kuntres*, 17. From the research aspect, see Solomon, "The Analytic Movement"; Brown, *HaḤazon Ish*, 315–21; Tikochinski, "Darchei," 57–65. Rishonim: Talmudic commentators preceding the Shulḥan-Aruch, that is, before the mid-sixteenth century.

19. Klibansky, *KeTzur*, 62–63; Klibansky, "Lama," 40–51, 62–63; Bialoblotsky, "R' Itzelle," 394–95; Bialoblotsky, "Merkezey," 197–98; Atlas, "Der Derech haHavone," 610; Tikochinski, "Darchei," 95–124. See also Mashbitzky, "Achsaniyot"; Don-Yiḥye, "BeYeshivat"; Shapiro, "R' Itzelle," 577.

20. For their names, see Klibansky, "HaYeshivot," 226–27.

21. Epstein, "Yeshivat Mir," 106–107; Meler, *HaRav*, II, 82, 91, 101; Meler, *Igrot*, 70; Levi, *Yeshivat*, 50; postcard: Kaplan to Berek, Sep. 29, 1933 (VHY/47); letters: Hirschowitz to Va'ad-HaYeshivot, May 9, 1937 (VHY/13), and Levinson to Berek, Dec. 12, 1935 (VHY/511). Kodshim is he order that deals principally with Temple sacrifices.

22. Desler, *Shenot*, I, 76. The book *Ḥidushei Rabeinu Ḥayim haLevi* [Novellae of Our Rabbi Ḥayim haLevi] was printed in Brisk. For requests to purchase it, see Klibansky, "HaYeshivot," 229n60. See also Edelstein, *Rabbi*, 80; Parush, *Orot*, 33–35; Frank, *Esah*, 476. Cf. Ovsey, *Ma'amarim*, "LiDe'muto shel R' Ḥayim miBrisk," 109–11.

23. *Edut—A Torah Anthology*, I (1987): 14–15. See also Klibansky, "HaYeshivot," 248–49.

24. Meler, *HaRav*, II, 80–81; Stefansky, *MiMir*, 99.

25. Edelstein, *Rabbi*, 64; Rozental, *Torah*, 75, 141.

26. Rosen, "HaGaon," 11. See Zinowitz, *Ishim*, 203; Bergman, *Shimush*, 230; Edelstein, *Rabbi*, 58, 99–100. Cf. Don-Yiḥye, "BeYeshivat."

27. Rozental, *Torah*, 74–76. See also Farber, *Olkeniki*, 218–19.

28. Rozental, *Torah*, 79; Yoshor, *HeḤafetz Ḥayim*, 686–87.

29. "HaRav R' Pesaḥ Horwitz," 221, 223; "HaRav R' Pesaḥ Pruskin," 227; Golan, *HaLaila*, 126. Cf. *TJO* (Dec. 1970): 21.

30. Reznick, *Klei Sharet*, 1H. See also Meltzer, *BeDerech*, 202; Zinowitz, "*Etz Ḥayim*," 451; Grossman, *Ki Im*, 26.

31. Barkai, "Naḥalat," 9. See also letter: Katz to Vaxman, June 1, 1923 (NWC/111); testimony: Bronznik; Ben-Yeminni, "In der Malchus," 29; Pomerantchik, *Yehegge*, preface (the author's letter); Weintraub, *BeSufa*, 168; Surasky, *Rabbi Shim'on*, 184.

32. Testimony: Bronznik; Segal, *VeEleh Toledot*, 52; Zariz, "Yeshivat," 207; Meltzer, *BeDerech*, 202.

33. *El haMevakesh* 6 (1939): 5 (according to the verses "The beginning of wisdom is the fear of the Lord" [Psalm 111:10] and "Watch over your heart with all diligence, for from it flow the springs of life" [Proverbs 4:23]).

34. A phrase from Rabbi Moshe-Ḥayim Luzzatto's *Mesilat Yesharim*.

35. *Tzu der Yugnt* 18 (Jan./Feb. 1936): 10–11 (from Yiddish). Cf. *HaOlam* 29, no. 8 (1940): 126; *HaNe'eman*, 3 (1928): 8.

36. Testimonies: Fortman and Bronznik; Herschberg, *Pinkes*, 336; Schwartzbord, *BaKodesh*, 78; Desler, *Sefer*, 24, 50. Cf. Katz, *Tenuat*, II, 201.

37. For details, see Klibansky, "HaYeshivot," 234–35. *Sha'arei Teshuva* [Gates of Repentance] was written by Rabbeinu Yona Gerondi.

38. The Musar talks in Telz were an exception. They were lectures on the aspects of fundamental religious ideas but were also meant to strengthen the faith-centered worldview of the talmid (Barkai, "Naḥalat," 11; Levinthal, *The World*, 4; testimony: Bronznik). For greater detail regarding the mashgiḥim, see chapter 5.

39. Ḥigger, *Sam*, 59; Epstein, "Yeshivat 'Sha'ar haTorah'," 299; Yoshor, "HaRav R' Eliezer," 131; Desler, *Sefer*, 151. Cf. Katz, *Tenuat*, II, 202–3.

40. Pomerantchik, *Yehegge*, preface (the author's letter); Barkai, "Naḥalat," 17–18.

41. Barkai, "Naḥalat," 17–18; Rozental, *Torah*, 119–20.

42. Etkes, *Rabbi Israel*, 309–12; Silman, "Torat," 297–304; Katz, *Tenuat*, I, 250–52, 257–58. Rabbi Lipkin's single work on Musar is *Gaon Yisrael*, known today as *Igerret HaMusar*. It should be noted that despite his involvement in character improvement as the basis for improving society as a whole, he did not discuss matters of social justice itself. See Etkes, *Rabbi Israel*, 153–73, 261–68; Salant, *Etz Peri*.

43. Testimony: Fortman. See also Report, Movshowitz-Wischnitzer, Dec. 28, 1938 (MWP); Carlebach, "Mussar," 351. Cf. Bloch, *HaTzadik*, 54.

44. Report, Movshowitz-Wischnitzer, Dec. 28, 1938 (MWP; English source).

45. Kremerman, *Beurei*, "BeSha'ar HaSefer"; Desler, *Sefer*, 45, 48, 54–56, 386, 392, 419; Carlebach, "Mussar," 351–52; Katz, *Tenuat*, II, 150–52, 178; testimonies: Fortman, Ben-Porat and Zuckerman.

46. Zaritzky, *Torat*, 20; Katz, *Tenuat*, II, 184; Desler, *Sefer*, 44, 51. Cf. Schwadron, *Lev*, 47.

47. Katz, *Divrei*, I, 192; Katz, *Tenuat*, IV, 194; Fishman, "Musar and Modernity," 42; Levin, *Novarodok*, 21; Gershuni, *Yahadut beRussia*, 135–36; Zilberg "Kat," II; Weintraub, *BeSufa*, 28; Ḥigger, *Sam*, 69.

48. Katz, *Tenuat*, IV, 236–37, 252, 279–82.

49. Zilberg "Kat," I; Katz, *Tenuat*, IV, 255, 285; Fishman, "Musar and Modernity," 48; Ben-Artzi, *Shivti*, 13, 45, 73, 92. Cf. Gotlieb, *Zichronotay*, 41.

50. Testimony: Ben-Artzi; Levin, *Novarodok*, 16; Ben-Artzi, *Shivti*, 21; Berman, *Siḥot*, 108; Zilberg "Kat," I. Cf. Dinur, *BeOlam*, 243; Shazar, *Kochvei*, 179–83; Broydes, *Vilna*, 204.

51. *Ohr HaMusar* 10 (1925): 63. Cf. Hurwitz, *Madregat haAdam beTikun haMiddot*, 57.

52. Nekritz, "Yeshivot," 273; Schwartzbord, *BaKodesh*, 227; Ben-Artzi, *Shivti*, 21. For details of this yearly calendar, see Klibansky, "HaYeshivot," 240–41. "Trust without making efforts": trust in aid from above without any need for human action. "Relinquishing ownership": relinquishing ownership of any personal property.

53. Nekritz, "Yeshivot," 273. See also Ben-Artzi, *Shivti*, 11–28; Levin, *Novarodok*, 17; Weintraub, *BeSufa*, 176.

54. These *ḥaburot* were immortalized in the novels of Shmuel Ben-Artzi (1915–2011; Ben-Artzi, *Shivti*, 50–59) and Ḥayim Grade (1910–1982; Grade, *The Yeshiva*, 251–65).

55. Ben-Artzi, *Shivti*, 21–22. See also Nekritz, "Yeshivot," 272; Zilberg "Kat," I; testimony: Ben-Artzi; Levin, *Novarodok*, 39; Fishman, "Musar and Modernity," 48. Cf. Leshovitz, *Volkovisk*, 62; Ba'al-Maḥshavot. "Grobin," 89.

56. Ben-Artzi, *Shivti*, 75; Nekritz, "Yeshivot," 272–73; Levin, *Novarodok*, 15, 39–40; Weintraub, *BeSufa*, 170–71; Gelbstein, "HaMishna," 135. Cf. Hurwitz, *Madregat haAdam beTikun haMiddot*, 56–57.

57. Katz, *Tenuat*, III, 122–23.

58. Brown, "Gadlut," 253–63; Tikochinski, *Lamdanut*, 113–18.

59. Zilberg "Kat," I.

60. Tikochinski, *Lamdanut*, 123–24. See also Alon, "Yeshivot," 7.

5

Leadership

The yeshivas achieved their renown in the interwar period due more to the two principal figures who led them, the rosh-yeshiva and mashgiaḥ, than for any other reason. Since the nineteenth century, the status of the rosh-yeshiva had gained strength thanks to the yeshiva's new model. According to this version, the yeshiva, which was supported by the Jews of the Pale of Settlement, drew its power from that community. The rosh-yeshiva was no longer just an instructor of a group of young men who received his salary from the local community and was dependent upon its opinion. Besides his traditional role in the yeshiva—delivering regular Talmud lectures, guiding his pupils in how to approach sugyot, and preparing them to become scholars—he was often regarded as a communal leader in the cultural milieu of Lithuanian Jewry. His involvement in central issues that concerned this Jewish public promoted the yeshiva's reputation and added to its renown, and this fame naturally attracted more students. Because not all of the students were well-off, the yeshiva was required to assist in their support, and as a result its expenses grew. As an institution that was maintained by contributions and lacked its own independent financial resources, it was natural that the rosh-yeshiva would assume the task of securing income and in this way be responsible for all of the yeshiva's contact with the outside world, which was for the most part related to funds and donations. These dealings and the expansion of the yeshiva forced him to appoint Talmud lecturers whose work was to deliver classes to the talmidim and lighten the burden of teaching. Alongside him, a supervisor was responsible for administration. He was in charge of discipline regarding prayer and sedarim, tested the level of new talmidim, and took care of their basic needs, such as their seats in the study hall and their lodging.

From the time that the Musar system penetrated the yeshivas, the Musar-mashgiaḥ became part of the administration staff as well. It was not simple for this supervisor to exert his authority over the students, and in quite a few yeshivas they created unrest in an attempt to restore the previous situation. Only in the years preceding the First World War did the position of the Musar-mashgiaḥ become established in the majority of the yeshivas.

In the interwar period, when the Musar approach had become an integral part of the study program in the Lithuanian yeshiva, the status of the Musar-mashgiaḥ also became stronger, alongside that of the rosh-yeshiva. One of the graduates of a Lithuanian yeshiva defined the division of labor between the two: "the rosh-yeshiva straightens minds and the mashgiaḥ straightens hearts."[1] Indeed, besides delivering weekly Musar talks to the talmidim, the Musar supervisor was the authority in everything relating to the inner world of the yeshiva, from determining its spiritual character to providing individual attention to each of its charges. His status was even comparable to that of the rosh-yeshiva in a certain sense, and sometimes it was he who became the very symbol of his yeshiva.

The individuals who were appointed to yeshiva positions and the criteria for their selection are the subject of this chapter. Attention will be paid to the complex factors behind their appointment to these positions in several of the yeshivas in the interwar period.

ROSHEI-YESHIVA AND THEIR APPOINTMENT

The rosh-yeshiva filled various roles in his institution, from giving weekly lectures to providing material support for each of his charges. Necessity often forced him to dedicate a significant portion of his time to the yeshiva's upkeep and solving its urgent financial problems rather than delving deeply into Talmudic issues in preparation for his lectures. But presenting his role in this way somewhat diminishes his true image, which was above all completely identified with his yeshiva. The yeshiva was named after him; he served as its sole representative internally and externally, and his standing at the head of the school was a lifetime position. This absolute confluence between the yeshiva and its head was not automatic, nor was it created in a day.[2]

According to the yeshiva tradition, when Rabbi Ḥayim of Volozhin laid the cornerstone of his yeshiva, he declared that through this action, his son Yitzḥak would be established in the new building. Indeed, Rabbi Ḥayim linked his son to the Volozhin Yeshiva, and the appointment of the son as its head when his father died in 1821 determined the familial character of its administration. After Rabbi Yitzḥak (1780–1849), his sons-in-law Rabbis Eliezer-Yitzḥak Fried (1809–1853) and Naftali-Zvi-Yehudah Berlin (known as *Netziv*; 1817–1893) stood successively at the head of the yeshiva. During the lengthy tenure of the Netziv, Talmud instructors who were members of his family were appointed, including his son-in-law Rabbi Raphael Shapiro (1837–1921), his granddaughter's husband Rabbi Ḥayim Soloveitchik, and his son Rabbi Ḥayim Berlin (1832–1912). The Jewish community accepted this customary nepotism within the yeshiva without protest. It was a number of members of the family of its founder who objected to particular appointments, which they demanded for themselves. Several famous figures were involved in these divisive steps, such as the charismatic Rabbi Yehoshua-Heschel Levin (1814/8–1883) and the sharp-witted Rabbi Yosef-Ber Soloveitchik (1820–1892), who saw themselves as worthy and deserving of the desired position. In the end, their hopes were not realized, and the position of rosh-yeshiva was exclusively passed down to either sons or sons-in-law.[3]

Passionate disagreements like this also took place in yeshivas beyond Volozhin. There was a struggle in the veteran Mir Yeshiva as well, after the death of its founders, Rabbis Shmuel Tiktinsky and his son Avraham, in 1835. These departures created a vacuum in the yeshiva's leadership. Another son of Rabbi Shmuel Tiktinsky, Ḥayim-Leib (1823–1899), was a young lad at the time and not fit to fill a position in the yeshiva. Therefore a temporary change was made in its familial administration, and the town rabbi of Mir, Yosef-David Eisenstadt (1767–1846), was appointed as rosh-yeshiva. This appointment contained the seeds of dissension that were to sprout in the next generation. Rabbi Eisenstadt shared the administration of the yeshiva with his son Moshe-Avraham. The son continued in this position after the death of his father and at the same time served as town rabbi. The difficulty in simultaneously serving in these two positions caused him to invite the now adult Ḥayim-Leib Tiktinsky in 1850 to serve as deputy rosh-yeshiva and administrator of the Mir Yeshiva. His appointment led to direct conflict between those who claimed ownership of the yeshiva, because several Eisenstadt family members were wary of providing a descendant of the yeshiva's founder with a foothold in the institution. The dispute eventually subsided, but tensions continued to rumble under the surface. They burst forth even more vigorously after the death of Rabbi Moshe-Avraham Eisenstadt in 1867. His position as town rabbi of Mir was passed on to his son-in-law, Ḥayim-Zalman Bressler, who also openly claimed his right to the yeshiva. This harsh disagreement ceased only when the beit-din, constituted of Torah authorities of that generation, categorically ruled to totally separate the rabbinate of Mir from the yeshiva located in the town. From that point on, Rabbi Ḥayim-Leib Tiktinsky was the head of the yeshiva and its administrator.[4]

This principle of inheriting leadership positions accepted in the supra-community yeshivas of Volozhin and Mir that became well-known to Jewish public due to the strident conflicts within them was also copied by the newer yeshivas. The principle itself was neither new nor unusual; this was customary at the end of the nineteenth century in the communities of the Pale of Settlement regarding the positions of rabbis and dayyanim. Its acceptance in the yeshivas was quite natural because the yeshiva was not dependent on a specific community that it served but rather on *Klal-Yisrael*—the entire Jewish world—that supported it, and it was the sole fruit of the labors of its head, who was required to be devoted to it, body and soul, in order to maintain it. He was justifiably considered the yeshiva's true owner, and with this authority he passed it down to his descendants, whom he trusted to continue his lifework. The capability of handing the yeshiva down not only to sons but also to sons-in-law allowed him great flexibility in choosing his future heir. It would have been difficult to ensure that his sons would achieve the appropriate level of scholarship needed to head his yeshiva. It was simpler and easier to choose a son-in-law from among his outstanding students. Indeed, most of the Lithuanian supracommunity yeshivas were family run, and the administrational positions were passed down from father to son-in-law or son.[5]

Hereditary Positions

During the First World War, the practice of passing down positions became especially pronounced in the Lithuanian yeshivas. The Mir Yeshiva moved to Poltava with Rabbi Eliezer-Yehudah Finkel at its head after his father-in-law, Rabbi Eliyahu-Baruch Kamai, decided to remain in Mir with his community. The Lomzhe Yeshiva was handed over to Rabbi Yeḥiel-Mordechai Gordon when his father-in-law, Rabbi Eliezer Shulevitz, went into exile in Ukraine with his older students. This practice did not change in the interwar period.

Moreover, the principle of inherited positions did not only apply to the position of the rosh-yeshiva. It was practiced regarding other teaching positions, and they were handed down to sons or sons-in-law as well. The position of Rabbi Baruch Hurwitz, a Talmud instructor in Slabodka, was handed down to his son Shraga-Faivel (1902–1941) in 1936; the position of Rabbi Ḥayim Rabinowitz (1860–1930), the senior Talmud instructor of the Telz Yeshiva, was inherited by his gifted son Azriel (1905–1941) in 1931.

This last appointment was not free of tension. The members of the Bloch family, the owners of the yeshiva, did not want to leave this position in the hands of the Rabinowitz family, and it was only the intervention of the rabbi of Kovna, Rabbi Avraham-Duber Shapiro, that forced them to accept the appointment of the young Talmud instructor. Indeed, he was pushed aside to a degree by the family-run administration and did not achieve the status that many of the yeshiva's students thought fitting for a Torah scholar of his stature.[6]

In Lomzhe as well, the principle of inheritance was not simple. When one of its Talmud instructors, Rabbi Yisrael-Leib Egulsky (1850–1935), became frail, the claim to his position in the administration was passed on to Moshe Schwartz, son of the yeshiva's founder; he promised the appointment as a dowry to the one who would marry his daughter. It is not clear whether this occurred due to the inappropriateness of the heirs of Rabbi Egulsky for the position of Talmud instructor, or whether the family of the founder wanted to keep external forces out of the yeshiva. In the end, this matter was put in order in a proper manner: Eliezer, Rabbi Egulsky's son, married another daughter of Moshe Schwartz and was appointed as the yeshiva's administrational supervisor.[7]

There was an additional peculiar instance of hereditary appointment in the Lomzhe Yeshiva that related to the mashgiaḥ Rabbi Moshe Rosenstein (1881–1941). The single position in the yeshivas that was not subject to hereditary claims was that of the Musar-mashgiaḥ. However, this practice would not be put into effect when Leib Pruskin was chosen to be the son-in-law of Rabbi Rosenstein. Although he was not appointed as mashgiaḥ in the yeshiva after his marriage, he was promoted to the honored position of Talmud instructor. It may be that he deserved this privilege by virtue of another claim: in his early years in Lomzhe, Rabbi Rosenstein served as a Talmud instructor as well as mashgiaḥ. Did the family of the yeshiva's founder maintain his claim on the position of Talmud instructor, or was it perhaps the friendly relationship between them that awarded his son-in-law with the honored position? There is no definite answer.[8]

The aforementioned instances show that the principle of inheritance was clearly in force only in reference to the appointment of the rosh-yeshiva and not with positions assumed by individuals who were not members of the founder's family. Hereditary claims were recognized to a degree regarding these positions, but appointments were made according to the considerations of the rosh-yeshiva or with his approval.

Hereditary appointments did not apply to all Lithuanian yeshivas. It is clear that the three Hasidic Lithuanian yeshivas were under the aegis of their admorim and in their absolute possession, and the Lithuanian Torah scholars who were chosen to head them were hired as employees. Hereditary positions were not the practice in a number of veteran yeshivas, such as Slonim, Remayle, and Brisk. The common denominator of the three was that they were sponsored by the local community. In the veteran Slonim Yeshiva, seven roshei-yeshiva served throughout its years of existence, and not one of them was a direct relative of his predecessors. They were all appointed by gaba'im from Slonim, for whom the principle of inherited positions was not decisive. The situation was quite similar in Remayle, a community yeshiva in Vilna, whose heads were also selected by gaba'im. When Rabbi Ḥayim-Ozer Grodzensky was appointed in 1887 as one of the halachic authorities in the city, a position he inherited from his father-in-law Rabbi Eliyahu-Eliezer Grodnensky (1831–1887), he became the yeshiva's patron. After World War I he searched out "attractive" candidates, and appointed a number of considerable Torah scholars who had no family connections with those who formerly occupied the position to serve as rosh-yeshiva successively.[9]

It is appropriate to examine the case of Brisk. The local yeshiva was established by the rabbi of the town, Rabbi Ḥayim Soloveitchik, and it was he who appointed Rabbi Moshe Sokolovsky as its head. In August 1915, the yeshiva was dissolved due to a decree that expelled the town's Jews. After the First World War, Rabbi Sokolovsky returned to Brisk and reestablished the yeshiva. From that point on, it was apparently owned by him. However, in practice it was still somewhat connected to officials in the town. The rabbi of Brisk, Rabbi Yitzḥak-Ze'ev Soloveitchik, sometimes helped maintain the yeshiva's upkeep and was a scholarly authority there. Each day he went into the yeshiva during his walk, and the students raised Talmudic questions before him and visited his home to hear him expound his teachings. Rabbi Simḥa-Zelig Rigger (1864–1942), the first halachic authority of the town, also had a connection with the yeshiva, and he ordained its students who wished to become rabbis.[10]

In the beginning of 1931, Rabbi Sokolovsky died without issue. A search began in Brisk for an appropriate candidate for the vacant position. The authority to appoint a successor was in the hands of the town rabbi, and not a few individuals contacted him and presented their candidacy. Apparently the decision was complicated because a great deal of time passed from the death of the rosh-yeshiva until the appointment in 1932 of Rabbi Yisrael-Ḥayim Kaplan (1891–1970), the son-in-law of Rabbi Yeruḥam Levovitz of Mir and the brother of the mashgiaḥ of Radin, Rabbi Eliezer-Ze'ev Kaplan. Even though all the matters concerning the yeshiva required the consent of the new rosh-yeshiva, Rabbi Soloveitchik stood in the background of its activities, and his name appeared on its letterhead beside that of Rabbi Kaplan.[11]

In actuality, it is difficult to define the case of Brisk regarding hereditary positions because Rabbi Sokolovsky had no heirs, and thus it is impossible to know the extent of his ownership of the yeshiva. But due to the situation that resulted upon his death, it was ruled over by the rabbi of Brisk, and therefore there was no further possibility of a hereditary position.

Struggles

As was already stated, not all the appointments in the yeshivas were accepted without controversy or dispute. Even during the interwar period, objections were raised to a number of problematic appointments from two directions:

- By talmidim: They thought that some of those who had been selected were unfit for their positions and did not bring honor to the yeshiva, and they expressed their opinion through protest
- By possible heirs: They saw themselves as deserving of a particular position in a yeshiva by virtue of inheritance from their father or father-in-law

Opposition by Talmidim

One of the more formidable obstacles that faced a rosh-yeshiva regarding the appointments he made in his institution was the opposition on the part of his students. An outstanding instance of this was the choice of Rabbi Ḥayim Berlin as a Talmud instructor in Volozhin, an appointment that was quite memorable among yeshiva graduates at the end of the nineteenth century. The Netziv had difficulty in fulfilling his responsibilities due to his advanced age. He wished to choose an heir and found this son to be a fitting candidate, but his students had their own opinions and thought otherwise. They exerted pressure, demonstrated against the appointment, and even showed disrespect toward the Netziv and his son. These rebellious actions were, in the end, one of the main factors in closing the yeshiva in 1892.[12]

But it was not only in Volozhin that students asserted themselves. The talmidim of Telz also acted in this way when a new Talmud instructor was needed there. Rabbi Eliezer Gordon wished to appoint his son-in-law Yitzḥak-Eliezer Hirschowitz to this position. Fierce opposition to the appointment did not deter him, and in the winter semester of 1904–1905 he carried out his plan. The fires of rebellion were ignited in the yeshiva. This violent opposition reflected the revolutionary tides washing over the Jewish community at the time, but there was also an element there in the forceful demand of the students to maintain the quality of their school, similar to the case of Volozhin. When studies were renewed after a short time, Rabbi Hirschowitz gave up his position.[13]

The tradition of rebellion in Telz did not fade even after the First World War. In 1921 Rabbi Yosef-Leib Bloch appointed his son Avraham-Yitzḥak to the position of Talmud instructor. This choice was not viewed favorably by the talmidim who were older than he was, but their reaction did not go beyond quiet grumbling. In 1927 the rosh-yeshiva went further and chose his eldest son, Zalman (1886–1941), as Musar-mashgiaḥ—an appointment that was accepted by the students without opposition. But when one year later he appointed his third son, Eliyahu-Meir (1894–1955), as Talmud instructor, the talmidim erupted. This son had decided to work in the textile trade in Memel (Klaipėda) after his marriage and had left the yeshiva. He did not consider returning, but his father insisted that he hold a position there. It was difficult for the talmidim to respect a Talmud instructor who had forsaken the world of Torah and gone into business, and the older students began to incite the others against the appointment. The struggle went on a long time until Rabbi Yosef-Leib Bloch decided to close the yeshiva. The students did not give up and went to study in the town's beit-midrash, and the older ones transferred to the yeshivas in Ponevezh and Kelm. The sides finally arrived at a compromise, but the bitterness regarding the appointment remained in Telz for many years more. The talmidim did not respect Rabbi Eliyahu-Meir Bloch, and many did not even stand up in his honor.[14]

Such stubborn opposition on the part of students was unknown in other yeshivas. At the very most, the talmidim expressed their indignation at the appointment of Talmud instructors who were their own age or slightly older. In Slabodka, displeasure was felt when Rabbi Yitzḥak-Isaac Sher appointed his son-in-law Mordechai "Tiktiner" Shulman as Talmud instructor in 1935. He was a senior student in the yeshiva, and after his marriage in 1929, he dedicated all his time to Talmud study. But when he began to deliver his lectures in the yeshiva, its veteran and strong-minded talmidim considered it below their dignity to participate, and only a few students attended the initial lectures.[15]

Let it be noted that it was not the lack of charisma or rhetorical abilities that spurred the aforementioned protests, but the students' assessment that the new appointments did not possess sufficient Talmudical ability. In contrast with this, there were no complaints regarding the appointment of figures considered great scholars of Torah. Rabbi Raphael Shapiro, for example, who was known as "the silent one" by virtue of his habit of speaking little, was appointed as Talmud instructor in Volozhin in 1870 with no contest. Moreover, he became rosh-yeshiva in 1899 there without any dissension on the part of the students.[16]

Discord in the Administration

During the interwar period, adversity affected two yeshivas, Slabodka and Radin, when fierce personal quarrels broke out in their administrations. Unlike the extensive involvement of talmidim in the passionate struggles that took place in the Volozhin yeshiva in the nineteenth century on the part of claimants to the sought-after position of rosh-yeshiva, the students' role was peripheral in these new disputes. In any case, they were influenced by the negative atmosphere created by the warring factions, which was sometimes expressed by spreading nasty rumors among the baḥurim and mutual accusations.

DISCORD IN SLABODKA

The efforts of Rabbi Moshe-Mordechai Epstein to establish a branch of the Knesset-Yisrael Yeshiva in Hebron and to provide for its upkeep and expansion necessitated his protracted absence from Slabodka. This created a complex situation in the mother institution, and in the course of time, a great clash even developed there, with his son-in-law Yosef Zusmanovitch, the "Jerusalemite," at its center.

Yosef Zusmanovitch was born in Jerusalem and studied in the local Etz-Ḥayim Yeshiva. His outstanding talents quickly came to the fore and these brought him to the famous Lithuanian yeshivas. In 1921 Rabbi Moshe-Mordechai Epstein met him and immediately recognized his exceptional ability. He convinced the young man to study in Knesset-Yisrael and that very year selected him as a bridegroom for his daughter.[17]

At that time, Rabbi Epstein planned to make aliyah to the Land of Israel with a group of his students, but the yeshiva's debts forced him to first solve its irksome problems by means of a fundraising trip to the United States. Military conscription to the Lithuanian army for older yeshiva students influenced his plan and pushed him to set up a branch of the yeshiva in Hebron. He planned to include his two older sons-in-law,

Rabbis Yeḥezkel Sarna and Moshe Finkel, in its administration, and he soon came to the conclusion that his younger son-in-law, Yosef Zusmanovitch, was the most fitting candidate to serve as his heir in the Knesset-Yisrael Yeshiva and as rabbi of Slabodka. After remaining for quite some time in the United States and leaving at the end of 1924 to go to Hebron, Rabbi Epstein decided to stop in his home and stay there for a short time. One can assume that this visit was connected to establishing his son-in-law's role in the yeshiva and the town rabbinate—two positions that had been intertwined for many years. Indeed, from that time Rabbi Zusmanovitch unofficially took his father-in-law's place as rabbi, and at the same time he began to deliver lectures in Knesset-Yisrael.[18]

From his debut in the yeshiva, the Jerusalemite, whose position was that the curriculum should be exclusively dedicated to Talmud study, was not in favor of Musar studies, and he even demonstrated a lack of respect for its young advocates, Rabbis Yitzḥak-Isaac Sher and Avraham Grodzensky. The seeds of discord had already sprouted between these rabbis and the Jerusalemite in those early days. It is logical to assume that the tension rose and even became outwardly visible when the founder of the yeshiva, Rabbi Notte-Hirsch Finkel, left for Hebron in summer 1925. The question of who would stand at its head hovered in the halls of the yeshiva: Rabbi Yitzḥak-Isaac Sher (Rabbi Finkel's son-in-law) or the Jerusalemite (son-in-law of Rabbi Moshe-Mordechai Epstein). I have no explicit reference on the part of these two senior figures regarding the proper heir. However, Rabbi Epstein's sudden return from Hebron to Slabodka at the end of the summer of 1925, which might have strengthened the status of his son-in-law, indicates more than anything else his position on this matter.[19]

The positions of the candidates themselves were clear: the Jerusalemite saw himself as the direct and natural heir of the rosh-yeshiva and its administrator, Rabbi Epstein. He was obliged to state his opinion publicly within a few years in an exceptional act when he published a pamphlet *The Law of Inherited Position,* in which he accused his rival of trespass. Rabbi Sher saw things differently—beyond his manifest right to inherit the position of his father-in-law, the founder of the yeshiva and its owner, he was already a senior Talmud instructor, headed the Beit-Yisrael Kollel attached to the yeshiva, and had even begun to serve as the unofficial director of the yeshiva in Lithuania, at least. Therefore his position and that of the other members of the administration was clear: he should stand at the head of the yeshiva. The administrators' position received additional support from the reservations of the Jerusalemite toward Musar study, which was considered the guiding light of the yeshiva, and his young age, which was the same as that of a number of the students and members of the kollel. The result was internal strife in Knesset-Yisrael.[20]

The talmidim themselves had an opinion on the issue as well. The genius of the Jerusalemite attracted quite a few talented young men (at the same time Rabbi Sher's presence was almost not felt in the yeshiva due to his many activities on its behalf and his frequently refraining from delivering lectures). In the opposing group were students who were faithful to their rabbis and the Musar approach and were not willing to deviate from the traditional ways of their Torah institution, even at the price of losing a brilliant rosh-yeshiva. As a result, division, or even a rift, developed from 1925 among the baḥurim, especially the senior ones, who hunkered down in their principled and opposing positions.

Rabbi Yeḥezkel Sarna decided to attempt to resolve the quarrel or at least cool it down, and he arrived in Slabodka from Hebron. When he came to the yeshiva, he found it afire with contention. He saw that he could exert no influence there, so he turned around and made the long journey back to Hebron. Some of the emotions felt in those tense times were expressed by the words of one of the senior talmidim, Shim'on-Shlomo Fenzter: "I call these events here a tragedy, since because of them the honor of Torah, its great ones and its students has been desecrated. If each one [of the talmidim] would only look at himself through the same lens that he looks at others—we would have not come to this."[21]

However, the dispute was not accompanied by loud upheaval, which often occurred in the yeshiva at the end of the nineteenth century and the beginning of the twentieth century. Many of the students, especially the young ones, were not actively involved, and perhaps they were not even completely aware of its severity because the controversy took place mainly below the surface.[22]

Apparently, all this was like nothing compared to the harsh events that occurred afterward. At the end of the summer of 1927, Rabbi Epstein came back to Slabodka after another long visit in the United States. This time he stayed in order to deal with the ongoing problems of the yeshiva and the community. It was not long before he was involved in a direct collision with the other members of the administration in the beginning of the winter semester. This was not about the position of the Jerusalemite, so one can assume that the struggle was over a more serious and distressing issue: the yeshiva's financial resources and the "competition" over them on the part of the Hebron branch.

The establishment of that branch led to the diversion of significant donations from those who had traditionally contributed to the Slabodka Yeshiva. Moreover, other donors did not distinguish between the two yeshivas, which shared the same name, and felt that contributing to one of them was sufficient to fulfill their obligation and ease their conscience. In addition, during his long voyages to America, Rabbi Epstein focused most of his efforts toward raising funds for the Hebron branch, and the yeshiva in Slabodka continued to suffer from a large deficit. In 1928 the deficit swelled to the huge sum of forty thousand dollars and brought the yeshiva to the brink of financial bankruptcy. As a first step toward escaping this economic quagmire, the administration demanded that Rabbi Epstein change the name of the Hebron branch and separate it from Knesset-Yisrael in Slabodka. This requirement clearly forced Rabbi Epstein to choose only one of the yeshivas as his own. It should be noted that the students took the part of Rabbi Epstein.[23]

Whether or not this disagreement influenced Rabbi Epstein's actions, he left for Hebron at the end of 1927, and on the Passover after his departure, he decided to resign from his positions in Slabodka. He informed the yeshiva of his decision in a letter and requested to be told who would serve as its head, so that he could update the yeshiva's friends and supporters about the changes. This letter surprised everyone concerned in the administration and amongst the students, because Rabbi Epstein had in effect relinquished the right of the Jerusalemite to the position of Talmud instructor. But he decided to retain for his son-in-law the last stronghold: the rabbinate of Slabodka. To that end, he wrote another letter to the members of the community where he made his opinion clear regarding the filling of that position.

As soon as the letter of resignation arrived, the administration immediately appointed Rabbi Yitzḥak-Isaac Sher as official rosh-yeshiva, and from that point onward the position was his without challenge. There was no apparent reason to continue the impassioned struggle. But matters were otherwise.[24]

As if on its own, dissension arose on the municipal front, and with good reason. For the past twenty years, the Slabodka rabbinate had been linked to and identified with the yeshiva, and the administration was convinced that the one who occupied the community rabbinical position would in the end also demand to be the head of the yeshiva. Therefore, they could not allow the Jerusalemite to receive this position, and they claimed that it was essential that the rabbi of Slabodka be a recognized rabbinical figure in the Orthodox world who would be able to attract donors to the yeshiva and save it from its heavy debts. They even presented names of famous rabbis who fit the "job description"—the well-known rabbi of the Hasidic community of Dvinsk, Yosef "Rogatchover" Rosen (1858–1936), and the rabbi of Lomzhe who was considered one of the greats of the Musar movement at the time, Aharon Baksht.[25]

The events occurred very quickly. When the differences of opinion arose regarding the issue of the rabbinical position, a meeting was immediately convened on April 29, 1928, in the New Kloyz in Slabodka. It was decided to set up a committee of one hundred people whose members would be democratically elected among the representatives of the Slabodka batei-midrash within a week. Their task would be to choose an appropriate candidate for the community's rabbinate. After the committee was elected, the yeshiva presented it with a proper list of candidates, and in addition to the two aforementioned names who were at the top of this list, it was graced by other notable and respected rabbis. Rabbi Epstein did not remain inactive and sent letters to the committee requesting its support for his son-in-law's candidacy.

The committee was not successful in choosing a candidate who was accepted by the majority of its members. The yeshiva administration therefore decided to choose on its own a rabbi for Slabodka. The individual chosen was Rabbi Zalman Osovsky (1883–1941), one of the senior members of the kollel attached to the yeshiva, and the letter of rabbinical appointment was signed by the yeshiva administrators and members of the kollel. When the opponents of this move saw this, they declared that the Slabodka rabbinate belonged to Rabbi Epstein's substitute, the Jerusalemite. The way to bitter dissension within the community was short.[26]

The sharp dispute was accompanied by a deep rift among the Slabodka residents, the establishment of a yeshiva competing with Knesset-Yisrael, and eventually a stormy election campaign for the suburb's rabbinate. Even after the Jerusalemite was officially chosen and granted government recognition as the rabbi of Slabodka, the members of the yeshiva community did not avail themselves of his halachic rulings; rather, they turned to Rabbi Osovsky, who was officially nominated as community dayyan, for legal decisions. This division was obviously uncomfortable for Rabbi Zusmanovitch, who had been completely distanced from the local circles of scholars. In the end, he could see no way other than to find a fitting rabbinical position elsewhere.[27]

At that time, the position of rabbi of Vilkomir became vacant. Because the Jerusalemite possessed excellent public speaking skills, he made a good impression on its residents and won the position. When he left Slabodka in 1937, the bitter, decade-long disagreement came to an end. At the center of this dispute stood the principle of inherited positions in the Slabodka Yeshiva, in which problematic aspects of relationships within its administration and even among its students found their expression.[28]

DISPUTE IN RADIN

The Radin Yeshiva was founded in 1869 by the Ḥafetz-Ḥayim, and in its early years it had the atmosphere of a study kibbutz. This character of the yeshiva underwent a change after the avrech Hirsch Levinson, who became the founder's son-in-law in 1886, was appointed as its administrator. He aspired to refashion it after the Volozhin Yeshiva, where he had studied formerly, and make Radin into a supracommunity yeshiva. However, the fundamental change to this Talmudic institution occurred only in 1904, when the Ḥafetz-Ḥayim chose as its head a scholar from outside, Rabbi Naftali Trop. Rabbi Trop's lectures to the students introduced an entirely new spirit to Radin and achieved renown throughout all the Lithuanian yeshivas.[29]

Rabbi Naftali Trop's sudden death at the end of 1928 raised the issue of the appointment of a new rosh-yeshiva. The "crown" had claimants from among Rabbi Trop's heirs: his son, Avraham Trop (1896/7–1978), one of the prominent talmidim in the yeshiva, and his son-in-law, Baruch-Yosef Faivelzon (1896–1933), one of the former *illuyim* of Knesset-Yisrael of

Slabodka, who was still being supported financially by his father-in-law at the time. However, due to the fact that they were not among the founder's descendants, their hopes went unfulfilled. The Ḥafetz-Ḥayim handed over the position to his young son-in-law, Rabbi Mendel Zaks (1893–1974), who had officially served as Talmud instructor for the past three years.[30]

The Ḥafetz-Ḥayim agreed to pass on Rabbi Naftali Trop's right to teach to one heir only, and under his direction the administration decided to give the Trop family the privilege of choosing the preferred candidate. The family was not content with this decision and saw the refusal to appoint the two heirs as Talmud instructors as an infringement of its rights. When the yeshiva administration did not accede to its demands, the family decided on an extreme measure: to request a *din-Torah* (halachic adjudication of litigation) from Rabbi Ḥayim-Ozer Grodzensky. The Ḥafetz-Ḥayim clung to his decision and wrote to Rabbi Grodzensky about three months after the death of Rabbi Trop:

> I have already made my decision that we should provide a teaching position to one person from the family [of Rabbi Trop] and beyond [the demands of] the letter of the law, to give some financial compensation to the other. In my opinion we have fulfilled our legal and ethical obligation by this. Their refusal [and demand] that both of them should be—this is impossible, since it relates to the yeshiva's very survival. I am asking that you deal with this matter and arrange it for the good of the yeshiva. . . . If there be, Heaven forbid, a quarrel and division between the yeshiva administration and the other party, then all the obligations are cancelled.[31]

It is reasonable to assume that Rabbi Grodzensky ruled according to the opinion of the Ḥafetz-Ḥayim. The Trop family was obliged to name a single candidate. They chose Baruch-Yosef Faivelzon to serve as Talmud instructor alongside the new rosh-yeshiva, Rabbi Mendel Zaks. However, Avraham Trop did not let go of his dream to serve as head of the yeshiva in his father's place. As a temporary solution, he would go over his father's lectures in a side room, and many baḥurim who enjoyed the lectures of Rabbi Naftali Trop came to hear them from his son. It is possible that the position of the head of the yeshiva's kollel, which had become vacant after Rabbi Zaks began to present lectures in the yeshiva, was a substitute for the financial compensation offered by the Ḥafetz-Ḥayim.[32]

In 1932 Rabbi Baruch-Yosef Faivelzon felt unwell, but despite difficulties in delivering lectures, he continued to teach. Less than a year later, he was forced to go to Warsaw to seek out a cure for his illness; he did not return from there alive. Rabbi Avraham Trop was not given the full position of Talmud instructor in his brother-in-law's stead, perhaps because he was the cause of the din-Torah in 1929, and he lectured only to ḥaburot. This situation lit anew the fires of disagreement. Though they were not openly visible to all, they flickered under the surface for the coming years.[33]

In 1937 it seemed that the ongoing dispute was about to be solved, as the yeshiva director Rabbi Yehoshua Levinson (1881–1944/5) wrote in his letter of that year: "I find it proper to point out to your honors that despite differences among the administrators—which we have not unfortunately been worthy of uniting—in the yeshiva itself, praise God, there is no division, and on the contrary, the yeshiva has grown and become stronger recently in the most excellent way . . . we are ready to turn over our issue to the beit-din that will settle, with God's help, all the conflicts and their causes."[34] I do not have the result of the legal proceedings, if they ever took place. However, the disagreement continued as long as the yeshiva existed, and it left its mark upon the talmidim as well.[35]

* * *

Even though there was no connection between the quarrels about heading the yeshivas in Slabodka and Radin, there was a common denominator between the two that is not found among the other yeshivas. The position of rosh-yeshiva was turned over at a certain stage of their history to an individual outside the immediate family of the founder. Over time, this caused in both the yeshivas a lack of clarity regarding the rules of inheritance and acrimonious disputes. Despite their severity, they were exceptions to the rule that most of the appointments to positions in the Lithuanian yeshivas during the interwar period were accepted with understanding and without real opposition.

THE MASHGIḤIM

From the day that the study of Musar was instituted in the yeshivas, the Musar-mashgiaḥ became a decisive figure in determining their character.

There was good reason to refer to him as the "director," because he served as a type of minister of the interior alongside the rosh-yeshiva. He also dealt with every detail of the lives of the talmidim, knew their virtues and weaknesses, and tried to guide them every step of their way during their student years and sometimes even after.

Unlike the roshei-yeshiva and the Talmud instructors who were appointed to their positions based on family connections, the powerful position of mashgiaḥ was not hereditary. Indeed, it had a unique aspect not found in other positions. Brilliant sons or sons-in-law were selected for teaching positions, and their exceptional scholarship allowed them to deliver lectures to the talmidim without concern or fear despite their young age. Yehoshua-Isaac "Vilner" Kostyokovsky (1907–1941), for example, married the daughter of Rabbi Yeḥiel-Mordechai Gordon in 1935 and was immediately appointed as Talmud instructor in the Lomzhe Yeshiva.[36] There was good reason for this, because he had already gained renown as one of the greatest scholars in the yeshiva world. But it was not possible to act in this way when it came to a mashgiaḥ, who needed to be an experienced Musar personality. The mashgiaḥ was the one who upheld all the yeshiva students spiritually, and he was the key figure who was responsible for the yeshiva's success. It is obvious that young sons or sons-in-law were not fit for this position, even if they were talented. The mashgiaḥ was chosen from an entirely different pool of individuals.

The Origin of the Mashgiḥim

The modern and familiar figure of the mashgiaḥ sprung from the Slabodka Musar Yeshiva, founded by Rabbi Notte-Hirsch Finkel. At the beginning of his career, Rabbi Finkel was appointed administrational supervisor in the Ohr-haḤayim Yeshiva-ketana in Slabodka. Even though its founder and rosh-yeshiva, Rabbi Hirsch Levitan (1840–1915), took care of his students' sustenance and welfare from the very beginning, the newly arrived supervisor began to make new arrangements, as if the yeshiva belonged to him. He allocated a fixed salary for Rabbi Levitan and brought a new approach to the school's administration. He set up a yeshiva for continuing studies for its graduates in Slabodka, and there he was the sole decision-maker.[37]

Rabbi Finkel saw the inculcation of Musar in his students as his main task in the new yeshiva. At its inception the yeshiva had the appearance of a study kibbutz, and occasional Talmud instructors gave lectures there. But when Rabbi Finkel felt a need to change his yeshiva's character, he appointed permanent Talmud instructors, among them figures who were known as great Torah scholars, such as Rabbis Ḥayim Rabinowitz and Yitzḥak-Ya'akov Rabinowitz, and later he appointed talented avrechim Moshe-Mordechai Epstein and Isser-Zalman Meltzer. He himself generally remained behind the scenes in the yeshiva and showed his presence chiefly through his Musar talks. Despite this concealed status, Rabbi Finkel made all the decisions relating to the inner workings of the yeshiva, and when it was necessary, he did not hesitate in splitting it and establishing a separate Musar yeshiva in Slabodka, Knesset-Yisrael. Over the years he went further and appointed Rabbi Epstein to be responsible for all the exterior issues of the yeshiva. Nevertheless, Knesset-Yisrael, unlike most of the other yeshivas, remained under the total ownership of its Musar-mashgiaḥ.[38]

Rabbi Finkel developed his approach to Musar under Rabbi Simḥa-Zissel Broyde of Kelm, even though he differed with his rabbi regarding its implementation in practice. In his yeshiva in Slabodka, Rabbi Finkel developed the "man's greatness" approach and handed it down to his many students. He placed quite a few of them in the Lithuanian yeshivas, and through them he worked to include the study of Musar in these Talmudic institutions. Many came out against his disciples, but his stubbornness bore fruit, and most of the yeshivas eventually adopted his vision. In the interwar period, all the Lithuanian yeshivas became Musar yeshivas, and this phenomenon clearly bore the seal of Rabbi Finkel.

Prominent among his students who led the revolutions of the Musar studies in the yeshivas were those whose spiritual growth took place not just in Slabodka but also in the Kelm Yeshiva. Rabbi Finkel was not satisfied with a short course of study for them with his rabbi, as his select students did in Kelm every year during the month of Elul.[39] He sent them for an extended period of study in the Kelm Yeshiva in order to inculcate in them the foundations of Musar instruction required for their role in the future. Indeed, the Kelm Yeshiva became a principal source of Musar development, and there the personalities of most of the senior mashgiḥim of the Lithuanian yeshivas were formed; among these were Rabbis Yeruḥam Levovitz, Eliyahu Dushnitzer, Yosef-Leib Nenedik, and Moshe Rosenstein, who were mentioned in previous chapters.

During the interwar period, young mashgiḥim arose who had acquired the main part of their Musar education from a member of the first generation of mashgiḥim, Rabbi Yeruḥam Levovitz. These had been his students in Radin and Mir before the First World War, and among them were Rabbis Eliezer-Ze'ev Kaplan, Shlomo Harkavy, Shlomo Matus and Yeḥezkel Levenstein. He had sent some of them to the Kelm Yeshiva, and their studies there had been a fine Musar completion of the Kelm-style education that they had received from him. Among the young mashgiḥim were only a few individuals who were the exception to this pattern, such as Rabbi Avraham-Ya'akov Gordon, who received his entire training from the two Musar thinkers Rabbis Notte-Hirsch Finkel and Yosef-Yozel Hurwitz, or Rabbi Avraham Grodzensky, who was unique in that he was solely the educational product of Rabbi Finkel.[40]

The Novardok yeshivas, whose principal goal was implementing the unique Musar system of Rabbi Yosef-Yozel Hurwitz, also had a mashgiaḥ. Several of these yeshivas were headed by the disciples of Rabbi Hurwitz, and as a matter of course they were the ones who gave regular Musar talks. It would seem that in these institutions, the role of the mashgiḥim expressed itself through personal Musar guidance rather than through delivering general Musar talks.

Characteristics of the Role

The phenomenon of mashgiḥim coming to the yeshivas to put Musar teachings into practice began at the end of the nineteenth century. The pioneer among them was Rabbi Leib Ḥasman, a disciple of Rabbis Notte-Hirsch Finkel and Simḥa-Zissel Broyde. The Telz administration invited him to serve as mashgiaḥ in 1897, and he attempted to include the study of Musar in a yeshiva that was neither prepared nor willing for this.[41]

It is surprising that Knesset-Yisrael, which had been founded by the mashgiaḥ Rabbi Notte-Hirsch Finkel after his yeshiva split in 1897, was also in need of Musar counselors. The impressive growth in the number of its talmidim required special organization in order to attract new students to Musar teachings. To this end Rabbi Finkel appointed individuals whose task was to strengthen the baḥurim in Musar. The first, in 1900, was Rabbi Zalman "Radiner" Dolinsky (1870–1910), a disciple of the Kelm Yeshiva.[42]

The principal stage of the spread of Musar in the yeshivas began as a result of the agitation in the Jewish street in the revolutionary period of 1905. Roshei-yeshiva turned to Rabbi Finkel with requests for help running their yeshivas according to Musar teachings in their war against the rebels from within. Knesset-Yisrael became a fortress from where forces went out to fill the breach that had opened in other yeshivas. These forces consisted of groups of students headed by mashgiḥim. However, Rabbi Finkel not only reacted by providing mashgiḥim upon request but also initiated sending missions proactively to yeshivas, and his students served as soldiers with a directive to turn them into Musar yeshivas.

An examination of those various types of missions repeatedly shows the names of the same mashgiḥim, who sometimes appeared in one yeshiva only to later show up in another. Indeed, in the years before the First World War, mashgiḥim were itinerant, and they were considered Musar personalities who came to fill the role of strengthening and transforming yeshivas until their next spiritual mission. Unlike the roshei-yeshiva who were connected to their institutions, the mashgiḥim were seen as independent of any particular yeshiva, even according to the outlook of Rabbi Notte-Hirsch Finkel.[43]

In the interwar period, with the exception of those that were Hasidic, all the Lithuanian yeshivas became Musar yeshivas. Did the role of the mashgiaḥ remain itinerant? Mobility was still a characteristic of the mashgiḥim, and only a few remained in one place throughout this period. Among those who did were Rabbis Moshe Rosenstein, who served in his position in the Lomzhe Yeshiva from 1912; Naftali-Ze'ev Leibowitz, who was appointed as the mashgiaḥ of Knesset Beit-Yitzḥak while it was still in Krementchug; Eliezer-Ze'ev Kaplan, who began his career in Radin when the yeshiva returned there from its exile; Avraham Grodzensky, who replaced Rabbi Notte-Hirsch Finkel in Slabodka in 1925; and Rabbis Zalman Bloch and Avraham-Ya'akov Gordon, who were appointed in 1927 to the position of mashgiaḥ, with Rabbi Bloch in Telz and Rabbi Gordon in Brisk. Three of the aforementioned had family ties to the head of their yeshiva: Rabbi Naftali-Ze'ev Leibowitz, the brother-in-law of Rabbi

Baruch-Ber Leibowitz; Rabbi Eliezer-Ze'ev Kaplan, son-in-law of Rabbi Hirsch Levinson and the husband of the granddaughter of the Ḥafetz-Ḥayim; and Rabbi Zalman Bloch, the firstborn son of the rosh-yeshiva of Telz. The fact that they were related can explain why these particular mashgiḥim continued in their positions in their respective yeshivas. Rabbi Moshe Rosenstein had no family connection to the head of the Lomzhe Yeshiva, and it would seem that he continued there for a long period of time thanks to his excellent relationship with its leaders, as he himself wrote in his introduction to the first section of his book *Yesodei haDa'at* (*Foundations of Knowledge*): "I have served with them for twenty-three years . . . and all those years have been with love, friendship and faithfulness towards them, and I have not found any injustice towards me all those years."[44]

Among the individuals mentioned, Rabbi Avraham-Ya'akov Gordon was unique due to place where he served as mashgiaḥ. Brisk was different from its counterparts because its program did not include a daily Musar session until 1927. This was apparently due to the historical lack of encouragement given to Musar studies openly shown by its founder, Rabbi Ḥayim Soloveitchik. It was its rosh-yeshiva, Rabbi Moshe Sokolovsky, who made the decision to have it conform to the other Lithuanian yeshivas of the time and establish there the position of mashgiaḥ. Besides the interest of the manner of implementing Musar teachings in this "non-Musar" yeshiva, it would seem that the description of Rabbi Gordon's activities makes it possible to understand the spread of the power and influence of the Musar-mashgiḥim over their talmidim in particular and their yeshivas in general. A short time after Rabbi Gordon, a product of the Musar systems of Slabodka and Novardok, began his work as mashgiaḥ, a significant change occurred in the Brisk Yeshiva. One of the local Talmud-Torah students described the yeshiva: "I was accustomed to go every night for Musar study and evening prayers. When I was still hundreds of meters away from the yeshiva, I already heard the sound and voices of the enthusiastic study of Musar. From nine until nine-thirty they studied Musar, and from nine-thirty until ten there were evening prayers. . . . How wonderful was it to see how the fine young men poured out their hearts before God in prayer, with enthusiasm and great intent, and all this was only done by Musar."[45] The addition of Musar-sedarim in the yeshiva did not suffice for the new mashgiaḥ. He immediately introduced all the characteristics of a Musar yeshiva, starting with a Musar talk every Saturday night and ending with influencing the setup of Musar-ḥaburot. One might think that student opposition could be expected, as was common in other similar yeshivas in the past, among them Volozhin and Telz. It would seem that there was something in the personality of the mashgiaḥ, which softened the acquaintance with Musar teachings and even awakened enthusiasm and the desire to accept them with joy. One of the talmidim at that time wrote:

> When he arrived in the yeshiva, a new spirit spread over it. He initiated the study of Musar in a sublime fashion, and the pleasantness of his sayings and talks, filled with the knowledge and fear of God, profound and broadly encompassing the words of our sages, were like life-giving dew to the hearts of the talmidim. His influence grew until all were drawn towards him . . . His influence on the older students, with whom individually he would discuss [Torah matters] back and forth was exceptional, and everyone was amazed by his leadership. There were baḥurim in the yeshiva at the time who were like dry bones, and he brought them back to life.[46]

The revolution of the mashgiaḥ described here did not end with teaching Musar and instilling moral traits. Its results went as far as a significant influence on Talmudic study in the yeshiva. When he came to Brisk, Rabbi Gordon was surprised to find a yeshiva-gedola with outstanding scholars—a yeshiva with the ability to bring its students up to a high level. He therefore demanded that they increase their diligence and effort in their studies, obligated all of them to produce *ḥiddushim* (novel interpretations), and established review sessions within the ḥaburot for the lectures of Rabbi Moshe Sokolovsky. Clarifying the material studied led to greater alertness in the lectures of the rosh-yeshiva and to lively give-and-take about the Talmudic sugyot. The influence of this revolution in the yeshiva raised the prestige of its students, and in 1930 Rabbi Sokolovsky could already write to Rabbi Ḥayim-Ozer Grodzensky, "The talmidim of our yeshiva excel everywhere; they are among the most outstanding in the yeshivas. [Even] now, when they do not accept any new student—those who come from here are always accepted with open arms."[47]

With Rabbi Sokolovsky's sudden death in 1931, the burden of the yeshiva fell upon the rabbi of Brisk. However, he could not run it in practice, even temporarily, and it was the mashgiaḥ who carried out all the actual functions there. The real task that Rabbi Gordon took upon himself was saving the yeshiva from collapse. By the end of Rabbi Sokolovsky's tenure, when the yeshiva's financial situation was difficult, the worldwide economic depression came and totally dried up its financial resources. The death of the rosh-yeshiva, who had taken care of all its needs up until then, brought the yeshiva to the brink of danger to its very existence. There is no doubt that the unique personality of the mashgiaḥ allowed the yeshiva to survive under those conditions for so long. Perhaps the mashgiaḥ felt a lack of gratitude because of the new appointments there, but he did not shake off the yoke or complain to the newly chosen rosh-yeshiva, Rabbi Yisrael-Ḥayim Kaplan. Rabbi Gordon continued to act on behalf of the yeshiva and its talmidim as if, on his part, nothing at all had happened; neither did he see the need to change positions until the last of the yeshiva's days in Brisk.[48]

SUMMARY

One of the principal objectives of a rosh-yeshiva consisted of delivering Talmud lectures and educating his talmidim in the ways of research and novel interpretation. In the interwar period, this role was dwarfed by his other activities, which related especially to the material aspects of the yeshiva. In the absence of tuition fees, most of the yeshiva's income relied on donations; a significant part of its budget was set aside for its students' upkeep. The constant growth of the student body in the yeshivas continued to inflate their debts, and all the Torah institutions suffered from financial deficits. From an economic standpoint, the yeshiva was not a profitable enterprise but rather a material burden that forced its rosh-yeshiva to wander overseas and to other countries to bring home bread from afar.[49]

Despite the weightiness of this burden, no rosh-yeshiva ever relinquished his position. Beyond his ideological considerations that were expressed through spreading Torah or personal considerations relating to prestige, his complete identification with the yeshiva stood in the background of the decision not to resign. Because the yeshiva was entirely in his ownership, he felt absolute responsibility toward it, and this responsibility

Table 5.1. Roshei-yeshiva and Mashgiḥim in the interwar period

Yeshiva	Location	Characteristic	Rosh-yeshiva	Mashgiaḥ
Slabodka	Lithuania		Moshe-Mordechai Epstein (1900–1928)	Notte-Hirsch Finkel (1882–1925)
			Yitzḥak-Isaac Sher (1928–1939)	Avraham Grodzensky (1925–1941)
Telz	Lithuania		Yosef-Leib Bloch (1910–1929)	Zalman Bloch (1927–1941)
			Avraham-Yitzḥak Bloch (1929–1941)	
Ponevezh	Lithuania		Yosef-Shlomo Kahaneman (1919–1940)	Yosef-Leib Nenedik (1920–1922?)
				Yeruḥam Levovitz (1922?-1924)
				Asher-Kalman Baron (1924–1931)
				Moshe-Ber Zefatman (1932–1941)
Kelm	Lithuania		Reuven-Dov Desler (1918–1931)	
			Daniel Movshovitz (1931–1941)	
Mir	Poland (Kresy)		Eliezer-Yehuda Finkel (1916–1940)	Yisrael Shlamovitz (1921)
			Ḥayim Shmuelevitz (from 1941)	Yeḥezkel Levenstein (1921–1924)
				Yeruḥam Levovitz (1924–1936)
				Yeḥezkel Levenstein (from 1937)

Radin	Poland (Kresy)		Naftali Trop (1904–1928) Mendel Zaks (1928–1941)	Eliezer-Ze'ev Kaplan (1921–1941)
Knesset Beit-Yitzḥak (Kamenitz)	Poland (Kresy)		Baruch-Ber Leibowitz (1904–1939) Reuven Grozovsky (1939–1940)	Naftali-Ze'ev Leibowitz (1918?–1941)
Slutsk-Kletsk	Poland (Kresy)		Isser-Zalman Meltzer (1897–1925) Aharon Kotler (1925–1941)	Asher Sandomirsky (1916?-1923) Yeḥezkel Levenstein (1924–1935) Yosef-Leib Nenedik (1935–1941)
Ohr-Torah of Korets	Poland (Kresy)		Yoel Shorin (1899–1927) Baruch-Mordechai Riz (from 1927)	Pesaḥ Plotnick (from 1926?)
Grodno	Poland (Kresy)		Shim'on Shkop (1920–1939) Moshe Shatzkes (1940)	Yosef-Leib Nenedik (1916–1920) Zvi-Yehuda Olshwang (1921?–1922) Eliyahu Lopian (1922) Shlomo Harkavy (1922–1941)
Volozhin	Poland (Kresy)		Ya'akov Shapiro (1922–1936) Ḥayim Valkin (1936–1941)	Yitzḥak Weinstein (1925–1930) Avraham Varshavsky (1930–1932?)
Kobrin	Poland (Kresy)		Pesaḥ Pruskin (1923–1939)	Yosef-Leib Nenedik (1923–1935) Shlomo Matus (from 1935)

(*continued*)

Table 5.1. (*continued*)

Yeshiva	Location	Characteristic	Rosh-yeshiva	Mashgiaḥ
Ostroh	Poland (Kresy)		Yosef Berkovitz (1931–1941)	David Ḥazanovitch (from 1931)
Ohel-Torah Baranovitch	Poland (Kresy)		Elḥanan Wasserman (1920–1941)	Yisrael-Ya'akov Liubtchansky (from 1922?)
Slonim	Poland (Kresy)	Community yeshiva	Shabtai Yogel (1906–1941)	Yitzḥak Weinstein (1924?–1925) Avraham-Zvi Listovsky (1926–1941)
Brisk	Poland (Kresy)	Community yeshiva	Moshe Sokolovsky (1919–1931) Yisrael-Ḥayim Kaplan (1932–1941)	Avraham-Ya'akov Gordon (from 1927)
Remayle (Vilna)	Poland (Kresy)	Community yeshiva	Avraham-Zvi Grodzensky (1890–1921?) Moshe-Menaḥem Kozlovsky (1921?–1924) Shlomo Heiman (1927–1935) Yisrael Levovitz (1935–1941)	Avraham-Zvi Listovsky Yitzḥak Waldschein
Beit-Ulpena Bialystok	Poland (Kresy)	Community yeshiva	Elḥanan Ya'akobowitz (1917–1935) Ya'akov Stolar (1917–1939)	Elḥanan Ya'akobowitz (1917–1935)

Bialystok	Poland (Kresy)	Novardok yeshiva	Avraham Yoffen (1921–1941)	Yisrael Movshovitz
Mezritch	Poland (Kresy)	Novardok yeshiva	David Bliacher (1921–1943)	Shmuel Panitch
Pinsk	Poland (Kresy)	Novardok yeshiva	Shmuel Weintraub (1927–1941)	Yitzḥak Waldschein (1928–1935) Yeraḥmiel Shulman (from 1935)
Ludmir	Poland (Kresy)	Novardok yeshiva	Shraga-Ze'ev Maggid (1923–1941)	
Lutsk	Poland (Kresy)	Novardok yeshiva	Moshe Reiss (1928–1941)	Yitzḥak Waldschein (1928) Ya'akov Zeldin (from 1928)
Dvinsk	Latvia	Novardok yeshiva	David Budnick (from 1931/2)	
Warsaw	Poland (Kongresówka)	Novardok yeshiva	Avraham Zelmans (from 1922)	
Ostrov-Mazovietsk	Poland (Kongresówka)	Novardok yeshiva	Ya'akov Kleinerman	Aharon Ogulnik
Ostrovtsa	Poland (Kongresówka)	Novardok yeshiva	Mordechai Shim'onovitz (from 1925)	Yitzḥak Waldschein (from 1935)
Lomzhe	Poland (Kongresówka)		Eliezer Shulevitz (1883–1923) Yeḥiel-Mordechai Gordon (from 1923)	Moshe Rosenstein (1912–1941)
Torat-Ḥayim Warsaw	Poland (Kongresówka)		Yitzḥak-Ze'ev Soloveitchik (1918–1919) Hirsch Glickson (1919–1939)	

demanded that he send frequent letters to foundations, go on fundraising trips overseas, convince local suppliers to continue their activities with the yeshiva, engage in confrontations with his students after reducing their support, exercise total control over its administration, and even push away individuals from outside the family who claimed the "right" to receive teaching positions and hand them over to talented sons or sons-in-law. This total ownership was usually accepted with understanding in the yeshiva world, but its results, which also included personal insults, sometimes caused quarrels within the yeshivas, dissension among the talmidim, and even absence from lectures. Nevertheless, these reactions were moderate in comparison with the rebelliousness expressed in the yeshivas in the first decade of the twentieth century, which was nurtured primarily by radical activity outside of the yeshiva walls.

The Musar-mashgiaḥ had a decisive role in the yeshiva as well. In the beginning of the twentieth century, he was still occupied in strengthening and disseminating Musar teachings in the yeshivas, and his mobility amongst them was great. After the First World War, Musar was already institutionalized in the Lithuanian yeshiva. By means of his being in charge of its internal operation, in practice the mashgiaḥ determined its character. A student in the Mir Yeshiva expressed his feelings based on his own experience: "How great and lofty is the importance of the mashgiḥim in the yeshivas, even more than those who deliver lectures."[50]

Despite their influence, the Musar supervisors' position continued to be impermanent, and there were many transfers also in the interwar period, as can be seen in table 5.1.[51] The mashgiaḥ of Mir, Rabbi Yeruḥam Levovitz, explained his feelings in one of his talks:

> [When] something is my responsibility, I do not rest until it is completely put in order. Maintaining the yeshiva's program—as long as I am in my position, I feel that this is the most crucial obligation, to the point of self-sacrifice. If something improper occurs in the yeshiva, it deprives me of all my rest and I do not calm down until the wrong and deficiency have been removed. Many times have I checked myself and thought about what my situation would be if I would, if it could be imagined, leave the yeshiva today, would I not leave it all as it is? And then, I would not worry about the spiritual fate of the yeshiva any more. . . . As long as the responsibility rests on me I will fulfill it completely, and the moment that the responsibility is taken away from me, I will do nothing.[52]

These words are, in effect, an example of the ambivalent relationship of the Musar-mashgiaḥ to his role: he felt great responsibility for his yeshiva and saw the need to be involved in it in every matter, big and small. However, there was always a sense of impermanence hovering over this intensive activity. Even though his influence over the yeshiva was often even more decisive than that of the rosh-yeshiva or the other Talmud instructors, he did not have any prior claim or ownership over it. He did not make decisions regarding appointments to its faculty but merely offered his advice; neither could he pass down his position to his son or son-in-law. Because he did not have a tangible stake in the yeshiva, he could decide to leave it at any time and go to a more fitting Torah-study institution to actualize his abilities. This explains the itinerant nature of the role of the mashgiaḥ, which is clearly shown in table 5.1.

An examination of the fate of the yeshivas where the mashgiḥim did not have permanent tenure does not provide a uniform picture: a few experienced crises that led to their collapse, but there were others that were very successful. In any case, it is possible to state that the permanence of a mashgiaḥ in his yeshiva contributed a great deal to its inner stability and the solidarity of its students from a social, emotional, and spiritual standpoint; such a yeshiva that experienced economic or leadership crises was able to overcome them successfully or with minimal damage.

NOTES

1. Schwartzbord, *BaKodesh*, 67.

2. Cf. Balosher, *Ḥayim*, 27.

3. These struggles were described in detail in Karlinsky, *HaRishon*. See also Shapiro, *R' Moshe*, 209.

4. Klibansky, *KeTzur*, 64; Epstein, "Yeshivat Mir," 90–91; Sh-o, "God," 230–32; Mirsky, "MeArchiyono," 139; Zinowitz, *"Mir,"* 39.

5. Menes, "Patterns," 403; Katzenelson-Nochimov, *Yitzḥak Katzenelson*, 126; Stampfer, *Families*, 313–14. Cf. Rabinowitz-Teomim, Seder *Eliyahu*, 104; Stampfer, *Lithuanian*, 240; Assaf, *Derech*, 100–117.

6. Testimonies: Shurin, Kremerman, and Bronznik; Kaplan, "HaRav," 116.

7. Rosenstein, *Ahavat*, 269–70, 281; Rabinowitz, "Yeshivat," 223, 225; *DoV*, Dec. 15, 1933, Dec. 27, 1935.

8. Regarding this relationship, see later, by note 44. See also Rabinowitz, "Yeshivat," 222; Rosenstein, *Ahavat*, 265; *DoV*, Feb. 9, 1934.

9. Klibansky, "HaYeshivot," 305.

10. Meler, *HaRav*, II, 58–59; Stern, *Gedolei*, III, 1141; Klibansky, *KeTzur*, 83.

11. Postcards: Gordon to Berek, Oct. 30, 1932 (VHY/48), and Kaplan to Berek, Oct. 22, 1935 (VHY/47) and June 29, 1936 (VHY/48); table of yeshivas, winter 1931–1932 (VHY/1107); Meler, *HaRav*, II, 51; Meler, *Igrot*, 70; Shulzinger, *Peninei*, 226; Sasson, *Naḥalat*, 526–27.

12. Stampfer, *Lithuanian*, 22. See also memoirs of Don-Yiḥye, Balosher, Zlotkin, and Turberg (Etkes and Tikochinski, *Yeshivot Lita*).

13. Assaf, "Shenot," 39; Friedman, *Sefer haZichronot*, 109–10. See also Etkes, "Yeshivot Lita," 54.

14. Testimonies: Bronznik, Kremerman, Shurin, Karno, and Ben-Porat; *IdL*, June 19, 1923. See also Surasky, *HaRav miPonivezh*, I, 173; Shoshana, "HaYeshiva," 287–88.

15. Testimony: Kremer; Grossman, *Ki Im*, 40, 50. Cf. Farber, *Olkeniki*, 242–43; Buksboim, *Sefer*, 48; Meltzer, *BeDerech*, 194.

16. Zinowitz, *"Etz Ḥayim,"* 255; Shapiro, *R' Moshe*, 84–86.

17. Zeidman, "HaRav Yosef," 28–31 (who was inexact); Bialoblotsky, "Merkezey," 205; Zusman, *Kuntres*; Levinthal, *The World*, 18; *Sha'arei Tziyon* 2, no. 1–2 (1921): 1; testimony: "Man of Kovna."

18. Klibansky, "HaYeshivot," 309n66; Blau, *Learn Torah*, 23. See also chapter 2, note 67.

19. *Sha'arei Tziyon* 5, no. 8–12 (1925): 15 (2); Sarna, Transcription; testimony: "Man of Kovna." See also "Vemn geit ihr, Slabodker birger vayln far a Rov!" [Whom are you going to choose to be the rabbi, Slabodka residents!] (LJC/1393); Zeidman, "HaRav Yosef," 31, 33.

20. *DIdS*, May 1, 1928; Zeidman, "HaRav Yosef," 33; testimonies: "Man of Kovna" and Kremer; "Undzer vendung tzu ale undzere Slabodker valbarechtikte" [Our appeal to all our Slabodka-ites who have the right to vote] (LJC/1393); Zusmanovitch, *Kuntres Mishpat*; letter: Fenzter to Katz, July 8, 1928 (SEA).

21. Letter: Fenzter to Katz, July 8, 1928 (SEA). See Sarna, Transcription; testimony: Kremer; Zeidman, "HaRav Yosef," 34; Blau, *Learn Torah*, 23. Cf. Ezraḥi, *HaMashgi'aḥ*, 153–54. For the character of Fenzter, see Klibansky, "HaYeshivot," 311n80.

22. Testimony: Kremer; Zeidman, "HaRav Yosef," 33. Cf. Katz, *Tenuat*, III, 43; Dvoretz, *HaGaon*, 25, 33–34.

23. Letters: Fenzter to Katz, July 8, 1928, and Grodzensky to Finkel, July 31, 1925 (SEA); *DIdS*, May 13, 1928; Klibansky, "HaYeshivot," 312n89; *DIdS*, May 1, 1928; Epstein, *Levush*, II, 6.

24. Letter: Fenzter to Katz, July 8, 1928 (SEA); *DIdS*, May 1, 1928; Oshri, "Yeshivat," 160 (Oshri concealed the issue of the quarrel); *Sha'arei Tziyon* 8, no. 3–5 (1927–1928): 14 (2); Epstein, *Levush*, II, 6; "Vemn geit ihr, Slabodker birger vayln far a Rov!" (LJC/1393).

25. Letter: Fenzter to Katz, July 8, 1928 (SEA); *DIdS*, May 1, 1928; Klibansky, "HaYeshivot," 313n98; testimony: Kremer. See also Blau, *Learn Torah*, 23; Tory, Getto, 304.

26. "Tzu ale Slabodker Idn!" [To all the Jews of Slabodka!] (LJC/1393); letter: Fenzter to Katz, July 8, 1928 (SEA). See also *DIdS*, May 3, 8, 9, 30, 1928.

27. For more, see Klibansky, "BeMakom," 331–40.

28. Testimony: "Man of Kovna"; Rosenblum, *Reb Ya'akov*, 145; Zusmanovitch, *Teru'at Melech*, preface. See also Zeidman, "HaRav Yosef," 33; *Sha'arei Tziyon* 17, no. 1–5 (1936–1937): 47.

29. Klibansky, *KeTzur*, 58–59.

30. Yoshor, *HeḤafetz Ḥayim*, 743–44; Poupko, *Michtavei*, 258; autobiography of M. Senderovitch (AJYP-3796).

31. Zaks, *Michtavim*, 151.

32. The Yeshiva reports until Jan. 1, 1929 and the report, Dec, 17, 1930 (VHY/1148); Zariz, "Yeshivat," 204; Farber, *Olkeniki*, 242.

33. Zariz, "Yeshivat," 205, 207; *Sha'arei Tziyon* 13, no. 10–12 (1933): 44. Cf. Yoshor, *He-Ḥafetz Ḥayim*, 703.

34. Letter: Levinson to "Members of the distribution committee," May 9, 1937 (VHY/511).

35. Testimonies: "Man of Kovna" and Zuckerman (see the same: Vagshel, *Yaḥid*, 140–41). See also Grade, *The Yeshiva*, 12–13; Farber, *Olkeniki*, 248.

36. See *DoV*, Dec. 15, 1933, Sep. 6, 1935.

37. Katz, *Tenuat*, III, 26–27.

38. Dvoretz, *HaGaon*, 19, 22, 29–31; Katz, *Tenuat*, III, 49.

39. *Eidenu*, 10; Katz, *Tenuat*, III, 19.

40. Grodzinsky, *Torat*, 10–11; Katz, *Tenuat*, III, 309. Another exception was Rabbi Asher-Kalman Baron (1887–1941), a Talmud instructor in the Ponevezh Yeshiva, who until 1931 had served there as Musar-mashgiaḥ, a profession he had acquired in his youth in the Kelm Yeshiva. Regarding Rabbi Gordon, see later in this chapter. See also Weintraub, *BeSufa*, 191; Plotnick, *Divrei*, introduction.

41. Dinur, *BeOlam*, 71–73.

42. Zinowitz, *"Mir,"* 159; Dvoretz, *HaGaon*, 34.

43. See Klibansky, "HaYeshivot," 324–25.

44. Rosenstein, *Yesodei haDa'at*, I, 7. See also ibid., II, 9; Lichtenstein, Degel, 14; Zariz, "Yeshivat," 196; Oshri, "Yeshivat," 155.

45. Zilber, *Torat*, 126. See Gordon, *Nefesh*, 8; report of Brisk Yeshiva, May 25, 1927 (VHY/1115); *HaPardes* 32, no. 1 (1957): 44–45.

46. Pomerantchik, *Yehegge*, preface (the author's letter). See also Gordon, *Nefesh*, 4.

47. Letter: Sokolovsky to Grodzensky, May–June 1930 (VHY/49). Cf. *Yeshurun* 2 (1997): 695.

48. Letter: Gordon to Berek, Dec. 13, 1932 (VHY/47); postcard: Gordon to Grodzensky, Jan. 22, 1932 (VHY/48); *Yeshurun* 2 (1997): 695.

49. See Grade, "Talmidei-Ḥachomim," II, 28. The growth in the number of yeshiva students will be discussed in chapter 6.

50. Hertzman, *Olam*, 114. Cf. Gardi, *Pirkei*, I, 37; Levin, *Zichron*, 37.

51. Notes to the table:

a) The table does not include the Hasidic-Lithuanian yeshivas because they did not employ Musar-mashgiḥim.

b) For Slabodka, the year 1900 marks the expansion of Rabbi Epstein's role from Talmud instructor to rosh-yeshiva and administrator. The faculty of the yeshiva established in Slabodka during the First World War, which eventually became part of the Knesset Yisrael that returned from Krementchug, is not mentioned here.

c) For Pinsk, this is the yeshiva from its settling in Pinsk in 1927 without its previous migrations.

52. Levovitz, *Da'at*, 257.

The Talmidim

Discussion regarding the students touches upon the most important and outstanding foundation of the yeshiva. The talmidim were the substance and body of their yeshiva as well as the factor that decided its fate. The history of the yeshivas indicates that in the beginning of the twentieth century, when the students of the Telz Yeshiva decided to set up an alternate institution of their own despite their esteem for their rabbi Eliezer Gordon, the yeshiva was empty for two months. When the talmidim in Volozhin and Kobrin during the interwar period felt that the directors had gone too far with their appointments and the strained relations amongst themselves, they left their yeshivas at once. In contrast, the fine scholars who occupied the seats in the Mir Yeshiva were the ones who made that institution the sought-after destination for talented young men from all over the yeshiva world.[1]

Is there any comparison between the characteristics of the talmidim who chose the path of the yeshiva after the First World War and those who studied in yeshivas at the end of the nineteenth and the early twentieth centuries? One of the obvious changes in the transition between the earlier and later periods was in the governmental-political area. Most of the yeshivas found themselves in new states, Poland and Lithuania, which offered their citizens freedom. Numerous educational possibilities were available in their cities, especially a variety of Jewish institutions that offered general and Jewish studies, as well as professional training. These schools presented a challenge to the yeshivas in their competition for the hearts of young people. The Jewish family was beset by a storm. It was far from certain that the sons of traditionally observant families in the towns of Lithuania and Poland would choose to join the yeshivas, just as it could not be taken for granted that all the sons of rabbis and religious functionaries would prefer that form of education. The surroundings and their powerful influence very often overcame the education that young people received at home.

Due to these exceptional developments, it is difficult to characterize all the talmidim in the Lithuanian yeshivas in the modern period. Nevertheless, detailed tallies of students make it possible to understand a few of their characteristics, and especially to answer questions such as "To what extent was the number of baḥurim in yeshivas influenced by the previously mentioned social changes?" or "Was there a change in the age of the talmidim or in the number of years they studied in yeshiva?" Another important measurable feature is the place of origin of these students. The political changes in the region had a decisive influence on this data. The barrier between Poland and Lithuania prevented the frequent transfer of baḥurim from one yeshiva to another. Also, the flow of students to the yeshivas in these countries from Russia and Ukraine was blocked by Soviet rule. However, the western borders opened up. Young men from all over the free world who aspired to the rabbinate had the chance to study in the Lithuanian yeshivas, which were considered the best training programs for religious professions.

Only a partial picture of the yeshiva baḥur will be presented here. The advantage of this limited characterization is its validity based on quantifiable parameters—the number of students, their ages, and their place of origin—and on statistical processing of these factors. An analysis of the changes that took place in them over the years makes it possible to identify the influence of the political, economic, and social transformations on the talmidim in Poland and Lithuania in the short but interesting period between the two world wars. However, the discussion of the characteristics of the yeshiva student cannot be limited to statistics alone. The typical talmid—an average of the characteristics, behavior, and thinking of the majority—in a yeshiva-gedola will be described on the basis of all the available sources. Moreover, every group has its exceptions, and a number of these will be portrayed in order to complete the picture.

In a chapter dedicated to the yeshiva student, it seems fitting to discuss the issues with which he would have had to deal each day when he went out of the study hall. As already mentioned, unlike other educational institutions, the yeshivas were not supported by tuition fees. On the contrary, they provided support for needy young men. In the interwar period, most of the talmidim came from the less well-to-do classes of Jewish society in Poland and Lithuania and required financial aid from their yeshivas. The needs of these students were not limited to room and board alone. They required additional vital help, and some lacked even the most basic items, such as clothing and travel expenses to return home for the holidays; their schools helped them in these circumstances as well. It is obvious that this extensive support was a weighty burden on the yeshivas' already feeble budget.[2]

POPULATION IN YESHIVAS

The natural population pool from which the yeshivot-gedolot drew their students was the yeshivot-ketanot spread throughout Poland and Lithuania. These yeshivot-ketanot prepared their charges for independent study for a number of years, and they even gave them tools to deal with the complex Talmudic sugyot discussed in the yeshivot-gedolot. The graduates of the yeshiva-ketana in Lithuania had a limited choice of institutions for higher learning: Slabodka, Telz, and Ponevezh. Nevertheless, they had a free hand in making their choice and were accepted based on their talents and accomplishments alone. This was not the case in the Kresy region of Poland. The Vilna Va'ad-HaYeshivot directed the yeshiva-ketana graduates to the many higher institutions. On the surface, this was not the original role of the committee. The unexpected supervisory task was assigned to it because there were dozens of senior and junior yeshivas in Polish Kresy, and their large number required exact and calculated streaming of the graduates of the yeshivot-ketanot to the yeshivot-gedolot. The Va'ad had the most up-to-date information regarding all the Kresy yeshivas, and on that basis it was possible to set acceptance quotas for each of the yeshivot-gedolot in order to intelligently direct the talmidim of the junior yeshivas to them. There was no other organization that was as qualified to do so.[3]

The task of setting quotas and referring students in Kresy was not simple. Va'ad-HaYeshivot had to deal with institutions in which there was a total of more than 5000 talmidim studying. After the Va'ad set an acceptance quota before each semester for the yeshivot-gedolot according to their relative size, it prepared the lists of students from the yeshivot-ketanot to be accepted. These lists were not only numerical but specified the talmidim by name. The Va'ad selected the yeshiva-gedola for the graduates and provided a letter of reference that would ensure their acceptance. In this fashion, the Va'ad had direct influence on the number of baḥurim in each of the yeshivas.[4]

The age of the students of the yeshivot-ketanot was parallel to that of the gymnasia students. Therefore there was room for competition (usually concealed) only between these two types of institution over the heart of the elementary school graduate from traditional homes in the towns of Poland and Lithuania. The "victory" of the gymnasia reduced nearly automatically the chances of the young man's future acceptance to a yeshiva-gedola, due to his lack of appropriate educational training. There are no statistics available showing the percentage of those who approached the gymnasia among these young people or those who preferred to work, or even the number of dropouts from yeshivot-ketanot. However, there is considerable data concerning those who chose yeshiva education, and this makes it possible to trace the developments in the population of the yeshivot-gedolot in the interwar years.

Choosing a Yeshiva

The student body of the yeshivot-gedolot was a dynamic element due to the constant stream of graduates from the yeshivot-ketanot joining the yeshivot-gedolot and the transfer of senior students from one yeshiva to another. Various motivations and considerations influenced those two groups of students in their choice of a yeshiva, and these were the decisive factors that determined its size.

As previously stated, the graduates of the yeshivot-ketanot of Lithuania freely chose the yeshiva where they would continue their studies. In contrast, the graduates from the Polish Kresy depended on the referrals of the Vilna Va'ad-HaYeshivot. Nevertheless, these graduates had their own aspirations as well; they did not stand by passively but made efforts to be accepted to the yeshivas they preferred. Naturally, the active involvement with many yeshivas prevented the Va'ad from consulting in advance with these yeshiva-ketana graduates regarding their preferences. Thus, decisions made for them were liable to create dissatisfaction not only for the graduates themselves but also for their roshei-yeshiva. Even though the decisions of the Va'ad were binding, the heads of the yeshivot-ketanot attempted to exert their influence. The referrals of Va'ad-HaYeshivot in the winter semester of 1928–1929, for example, did not suit three of the graduates of the yeshiva-ketana in Ivye, when two of them were sent to the Slonim Yeshiva, and one to the Kobrin Yeshiva. Their rosh-yeshiva, Rabbi Yehoshua Lev, requested that they not be sent to those yeshivas and suggested a preferable substitute: "Those yeshivas do not have a good reputation among the talmidim, and they absolutely do not want to go there, and we think that they are right. . . . I request, for the good of our yeshiva, to give them a place in the Radin Yeshiva or the kibbutz [class] in Baranovitch . . . and if Rabbi Elḥanan [Wasserman] insists on not accepting new talmidim to his kibbutz, it would be better in my opinion in his sixth class than in those yeshivas."[5] The rosh-yeshiva advised to refer his students to the sixth class in the Baranovitch Yeshiva, where talmidim still studied under the guidance of a Talmud instructor, and not to the Slonim or Kobrin Yeshiva-gedola. Graduates of the yeshiva-ketana in Rovne took an entirely different position in advance of the winter semester of 1931–1932. Two of them asked to be referred to only one yeshiva, Slonim![6]

These two examples, as well as others, leave the impression that the yeshiva-ketana graduates attributed great importance to the institution where they would continue their studies. It would seem that its geographic location played a small part in their considerations. The talmidim in yeshivot-gedolot remained in their yeshivas for the entire term in any case, and sometimes for several semesters. They spent their vacations together in a common vacation site and returned home quite rarely. The traveling distance from their homes was a negligible factor in their decisions. Proof of this can be found in Polesia, which was located on the edge of the Lithuanian Jewish area and next to Vohlin. There, near medium-sized yeshivas such as Brisk and Kobrin, towered the sought-after Kamenitz Yeshiva, which was one of the largest in Kresy by the second half of the 1930s.[7]

Other factors had a place in the preferences of the yeshiva-ketana graduates. These students were guided by rumors, image, reputation, or hope of material support. Naturally, most of them preferred the most well-known yeshivas, and it seems that many realized their hopes. The most well-known and sought-after yeshivas were the largest, and hence they had the biggest quotas. It was therefore very likely that the graduates would be referred to these yeshivas rather than the smaller and less attractive institutions.[8]

We shall see later that these yeshivas, such as Mir or Kamenitz, shut their doors in the face of the yeshiva-ketana graduates in the late 1920s and early 1930s, and the Va'ad's referrals did not help either. Ya'akov Reif from Lubavne wrote a typical letter to Va'ad-HaYeshivot after he had been rejected by the yeshiva that was designated for him, Mir:

> I request from your great honors to send a letter for me here [in Mir] to the administration of the Radun [Radin] Yeshiva regarding my acceptance to the Radun Yeshiva, as it is impossible to stay here, since the rosh-yeshiva, may he live, despite all my efforts and pleading, has not fulfilled my request to accept me, as they do not accept any of the new [students] who also have letters from Va'ad-HaYeshivot. Therefore I have decided on Radun, because it will be more comfortable for me to go in there and manage. Since the term has already begun, and every day that passes is a waste, please answer me as soon as possible so that I will know what I must do.[9]

Young men who did not receive what they wanted tried to find an alternate yeshiva that was likely to compensate them in another fashion, for example with material support.

Not only yeshiva-ketana graduates knocked on the doors of the yeshivot-gedolot; talmidim who had studied several years in one of the other senior yeshivas did so as well. Unlike the young yeshiva-ketana graduates, these students did not have to rely on rumors or "childish" reasons in order to choose their preferred yeshiva. They could receive information from conversations and correspondence with their friends in other yeshivas and form clear ideas regarding alternative institutions. One of the motivations of these young men who wished to change their place of learning was the desire to study under a renowned rosh-yeshiva. After a few years in yeshiva, the talmidim had already gotten to know their rabbi's method and wanted to learn other approaches to the Talmudic sources. A number of well-known personalities whose methods were different one from another stood at the head of the Lithuanian yeshivas, and listening to each one of them was an intellectual challenge for talented students, as well as a means of gaining essential knowledge on the way to achieving Torah scholarship.[10]

Indeed, several young men migrated among these famous yeshivas, although an examination of the number of students in them does not show a large influx. In the Knesset Beit-Yitzḥak Yeshiva, whose head, Rabbi Baruch-Ber Leibowitz, was known as one of the pillars of the Lithuanian Yeshiva world, there were about eighty baḥurim before it moved to the town of Kamenitz. In the Grodno Yeshiva, which was headed by one of the leaders of the yeshiva world, Rabbi Shim'on Shkop, fewer than two hundred talmidim studied in each one of the years that it existed. Sometimes the yearning of the best students to study in the presence of great Torah scholars was impeded by various forces, principal among them the material support promised to them. Talented young men already in their twenties did not want to live like teenagers, and economic considerations were likely to be decisive.

It was not only the oppressive material factors that determined the preferences of the senior students. Many had already acquired advanced scholarship and the skill of discovering novel interpretations in Talmudic sugyot in their yeshivas. The lectures of the rosh-yeshiva were no longer the basis of their daily schedule. They saw incomparable importance in finding peers in abilities and knowledge and making progress through them and with them in their Torah learning.

The Mir Yeshiva became a place like this where the best of the scholars congregated. It will be shown that from the mid-1920s, this institution began to be the foremost of the Lithuanian yeshivas in terms of its size, and in the winter term of 1935–1936, its talmidim numbered 402, particularly thanks to the mashgiaḥ Rabbi Yeruḥam Levovitz. Following his sudden death in 1936, there was a significant decrease in its students, however by the 1938–1939 winter term, the yeshiva had recovered, and 403 talmidim studied there. It may be that the appointment of the veteran mashgiaḥ Rabbi Yeḥezkel Levenstein in the place of Rabbi Levovitz helped stabilize the yeshiva, however a more significant factor is that the best students did not leave the yeshiva upon their Musar supervisor's death. From their point of view, it continued to serve as their spiritual home, and they found their satisfaction in scholarly discussions among themselves. This group of exceptional scholars preserved the reputation of the Mir Yeshiva. The yeshiva was never again dependent on its heads and leaders, and it was the senior students who attracted young people from within and without.[11]

Changes in the Relationship between Talmidim and Their Yeshivas

The early years of the twentieth century were unique in terms of the extreme changes that took place in the yeshivas—their shrinking due to the pull of socialism and Zionism on their talmidim, and their stabilization as a result of reaction in Russia. Verified statistical data is unavailable regarding the number of yeshiva students before the First World War, but from the scant sources that are accessible, it is possible to reach some interesting conclusions relating to the size of the yeshivas. Exact numbers exist for Knesset-Yisrael of Slabodka, where 328 talmidim appear in its class picture in 1914. The figures for the other yeshivas are round numbers, and these should be seen only as general estimates. Among these are 400 in Mir, the same number in Slonim; 300 in Radin; 220 in Telz; and 200 in each of the yeshivas of Novardok, Slutsk, and Knesset Beit-Yitzḥak of Slabodka. In the interwar period, only the last four succeeded in significantly increasing the number of their students. From this we see that several yeshivas were already functioning at maximum capacity before the First World War, and the limitations on their capability to absorb more talmidim and economic constraints made it difficult for their numbers to grow.[12]

During the First World War, there was again a great change in the size of the yeshivas. Although there is no hard data regarding the number of students in the early war years, it is certain that there was a significant decrease. There is data that is apparently quite precise for three yeshivas, particularly for the end of that period: there were about one hundred talmidim in the Mir Yeshiva when it was located in Poltava, a similar number studied in Knesset-Yisrael a short time before it left Krementchug and returned to Lithuania, and there was an even lower number of students in Radin on its way back from exile.[13] A comparison between these numbers and those in the period before the war highlights the mortal blow visited upon these yeshivas during the extended emergency period. This was the abysmal situation in three of the largest institutions in the yeshiva world before the war. How much worse was it in the others that had gone into exile or remained in situ during the years of German occupation? In view of such sharp transitions in the yeshivas from periods of growth to situations of dire crisis, and notwithstanding their ability to endure, it is not surprising to see that they survived in the interwar years as well.

The quantitative data allows lateral graphic comparison between the yeshivas in those years of the interwar period and identification of changes in their size by presenting the number of students in them. These comparisons show that not a few of the yeshivas experienced severe crises. To understand these events and their causes, the first two graphs—of the Mir and Grodno Yeshivas—whose axes have been calibrated for easy comparison, are presented in figure 6.1.[14]

Each yeshiva had its own special background. Mir was one of the most veteran yeshivas in the region of Lithuanian Jewish culture and one of the largest in the years before the First World War. In contrast, the Grodno Yeshiva was established during the German occupation by a group of students, and it lacked the tradition of age and renown. Neither of these institutions escaped the period of uncertainty after the First World War. Mir lost most of its senior baḥurim in the waiting period in Vilna in the summer of 1920, and Grodno was nearly shut down during the Russian occupation of the city in 1921. It was only after Polish rule became soundly established in Kresy in the second half of 1921 that the two yeshivas were stabilized once more. From that point on, they saw a similar and continuous trend of increase in the number of students. This was the pattern in a number of other yeshivas, such as Kamenitz, Kletsk, and Brisk.[15]

Did similar growth skip over the rest of the yeshivas? The quantitative data relating to the yeshivas that did not fit this trend of growth will be examined. Figure 6.2 shows the situation in Radin and Kobrin.

Despite the difference in the relative size of these two yeshivas, it is possible to see the identical trend of growth in them as in the previous

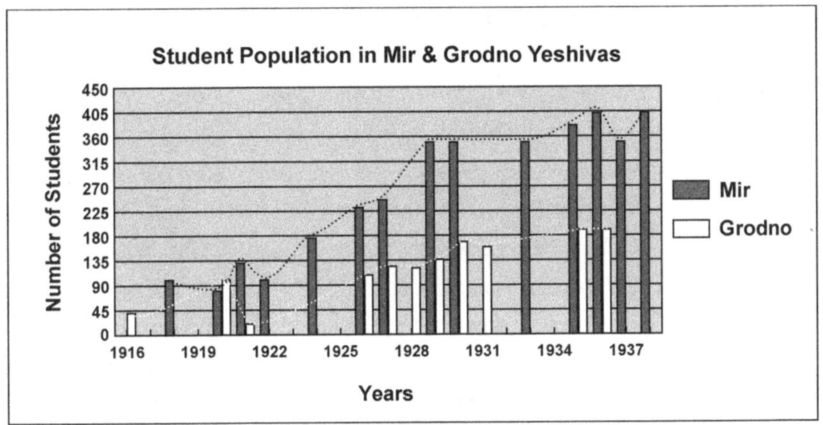

FIGURE 6.1.

Student population in Mir and Grodno Yeshivas.

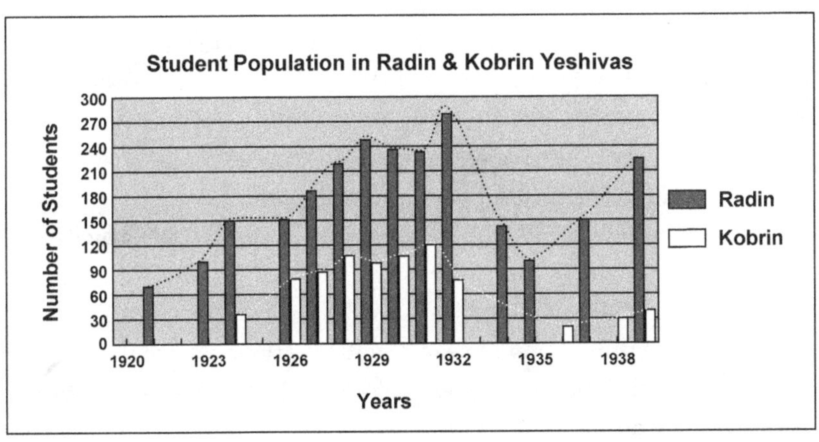

FIGURE 6.2.

Student population in Radin and Kobrin Yeshivas.

yeshivas mentioned, but only until the beginning of the 1930s. From then onward, a significant decline is observable, and only in the final years of their existence is there a partial recovery. A similar picture can be seen in the Volozhin and Remayle Yeshivas. Indeed, difficult administrational problems cast their shadow upon the ability of all these yeshivas to attract talmidim in the 1930s. As an example of this, the events in the Radin

Yeshiva that were described in the previous chapter under other circumstances will be presented.

This yeshiva became well-known in the 1920s thanks to two unique figures: its rosh-yeshiva, Rabbi Naftali Trop, and its founder, the Ḥafetz-Ḥayim. The latter had no official position in the yeshiva, but his name drew quite a number of talmidim from afar, as well as donations. The death of Rabbi Trop in 1928 was a severe blow to the students. Many felt that they had lost not only their academic instructor but also their guide in dealing with personal problems. Above all, his demise struck the senior baḥurim, who were better able than their fellow talmidim to appreciate the qualities of their rabbi. They understood that a rosh-yeshiva who could fill his place would not be found, and they prepared to leave Radin and transfer to other yeshivas. Nevertheless, only a small decrease in the number of students is discernible in the following two years. The places of the senior baḥurim were quickly filled by younger men, and in the winter term of 1931–1932, there were 279 talmidim studying in the yeshiva—a record number. It is clear from this that it was not only the talents of the famous rosh-yeshiva that filled the benches of Radin in the past but other reasons as well, such as the personality of the Ḥafetz-Ḥayim, the attitude of the yeshiva to its students, and the financial support it offered them.

However, the crises in Radin were not over. In 1933 Rabbi Baruch-Yosef Faivelzon, a brilliant Talmud instructor in the yeshiva, died. The memory and untimely passing of his father-in-law, Rabbi Trop, were still fresh, and the death of the young son-in-law was another serious blow to the yeshiva's students. A month had not passed before the Ḥafetz-Ḥayim became ill with relatively minor illnesses, but they worsened his condition and thus began his demise. Even though he had no longer appeared in the yeshiva in recent years and his talks were given only in his home, he continued his activity on behalf of the Jewish people and turned to the yeshiva's donors to support it. The talmidim knew that it was his name that created the yeshiva's reputation throughout Poland and the Jewish world, and they understood that the death of the father of the yeshiva would seriously damage it. Indeed, Radin's economic decline while its debts skyrocketed to fifteen thousand dollars was keenly felt. It would seem this situation influenced the number of the students more than any other factor, and in the summer term of 1934, that number decreased to only 142.[16]

In a single moment, the Radin Yeshiva had gone from being one of the largest Lithuanian yeshivas to an institution in serious decline. Its young administration, which had to deal with this situation, was unsuccessful in the task. One year later, the mashgiaḥ, Rabbi Eliezer-Ze'ev Kaplan, wrote these pointed words: "We simply have no rest. The young men ask for bread and the bakers do not want to give them any more on credit, and the landladies do not want to cook for them, since they have not gotten what they deserve for a long time."[17] The yeshiva's financial network was near total collapse. It is not surprising that rumors circulated among the public that there was a sharp decline in the number of students in the winter term of 1935–1936 to only one hundred![18]

Even in the other yeshivas, the material situation was difficult and continued to be quite severe throughout the 1930s. Nevertheless, when their talmidim saw the administration's determination, they felt a glimmer of hope for a better future. In contrast, in Radin and similar yeshivas, the baḥurim had lost faith in their leaders. The young men distanced themselves from these yeshivas, and this widespread abandonment did not encourage new candidates to apply.

Despite the collapse of the aforementioned yeshivas, their graphs show somewhat of an increase in the number of students in the second half of the 1930s. The efforts of their administrators to improve the situation and attract new talmidim definitely helped in expanding their reduced dimensions. However, this growth also shows the general trend of expansion in the yeshiva world in those years, which is reflected in the first two graphs of the Mir and Grodno yeshivas that appeared previously. New students preferred the famous yeshivas such as Mir, but when there was no other alternative, they agreed to study in other yeshivas as well, especially in those that had a glorious past, such as Radin or Volozhin.

AGE OF THE TALMIDIM

After the First World War, a significant change occurred in the organizational makeup of the yeshivot-gedolot. Only a few years earlier, talented bar-mitzvah-aged lads studied together with young men in their twenties. This phenomenon disappeared in many of the yeshivas. The change occurred not by preventing the young students from studying in the yeshivot-gedolot but by creating an internal division and designating the yeshiva-ketana for these younger talmidim. This division had various expressions, such as complete separation between the mother yeshiva and the new yeshiva-ketana, a situation that was familiar even before the First World War, or merely formal separation for budgetary reasons. There were two motives for this organizational change:[19]

1. Pedagogic
   - The modern organization of the new Jewish schools gave incentive to the yeshivas that felt the hidden competition to organize their institutions in a more balanced fashion and divide the talmidim according to age.
   - The obligation to provide general studies for students aged seven to fourteen in schools in Poland and Lithuania compelled the yeshivas to part with the talmidim of compulsory education age in order to maintain the Talmudic institutions' pedagogic independence.
2. Financial
   - Separating the younger students in a secondary institution and placing this institution on the shoulders of the local community lightened the burden on the yeshivas' deficit finances.
   - Fashioning the yeshivot-gedolot as institutions of higher learning for training rabbis, where only adult talmidim studied, made them more attractive to American donors.
   - The separate budget in Va'ad-HaYeshivot for the yeshivot-ketanot of the Polish Kresy encouraged a number of yeshivot-gedolot to create a division in their schools, which was only a formality in order to receive additional funding.

Jewish children in Poland and Lithuania acquired their education in Jewish elementary schools, or *ḥadarim,* whose curriculum was approved by the government. Studies there usually lasted four years until the age of eleven, and then their graduates could choose to go out and work or study in an academic program, such as the Jewish gymnasia or yeshivot-ketanot.[20] Youngsters who chose a yeshiva-ketana absorbed the foundations of Talmudic inquiry and within a few years were prepared to study

Talmud without an instructor. The age of the students in the yeshivot-ketanot was twelve to sixteen, and in this aspect these institutions were similar to the gymnasia. Their graduates were eligible to be accepted to the yeshivot-gedolot, where they would already study entirely on their own. Studies in those yeshivas started at age seventeen, and it was possible to continue learning there until the talmid's marriage in his twenties. In terms of the age they served, the yeshivot-gedolot were similar to the final grades of the gymnasia or the universities.

The sharp and clear division in age of the students in the yeshivot-ketanot and that of the baḥurim in the yeshivot-gedolot existed only in theory. In actuality, this division changed in the 1920s and 1930s as a result of the constraints with which the yeshivot-gedolot had to cope.

Younger Talmidim

Each yeshiva had its own way of separating the younger talmidim from the older ones. Grodno, Telz, and Slabodka established ancillary preparatory schools whose heads were in close contact with the yeshiva-gedola administration. In this way, the leadership of the preparatory school, the mechinah that was set up in Grodno in 1921, was given over to Rabbi Moshe-Mordechai Shkop (1882–1975), son of the rosh-yeshiva. He divided it into three classes, and the young yeshiva students were transferred into them. The two institutions were separated when the mechinah was moved to a study hall in the courtyard of the local industrialist Shershevsky, while the yeshiva remained in its place in the Alsheich Beit-Midrash. Despite the physical distance, the preparatory program was organizationally an inseparable part of the yeshiva-gedola. Their administrations were consequently able to ensure the optimal division of the talmidim, as demonstrated in the histogram of the ages of students in the yeshiva-gedola in the second half of the 1920s (figure 6.3). As is to be expected, there were no baḥurim in the yeshiva younger than seventeen—students of that age studied in the mechinah.[21]

In contrast to this preparatory school, which was just like a regular yeshiva-ketana, the mechinah in Slabodka, established in 1923, played a role that was unique and better fit its name. Its training was a transitional stage upon the completion of studies in the Even-Yisrael Yeshiva-ketana,

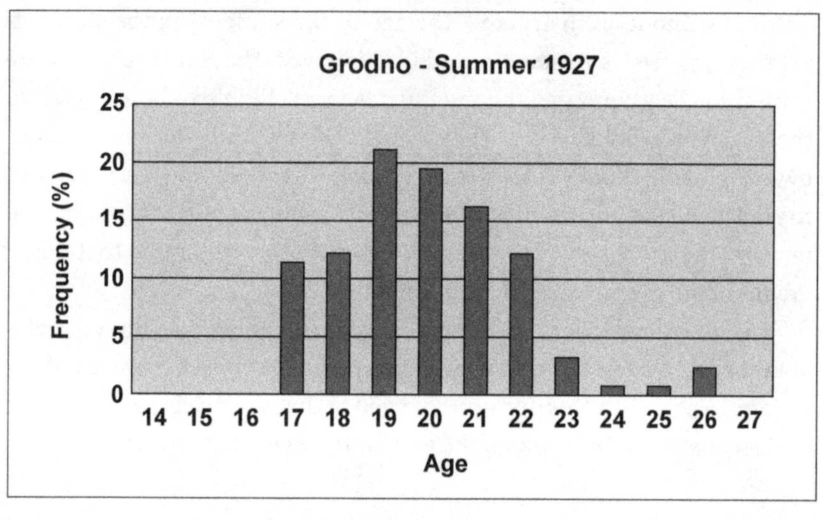

FIGURE 6.3.

The age of students in Grodno Yeshiva in the summer of 1927.

and it was intended to raise the level of young graduates before they began their studies in the Knesset-Yisrael Yeshiva-gedola. For years this senior yeshiva had the character of an institution for older baḥurim, and only occasionally were a few outstanding younger talmidim accepted. Its nature was even more sharply defined after the mechinah was established and absorbed the young men aged sixteen to nineteen in its classes. There is no available data regarding the ages of the yeshiva-gedola students throughout the years that it existed. From a source in 1938, it is possible to conclude that in that year the talmidim were aged nineteen to twenty-seven.[22]

Unlike the aforementioned yeshivas, which had a close relationship with their preparatory schools, it appears that the veteran yeshivas in the Kresy region were not so connected with the yeshivot-ketanot, adjacent to them in terms of location but separate in terms of their administration and finances. One of these was the Radin Yeshiva, which had a clear boundary between it and the local yeshiva-ketana. The histograms in figure 6.4 show the age of the talmidim in the yeshiva-gedola.[23]

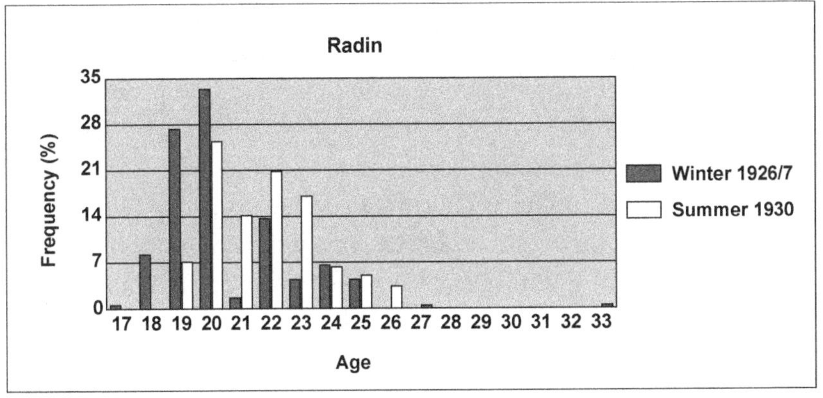

FIGURE 6.4.

The age of students in Radin Yeshiva.

During the winter semester of 1926–1927, there was only one talmid seventeen years of age in the Radin Yeshiva, and three years later there were no young people under the age of nineteen. This data apparently indicates the lack of a fruitful connection with the local yeshiva-ketana, which was meant to graduate students at age seventeen, because they never arrived at the adjacent yeshiva-gedola. A comparison with the graphs of other veteran yeshivot-gedolot shows that this phenomenon was part of a trend of decreasing acceptance of new talmidim to the senior yeshivas and, as a result, a gradual rise in the age of students in most of the yeshiva world.

To understand how such a rapid change took place in the age of the talmidim when tens of students graduated from the yeshivot-ketanot each year, the situation in the Mir Yeshiva in the early 1930s will be examined. Already at the time that the yeshiva was temporarily located in Vilna in 1920, its head, Rabbi Eliezer-Yehudah Finkel, refused to accept young baḥurim. He claimed, "There is no room in our yeshiva for boys. The Mir Yeshiva is a yeshiva for young men who study Talmud with commentaries and legal rulings."[24] In an exceptional case, the rosh-yeshiva accepted a youngster of fifteen, and the boy stood out among his older fellow students because of his age.[25] Rabbi Finkel continued to cling to this restrictive policy when the yeshiva returned to the town of Mir. He even refused to establish a preparatory school adjacent to the yeshiva and stated, "It is impossible to carry this out for a number of reasons, especially since it will reduce the prestige of the present yeshiva, when young lads join it."[26] Indeed, when the journalist Ḥayim Shoshkes visited the yeshiva in 1925, he found there baḥurim of nineteen to twenty-five years old and did not mention any younger students in his report.[27] This trend became more pronounced over the years as outstanding talmidim from other yeshivas came to study in Mir, and it gained renown for its older baḥurim. However, like the other yeshivot-gedolot, it was also obliged to accept its quota of graduates of yeshivot-ketanot each term, as stipulated by Va'ad-HaYeshivot. Most could expect difficulties in studying there. The veteran talmidim set the institution's high level, and the younger ones needed a great deal of help to raise their knowledge to the standard necessary for the yeshiva's studies. Rabbi Finkel was aware of this complex situation and requested Va'ad-HaYeshivot make a revolutionary change: "I wish to inform your great Torah eminences that since it is our opinion that it is not worthwhile for the students of yeshivot-ketanot to study in our yeshiva, we have made an agreement with the administration of the Baranovitch Yeshiva that the five talmidim that we would have accepted through Va'ad-HaYeshivot will be accepted by the Baranovitch Yeshiva, and that we will send the support there that they would have received here, and I request from your great Torah eminences not to send any students here."[28] The capacity of the Baranovitch Yeshiva to absorb talmidim was also limited, and it was not able to carry out this creative method in full with the large quota of students assigned to Mir. To illustrate this, toward the winter semester of 1929–1930, Va'ad-HaYeshivot sent ten yeshiva-ketana graduates to Mir, and for the summer term it sent fifteen young people, together making up a total of 7 percent of its students that year! These quotas created an imbalance in the age of the talmidim there, and this was what Rabbi Yeruḥam Levovitz meant when he asked in 1933 that Va'ad-HaYeshivot not send new students to Mir because of "various reasons regarding the essentials of our yeshiva."[29]

The reasons that Rabbi Levovitz concealed were already revealed in the words of another mashgiaḥ, Rabbi Naftali-Ze'ev Leibowitz of

Kamenitz in 1929. When Kamenitz began to be replete with new baḥurim, he expressed his concern for the institution's serious image: "We cannot accept any more talmidim from the yeshivot-ketanot because we have already accepted 17 new students this semester, among them many from yeshivot-ketanot, and it is likely that we will have to accept some more against our will. Last term we accepted many from the yeshivot-ketanot and we cannot reduce the stature of our yeshiva due to the increase of young students. Therefore I must inform your Torah eminence that it is impossible to fulfill the regulation of the Va'ad at this time, so please do not send us any, since they will not be accepted."[30] To explain this reaction, it should be clarified that these seventeen new talmidim, who mostly came from yeshivot-ketanot, made up 14 percent of the student body of Kamenitz. The mashgiaḥ was rightly concerned that this rate of flow would distort the balance in the yeshiva toward the lower age bracket and change its image to that of a yeshiva for younger people.

The involvement with image was only a concern in a few yeshivas, among them Mir and Kamenitz. More vital matters worried the other Torah institutions. The most serious issue with which they had to deal was the burgeoning number of students that increased expenditures from their limited and deficit-riddled budgets. The yeshivas found no other solution than to shut their doors in the face of the yeshiva-ketana graduates. This explains the upward shift of the age of the talmidim.[31]

Youngsters in the Multiage Yeshivas

A few yeshivas did not join the general trend of separating the younger talmidim from the older ones. Among them were the Hasidic Lithuanian yeshivas, the yeshivas of Vohlin (which did not need this separation), and even some of the veteran Lithuanian yeshivas. Slonim, which was divided up into younger classes that remained in the yeshiva building and a kibbutz class that met in the beit-midrash, was already mentioned. However, this separation had no administrational or budgetary value, and Slonim continued to appear in its documents as a single, combined yeshiva. Actually, in 1929 its rosh-yeshiva, Rabbi

Shabtai Yogel, divided the two lower classes and the rest of the yeshiva, but this was purely a formal move in order to receive funding for his yeshiva-ketana.[32]

Another outstanding yeshiva that maintained its original form with no change was Lomzhe. There is no mention of an adjacent yeshiva-ketana. In the 1920s, there was only a one-class preparatory program that was located in the yeshiva building, and its fourteen- to fifteen-year-old graduates enrolled in the yeshiva-gedola, which had four classes. The young talmidim studied in grades two through four, and the older baḥurim (aged seventeen and up) were in grade five. After the Talmud classes given by the instructors in the classrooms, all the talmidim would continue their studies in the yeshiva's large study hall. The younger ones sat close to the front of the hall, and the older students sat behind them. Data is available regarding the ages of the talmidim from the second half of the 1920s alone; figure 6.5 is a representative sample.[33]

The graph indicates a large percentage of younger students; among the talmidim of the usual age for a yeshiva-gedola, the younger group—those aged seventeen to nineteen—stands out. It can be hypothesized that this picture changed to one that was better aligned with the trend in the other yeshivas during the 1930s.

Ohel-Torah of Baranovitch was the exception among the multiage yeshivas. Like its neighboring institution, the Hasidic Torat-Ḥesed, and the other multiage yeshivas, it had separate classes that divided the talmidim—six classes and a kibbutz class. Like most of these multiage yeshivas, it was considered a yeshiva-gedola, and it was classified as such in the table of financial allocations of Va'ad-HaYeshivot. However, the histograms of the ages of the three upper classes and the kibbutz class, which together made up the yeshiva-gedola, show in figure 6.6 an entirely different situation.[34]

Besides the significant increase in the number of students within a decade (approximately 70 percent), no essential change occurred in the main criteria of age that was predominant in the yeshiva. It remained sixteen years old, and that clearly shows the difficulty of listing this institution as a yeshiva-gedola, especially because the talmidim aged nineteen and older were only 9 percent of the student body in the summer of 1936. Actually, many saw this institution as a yeshiva-ketana, or more precisely

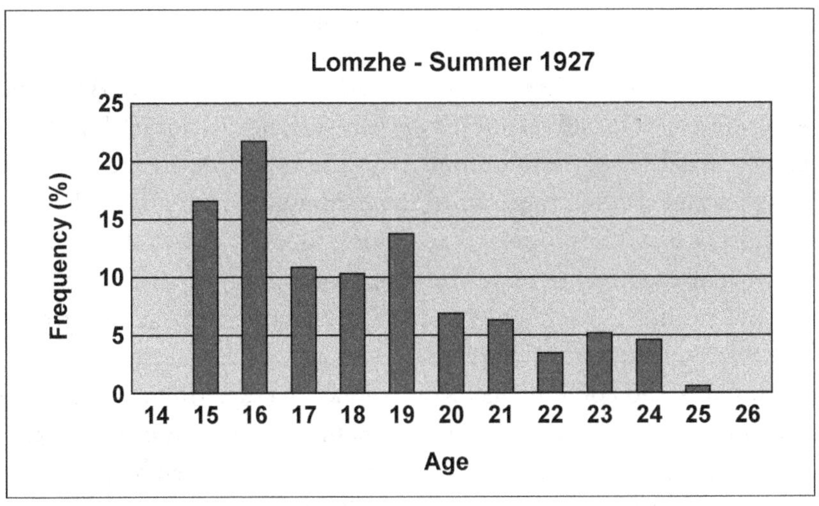

FIGURE 6.5.

The age of students in Lomzhe Yeshiva in the summer of 1927.

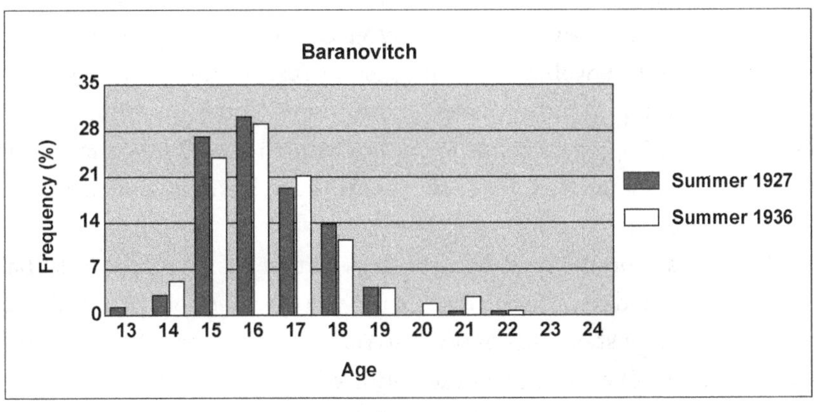

FIGURE 6.6.

The age of students in Baranovitch Yeshiva.

as an excellent preparatory program for the yeshivot-gedolot, thanks to its head, Rabbi Elḥanan Wasserman, who was well-known for his excellent elucidation of the material. The graduates of its upper classes, which were instructed by him, had the reputation of being fine scholars, and they usually chose not to remain in the yeshiva's kibbutz class for a long time but transferred to the more renowned yeshivot-gedolot.[35]

Older Talmidim

When a new student arrived at one of the yeshivot-gedolot (with the exception of Telz and the multiage yeshivas), he did not find separate classes that divided the talmidim. All students participated in the same lectures and studied together in the common study hall. In the Mir Yeshiva, students were seated according to level, like in the Lomzhe Yeshiva already mentioned. The veteran and senior baḥurim in their thirties sat in the back rows, and the younger yeshiva-ketana graduates were seated in the front.[36] This emphasized hierarchy expressed remoteness and condescension, as well as an educational message to the younger students, instilling in them the aspiration to rise to a higher station in the yeshiva. The senior baḥurim even helped them to advance, showing interest in their situation and assisting them in their studies and their understanding of the lectures and Musar talks. This ambivalent approach toward the young talmidim was described from a distance of years by one of the graduates of Mir: "Attention was given in order to help them; by virtue of the obligation to help one's neighbor as well as from a sense of responsibility to maintain the educational climate in the yeshiva—everyone saw himself as a 'social mashgiaḥ' in terms of his fellow student. . . . The concern for the yeshiva as a whole and its success was the business and worry of each individual."[37]

There was a sort of esprit de corps shown in the actions of the older baḥurim; they tried to raise the level of the younger ones out of a desire to keep up the high standards of the Mir Yeshiva. Their contribution to the yeshiva's atmosphere and the preservation of its primacy in the Lithuanian yeshiva world raises the question of their age and their relative percentage among the student body. Unfortunately, the ages are missing in the lists of the talmidim in Mir, and one can only quote from Ḥayim Grade's poem, "Torah Scholars in Lithuania," which exemplifies the image of their advanced age more than anything:

> The rosh-yeshiva of Mir is going! The one who uproots mountains,
> Who prepares his lectures on the deck of the ship to America.
> He goes there to collect money,
> and poor and rich give to him
> For his 35 year-old baḥurim.[38]

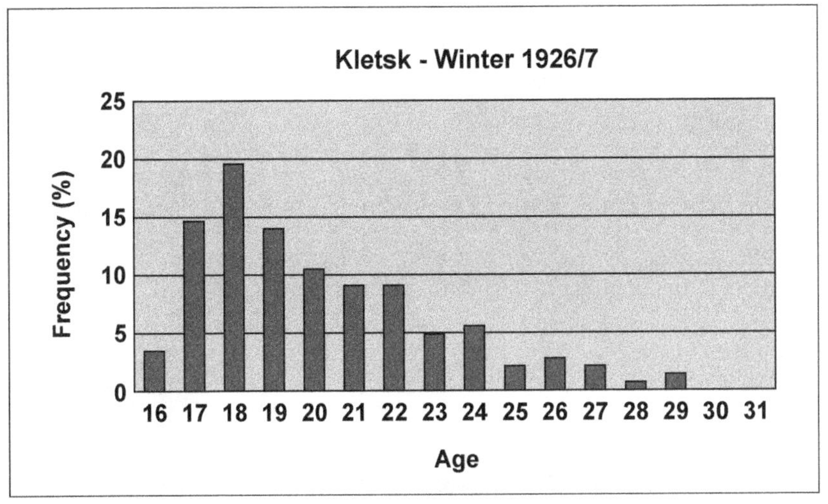

FIGURE 6.7.

The age of students in Kletsk Yeshiva in the winter of 1926–1927.

The data relating to the Mir Yeshiva is unavailable; consequently, the statistics of older students in other famous yeshivas will be examined, because senior baḥurim were likely to be concentrated there as well. Figure 6.7 shows the ages of the talmidim of Kletsk.

The graph indicates that in the second half of the 1920s, only a few students aged twenty-eight to twenty-nine studied in the yeshiva. This situation underwent a total change in the 1930s. The number of the older baḥurim in Kletsk increased continually, until at the end of the 1930s there were twelve talmidim (approximately 5 percent) aged twenty-nine and older. A similar and even more extreme development took place among the ages twenty-six to twenty-eight: in the winter of 1926–1927, there were only eight students in this age bracket (approximately 5 percent), but in 1938 there were forty-three (approximately 16 percent).[39]

The head of the Kletsk Yeshiva was Rabbi Aharon Kotler, a profound scholar whose lectures could be understood only by veteran baḥurim who had already studied in yeshivot-gedolot for quite a few years. Was it only his personality that attracted older talmidim to Kletsk?[40]

In order to answer this question, figure 6.8 will present the latest histograms available of the ages of students in the Radin Yeshiva, which in the

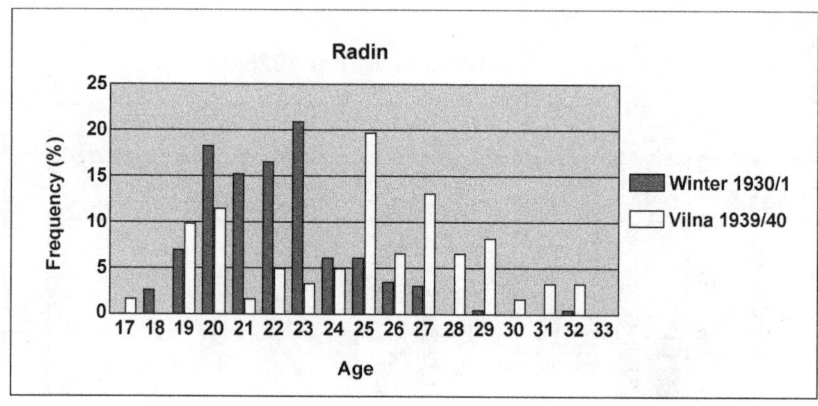

FIGURE 6.8.

The age of students in Radin Yeshiva in the 1930s.

1930s lacked a pronounced scholarly figure like its former rosh-yeshiva, Rabbi Naftali Trop.

From the Radin graphs earlier in the chapter, it is possible to see that in the winter of 1926–1927, there were no talmidim in that yeshiva above the age of twenty-five. According to the winter of 1930–1931 graph, there were already seven (3 percent) twenty-seven-year-olds, as well as another few that were older than that. After the war broke out in 1939 and the Kresy region was occupied by the Soviets, the yeshiva left the town of Radin and broke up into two groups. One group settled in Eishishok, and the other settled in Vilna. Data is available regarding sixty-five students, who made up two-thirds of the Vilna group. It is possible to see from the 1939–1940 graph that among these talmidim, there were two main age groups, nineteen to twenty and twenty-five to twenty-nine, as well as a few who were aged thirty to thirty-two. Assuming that this data reflects the original Radin students from before the war, the graph indicates a significant rise in age and the readiness of young men to remain in yeshiva until a relatively advanced age, even though there was no charismatic rosh-yeshiva who could draw the best of the students toward him. It would seem that the attitude of the older talmidim toward their yeshiva was not a function of the personality of the rosh-yeshiva, nor was he the main reason that they remained there.[41]

It is natural that each year, older baḥurim were meant to complete their studies in the yeshiva, marry, and go on to work as religious functionaries or in secular professions. It would then have been expected that the attempts to reject many of the graduates of yeshivot-ketanot and close the gates of the yeshivas in their face would lead to a gradual decrease in the student population of the yeshivot-gedolot. In reality, the situation was completely different. In the beginning of this chapter, a continuous increase in the yeshivas was presented, and the only explanation for this is that the older talmidim remained there. This is the reason for the surprising upward drift of the average age of the students in many of the yeshivas.

This preference of older baḥurim to delay marriage and earning a livelihood in order to continue their studies had significant financial implications for their yeshiva. They received greater support than did their younger counterparts, and their remaining in yeshiva was a burden on its finances. More serious than this, their extended stay in yeshiva prevented a regular changeover of talmidim and the acceptance of new students. This phenomenon was mentioned outright by the rosh-yeshiva of Mir, Rabbi Eliezer-Yehudah Finkel: "If it is necessary to bring the students of the yeshivot-ketanot into the yeshivot-gedolot, then we should ensure that there are vacant places for them in the yeshivot-gedolot, and we must organize things so that many of the talmidim of the yeshivot-gedolot leave each term."[42]

The older baḥurim remained in their yeshivas in Poland and Lithuania because after years of education, they began to understand the difficult situation waiting for them at the end of their studies due to their lack of prospects in religious professions. There were very few rabbinical positions available, and there were no other equivalent alternatives. The author David Zaritzky, a graduate of Radin, wrote about these young men: "There were many opportunities to marry the daughters of respected ba'alei-batim [householders], and to become a member of society or even a community leader in this town or that city. But this meant becoming separated from the Torah, because a ba'al-bayit [householder] becomes immersed in everyday life, his world becomes an everyday world, and his thinking becomes everyday thinking. But a Torah scholar is not like this, his thoughts are not everyday thoughts . . . and he is not satisfied with what a ba'al-bayit is satisfied."[43] The possibilities that lay before a yeshiva graduate are described quite optimistically here. In the practicality-oriented atmosphere of the interwar period in Poland and Lithuania, older baḥurim found it difficult to make a decent match. The daughters of respected ba'alei-batim and even those of rabbis usually studied in gymnasia, and many preferred husbands who had a profession rather than yeshiva students who were unprepared for the struggle for existence. Even the talented ones among the older talmidim could no longer hope for wealthy fathers who waited in line to receive a choice son-in-law from the rosh-yeshiva. Neither did they wish to marry a poor girl and work to make a secular livelihood. In actuality, many of them who had reached an advanced age stayed in their yeshivas and did not marry.[44]

BACKGROUND OF THE TALMIDIM

Most of the yeshivas in Lithuania and Poland in the interwar period were populated by local baḥurim, as could be expected. But in quite a few of those institutions, two groups were an exception to this rule: those who had left Russia and Ukraine, and those who had been born in countries outside Eastern Europe, of whom only a few were to be seen in the yeshivas in earlier days.

Migrant Talmidim

The exile of Lithuanian yeshivas during the First World War created a very fascinating phenomenon: the "migrant talmidim." These were local young men who joined the yeshivas that were temporarily located in Russia and Ukraine; became attached to the roshei-yeshiva, the students, the manner of studying Torah; and did not wish to leave the yeshivas when they returned to Lithuania and Poland. The rise of the Bolsheviks to power and their attitude to the Jewish religion also convinced parents that it would be a good move for their sons to go to the neighboring free countries. In quite a few cases, local young talmidim, especially those who studied in the Novardok yeshivas, migrated with their friends over the border without saying goodbye to their parents, either because of the suspicion that they would not receive permission or because of geographical distance. After arriving in Poland or Lithuania, these immigrants would have nearly no contact with their families, and their yeshivas became the substitute for their homes in Russia or Ukraine.[45]

The appearance of young men from Russia in the Lithuanian yeshivas was not new. Already in the second half of the nineteenth century, rabbinical emissaries had spread the yeshivas' reputations throughout the Russian Empire and even among Jewish communities in the God-forsaken regions of Siberia and Manchuria. Rabbi Shabtai Yogel described the new talmidim in his yeshiva in Slonim: "In addition to the baḥurim from Lithuania, Reisen, Vohlin, etc., yeshiva students carrying daggers and lances have appeared, just like Circassians in every way. Indeed, the yeshiva's praises have reached as far as the Caucasus, and from there Georgian Jewish youth have come to the home of the Torah in Slonim. . . . Moreover, even several converts from among the Subbotniks [Sabbath-observing Russians] from the Voronezh Province in Central Russia, converts wearing farmers' aprons and fur hats [have come]."[46] The unique costume or unusual accent of these exotic baḥurim attracted the attention of the other talmidim and earned a place in memoirs. But even the ordinary young men from Russia succeeded in rousing the interest of the other students due to their different background from those who were natives of the Pale of Settlement. Persitz, a student from Moscow University, found his place among the memories of the talmidim of the Telz Yeshiva: "The student with the black beard from Moscow, Shmuel [*sic*: read Yosef] Persitz (the future husband of Shoshana Persitz née Zlatopolsky), who came each year during the university vacation in a uniform with shiny buttons, like an officer, to study in the yeshiva—to the amazement and pride of the yeshiva baḥurim and the town residents that this young man from a privileged background desires to learn Torah and keeps the commandments religiously—is one of our own, attached to the talmidim and like a member of the rabbi's household."[47]

These cases were exceptional and completely unlike what occurred after the war's conclusion. When the yeshivas returned from their exile, there were many migrant talmidim. The Mir Yeshiva stood out in its number of immigrant students compared to the other yeshivas that had returned to their original locations. At the end of the summer term of 1924, ninety-five migrant talmidim attached themselves to the yeshiva, making up nearly 60 percent of the student body. From that time a precipitous decrease took place in their number: in 1926–1927 it fell to fifty to sixty, and it remained stable until the beginning of the 1930s. Despite this decrease, the Mir Yeshiva was still considered to have had more immigrant talmidim than the other yeshivas. Their number motivated the rosh-yeshiva, during his stay in the United States in 1926, to raise this issue before the leaders of the JDC and Central Relief and request increased support on their behalf. Indeed, the cost of their maintenance was higher than costs for other students. Obviously, they received no material support from their parents, and all their expenses were paid by the yeshiva, which even had to deposit sureties with the authorities for residence permits in Poland. It was only in the 1930s that they were no longer mentioned in the yeshiva's correspondence, either because their numbers dwindled as part of a natural process or because this issue became marginal among the plethora of the yeshiva's economic problems.[48]

Many migrant talmidim were in the Kletsk Yeshiva as well. When the large group of tens of baḥurim left Slutsk to settle in Kletsk, this group naturally included many natives of Russia. Over the years, the number of students in Kletsk increased, especially from among young men from Poland but also from the Slutsk refugees who continued to cross the border. In 1924 there were 73 migrant talmidim among the 156 students in the yeshiva. Over the years their number decreased, and in the winter of 1932 there were only thirty-one immigrants.[49]

Also in Knesset-Yisrael of Slabodka, there were many natives of Russia and Ukraine, who had arrived with the yeshiva from Krementchug to Lithuania. Other migrant talmidim joined them in illegally crossing the Lithuanian border. In this way there was a large concentration of them in the yeshiva, even though their exact number is unknown. In 1923 the Lithuanian government began a series of steps to expel the illegal immigrants from its borders. First it required organizing lists of all residents, and afterward the Lithuanian minister of the interior issued an order for natives of Russia to leave the country. The police ensured that this order was carried out. In their investigations, they arrived in the suburb of Slabodka and even seized a few yeshiva students, arresting them. Rabbis Notte-Hirsch Finkel and Moshe-Mordechai Epstein immediately began to lobby for their release and succeeded in their goal, but in return they were forced to commit themselves to the expulsion of all the undocumented talmidim.

Indeed, a number of those students scattered to other yeshivas in Lithuania, and others attempted to steal over the border into Poland.[50]

The migrant talmidim also had an important place in the other yeshivas that had a similar past, among them Radin, which had returned from exile to its town, or Knesset Beit-Yitzḥak which had settled in Vilna. Russian natives, who had formerly been talmidim in Amtchislav, were successful in arriving at the Kobrin Yeshiva, which was established by their rosh-yeshiva Rabbi Pesaḥ Pruskin in 1923. In these three institutions, the migrant talmidim made up 20–25 percent of the student body in the middle of the 1920s.[51]

Unlike the aforementioned yeshivas that were filled with migrant baḥurim, only a few studied in those that had not experienced exile. This was the situation in Slonim in the 1920s, which had remained in its place during the First World War. In the Brisk Yeshiva, which had been reestablished, the first three migrant talmidim appeared in the winter term of 1927–1928. Remayle Yeshiva was the exception among those yeshivas. Even though it had not gone into exile during the war, it had a large number of migrant baḥurim. Twenty-five studied there in the summer of 1926 and made up 15 percent of the student body. It was only in the 1930s that their portion decreased to 10–12 percent of the whole. What attracted the migrant talmidim to this yeshiva? As mentioned in the first chapter, Vilna served as a place of assembly and transit for the young men who had returned from their exile in Russia and Ukraine, and a few took advantage of the opportunity and chose a yeshiva according to their preferences. The advantage of Remayle Yeshiva was its dormitory. This was very important to the migrant students because the connection with their families had been cut off, and they needed the full support of their yeshiva. Hence quite a few chose to study in this Vilna yeshiva.[52]

In these last mentioned yeshivas, the immigrants were indistinguishable among the other talmidim and did not make their own mark. However, even their large number in some of the yeshivas was not emphasized in memoirs, and it would seem that they did not affect the character of those yeshivas. This was not the case in the Novardok network. During the First World War, its yeshivas were spread all over Russia and Ukraine, and their chief aim was to gather local Jewish boys and bring them to study in a yeshiva. These youngsters took upon themselves the Novardok Musar system, and during the long and dangerous illegal border crossing of their yeshivas from Russia to Poland, they joined the flight as well. The theme of talmidim who audaciously stole across borders was well-known in the world of Novardok, and these baḥurim also made their mark in the considerable literature that was written about those years. This is an example from the writings of Mordechai Strigler, who heard this oral tradition when he studied in the Novardok Yeshiva of Lutsk:

> It is as if a ray of light came down from heaven and it immediately became clear to the *Musarnik* leaders that that's it—there's nothing left to seek and to find in that country. They must part from the places where they had established themselves. . . . The roshei-yeshiva, the mashgiḥim, the older students have all escaped, but usually they have taken with them the young ḥaburot, to the extent that it was possible to reach them. Even a few pre-bar-mitzvah boys joined them. Some of these boys did so with the agreement of their worried parents, but others joined the group without asking anyone. Their homes were far away and cut off by warring armies, and it was not possible to consult any relative. Many more had already become orphans, their families lost through slaughter and plague, and the yeshiva remained their only home. And when the home moved from its place, they only stuck their *tefillin* bag or a few booklets in their pack, and the rest they left to God's mercies.[53]

These young migrant baḥurim grew up during the time that the Novardok yeshivas were being set up in Poland, and several of them became senior talmidim there. They directed the Musar-ḥaburot, and the independence that they acquired made it possible for them to be among those who established their centers' branches. The few who survived the Shoah even became roshei-yeshiva and mashgiḥim.[54]

Westerners

Before the First World War, young men from Western European countries or the United States were a rarity in the Lithuanian yeshivas. These Talmudic institutions were located in areas under the control or protection of the Russian Empire, whose attitude toward Jews, particularly after the murder of Tsar Alexander II in 1881, made this region an insecure place to live. Even if these yeshivas gained renown and respect among Jewish communities overseas, their members did not consider it a good idea to endanger their sons and send them to this "wilderness" to study. A significant change took place in this attitude after the war, and even the Ḥafetz-Ḥayim himself was moved by this phenomenon:

> And were the majority of them already filled up with foreign wisdom in the schools there, where they poison the mind of a person while he is still young?! This is one of God's miracles that especially after the war (WWI) and the Russian Revolution with every poisonous heresy that spread from there to the ends of the earth, many young Jews from enlightened countries, even Germany, the source of the Enlightenment which laid Judaism waste, woke up and came to Poland in order to quench their thirst from the springs of Torah in Lithuania and Poland. There are even exceptional and God-fearing [students] among them.[55]

This new trend did not spring forth ex nihilo. Up until the First World War, the rabbis of Germany sought to separate themselves from the *Ostjuden* and regarded them as second-rate relations who were unworthy of their company. As the German occupation administration spread over the Lithuanian provinces, the German rabbis began to be appointed to field positions there, and they had the opportunity to come in contact with the unique quality of local Torah learning. They radically changed their estranged attitude and even extended help to the Slabodka, Grodno, and other yeshivas.[56] The favorable impression that these yeshivas made upon them trickled down to German Orthodoxy. When the war was over, its rabbis found in the adjacent Lithuanian yeshivas the best rabbinical training institutions for their youth. This approach was reinforced by great Torah scholars who had graduated from these yeshivas, among them Rabbis Avraham-Eliyahu Kaplan (1889–1924) and Yeḥiel-Ya'akov Weinberg, the heads of the Talmud faculty in the Berlin Rabbinical Seminary. Their special Talmudic instruction prompted their talmidim to go and study in the Torah institutions in Lithuania and Poland.[57]

The geopolitical changes in the region further strengthened this trend. After the war, the Lithuanian yeshivas were located in free and independent states, where the Jews were equal citizens in many senses. There was no longer any reason for concern about going from Central Europe to Lithuania or Poland to study for a number of years in one of the famous yeshivas there. Indeed, in the late 1930s the reputation of these yeshivas spread throughout Europe, and religious authorities who knew the

Lithuanian Torah world well encouraged young men from local Orthodox communities to go there to complete their studies.[58]

American Orthodoxy came to the same realization as well. Graduates of Lithuanian yeshivas arrived in the United States among the waves of immigrants from Russia at the end of the nineteenth century, and a number of them became respected community leaders in local congregations. In their aspiration to create a new Torah world in their country, they saw raising a generation of scholars as a vital need. However, there were only a few yeshivas in the United States after the First World War, and those that existed did not reach the same level as the yeshivas they knew from their youth. It was obvious to them that the natural place for nurturing Torah leaders was at that time in Lithuania and Poland, where the yeshivas had been rehabilitated. This approach was encouraged by the roshei-yeshiva as well. Economic difficulties and large debts of their yeshivas in the 1920s had forced them to travel to America to raise funds essential for the Torah institutions' functioning. Their extensive appearances in American congregations gave publicity to the Lithuanian yeshivas, which had been unfamiliar to many until then. Among their audiences and the community activists who aided the yeshivas, there were those who were impressed by the personalities of their guests and convinced to send the young sons to their institutions in Lithuania and Poland for rabbinical training.

It was not only to these yeshivas that the American and European candidates arrived to complete their rabbinical studies. From the time that the Ḥebron branch of the Slabodka Yeshiva was established in 1924, not a few candidates chose to study there. However, the serious blow the yeshiva was dealt by the Arab riots of 1929 reduced the attraction of studying in Eretz-Yisrael, and from that point there was only one destination: the Lithuanian yeshivas of Eastern Europe.[59]

Among the students who began to appear in these yeshivas were two main groups, those from Germany and from the United States. They came with the sincere intention to intensify their knowledge of Talmud and Musar, but they all had the identical goal: to receive ordination that was meant to open the doors of the communities in their countries of origin and procure for them respected rabbinic positions. Besides this common purpose, these groups were quite different one from another.[60]

The talmidim from Germany were from well-to-do families that had preserved their identity as members of Orthodox congregations. Despite their separatist orientation, their youth had been brought up in German culture, had received a general education, and had graduated from gymnasia. Some had even studied in universities and received doctorates. In the yeshivas, they were outstanding in their punctiliousness, their dedication to the studies, and their piety. Most of them did not have a yeshiva background, and they were not on the level of a yeshiva-gedola. These German baḥurim had to begin their Talmud studies from the foundation, but thanks to their abilities and their prior academic experience, they overcame these natural difficulties; the gifted ones among them even acquired the ability to study independently in a relatively short time.[61]

This education of the talmidim from Germany was funded by their parents, and therefore they were considered "wealthy" by the others who surrounded them. Their impressive economic circumstances were completely transformed in the years following *Kristallnacht*. In those years the yeshivas were obliged not only to take care of all their needs—similar to their support for local students—but even to pay for private tutors from among their peers. The Telz rosh-yeshiva, Rabbi Avraham-Yitzḥak Bloch, complained about this to the Joint in the beginning of 1936:

> It is understood that we make no distinction between one student and another in matters pertaining to food or clothing. As much as we can we extend this to all the poor pupils alike. Nevertheless, the German students whose parents became poor and are unable to send anything to their sons, even if they would like to, became quite a problem to the Yeshiva whose treasury is depleted as it is. The German youth is a community obligation and they are looking forward especially to your aid. If not for the worries how to provide for the German students, their number in our Yeshiva would increase greatly, as many who are still in Germany are appealing to us to save them from the German Hell and give them higher education as we did to their friends.[62]

The JDC had budgeted special funds to support the talmidim from Germany, but these funds were insufficient to cover the expenses of the yeshivas that continued to swell as more refugees arrived from that country.[63]

Most of the American talmidim were university graduates from middle-class families, and a few were the sons of congregational rabbis.

They were different from their fellow students from Germany and the rest of the talmidim in their loudness, their lack of manners, and the way they spoke to their elders. Their absorption in the yeshiva was not easy. They were liable to experience culture shock as they encountered "primitive" conditions in the remote town where their yeshiva was located. Their highest concentration was in Mir, and an article that appeared in an American newspaper described their first meeting of this Polish town: "When they arrived in Mir, a place that does not even appear on a map, they had to change their entire way of life. Hot baths, sports facilities, cars, a pressed suit and the theater—all these are unknown in Mir. . . . In the beginning, it was hard for them to get used to this kind of life. They especially suffered because they did not find clean bathrooms."[64] After the initial pains of absorption, the American young men succeeded in adapting somewhat to this new way of life, and a change was even seen in their personalities and behavior. Their desire to succeed in their studies was strong, and their broad general knowledge helped them approach the Talmudic material. Nevertheless, it was hard to break old habits. One day an incident occurred that was described in the same article:

> It was about a football game. A Harvard graduate knows that it is possible to study science and still go outside between lectures and play a little ball. But in the Mir Yeshiva they don't agree with this approach. This is what happened: five or six Americans wanted to get some air and, with great gusto, started to play football right in front of the yeshiva. Their Polish friends and householders from the town stood and stared with amazement. This was the first time that they had seen the combination of students and ball-players. . . . Immediately the administration informed the young men that they "had gone too far." After a quiet protest, the group gave in.[65]

They had to restrain themselves and refrain from games until the summer, when the yeshiva baḥurim went to vacation sites in the nearby forests. There they could return with enthusiasm to their beloved ball games.

The Mir Yeshiva was noted for attracting not only Americans but also other foreign students. The largest groups among them created their own separate "colonies" and kept their distance from the local talmidim to a certain degree. But when these students had to improve their level of learning, they required the help of their counterparts from Poland and hired them as private tutors. Some American baḥurim would even pay the locals to copy summaries of the lectures and the Musar talks that were meant to serve them when they returned to their home country. The income from these services helped the poor talmidim from Poland a great deal, especially considering the difficult financial situation in the yeshiva. Moreover, the joint activity brought the locals and the foreign students closer one to another, and was mutually fruitful. The Polish baḥurim found an opportunity to express their abilities in teaching and exerting spiritual influence, and to change their bashful nature. At the same time, they adopted from their "students" a broader frame of mind and much general knowledge that they did not have before. Thus the "residents of the colonies" not only received (because those who studied for a number of years in yeshiva achieved a high level of scholarship) but also contributed to the social atmosphere there.[66]

Complete lists of the students in Mir from two different periods—from the middle of the 1920s and from the second half of the 1930s—indicate their origin. It is difficult to postulate the number of foreign talmidim between these two periods. What's more, a brief perusal of the first list shows that there were no foreign baḥurim at all at that time. Consequently, there is only one period in which the number of these students can be observed in Mir, and the general picture may only be filled in by anecdotal material. Table 6.1 shows data regarding Mir talmidim according to testimonies from the beginning of 1932 and the fall of 1934, followed by precise lists from the winter term of 1935–1936 and 1938.[67]

The surprising data in the table is the percentage of foreign baḥurim, which in the 1930s was approximately a quarter of the student body. As could be expected, two main groups stood out: from Germany and from the United States. There is an obvious opposing trend in each of them: the number of students from Germany continually increased, whereas the Americans began to decrease significantly from the middle of the 30s until they lost their numerical superiority among the foreign students in the yeshiva. The presence of American talmidim was presumably the fruit of Rabbi Eliezer-Yehudah Finkel's lengthy visit to the United States in 1926. The strong bonds that he formed with the leaders of local Orthodox Jewry and its activists motivated several of them to send their sons to his yeshiva. Parallel to this, the rise of the Nazis to power in 1933 was what caused the

Table 6.1. Origin of the Mir Yeshiva students in 1932–1938

Origin of Students	**1932**	**1934**	**1935/6**	**1938**
Poland and Russia	[255]	[~278]	312	325
Germany	~25	~30	39	53
United States	31	~40	20	21
Belgium	-	4	8	6
England	7	8	5	7
Ireland	-	3	3	3
Scotland	-	2	1	2
The Land of Israel	-	-	4	1
Lithuania	8	-	-	-
Latvia	~10	-	3	2
Canada	-	2	3	1
Austria	-	6	2	2
Hungary	3	-	1	1
Czechia, Finland	1 (Fin)	-	1 (Cze)	3 (Cze)
Switzerland	2	-	-	2
France	5	3	-	-
Holland, Denmark	~3 (Hol)	1 (Den)	-	-
Sweden	-	1	-	-
South Africa	-	2	-	-
Total Foreign Students	~95	~102	90	104

constant increase of the number of baḥurim from Germany in Mir; the newer ones were penniless refugees when they arrived there. They stood out in their numbers as well as in the financial burden they imposed on the yeshiva. Only from 1936 onward did the yeshiva begin to receive support for them from a few outside organizations.[68]

Two yeshivot-gedolot in Lithuania, Slabodka and Telz, were graced by a number of foreign students. Talmidim from Germany had been studying in Knesset-Yisrael of Slabodka since the 1920s. The first student from America arrived there in 1927. In the early 1930s, the presence of American baḥurim in Slabodka was so noticeable that the American consul in Lithuania found it necessary to take part in the laying of a cornerstone for its new building in 1934. Four years later, thirty-one

Table 6.2. Origin of the Telz Yeshiva students in the interwar period

Origin of Students	1918–1929	1936/37
Lithuania	-	235
Germany	18	29
United States	-	5
Belgium	-	1
England	-	6
The Land of Israel	-	2
Poland	-	7
Latvia	14	5
Estonia	1	-
Hungary	-	4
Czechia	-	2
Switzerland	2	3
France	-	1
Holland	1	1
South Africa	-	1
Brazil	-	3
Total Foreign Students	36	68

foreign baḥurim (11%) studied in Slabodka, among them five Americans and only two Germans.[69]

There are lists from the Telz Yeshiva showing the origin of its talmidim from two distinct periods, one from the years 1918–1929, and the other from the years 1936–1937.[70] Unlike the second list, which is exact, the summarizing data from the 1920s provides only a general picture of the foreign students in the yeshiva, but it can be used to help identify trends.

In table 6.2, which shows data regarding Telz talmidim according to the two existing lists, the number of foreigners stands out, making up 22 percent of the student population of the yeshiva in the second half of the 1930s. American baḥurim were not enrolled there at all in the 1920s, and in 1936–1937 they were quite few. Obviously, it is not possible to estimate the number of American students in the first half of the 1930s, but based on other sources, this appears to be insignificant as well. In the two lists, the talmidim from Germany stand out. Students from that neighboring country were enrolled in the yeshiva from the beginning of the 1920s, and their numbers increased in a fashion similar to that in the Mir Yeshiva.[71]

An examination of the enrollment in the Lithuanian yeshivas shows that only a few of those institutions attracted foreign students, mainly Mir, Telz, Slabodka, and Kamenitz. The data available does not explain this phenomenon, and one can assume that the attractiveness of the yeshivas was related to the visits of their heads overseas or the renown of their mashgiḥim. However, it would seem that the main influence in choosing to attend these institutions was from the recommendations of rabbis and community leaders overseas who knew the yeshivas well and could direct the young people in their communities to the appropriate institutions of Torah learning. When "colonies" formed among them, these colonies then drew more talmidim, and this was what determined the trend relating to their numbers in the Lithuanian yeshivas.

IMAGE OF THE YESHIVA STUDENT

The picture of the yeshiva baḥur as he appears in the imagination—an adolescent youth so frail that he could be knocked over by a gust of wind—is far away from the image of the actual talmidim who studied in the Lithuanian yeshivot-gedolot between the wars. On the contrary, they were young adults who were, on the average, in their early twenties, and their personalities had already been seriously influenced by the Musar talks of the mashgiḥim in their yeshivas. These teachers had a significant role not only in strengthening the spiritual sides of their students' personality but also in developing their sense of self-worth, which was expressed in many different ways in their lives, from modern dress to argumentative interjections during public meetings.[72]

It is appropriate to open with the impressions of the journalist Ḥayim Shoshkes, who visited Mir in 1925. For the first time in his life, he saw a Lithuanian yeshiva from the inside; before this, he had known about its world from Enlightenment literature alone. These works described the yeshiva baḥur as an unfortunate, bent-over creature who wasted his days next to useless books and who depended on ba'alei-batim to provide him with meals at their impoverished table. Shoshkes was surprised to discover an entirely different picture in the yeshiva:

> About one hundred young men dressed in short suits sitting in groups by lecterns with books and involved in a lively discussion, but all their movements and behavior while they are studying are saturated with a certain culture and discipline. One group does not drown out the voice of another, and the general picture of this study-hour is not inferior to that of a seminar on Roman law in an ancient German university. . . . If it were not for the brimmed hats the young men were wearing, it would be possible to think according to their outward appearance that these are students in one of the institutions of higher learning—so much intelligence is expressed in their faces.[73]

The outward appearance of the individuals described was not unique to the Mir Yeshiva. Its talmid Moshe Ḥigger transferred to the Slabodka Yeshiva in 1923 to continue his studies there, and wrote, "Even the Elder [Rabbi Notte-Hirsch Finkel] made sure, like Rabbi Yeruḥam [Levovitz] of Mir, that the baḥurim wear clean clothes, and, to the extent possible, according to the latest fashion. They all had suits (not necessarily black) and wore ties around their necks and brimmed hats on their heads."[74]

In these quotes, the yeshiva students' modern appearance is emphasized. But their modernity was expressed not only in their clothing. In a few yeshivas, the local talmidim read newspapers and were conversant with current events. The director of the Vilna YEKOPO, the Jewish Committee to Aid Victims of the War, visited the Mir Yeshiva at the end of 1929 and was surprised by "the familiarity of not a few baḥurim with newspapers, politics and international events."[75] This was not being done surreptitiously, as was the case in the past; in the Telz Yeshiva it was customary even during meals in the dining hall.[76]

A comparison of these descriptions with the persecution and investigation of those who read *Haskalah* books and newspapers at the end of the nineteenth and the beginning of the twentieth centuries shows that the involvement with the Enlightenment had ceased to be a central issue in the yeshivas in the interwar period, as was written about the Kamenitz talmidim: "Even the least serious among them . . . even if they read secular books, neither Haskalah nor disgusting books and materials, but about general topics, one can see that they are intelligent."[77] It is reasonable to suppose that the general knowledge of these yeshiva baḥ urim was further broadened through the influence of the foreign students previously mentioned.

Yeshiva-gedola talmidim were measured by their peers and teachers by the level of comprehension they showed in their studies and their ability to think profoundly and come up with novel interpretations. It was very difficult for students who were not sufficiently talented to survive in an institution where the entire social experience revolved around scholarship and academic success; the psychological pressure they experienced encouraged them to leave sooner or later. Baḥurim who did not find satisfaction in intellectual pursuits and aspired to goal-oriented success were likely to cease their studies as well and quickly go out into the big world. Those who continued in the yeshivas naturally had a high aptitude for study and a strong personality. But no matter how talented they were, they could only advance and succeed in achieving outstanding accomplishments through dedication, continual study, profound analysis, and review. Several testimonies from the interwar period describe this sort of devotion to study among the yeshiva talmidim. The daily studies in Kamenitz and Telz extended to the "third seder" into the night; baḥurim in Grodno set up a special afternoon seder on Fridays, when most other students were busy preparing for the Sabbath; and Rabbi Yeḥiel-Mordechai Gordon was forced to lock the doors of the Lomzhe Yeshiva on summer evenings in order to take all his students on a daily one-hour excursion.[78]

There were young men whose academic accomplishments were outstanding, and their names were well-known throughout the yeshiva world. However, only a few were considered real illuyim who could almost instantaneously comprehend a profound sugya. One of these special young men was Mordechai Pogramansky, who may have been sui generis in the yeshivas during the interwar period. He arrived in Telz as a young man after the First World War. A short time later, he earned the sobriquet "the Tavrig illuy" and became completely familiar with the Talmud and legal works. When he got older, he continued his studies in his room. He rarely visited the yeshiva, and whenever he entered, he was surrounded by the many baḥurim who wished to pose difficult questions or hear his Torah teachings. He was not content with the routine yeshiva study but delved profoundly into Musar and Kabbalistic works until he formed his own philosophic Musar-Kabbalistic system. This is how the rabbi of Kovna, Avraham-Duber Shapiro, described him in one of his writings: "There is in our country [Lithuania] a young man who is a great and superb illuy, not just like someone who is called an illuy today, but a true illuy like one who lived hundreds of years ago. He excels in his broad knowledge, profundity and wondrous comprehension, and his original novel insights are like those of one of the outstanding giants. Besides this, he is an exceptional and wonderful fearer of God, a mouth that gives forth pearls of sublime knowledge in the ways of Musar, and an exceptionally refined person."[79]

Another unique figure whose talents were expressed in his philosophical thinking was Yitzḥak "Varshever" Hutner, who arrived in Slabodka at the end of 1921 when he was fifteen or sixteen years old. He was accustomed to writing down his impressions and thoughts, which were imbued with his most profound life experiences, in his personal diary. Even though he wrote these thoughts for himself, he would polish them a number of times until they seemed like lyric prose. About two years after his arrival in Slabodka, he wrote words that reflect the influence of Rabbi Notte-Hirsch Finkel's Musar talks:

> As I perceive today this image of a world set in motion by some individual force that occurred by happenstance one day, I see the vision of the entire weight of the slightest movement of human life, and in my ears I hear the storm of worlds being propelled, hidden and folded up in the force of an individual hand that occurred one day. This is because a man's life is not just an every-day occurrence. Man is everlasting, every partial segment of his action, whether emotional or physical, is everlasting. Each of a man's steps in the world holds within it a complete eternity of existence. A man's slightest motion, a quiver of feeling in the heart—this is no hasty leap above or around the world's mechanism, [but] an endless store-house that contains a primeval force of eternal motion. This is the true face of the story of human action.[80]

Despite their uniqueness, these talmidim did not step outside the accepted scholastic boundaries of their institutions. Highly intelligent yeshiva students were often gifted with other outstanding abilities as well, but those talents were usually stifled by the pressured and achievement-oriented curriculum. However, there were exceptions among these baḥurim, usually individualistic personalities who were unable to hide their abilities, and they brought them to the fore on various occasions. One of these was a student in the Mir Yeshiva, Ḥayim "Tiktiner" Semiatitzky (1908–1943), a future poet. Because he was an individualist, he would study Talmud on his own rather than with a study partner. His career as a poet began within the walls of the yeshiva. He composed his first poems around 1930, and his writing was known among the talmidim. One of his poems was once even shown to Rabbi Eliezer-Yehudah Finkel. The rosh-yeshiva was impressed by the work but found a Talmudic sugya to be more to his liking; Semiatitzky left Mir circa 1934. A book of his poetry was published in Warsaw a little while later, in 1935. Other talmidim with great literary talent studied in the Novardok yeshivas in particular, among them Ḥayim Grade and Mordechai Strigler. A short time after they completed their yeshiva studies, they also published their first literary works.[81]

The young men spent most of their time in yeshiva in the study of the Talmud and its commentaries, and quite a number of them even published their own novel Torah interpretations in religious journals. A few had the privilege of collecting their novellae in books, and these books were published.[82] Besides their writings in distinctly Talmudic language, several baḥurim developed a refined eloquent style and an exceptional ability of expression in the elegant Hebrew, which they had learned in elementary school and through studying the Holy Scriptures. The principal virtues of their writing were expressed in the letters they wrote to their friends, sometimes showing aspects of lyricism.

It is natural that the yeshiva students who were intellectually gifted did not excel in physical culture, but where possible they also showed athletic abilities. The talmidim in Telz used to go in the summers after the sedarim or on Friday afternoons, with the permission and even the encouragement of their teachers, to the local Mastis Lake for swimming and boating. Also in Lomzhe Yeshiva, which was situated on a hill over the Narev River, the young men found an opportunity to show their abilities on hot summer days. The swimming season began every year on the day before Shavuot, when the talmidim would immerse themselves in the river before the festival. They took advantage of breaks in their studies, especially on Fridays, for bathing there in groups, teaching the new students how to swim, and crossing the breadth of the river. The Lomzhe talmidim had the reputation of excellent swimmers. When the rumor spread that the yeshiva students were going down to the river, many local residents joined them in order to enjoy safe swimming in the water. One of the yeshiva graduates wrote, "In the end, there was not a yeshiva student who didn't learn how to swim in deep water—besides his ability to swim well in the 'sea of the Talmud.'"[83]

THE YESHIVA'S SUPPORT OF ITS STUDENTS

One characteristic of the talmidim that cannot be found in the long lists of their names, ages, and origins is the socioeconomic status of their families. It is possible to learn from other sources that the majority of the yeshiva students in the interwar period were from families lacking in means from lower middle-class, and they were obliged to rely on their yeshiva's material support. For these baḥurim to continue with their studies, the yeshiva provided them with room and board and other occasional needs that were no less essential.

Already in the early part of the nineteenth century, the Volozhin Yeshiva provided its students with regular economic maintenance. This was intended to fill the lack of two supplementary facilities within the yeshiva: a dormitory and a dining hall. By means of a monthly or weekly stipend, called *ḥaluka* (distribution), the talmidim were able to rent rooms in the town's houses and pay for meals in private homes or for food prepared by cooks for a number of baḥurim. This arrangement was copied as well in Mir and other supracommunity yeshivas that were established afterward. In a number of them, the amount of the ḥaluka was determined according to the student's place of origin and the number of talmidim from that place studying in the yeshiva. This system underwent change over the years, and support was provided based on a scale according to the seniority of each student and his excellence in Talmud study and Musar. However, the ḥaluka was inadequate for providing basic needs, and students' memoirs tell of the need for supplementary help from family in the form of money and food packages.[84]

In the interwar period, this situation further deteriorated, and most of the talmidim could not depend on the economic help of their parents. Consequently, the ḥaluka became their main financial resource and was supposed to fulfill the basic needs of room and board and provide the peace of mind necessary for studying Talmud. The extent to which the ḥaluka could provide for a student's needs is shown by statistical data collected by representatives of the YEKOPO when they visited the Mir Yeshiva at the end of 1929. The cost of a baḥur's room and board in Mir was fifteen dollars per month, and the scaled support for 350 yeshiva students was divided as follows: 20 needed no support, 150 received ten to twelve dollars each month, 100 were granted eight to ten dollars, and 80 received six to eight dollars. This data proves that the ḥaluka did not cover students' needs. Even senior or outstanding talmidim, who received preferential financial treatment, were required to supplement their income from other sources, such as private lessons to foreign students or loans from local financial aid funds. It is also possible to see that only a few (just 6 percent) could cover their expenses from their own pockets, and it would seem that these were the sons of industrialists from Lodz or others similar to them.[85]

Analysis of reports from other yeshivas reflects a similar picture, and at times a harsher one, because nearly all of their talmidim were in need of ḥaluka: 93 percent of the baḥurim in Grodno were given this stipend, and approximately 96 percent in both Radin and Kobrin received it. Ostensibly Brisk should have stood out with fewer students requiring support, because many of its talmidim were local and could sleep and eat at home. However, due to the deteriorating economic situation, even they could not depend on their families' help anymore. The yeshiva was obliged to support them, as its head, Rabbi Moshe Sokolovsky, wrote at the end of 1927: "Nearly all of them, even those from this city, are from poor families and are simply in need of support for bread."[86]

An examination of the yeshivas' expenses shows that the ḥaluka was a major item, and in Mir, Kamenitz, and Kletsk it made up more than 60 percent of the budget.[87] It is obvious that such a large expenditure was a burden on the yeshivas' very narrow shoulders, especially because the administrations' salaries came to just 10–20 percent of their budget. The continual growth in the numbers of the talmidim increased the total expense necessary to maintain them. In this dire situation, there were insufficient funds to pay the baḥurim, and the yeshivas often had to postpone the ḥaluka until the end of the term. With great concern, Rabbi Shlomo Matus, a Talmud instructor in the Kobrin Yeshiva, wrote to Va'ad-HaYeshivot at the end of the winter term of 1933: "And now we are in dire straits and we cannot hold back regarding our yeshiva's talmidim who have not received anything all term, and now when they are planning to go home for the festival, we are obligated to give them at least half or a third of what they deserve. Have mercy on us and save us from aggravation and inconceivable agony, and provide us with at least what is coming to us from the last term and a bit from this present term."[88] The hosts in the towns were already accustomed to repeated delays in payment for their services and knew how to wait patiently. Indeed, the end of term in the Kresy yeshivas became the set time for the pressures exerted by the roshei-yeshivas on the Va'ad in Vilna. They demanded that the committee pay the debts to their institutions to make it possible to distribute the ḥaluka, or if this was not possible, to at least cover the cost of the students' travel to their distant homes.

As mentioned, the ḥaluka was a major budgetary item in the yeshivas' expenditures and was subsequently the main "victim" in the round of budget cuts that they made in times of crisis. The talmidim did not sit with their hands folded; rather, they raised their voices. When the younger students in Telz received a reduced ḥaluka in 1938, it was the baḥurim in the second class who loudly expressed their protest, as befitting the tradition of this class in the distant past. When the ḥaluka was decreased in the Mir Yeshiva in 1931, the talmidim there did not quietly accept the decree but began to disturb the regular study seder in part. Things reached a boiling point between the afternoon and evening service: the lights were extinguished, and calls of "sha-sha" filled the air while students drummed rhythmically on their lecterns. This was a characteristic scene of protest from the early twentieth century. However, as was befitting to the serious Kelm-like image of the baḥurim of the Mir Yeshiva, the protest did not deteriorate into violent acts such as were previously seen in the yeshivas: turning over lecterns, breaking windows, or attacking the yeshiva staff.[89]

Similar reactions were repeated in Radin in response to the termination of support to its students. Thus wrote the son of the Ḥafetz-Ḥayim, Rabbi Leib Poupko (1861–1938), to the rabbi of London in 1934:

> Indeed, after the death of my father of blessed memory [the material situation of the yeshiva] worsened even more, and the talmidim are actually hungry for bread because the bakers stop providing bread many times, and the owners of the lodgings lock the door as they did not get what they deserved for several months, and even more so, the butchers and store owners stop giving on credit. It is understandable that because of this the

> yeshiva students begin to quarrel with the administrators and put the blame on them, and they really did not sin at all, only the crisis in all the countries, especially America, brought on all this evil.[90]

A similar protest against not paying the ḥaluka in the scholarly Kamenitz Yeshiva at the end of 1931 was expressed in a silent strike. All of its students decided to absent themselves from the study hall for a day. The administration gave in and accepted their demands. Thus the ḥaluka became an integral part of the Lithuanian yeshiva tradition, to the point that the talmidim saw it as one of their natural rights and did not hesitate to vocally demand it.[91]

Besides the ongoing ḥaluka, the yeshivas' budgets dealt with two additional common forms of maintenance for the students: payment for medical bills (examinations by doctors, operations in hospital and convalescent care) and bribes to release baḥurim from the draft. The yeshivas obviously could not fund all these expenses in total. However, they saw it proper to participate in them in part, and this expense was not slight.[92]

SUMMARY

A comparison of the student bodies in several yeshivas shows a significant trend of growth from the end of the 1920s. Even those yeshivas that suffered economic pressures or internal issues returned, for the most part, to the increased growth trend in the second half of the 1930s. Unlike the process of leaving that was usual in the Lithuanian yeshivas at the beginning of the twentieth century, this trend was reversed in the interwar period. Moreover, the yeshivas even had to partially close their doors to new students, and repeated appeals to open them were common. The rabbi of Suvalk, Rabbi David Lifshitz (1906–1993), expressed this well: "Times have changed. If in the past a question nagged at us: Where can we find young Jewish men who will dedicate their lives and strength to Torah, today the cycle is reversed and the order has changed. Precious baḥurim, great in Torah and knowledge, are knocking on the gates, but unfortunately the most essential means are lacking in order to be able to accept them."[93]

The overwhelming cause of this swell in the number of students in the yeshivas was the desire of many yeshiva-ketana graduates to continue their Torah studies. The older baḥurim in the yeshivot-gedolot had a significant influence on this process as well. Moreover, their long stay in the yeshivas not only contributed to the swelling of the student population but also prevented the natural exchange of one generation of talmidim for another, and as the years went by, there were fewer young students aged seventeen to eighteen in the yeshivot-gedolot. The dynamic that took place at both ends of the age scale brought about a clear trend of aging in the student population of the yeshivas.

This aging was not the only significant change in the characteristics of the yeshiva talmidim between the wars. In addition, there was the variety in their place of origin. In the beginning of the twentieth century, the majority of yeshiva students came from the cultural habitat of Lithuanian Jewry, and only a few came from the center of Poland or Russia. After the First World War, the "foreigners" became a significant force. Among them there were migrant talmidim who joined the yeshivas when they were in Russian and Ukrainian exile. In the first half of the 1920s, they were a significant percentage of the student population in a number of yeshivas, but as the decade went on, their numbers dwindled, and they did not leave their mark as a defined group. It was only in the Novardok movement that they were prominent in filling senior positions as heads of Musar-ḥaburot and even directors.

At the same time that the number of migrant talmidim decreased in the Lithuanian yeshivas, Westerners took their place, especially students from Germany and the United States. The lack of an appropriate background in Talmud learning of these gymnasia or university graduates made them work assiduously at their studies, and a number of them achieved fine results. But unlike the studies of the natives of Lithuania or Poland, which were not directed toward any practical goal, the chief purpose of the foreign talmidim was to receive rabbinical ordination from their roshei-yeshiva to serve in rabbinical positions when they returned to their countries. It is therefore surprising that they were also eager to be accepted to the Kelm Yeshiva, which was directed not at reaching a high level of achievement in Talmud study but toward character development. Despite their practical image, Rabbi Daniel Movshovitz, the head of the institution, was able to state about those who had been accepted, "All of them, like the others, came to the Talmud-Torah to develop their skills in the unique work that is being done here."[94]

Another characteristic of the yeshiva students is observable in the interwar period: many of the baḥurim came from families from the lower middle socioeconomic class in small towns in Poland and Lithuania. As economic conditions worsened in Eastern Europe, their families found it difficult to help them, and their material support fell upon their yeshivas. The ḥaluka that was distributed provided only the most basic necessities. Moreover, the yeshivas were obligated to provide not only room and board but also many other expenses, from clothing and shoes to a visit to a vacation site in the summer. It is clear that their support for the talmidim became a heavy burden on their budget.

What is the significance of the unique and multifaceted support, unparalleled by any other educational institutions in Eastern Europe, that the yeshivas provided for their students? Why were the yeshivas obligated to do so when their material situation was so miserable and this support only deepened their deficit? Even more amazing is the help the Mir Yeshiva was ready to provide the parents of a talmid who had died in 1935 while he studied there. The community demanded a large sum of money from his parents to erect a tombstone, but they were unable to find the necessary funds. The rosh-yeshiva, Rabbi Eliezer-Yehudah Finkel, came to their aid and wrote to Va'ad-HaYeshivot, "We regard taking care of this important matter as our task, and through you we are approaching the community leadership with the attached letter concerning permission to erect a tombstone without payment, while we stress that we have turned over this matter to Va'ad-HaYeshivot. It is impossible to describe the pain and abject sorrow caused to the parents by the great difficulties in setting up a monument for their late dear son, and therefore give your attention to carrying this matter out as soon as possible, since the extreme delay involves the desecration of the yeshiva's honor."[95] To answer those questions regarding the extent of the yeshivas' support, one needs to view the relationship of the yeshiva with its talmidim in a new light. Surprisingly, the yeshiva did not see them as transitory students who happened to enter its gates for the purpose of acquiring knowledge for a fixed period of time but as members of the yeshiva family. The support given to baḥurim was therefore part of its obligation to them. In the same way that the yeshiva heads made their own livelihood from it, it became accepted that the yeshiva was committed to providing a significant portion of the most essential and basic needs of its talmidim. Therefore it is no wonder that in difficult times, the students demanded what they "deserved" from the directors of their yeshivas, at times even through demonstrations and strikes.

NOTES

1. Assaf, "Shenot," 41; Shelli, "Resisei," 430–31; letters: Volozhin students to Grodzensky, Oct. 11, 1932 (VHY/723), and Hindes to Voronovsky, Oct. 31, 1935 (VHY/145).

2. Postcard: Platchinsky to Berek, March 1935 (VHY/373). Cf. Wischnitzer, "Di Banayung," 34–35.

3. For the development of the tasks of Va'ad-HaYeshivot, see Klibansky, *KeTzur*, 236–237, fn. 89.

4. Over the years, changes occurred in the numbers: In 1929–30 there were 58 yeshivas in Kresy, in which 5640 students studied (Shalitt, *Oif di Ḥurves*, 700); in 1936 there were 67 yeshivas with a student body of 5300 in total (report, Dec. 22, 1936 [VHY/1107]).

5. Postcard: Lev to Va'ad-HaYeshivot, Oct. 16, 1928 (VHY/178). See also *Hatzoffe*, Aug. 6, 1957.

6. Letters: Gelbor to Va'ad-HaYeshivot, Aug. 28, 1931, and Sep. 18, 1931 (VHY/528).

7. See Golan, *HaLaila*, 216.

8. This policy of Va'ad-HaYeshivot therefore reinforced the existing situation and did not create substantial changes in the size of the yeshivas.

9. Postcard: Reif to Va'ad-HaYeshivot, May 16, 1932 (VHY/373).

10. Cf. a similar habit of students wandering from university to university until the later thirteenth century (see Fletcher, "University Migrations," 164).

11. Letter: Finkel to Va'ad-HaYeshivot, Dec. 31, 1935 (VHY/371); Yeshiva report, 1938 (MWP/Mir); Gugenheim, *Letters*, 95. Cf. Berenstein, *Yeshivat*, 1011–1016.

12. See Klibansky, *KeTzur*, 74, table I. There are exact numbers available for the Lida Yeshiva as well, but because of its demise during WWI, it is not mentioned here. For shrinking of yeshivas in the first decade of the twentieth century see e.g., Shulman, "HaRuaḥ," 144, 147.

13. "Geschichtlicher Ueberblick," 3; Rozental, *HaZvi*, 280; Zariz, "Yeshivat," 195.

14. The graphs in this chapter (and specification of their data in the text) are based on the number of talmidim in the yeshivas' reports and summary tables (VHY) and in Shalitt, *Oif di Ḥurves*. The use of other sources will be mentioned ad loc.

15. Epstein, "Yeshivat Mir," 99; Agudat haRabbanim, *Sefer*, 78; Daniel, *HaSar*, 26.

16. Announcement for the first anniversary of the death of the "Ḥafetz-Ḥayim" (VHY/510); Zaks, *Michtavim*, 165; Shapira, *Igrot*, 211–12; Zariz, "Yeshivat," 203, 205; *Sha'arei Tziyon* 13, no. 10–12 (1933): 44.

17. Yoshor, "HaRav R' Eliezer," 129.

18. Letter: Hindes to Voronovsky, Oct. 28, 1935 (VHY/145).

19. *HaMizraḥi*, Oct. 5, 1922: 6; *HaNe'eman* 2 (1927–1928): 13; Levinson, *HaTenu'a*, 58; Klibansky, "HaYeshivot," 260n43; Stampfer, Shalosh Yeshivot, 223–30. Cf. Zaritzky, *Lema'alah*, 89–90.

20. Levinson, *HaTenu'a*, 363. Cf. *IdL*, Sep. 9, 1934; *DoV*, Nov. 8, 1935.

21. Yeshiva reports, 1926–1928 (VHY/1126; nevertheless, in a number of those years, the yeshiva opened its doors to a few youngsters aged sixteen years or younger thanks to their exceptional abilities). See also Epstein, "Yeshivat 'Sha'ar haTorah'," 298; Buksboim, *Sefer*,

24; HaMerkaz haOlami, *Keren*, 23. The frequency in the histogram is the percentage of talmidim of any given age among the yeshiva students.

22. Yeshiva report, 1938 (MWP); testimony: Kremer; letter: Katz to Vaxman, Apr. 19, 1923 (NWC/111); Blau, *Learn Torah*, 22; Assaf, "Shenot," 40; Shoshkes, *Lender*, 273; Tau, *Sefer*, 4; Ḥigger, *Sam*, 64.

23. Yeshiva reports, Nov. 7, 1926 (VHY/511), and Jun. 25, 1930 (VHY/1148).

24. Ḥigger, *Sam*, 57.

25. Ibid., 57–58.

26. Finkel to Ḥasman, Dec. 9, 1921 (VHY/371).

27. Shoshkes, *Lender*, 229.

28. Letter: Finkel to Va'ad-HaYeshivot, Apr. 17, 1932 (VHY/371).

29. Postcard: Levovitz to Schuw, Apr. 5, 1933 (VHY/371; in that time Rabbi Levovitz took Rabbi Finkel's place in the yeshiva, because of the latter's absence due his visit to the Land of Israel). See also letter: Finkel to Schuw, Apr. 24, 1930 (VHY/371).

30. Postcard: Leibowitz to Va'ad-HaYeshivot, May 10, 1929 (VHY/212; Rabbi Naftali-Ze'ev Leibowitz had also taken the place of the rosh-yeshiva, Rabbi Baruch-Ber Leibowitz, who was collecting donations in the United States at the time).

31. Table of yeshivas, winter 1931/2 (VHY/1107). Cf. *DIdS*, Jan. 29, 1932.

32. See chapter 1, by notes 30, 31.

33. Yeshiva reports, 1926–1928 (VHY/1136). See also report, Jan. 19, 1939 (MWP/Lomzhe); testimony: Ḥamiel.

34. Yeshiva reports, Jun. 8, 1927, and Jun. 11, 1936 (VHY/1114). See also HaMerkaz haOlami, *Keren*, 22; Schwartzbord, *BaKodesh*, 149. Regarding the yeshiva prior to the First World War, see Klibansky, *KeTzur*, 67.

35. Schwartzbord, *BaKodesh*, 149; Golan, *HaLaila*, 126–28; Postcard: Lev to Va'ad-HaYeshivot, Oct. 16, 1928 (VHY/178); *TJO* (Jun. 1970): 15.

36. E.g., Buksboim, *Sefer*, 36. Compare to the Telz Yeshiva where the older students sat near the eastern wall in the study hall, that is, in the front section (testimony: Bronznik).

37. Hertzman, *Nes*, 26. See also Stefansky, *MiMir*, 302.

38. Grade, "Talmidei-Ḥachomim," I, 13–14 (uproots mountains—analyzes the Talmudic text with brilliance). Cf. Grade, *The Yeshiva*, 14; testimony: Volbe.

39. Yeshiva reports, Oct. 28, 1926 (VHY/1130), and 1938 (MWP/Kletsk).

40. Testimony: Fortman. Cf. Grade, *The Yeshiva*, 11.

41. Lists of talmidim in Vilna and Yeshiva report, Dec. 17, 1930 (VHY/1148). See also Nishri, *Me'ir*, I, 199, 298–300.

42. Letter: Finkel to Schuw, April 24, 1930 (VHY/371).

43. Zaritzky, *Lema'alah*, 208. See Gardi, *Pirkei*, II, 145.

44. Nishri, *Me'ir*, I, 198–99, 298–300; Shalitt, *Oif di Ḥurves*, 702; Gugenheim, *Letters*, 86. Regarding this phenomenon see Stampfer, *Families*, 13; Stampfer, "Marital Patterns"; Kaubrys, *National Minorities*, 56; Research Institute, "Jews," 4.

45. See *DoV*, Mar. 30, 1934.

46. Lichtenstein and Rabinowitz, *Pinkas*, 129.

47. Shelli, "Resisei," 424. Cf. Assaf, "Shenot," 42. See also Zak, "HaYeshivot," 105; Eisenstadt, "Yeshivat Volozhin," 166; Mashbitzky, "Achsaniyot"; Rolnik, *Zichrones*, 74; Olitzky, *Yeshive-Layt*, 208; Zolf, *Oyf Fremder Erd*, 115–16.

48. Letters: Kalmanowitz to Teitelbaum, Mar. 11, 1927 (CRC-129/7), and Greineman to Va'ad-HaYeshivot, Aug. 31, 1924, and Jan. 2, 1927 (VHY/371); list of talmidim, Apr.–May

1926 (VHY/1142). For their numbers due to the proximity to the border, see Epstein, "Yeshivat Mir," 114.

49. Klibansky, "HaYeshivot," 272n107, 272n108.

50. *Baricht*, 101; Ḥigger, *Sam*, 65–67; Rozental, *HaZvi*, 281.

51. Letter: Nenedik to Va'ad-HaYeshivot, Aug. 19, 1924 (VHY/239); yeshiva reports of Radin, May 14, 1926 (VHY/1148), and Knesset Beit-Yitzḥak, Nov. 9, 1926 (VHY/1129).

52. Remayle Yeshiva reports (VHY/699, 1162); Brisk Yeshiva report, Nov. 24, 1927 (VHY/1115); table of yeshivas, winter 1931–1932 (VHY/1107); letter: Yogel to Va'ad-HaYeshivot, Aug. 18, 1924 (VHY/580).

53. Strigler, "Farshverer," I, no. 1551, 6–7 (from Yiddish; the letters "that's it" are with wider spacing in the original). See Klibansky, "HaYeshivot," 88–90, 215–16.

54. Nekritz, *Lev haAri*, 40; Levin, *Novarodok*, 39; Valach, "HaMaor haGadol," 3–5; letter: Bliacher and Glick to Kahn, Feb. 1, 1931 (AJJDCA/353).

55. Vaxman, "BiMeḥitzat," 422–23. See Agranovsky and Leiman, "Three Lists," 12; Zaltzman, *Min heAvar*, 112; Mashbitzky, "Achsaniyot"; *Hamodi'a*, Mar. 7, 1912; Zolf, *Oyf Fremder Erd*, 116.

56. *HaTzefira*, Jan. 31, 1916; *Deutsche Israelitische Zeitung*, Feb. 17, 1916; Epstein, "Yeshivat 'Sha'ar haTorah'," 292; Breuer, *Eida uDeyokanah*, 59–61.

57. *Hane'eman* 16–17 (1929): 3; Surasky, *Ohr*, I, 124n22. Cf. Breuer, *Eida uDeyokanah*, 336; Eisner, "Reminiscences," 41.

58. *Hamodi'a*, Sep. 24, 1999; Yakobzohn, *Zichronot*, 117.

59. Parush, *Orot*, 25. See also Brezin, *Tzum Yidishn Folk*, 11.

60. See Gliksman, *A Tale*, 97n53. Cf. Schwartz, "Bein Berlin," 1086; Grade, *The Yeshiva*, 14–15; testimony: YBB.

61. Ben-Yemini, "In der Malchus," 27; Epstein, "Yeshivat Mir," 107; Golan, *HaLaila*, 208, 210.

62. Letter: Bloch to JDC, 1936 (CRC-213/1; translated to English source; the Hebrew original of the words "community obligation" was mistakenly translated as "a public victim" in this source).

63. Epstein, "Yeshivat Mir," 115; letter: Finkel to Grodzensky, May 17, 1939 (VHY/373). See also *IdL*, Mar. 27, and Dec. 25, 1936.

64. "Fun Amerikaner Universitetn," 531 (from Yiddish). See also page 530; Gardi, *Pirkei*, I, 32.

65. "Fun Amerikaner Universitetn," 532 (from Yiddish). See also Ben-Yemini, "In der Malchus," 27.

66. Epstein, "Yeshivat Mir," 104, 107; Ben-Yemini, "In der Malchus," 27. See also Zinowitz, *"Mir,"* 134.

67. List of Mir talmidim, winter 1935–1936 (VHY/1162); Berenstein, *Yeshivat*, 1011–16; *HaPardes* 5, no. 11 (1932): 5; Domb, *Memories*, 50, 56. See also the lists of Mir talmidim, Apr.–May 1926, and Nov. 7, 1926 (VHY/1142).

68. Epstein, "Yeshivat Mir," 114–15; Gugenheim, *Letters*, 104–5, 147.

69. List of Slabodka talmidim, 1938 (DSA/S-21); Boi-Komitet, *Heichal haTorah*, 14, 21; Blau, Learn Torah, 18; Teitz diary (MPTA); *IdL*, Jun. 3, 1934.

70. Levinthal, *The World*, 18–26; Yeshiva report, Dec. 14, 1936 (CRC-224/10; cf. *Hayntike Nayes*, Mar. 3, 1937).

71. Alperowitz, *Telz*, 211; Wischnitzer, "Ḥomer," II, 606; Blau, *Learn Torah*, 69. The number in brackets of Czechian students is taken from *Hayntike Nayes*, March 3, 1937. Cf. the number of German students in Slabodka around the same time (this chapter, by note 69).

72. Mishkinsky, "Fun der Mirer Yeshive," II, 19; Alperowitz, *Telz*, 64; Nishri, *Me'ir*, I, 193.

73. Shoshkes, *Lender*, 229 (from Yiddish). Cf. *HaHed* 7, no. 9 (1932): 9.

74. Ḥigger, *Sam*, 63. Cf. Oshri, "Yeshivat," 150; Grodzinsky, *Shevilim*, 124, 155.

75. Shalitt, *Oif di Ḥurves*, 701 (from Yiddish). See Shoshkes, *Lender*, 232; postcard: Rach to *DoV*, Apr. 7, 1930 (VHY/373); Alperowitz, *Telz*, 64. Cf. Tikochinski, *Lamdanut*, 160–64.

76. Testimonies: Melamed and Bronznik.

77. Levin, *Zichron*, 34. See Katz, *Toledotai*, 5; Alperowitz, *Telz*, 64; Endlin, *Oif di Vegn*, 45–46; testimony: Klibansky.

78. Ben-Yemini, "In der Malchus," 27–28; Alperowitz, *Telz*, 60; Rozovsky, *Zichron*, 576; Rabinowitz, "Yeshivat," 224; Krone, *Ishim*, 18.

79. Letter: Shapiro to Rosenberg, Jan. 4, 1937 (IRC/box 5). See, e.g., Blau, *Learn Torah*, 22; Shurin, *Morei haUmah*, 172–73; testimonies: Karno and Kremerman.

80. *Tevunah* 2 (1932): 3. See also Tau, *Sefer*, 7, 339.

81. Grade: *Ya: Lider*; Strigler: *Geklibene Droshes*; Semiatitzky: *Oisgeshtrekte Hent*. See also *Idisher Kemfer* 66, no. 2575 (1987): 25; Mishkinsky, "Fun der Mirer Yeshive," II, 19; Golan, *HaLaila*, 211; Zak, *Knecht*, 127; *DoV*, Feb. 9, 1934.

82. For a detailed list, see Klibansky, "HaYeshivot," 285n195–96.

83. Levinsky, "Pirkei," 57. See testimonies: Kremerman and Bronznik; Alperowitz, *Telz*, 64. Cf. Gugenheim, *Letters*, 160 (for Mir).

84. Assaf, "Shenot," 42; Reines, "Achsaniyot," 15–16; Ovsey, *Ma'amarim*, 129; Zuckerman, *Zichreines*, I, 67–68.

85. Shalitt, *Oif di Ḥurves*, 702. Cf. Shoshkes, *Lender*, 229–230; Golan, *HaLaila*, 204.

86. Letter: Sokolovsky to Grodzensky, Nov. 10, 1927 (VHY/49). See also the mentioned yeshivas' reports, 1926–1931 (VHY/238, 1115, 145, 511, 1126, 1131, 1148). Cf. *IdL*, Jun. 4, 1937.

87. According to the reports of the three yeshivas, 1926–1931 (VHY/1129, 1130, 1142) and 1938 (MWP).

88. Postcard: Matus to Schuw, Mar. 19, 1933 (VHY/239). See letter: Pruskin to Grodzensky, Mar. 9, 1926 (VHY/238); Nishri, *Me'ir*, I, 299. Cf. *HaMelitz*, Sep. 9, 1902.

89. Mishkinsky, "Fun der Mirer Yeshive," II, 20; testimony: Bronznik. Cf. Gardi, *Pirkei*, I, 10; Assaf, "Shenot," 36, 38–39.

90. Zaks, *Michtavim*, 165.

91. Levin, *Zichron*, 34; Letter: Sokolovsky to Va'ad-HaYeshivot, Dec. 26, 1928 (VHY/49).

92. For an itemization of these payments, see Klibansky, "HaYeshivot," 289–95.

93. Agudat haRabbanim, *Sefer*, 79. Cf. Sheinfeld, *HaKnessiah*, 12.

94. Kelm Yeshiva report, 1938 (MWP/handwriting; English source). The yeshiva was named Talmud-Torah.

95. Letter: Finkel to Va'ad-HaYeshivot, Aug. 20, 1935 (VHY/371). See also *DoV*, Sep. 29, 1933.

III

The Beginning of the End

The beginning of the Second World War marked the opening of the last chapter of the Lithuanian yeshivas in Eastern Europe. Their actions, taken as a consequence of the initial course of the war, were a reproduction in miniature of the actions they took only one generation earlier, during the First World War. Once more the talmidim were forced to bear wandering and exile, and this time they dealt with the new conditions together. The scene of the infinite expanses of Russia and Ukraine that opened before them in the early years of the last war were reduced in this exile to the picture of the peaceful towns of tiny Lithuania. Just as before, a Bolshevik government's takeover of the yeshivas' new place of residence created a suffocating feeling and made it clear to the roshei-yeshiva that they must seek out a way for themselves and for their talmidim to escape. Most of them learned quickly that the road to salvation was difficult. However, even those who had already experienced wandering and exile, famine and pogroms, shooting and extreme danger during the First World War could not imagine that this time the horrors of war would reach such a tragic end.

This section, consisting of two chapters, will explore the wanderings of the Kresy yeshivas until the yeshiva world shrank into the narrow borders of Lithuania, and it will examine the internal and external efforts made to rescue them during the periods of Lithuanian independence and Soviet occupation to the beginning of their total annihilation.

7

Return to Wandering

August 1939 marked twenty-five years from the outbreak of the First World War. Tension filled again the air in Europe, and sounds that hinted of conflict could be heard. Most of the roshei-yeshiva still remembered the battles between the Russian and German armies during the last war, as well as the severe changes that took place in the yeshiva world because of it, but they carried on with their routine undertakings. They continued to attempt to balance their institutions' deficit-ridden budgets, implement plans to build and renovate their yeshivas, arrange conferences on Torah subjects, and go on with their everyday activities. Despite their attempts to ignore the explosive state of affairs, there were numerous indications of the direness of the situation. One of these was the call by the American embassy in Warsaw for the American students to leave the yeshivas in Poland as soon as possible due to the danger of war. The hurried departure of these talmidim filled their local counterparts with apprehension, especially in the yeshivas that were popular among the foreign students. Another bad omen was the conscription of young men at the end of August, including yeshiva baḥurim. A talmid in Kletsk described his feelings at the time: "We yeshivah baḥurim that summer were perhaps among the first to realize the seriousness of the political situation, because many of our classmates who previously had been exempt from military duty suddenly received draft notices from the Polish army."[1]

Most of the yeshivas took no steps of any kind in response to these indications. The graduates of Mir went so far as to fill the yeshiva in advance of the month of Elul, as was their custom every year. It would seem that Lomzhe was the only one to prepare for the future, and the administration instructed its talmidim to return home immediately until the troubles passed. Indeed, many obeyed this instruction, and only about one hundred baḥurim who had nowhere to go remained in the yeshiva and continued their regular studies.[2]

These portents of what was yet to come were not empty. On the morning of Friday, September 1, 1939, the Second World War began with a massive German attack on Kongresówka towns. The Kresy region, farther from the border, was not exempt from aerial bombing, and this cast a dark shadow over the yeshivas. The shadow was further intensified on that Sabbath, when the Torah reading included the dreadful punishments mentioned in Deuteronomy 28.[3]

Those areas adjacent to Germany were the first to feel the fearsome, face-to-face contact with its motor corps and infantry. A bitter conflict between Poles and Germans opened in Lomzhe on September 7, and in the following days the town was bombed from the air; most of its houses were destroyed. The yeshiva building was one of the few that remained standing in the immediate area. Under cover of darkness, the roshei-yeshiva and talmidim escaped to one of the nearby villages and remained there until the eve of Rosh HaShana, September 13. On their way back to Lomzhe, they met German soldiers. The soldiers took this opportunity to torment the roshei-yeshiva, and only in the late hours of the evening was the frightened group able to reach the yeshiva's building, where they hid until after Yom Kippur. The experience of stumbling upon German soldiers who were rapidly moving eastward was not limited to the heads of the Lomzhe Yeshiva, but they were the only members of the Lithuanian yeshiva world to feel the heavy hand of the conquerors at such an early stage.[4]

A few days before Rosh HaShana, the Germans bombed the city of Bialystok in the Kresy region—only a few days after the dedication of the building of the local Beit Yosef Yeshiva. Talmidim from the Torah institution wanted to flee eastward to distant Baranovitch, and there were those who did so, but the mashgiaḥ, Rabbi Yisrael Movshovitz, instructed the baḥurim to remain in the new building and continue on with their studies according to the schedule of the month of Elul.[5]

In the Kamenitz Yeshiva, which adjoined the fortified town of Brisk where a small Polish force prepared for the German attack, similar deliberation took place. Kamenitz was filled with refugees who brought with them an atmosphere of panic and ideas of flight from the approaching German army. The rumors about its acts of destruction and the sight of the local youth leaving the town and joining the streams of refugees on foot motivated the yeshiva students to discuss a similar solution with their rosh-yeshiva. However, Rabbi Baruch-Ber Leibowitz decided to remain in Kamenitz, and the talmidim gathered in his home and recited psalms. On the eve of Rosh HaShana, in the early hours before dawn, German soldiers entered the town. Even though they confiscated foodstuffs, they did not harm the populace, and most continued on to Brisk.[6]

The two Kresy yeshivas mentioned, Bialystok and Kamenitz, were located near the territories of the Kongresówka. Nonetheless, the effects of war soon arrived at a number of the eastern border towns of the Kresy as well. One of the first was Baranovitch, which was heavily bombed by the Germans from the afternoon of the first day of Rosh HaShana, Thursday, September 14. Most of the younger talmidim of the local Ohel-Torah Yeshiva had gone home, and some of the older ones scattered. At the end of the second day of Rosh HaShana, Friday, September 15, even its heads, together with a group of baḥurim, fled in wagons in the direction of Mir. As a result of the bombing, the neighboring towns began to prepare for the coming events, and in this way residents of Kletsk, including some of the local yeshiva students, were recruited for digging shelters on the morning of the Sabbath after Rosh HaShana.[7]

However, these efforts toward preparation and flight were for naught at that stage. The next day, Sunday, September 17, the Russian Army began to fulfill its part in the Molotov-Ribbentrop Pact for the division of Poland. Until then, the Soviet army had allowed the Germans to advance and occupy most of its territory; it went into action only after the Polish army had become totally exhausted. On that day, the residents of the towns adjacent to the eastern border, including Mir and Kletsk, were surprised at the appearance of Soviet airplanes and tanks; the Russian army advanced along the entire length of the front line.[8]

The Germans evacuated Bialystok and made it possible for the Russians to enter the city before Yom Kippur, and the prayers on the Day of Judgment, September 23, were loudly recited in the Beit Yosef Yeshiva. Kamenitz saw the appearance of the Russian army on the very day of Yom Kippur. Once again the students in the local yeshiva debated about what to do; this time the question was whether to flee to western Poland, which was under German control. Rabbi Baruch-Ber Leibowitz again thought that they should not panic and decided to remain in the town. On October 5, the festival of Shemini Atzeret, the Russian army succeeded in reaching Lomzhe as well, and its residents were able to leave their cellars with open joy and dancing.[9]

The joy of the inhabitants in Kresy did not last. The days of privation, characteristic of the Soviet state, soon arrived. The yeshiva students began to need the help of local Jews in getting food, and some were permitted to collect the remnants of the harvest that were still in the fields. In this way the baḥurim from Kletsk, for example, were successful in filling the storerooms of their yeshiva with a large emergency supply of vegetables, and this provided them with basic food and at times their only nourishment. However, the ravages of the conflict were not only material. The border with Lithuania passed near Radin, and a significant Soviet military presence was evident in the town. The army created an atmosphere of trepidation in the yeshiva and soon requisitioned its large building, making it into the police headquarters. In order to not stand out, its talmidim and administration began to wear simple caps, and study nearly ceased.[10]

Even in less sensitive areas, the new authorities began to constrain the yeshivas, and the buildings of Kamenitz were confiscated, as were those of the Baranovitch Ohel-Torah, the Lutsk Yeshiva, and even the not-yet-dedicated structure of the Pinsk Yeshiva. However, these confiscations were the sole means of pressure in those early days. The new government had not yet succeeded in consolidating its status and had not decided to interfere with the regular studies in the local yeshivas. Moreover, the festivals, especially the holiday of Simḥat Torah on October 6, were an opportunity for the yeshiva students to dispel some of the tension they felt by rejoicing and dancing enthusiastically despite their concern about being observed by outsiders. A talmid from the Ḥachmei-Lublin Yeshiva, who managed to flee his city that was under Nazi rule, wrote about the Simḥat Torah celebrations in Baranovitch:

> We arrived in Baranovitch for Shemini Atzeret and Simḥat Torah and spent [the holidays] in the yeshiva together with the Gaon Rabbi Elḥanan Wasserman, may he live a good life. There, inside the walls of the yeshiva, we forgot about the world, the war, politics, and we sloughed off all material concerns, and we really had days that were entirely good. . . . The true Jewish soul is incomparable. We were shown this clearly by a few [Jewish] Red Army soldiers who came to participate in the *hakafot* (dancing with the Torah-Scrolls) in the yeshiva on the night of Simḥat Torah, despite the unpleasantness that was in store for them had they been caught.[11]

This "coexistence" between the new Soviet government and the yeshivas would soon end. However, surprising adjustments in the Molotov-Ribbentrop Pact brought dramatic change to the situation.

FLIGHT TO VILNA

The secret protocol of the Molotov-Ribbentrop Pact from August 23, 1939, included the state of Lithuania in the area of German influence and set its northern border as a barrier between Russian and German control. However, the military developments in the field led to preparing a corrected version of the pact on September 28, and in a supplementary protocol Lithuania was transferred to the Russian area of influence in exchange for handing over the Lublin region and a portion of the land surrounding Warsaw to the Germans. As a result of these adjustments, a mutual assistance treaty between Russia and Lithuania was signed on October 10, with its first paragraph stating that Vilna and its surroundings would be handed over to the Lithuanian state.[12]

Until then, the eastern regions of Poland, occupied by the Russians, drew hordes of Jewish refugees. The refugees went as far as Vilna immediately after it was occupied by the Russians on September 18, but in smaller numbers due to the fact that it was a less attractive destination. The publication of the mutual assistance treaty aroused great attention among those refugees and encouraged thousands of them to move toward that city this time.[13]

In the Mir Yeshiva, the existence of the treaty became known when one of the talmidim heard about it on a British radio broadcast. Immediately suggestions to secretly escape to Vilna were raised in the yeshiva, and these awakened a lengthy give-and-take among the baḥurim. However, beyond all the uncertainties, it was clear to everyone that the yeshiva had no hope of survival for long under Soviet rule, and the idea of Vilna was the lone possibility in the present circumstances. The implementation of this plan did not seem complicated either, because trains moved freely between that city and the Soviet Kresy region. Yosef-David Epstein, the yeshiva secretary, wrote about the atmosphere in Mir:

> At once, a single idea took over the minds of all the yeshiva students: the idea of running off to Vilna. If there is an opening before you—you must run. Who knows, perhaps the fate of Lithuania is to remain non-aligned, and you're saved. . . . This is not a time for thinking, and the yeshiva baḥurim are packing their suitcases, and all around them is the rush to travel. . . . Now that the yeshiva is under Soviet rule, extra care is needed, since who knows what will happen if hundreds of religious talmidim run away? However, the titanic force of flight that seized hundreds of yeshiva students has swept away the presence of mind of the elders, the administration. The talmidim flee, and their rabbis after them.[14]

Clandestine vigorous preparations for departure began in the yeshiva, and after the Sabbath of October 14, in the middle of the night, most of the students left the town. A short while afterward, the rest of the baḥurim left with the roshei-yeshiva and their families, and only Rabbi Avraham-Hirsch Kamai decided to remain with his community in that difficult time.[15]

When the baḥurim of Mir reached Vilna, they were surprised to find that faster yeshiva students had preempted them, in particular talmidim from Kletsk. How did this happen? Immediately after the festivals, on October 8, the Kletsk rosh-yeshiva was urgently summoned by Rabbi Ḥayim-Ozer Grodzensky to discuss saving the yeshivas from the Soviets. On October 11, the participants in the discussion became aware of the transfer of Vilna to Lithuanian control, and Rabbi Aharon Kotler sent a telegram in which he requested that his family and all his talmidim join him without delay. Even though they did not understand the reason for these instructions, they recognized his good sense and prepared to depart.

The next evening, a convoy of wagons awaited to take most of the yeshiva students to Baranovitch, and from there they succeeded in reaching Vilna by train on Sabbath morning, October 14. All of them spent their Sabbath in the city's train station.[16]

The other yeshivas did not yet sense the urgency of the situation and acted more slowly, but soon they also migrated to Vilna. Had Va'ad-HaYeshivot instructed them to leave their towns and gather in its city? It is reasonable to assume that following the consultation in the house of Rabbi Grodzensky, telegrams were sent not only to Kletsk but also to the other yeshivas, although it is unclear how much these influenced their moving. It would seem that local pressures were the deciding factor. Rabbi Baruch-Ber Leibowitz was obliged to leave his home, which had been requisitioned by Soviet policemen, and left Kamenitz for Vilna between October 15 and 17. Following his lead, a wagon convoy of the yeshiva's students and its heads set out on the night of October 19 for the railroad hub in Brisk and arrived in Vilna by way of Bialystok in the middle of the Sabbath of October 21. The constant migration of many yeshiva baḥurim through Radin influenced the local talmidim and encouraged most to move to the neighboring Lithuanian town of Eishishok; some chose to remain there, whereas others, headed by Rabbi Yehoshua Levinson, continued on to Vilna.[17]

Even roshei-yeshiva who did not immediately suffer from Soviet rule saw the need to leave the area under its control because most had personally experienced its viciousness and persecutions at the end of the First World War, which were the main reason at that time for leaving Russia and Ukraine. The escape of their yeshivas to Vilna was therefore, in their eyes, the logical solution in the short run and perhaps the start of the process of moving them to a distant land of refuge.[18]

Not all the yeshivas reached Vilna in their entirety. Similar to that which had occurred during the First World War, some thought it best at this time to reorganize and split up in light of the students' constraints. In this way, most of the talmidim of the Lomzhe Yeshiva left for Vilna, except for the local ones, which were divided into two classes and studied in a regular fashion in the available upper rooms of the yeshiva building. This situation lasted until Purim 1940, when the Soviet authorities decided to commandeer the building and turn it into a storehouse. The two last

Talmud instructors, Rabbis Yehoshua-Zelig Ruch and Yisrael Rabinowitz, immediately left Lomzhe in an attempt to cross the border and join the yeshiva's branch in Vilna. The former chose to go through the town of Oshmiana and succeeded in reaching Lithuania; the latter, who tried his luck going through Lida, was seized at the border by the Russians, arrested, and sent to Siberia. The Bialystok Yeshiva was split into two as well: most of its students set out early with Rabbi Avraham Yoffen to Vilna, and quite a few baḥurim, supplemented by talmidim from other yeshivas, remained under the supervision of the mashgiaḥ, Rabbi Yisrael Movshovitz, in the town. This group left for Vilna only in midwinter. The situation was more complicated in the Mezritch Yeshiva, one of the only Lithuanian yeshivas that found themselves under German rule. Its head, Rabbi David Bliacher, decided to divide the yeshiva in two and sent his brother-in-law, Rabbi Shmuel Panitch, with about one hundred baḥurim to Vilna. He himself remained in Mezritch and continued the studies of the yeshiva underground. The students numbered, along with talmidim from other yeshivas who joined them, about two hundred.[19]

In keeping with the treaty between the Soviet Union and Lithuania, the Russian army left Vilna on October 28. The borders between the Vilna region and the areas of Russian occupation, which had been open until then, were closed in mid-November. In the short time of the month that passed between the publication of the mutual assistance treaty and this official border closing, about 1,500 yeshiva students and their teachers arrived in Vilna. Only those who had lingered were forced to then travel by train to Lida and from there attempt to cross the border with the help of professional smugglers to Lithuanian Eishishok. This perilous trip continued to take place in the frigid weather of that winter until the nearly hermetic sealing of the border in mid-January 1940. Many yeshiva students succeeded in crossing the border in this interim period, and by its end, they totaled about 1,900, not counting teachers.[20]

A similar number of *ḥalutzim* from Poland had also arrived in Vilna, crossing the border by stealth as well. These two out-of-the-ordinary groups were exceptional amid the sea of refugees in Vilna because of their mobility, which was a result of their youth, the ongoing separation from their parents' homes, and the absence of any family responsibilities. But their overriding uniqueness stemmed from their membership in organized and supportive frameworks that could make their time in Lithuania easier, especially during the early period, which was replete with difficulties experienced by the refugees in Vilna.[21]

Va'ad-HaYeshivot served as an organizational framework for the migrating yeshivas and saw its role as extending basic aid to their numerous talmidim, finding appropriate lodgings, and renewing regular studies for them. This last task was not simple because a few of the yeshivas numbered hundreds of baḥurim who required especially large halls for study, and these were rare. Arranging the material aspects of the students' needs was also not simple in the period of privation while under Soviet rule. It was only when Vilna was handed over to Lithuania that the work of the Va'ad became easier. It organized the baking of bread from the bags of flour that had been obtained through the initiative of Rabbi Aharon Baksht, rabbi of Shavl, and it set up special kitchens besides each yeshiva so that the baḥurim would not have to wait for food in the long lines of refugees. They even received appropriate clothing from a few different sources, and, similar to the others from Poland, were placed on the lists of the refugee committees and began to get regular financial support.[22]

The solution to problems of food, clothing, and location made it easier for the yeshivas to reorganize, and the Talmud instructors and mashgiḥim once again gave their regular classes and talks. A talmid from Kamenitz wrote about this period:

> Living in the shadow of "the Russian Bear," whose great paws might at any moment choke the freedom of Lithuania and our ability to pursue our studies, we felt an added urgency to study and to learn. Not a moment was wasted. The yeshiva routine, beginning with *Shacharis*, the morning prayers, at down, continued through the day, with well-attended lectures and the sing-song repetition of the questions and answers of the Gemara. The day ended late, with a frugal meal and *Ma'ariv*, the evening prayers. It seemed as if the spirit of Kamenitz had been transferred, intact, to its new location.[23]

Indeed, it was an unusual sight when Vilna was full with eighteen active Lithuanian yeshivas that were organized in separate batei-midrash, and each continued to maintain its uniqueness. In addition, other yeshivas arrived from the area under German occupation: the Lubavitch Hasidic Tomchei-Temimim Yeshiva from Otvotsk, the remnants of the

Ḥachmei-Lublin Yeshiva of Lublin, and the Beit-Shmuel Yeshiva from Warsaw. In October–November 1939, Rabbi Yitzḥak-Ze'ev Soloveitchik, who had succeeded in fleeing bombed-out Warsaw, arrived in the city and started his kibbutz anew. He began to deliver his profound lectures on the order of Kodshim to fifty or sixty of the finest talmidim who had concentrated in Vilna, and he kept this up for about a year, until December 1940.[24]

In this period of reorganization, the yeshiva world lost two of its principal pillars. On October 22, Rabbi Shim'on Shkop, who had remained in Soviet Grodno with only a few talmidim after his health prevented him from joining the students in flight, died in his town. The second was Rabbi Baruch-Ber Leibowitz, who had managed to deliver one lecture in Vilna and then suddenly became ill and died on November 17. Unlike Rabbi Shkop, who under the circumstances was buried with only a limited number of people in attendance, Rabbi Leibowitz was honored with a funeral in which more than a thousand students from the migrant yeshivas participated. But this brought little consolation to the participants. The demise of these great roshei-yeshiva one after the other seemed an evil omen to many of them and intensified the sense of the temporary nature of their stay in Vilna.[25]

DISPERSION TO THE TOWNS

The presence of so many Polish refugees in Vilna greatly disturbed the Lithuanian authorities, who aspired to change the demographic makeup of their old-new city. On December 20, 1939, the recently appointed commissar for refugee affairs, Tadas Alekna, issued a government decree that ordered them to register at police stations; in fact, it was intended to disperse them throughout the country. This decree applied to the students of the many yeshivas in the city as well, but already some time before its publication, a few yeshivas had begun to make efforts to spread out to the Lithuanian towns. One of these was the Mir Yeshiva. After the initial stages of reorganization in the building of the Remayle Yeshiva, it also received the large beit-midrash in the suburb of Novogrod, which had hundreds of seats and was well adapted for the yeshiva's large number of talmidim. Notwithstanding, its head, Rabbi Eliezer-Yehudah Finkel, preferred to find a quieter place for it in Lithuania. The yeshiva's size required a large town that could provide housing for all the talmidim. The district capital Keidan, where Rabbi Finkel's brother-in-law Rabbi Avraham-Hirsch Kamai served as rabbi in the years before the expulsion of the Jews from the Kovna Province in the First World War, was chosen as the place to relocate the Mir Yeshiva. It would seem that this early choice was not a simple one, and it required bribes and the special intervention of the secretary of the Lithuanian Rabbis' Association, David Itzikovitz (1903–1944/5), with the upper echelon of the Lithuanian authorities. By December 10 the yeshiva already had a transit permit to Keidan, and a few days later, on Hanukkah, it transferred from Vilna to its new location. The yeshiva set itself up in the town's beit-midrash, and the 2,500 Jews of Keidan—a similar number to those of the town of Mir—prepared to host about 260 talmidim, in addition to the families of the administration.[26]

Another yeshiva that chose to leave Vilna at that time was Ohel-Torah of Baranovitch, moving its location to the adjacent town of Trok. Rabbi Aharon Kotler decided on a similar step, and on December 10 his yeshiva was granted permission to settle in one of the Lithuanian communities. His choice was the town of Yaneve, but for some reason he delayed his move there for quite a while, and it was only in February 1940 that most of the talmidim of the Kletsk Yeshiva got on rented trucks and settled there.[27]

The rest of the yeshivas began to move toward the interior of Lithuania as a result of the government decree. Even though the move from Vilna involved a great deal of bother as well as distance from the centers of activity and decision-making at this very sensitive time, there were also positive aspects, as Rabbi Ḥayim-Ozer Grodzensky said: "The desire of the instructors themselves is to move, since dwelling in a large city is harmful to the spirituality of the yeshiva, while in a small town they have no distractions and learn with great diligence. The Joint which supported the refugees until now—will support the yeshivas wherever they may be."[28]

The yeshivas did not need to take great efforts in choosing a place to settle, as was noted by an eyewitness: "Each town sent emissaries to the yeshiva administrators asking them if they would be willing to bring their Torah to dwell there. The towns actually fought among themselves over the privilege of hosting one yeshiva or another."[29] However, for the majority of the yeshivas, their size dictated the choice of a district capital such as Keidan. The Radin and Pinsk Yeshivas remained in Vilna longer than

MAP 7.1.

Deployment of the Lithuanian yeshivas in independent Lithuania, spring 1940.

the other ones, and the last to depart was Lomzhe, which chose to move to the town of Plungyan only after Passover of 1940.[30] The new deployment of the yeshivas is shown in map 7.1.

Despite this mass exodus from Vilna, several yeshivas remained there, including the three non-Lithuanian ones. How did they evade the government decree? In order to answer this question, table 7.1 shows the yeshivas arranged according to the number of their talmidim at the end of the winter of 1940. To illustrate the influence of the war on the size of the yeshivas, partial data has been added from 1938.[31]

It is simple to see that all the Vilna yeshivas can be found at the bottom of the table. It would seem that their low number of students made it possible for them to disappear into the large community of refugees in

Table 7.1. Deployment of the migrating yeshivas in independent Lithuania

Yeshiva	Final Location	Number of Students			
		1938	Nov. 23, 1939	Beginning of 1940	March 1940
Mir	Keidan	403	285	264	273
Kletsk	Yaneve	260	200	225	241
Kamenitz	Rasein	306	195	180	235
Radin	Utyan and Eishishok	225	160	164	198
Bialystok	Birzh		175	166	186
Ohel-Torah Baranovitch	Trok		115	150	145
Pinsk	Vilkomir		120	104	128
Lomzhe	Plungyan		155	99	125
Mezritch	Nementchin		120	72	94
Grodno	Vilna		40	65	75
Ostroh	Vilna			37	57
Remayle (Vilna)	Vilna	115	200	55	53
Torat-Ḥesed Baranovitch	Tavrig			43	49
Lutsk	Vilna			34	43
Ostrov-Mazovietsk	Vilna			42	42
Volozhin	Vilna	55	40	37	41
Slonim	Vilna		50	45	38
Brisk	Vilna	125		[50]	27
Ḥachmei-Lublin	Vilna			46	63
Tomchei-Temimim	Vilna			46	43
Beit-Shmuel	Vilna				40
Total				**1924**	**2196**

the city without drawing much attention. The medium size of the Lomzhe and Pinsk yeshivas, as well as the Vilna branch of the Radin yeshiva, can explain their aforementioned tarrying in Vilna until they were also forced to leave the city. Missing from the table are several yeshivas that were located in the Kresy region before the war, including Luninets, Stolin, Korets, and Kobrin. There is no information available about the first three that describes their activities during the Soviet occupation, but it is clear that they did not move to Vilna. Regarding Kobrin, its rosh-yeshiva, Rabbi Pesaḥ Pruskin, became debilitated when the Russians entered the town, and he died shortly afterward. The lack of leadership and the small number of the students—only forty in 1939—prevented it from moving in an organized fashion to Vilna like the other yeshivas.[32]

The warm welcome that the Polish refugees received from the Lithuanian Jews is reflected in the many books that were written about this period. Similarly, the hospitality extended to the exiled yeshivas in the towns made a very favorable impression in the collective memory. These communities allocated batei-midrash for study and lodging places that at times were spread out in the homes of the majority of the Jewish town residents. One example of this is the Kamenitz Yeshiva, whose move from Vilna was well documented in several sources. The large number of its talmidim necessitated finding a town of sufficient size to house the yeshiva, and the county capital Rasein, home to some two thousand Jews, was chosen. An initial group was sent there to organize places for study and appropriate lodging for the 183 baḥurim and 23 family members of the administration. After completing this task, the yeshiva left its place in the beit-midrash in the Lukishok suburb, and the rabbis and their students got on the train that left Vilna for Rasein. The town's Jews greeted those arriving warmly, and the baḥurim were sent to homes. An old beit-midrash that had been renovated was set aside for the yeshiva, and within a few days the talmidim returned to their regular activities. They could once again devote all their time to study, and on Fridays they could even relax by swimming in the river that was some distance from the town.[33]

Despite this tranquil picture, there is no doubt that the students' peace of mind was disturbed by news of what was happening on the other side of the border, in the places where their families remained, whether on the Russian or German side. But more than anything else, many did not understand the point of staying in quiet Lithuania. One who was very concerned about this situation was Rabbi Eliezer-Yehudah Finkel, who did not let the pleasant atmosphere delude him, and he expressed his trepidation in this letter from Keidan: "Indeed, we have meanwhile obtained a permit to stay here in a small town called Keidan, but this stay even now cannot be called a stay in a dwelling-place, but rather a stay in prison, since our feet are bound in iron chains, and we have no idea, even the faintest, about the future. Not [only] this, but the danger of an expulsion decree, God forbid, hovers over us, and we cannot know what is happening behind our backs and what is waiting for us tomorrow.[34]" These worries were expressed by several of the roshei-yeshiva in the imploring letters they sent to save their Talmudic institutions from the trying situation in which they found themselves. However, in their desire not to hinder the regular function of their yeshivas as educational institutions, they did not encourage their talmidim to be involved in communal affairs in any way. This was the polar opposite of the refugee community, which roiled at the time in Kovna and Vilna in their frantic attempts to leave.[35]

TO THE LAND OF ISRAEL?

A number of the yeshiva heads found an opportunity in their transfer to Vilna to move their yeshivas to the Land of Israel. The first two to announce this publicly were Rabbis Finkel and Leibowitz, and later on Rabbi Kotler joined them. The active one was Rabbi Finkel, who turned to several sources to obtain immigration certificates to Palestine. However, the community activists from the Land of Israel on behalf of the yeshivas knew the actual situation. They saw no purpose in waiting to procure so many certificates when, in their opinion, there was no chance of obtaining them, and they made efforts to gain entry permits for the roshei-yeshiva themselves. The pressure they exerted toward choosing this solution can be seen in a letter from Rabbi Ḥayim-Ozer Grodzensky to Meir Bar-Ilan: "I will not argue with my friend, your honored Torah eminence, in your opinion that the roshei-yeshiva should go to the Holy Land and leave their students overseas. Their entire existence depends on the talmidim, and the entire existence of the talmidim depends on their rabbis."[36]

Among the few who benefited from the meager allocation of immigration certificates by the British for the period October 1939–March 1940 were Rabbis Finkel and Kotler. Their reactions were different: Rabbi Kotler did not take advantage of the certificate he received and waited to see the results of the attempt to obtain permits for his talmidim, whereas Rabbi Finkel seemed to have given up on outside help. He decided to go to Eretz-Yisrael and act from there directly to save the students of his yeshiva. It was only the injury of his wife on the ramp to the airplane in Riga that prevented carrying out his plan at that stage.[37]

Besides Mir, Kamenitz, and Kletsk, it would seem that other yeshivas also hoped to make aliyah to the Land of Israel. These hopes were mentioned by one of the heads of the Pinsk Yeshiva and in aliyah requests from the Lomzhe Yeshiva, which already had an Eretz-Yisrael branch. The Volozhin Yeshiva, which had stayed in Vilna, did not remain idle, and its head, Rabbi Ḥayim Valkin (1898–1941), pressured his brother-in-law, Rabbi Shim'on Langbordt (1892–1983), director of the Ge'onei Volozhin Yeshiva in Tel-Aviv, to procure permits for all his students. But all these were random attempts, and the lack of an organized, comprehensive plan that included all the yeshivas was evident. The one who could have put this plan into motion—the spiritual father of the yeshivas, Rabbi Ḥayim-Ozer Grodzensky—doubted the necessity of leaving Lithuania, as Zeraḥ Warhaftig, the head of the Eretz-Yisrael Refugee Committee in Kovna, wrote at that time: "He hesitates to bring the yeshiva students to the Land of Israel [out of concern] whether this will be for the good of Torah study, he fears the atmosphere of Eretz-Yisrael. He still believes in the Diaspora, deluding himself with the hope that the yeshivas will find a secure refuge in Lithuania until the end of the war, and then return to Poland. Because of these doubts he thinks it is better to leave the matter of the aliyah of yeshiva students to each yeshiva."[38] This position of Rabbi Grodzensky not to undertake organized emigration was apparently decisive among the roshei-yeshiva. The local yeshivas in Lithuania, which throughout their years of existence had always acted independently and without an umbrella organization, adopted the same policy. Each of their heads attempted to exert his influence on organizations or individuals in the Land of Israel or the United States. However, those organizations directed their attention toward the migrating yeshivas that had been uprooted and therefore required more immediate assistance.[39]

It would seem that the profound conviction of Rabbi Finkel that it was necessary to act urgently to save his yeshiva and bring it to the Land of Israel motivated him to exert more pressure than his colleagues. His efforts were clearly expressed when he urged and rebuked Moshe Shapiro (1902–1970), the head of the Aliyah Department of the Jewish Agency: "At this hour of great responsibility one should not delay because of the conditions of the time, but rather proceed to take this step with deep faith and confidence. If the self-sacrifice required to rescue the 'tent of Torah' exists, then certainly God will show one the way which is above the [ordinary] process [to accomplish this]. . . . One should rush, with all the strength in the world, to carry out our immigration to our Holy Land, and may our Father in Heaven have mercy!"[40]

Rabbi Finkel practiced what he preached. He understood that there was no sense in sitting idly in Lithuania and waiting for salvation to come from elsewhere. He installed one of his students, Eliezer Portnoy, in Kovna in order to investigate the possibility of aliyah to Eretz-Yisrael. Among his other activities, Portnoy met with Zeraḥ Warhaftig regarding the execution of Rabbi Finkel's plan. Portnoy was amazed to discover that this was an empty hope. He put pressure on Warhaftig to go to Keidan and present his assessment of the situation directly to the rosh-yeshiva. Warhaftig agreed and traveled to Keidan, and this is how he described the emotionally fraught meeting:

> I tried as best as I could to infect him with the anxiety that I felt, the need to act, to prepare documents and visas for all the yeshiva students despite only a slight chance of their practical value. Not to wait for a miracle, but to draw near to a miracle. . . . It was a difficult conversation, at times stormy. I saw and felt the doubts of the rosh-yeshiva. It was hard for him to step forward among the other roshei-yeshiva who were sitting complacently, to spend money on a dream, and the main thing, to cause several yeshiva students who would have to dedicate all their time to running around Kovna to neglect their Torah study.[41]

This conversation did indeed motivate Rabbi Finkel to engage in practical activity, however it was more his senior students who became convinced in the necessity of their involvement. The impression is that from the time this conversation took place, they entered the thick of things and began to act energetically, independent of their rabbi. The first task was to secure passports for all the yeshiva baḥurim, a necessary condition for the possibility of their exit from Lithuania. The office of the Polish government-in-exile was located in the British consulate in Kovna; it was ready to provide substitute papers for their old documents, which had been rendered worthless due to the dissolution of the Polish State. One talmid, Ya'akov Ederman, who spoke fluent Polish, was appointed as liaison to this office. He was successful in arranging substitute passports in February 1940 for all the yeshiva students without their having to appear personally at the consulate. However, a short time later, the exit routes from Lithuania westwards were closed, and the possibilities for emigration became quite murky.[42]

MATERIAL OR PHYSICAL RESCUE?

The large refugee community in Lithuania was materially helped by a number of groups. The principal among them was the Joint Distribution Committee, and the yeshiva students benefitted from its funds as well. These baḥurim attracted the attention of two other important organizations, which had differing interests and opposing approaches at times to the issue of rescue. One was the American Union of Orthodox Rabbis, which took upon itself the goal of supporting the migrating yeshivas materially and organized a new body for that purpose, Va'ad-Hatzalah (Rescue Committee). The second was the Chief Rabbinate of the Land of Israel, which saw the immigration of yeshiva students to Eretz-Yisrael as the only solution to the dire situation of the migrating yeshivas. These two rescue activities have already been discussed in the research but will be dealt with here in brief in order to present a more complete picture.[43]

"Va'ad-Hatzalah"

The news about the war and the rapid chain of events in Poland motivated the American Union of Orthodox Rabbis to return to its historic task that began during the First World War, when it established significant assistance organizations for the refugees, rabbis, and yeshivas in Eastern Europe.[44] The beginning was a notice in the newspapers calling for generous donations to the yeshivas in Poland to prevent their destruction. But then telegrams began to arrive from Lithuania with information about the migrations of those yeshivas to Vilna and requests for urgent help. This convinced the executives of the union to dedicate its biannual convention on November 13, 1939, to the issue. At the convention, it was decided to establish the Va'ad-Hatzalah under the presidency of Rabbi Eliezer Silver (1882–1968), rabbi of Cincinnati, and its purpose was to provide first aid to the migrating yeshivas. As a first step, the participants were requested to dedicate at least two weeks of their time to spreading information and fundraising in American communities for these yeshivas.[45]

The new committee, which brought together rabbis from Zionist HaMizraḥi and non-Zionist Agudat-Yisrael in its activities, was meant to be a unique instrument for supporting the yeshivas. In order to determine its optimum modus operandi, Rabbi Silver suggested that a special representative be sent to Lithuania, and he recommended Dr. Shmuel Schmidt, a well-known Cincinnati community activist from the Po'alei-Tsiyon Labor Zionist movement and an editor of a local Jewish weekly. Schmidt agreed to take on the position and set off for Vilna by way of the Scandinavian countries. He arrived there on February 27, 1940; met with Rabbis Ḥayim-Ozer Grodzensky and Avraham-Duber Shapiro; and visited several of the yeshivas in order to learn about their condition and needs. He found Lithuania to be a safe place for the talmidim and did not sense danger to them there, so he channeled his efforts at obtaining material aid for them. In his telegrams, he requested that the funds that had been raised be sent to Lithuania as soon as possible, out of concern that the channels for transferring them would shut. After he returned to the United States, a special meeting of the Va'ad-Hatzalah convened on July 2, 1940. There he reported on his mission and emphasized that he was profoundly impressed by the dedication of the talmidim to Torah study despite their difficult material conditions.[46]

Apparently Dr. Schmidt's mission did not reveal anything new, but the communication of his feelings regarding the difficult conditions in the yeshivas and his message that actually reflected the position of Rabbi Grodzensky spurred the members of Va'ad-Hatzalah on in their activities and efforts. Moreover, the recent occupation of Lithuania by the Soviet Union on June 15, 1940, led them to conclude that the time had come not only for financial aid but also to actually save the lives of the students.

The Activities of Rabbi Herzog

The presence of the yeshivas of Poland in the field of conflict roused the chief rabbinate of the Land of Israel to action, especially its head, Chief Rabbi Yitzḥak-Isaac Herzog (1888–1959), who because of his position felt responsibility for the well-being of the Torah world. Unlike the characteristic American approach of the Union of Orthodox Rabbis, which immediately decided to call for comprehensive financial aid for the yeshivas, Rabbi Herzog directed his efforts toward their physical rescue. Already on October 8, 1939, when all the yeshivas were still in their places in Poland with nowhere else to go, he contacted the British colonial secretary, Malcolm MacDonald (1901–1981), requesting his authorization for their immediate transfer to Palestine and promising their material maintenance on the basis of the support of the Jewish world. MacDonald rejected this proposal but promised to reconsider after the renewal of the Jewish immigration quotas in March 1940.

In the meantime, the yeshivas began their migration to Vilna and their reestablishment there, and a few of their heads contacted Rabbi Herzog with urgent requests to facilitate their yeshivas' aliyah. This led him to prepare a new emergency plan in December 1939 to bring all the students in the migrating yeshivas to Eretz-Yisrael. Three areas of activity were necessary for its implementation:

- Convincing the British government to provide entrance permits independent of immigration quotas
- Arranging transit visas with the Russian authorities by way of the Soviet Union
- Recruiting philanthropic organizations in the Jewish world for the formation of an appropriate economic base for supporting the immigrant talmidim

Rabbi Herzog set off for London on February 6, 1940, to obtain government cooperation and promote his plan. On February 21 he met with Secretary MacDonald, but the latter rejected his plan and made it clear that the immigration of the yeshiva students would be accomplished only within the regular immigration quotas, and it was conditional on ensuring their economic maintenance.

It was not only Rabbi Herzog's contacts with the British that ended in disappointment. When he turned to the Jewish philanthropic organizations in the United States through Meir Bar-Ilan, the result was similar: Va'ad-Hatzalah offered only general promises, and the Joint refused outright. It would seem that his only success was in his meeting with Ivan Maisky (1884–1975), the Russian ambassador in Great Britain. Maisky expressed an optimism regarding the transit visas for the yeshiva students—if they would indeed receive immigration certificates to Palestine—and promised that he would pass on the request to the authorities in Moscow for their perusal.[47]

SUMMARY

Soviet occupation of eastern Poland in 1939 did not immediately bring with it an expulsion decree or the large-scale fighting that would have spurred a sudden exit of the yeshivas from their towns, as had happened during the previous war. Still, among a few of them, there was a sense of panic and worry about saving life and limb to the point that they decided to flee and travel on the Sabbath, as one witness wrote: "It was a strange sight to see rabbis and roshei-yeshiva getting off the train on the Sabbath in the regal capital city of Vilna."[48]

Most of the talmidim together with their roshei-yeshiva succeeded in arriving in Vilna by train in organized groups, and it was only those who were late in leaving their towns who were obliged to make their way on their own over borders and past armed guards in the freezing winter of that year. Finding places on the trains for such large groups despite the emergency situation was made possible by the lack of uniformity in the directions of migration. Many of the refugees streamed toward the area of Soviet occupation, however not a few crossed the border into the area of German rule out of a desire to be united with their families or out of fear of the Bolsheviks. An eyewitness described this "confused" movement: "People did not know the right direction. They were unable to see road markers in those frantic days."[49] This sentence is the key to understanding the processes and behavior of many of those involved as the events unfolded.

At the start of the journey, the yeshivas knew the proper direction. As soon as they heard that Vilna had been handed over to the Lithuanians, the rabbis and their talmidim moved toward that city in the hope to find there the path to freedom. Vilna was the seat of Va'ad-HaYeshivot and its head, Rabbi Grodzensky; indeed, they provided valuable organized logistical help to twenty yeshivas that were concentrated in Vilna in late 1939.[50] This help did not end even when half of the yeshivas left Vilna for the provincial towns spread throughout Lithuania. However, the hopes of the yeshivas to be rescued from the fragile bubble in which they found themselves did not materialize. From the time that the "road markers" became invisible, the organized and uniform direction provided by Va'ad-HaYeshivot was lacking, and each yeshiva was granted complete autonomy in its actions to ensure its future.

Could this sort of direction with the help of world Jewry have yielded proper results? The awakening to the need to rescue the students of all the yeshivas came from the chief rabbi of the Land of Israel, Rabbi Herzog, but his pressure on the British authorities and on Jewish philanthropic organizations did not bring the hoped-for results. It is possible that the recruitment of American Orthodoxy to this cause by Rabbi Grodzensky would have changed the picture. Nevertheless, even if this had not helped, organized and uniform activity of the yeshivas at that time was likely to have been decisive in future stages, as will be shown in the next chapter.

NOTES

1. Pekier, *From Kletsk*, 15 (English source). See also Hertzman, *Nes*, 32–33, 99; Rabinowitz, "Yeshivat," 225; Edelstein, *Rabbi*, 75; letters: Kaplan to Berek, May 19, 1939 (VHY/46), Matus to Va'ad-HaYeshivot, Feb. 20, 1939 (VHY/238), Epstein to Va'ad-HaYeshivot, Jul. 28, 1939 (VHY/373), Lev to Berek, Aug. 9, 1939 (VHY/43), and Meshulam to Va'ad-HaYeshivot, May 23, 1939 (VHY/230).

2. Rabinowitz, "Yeshivat," 225–26; Hertzman, *Escape*, 3. At the beginning of 1939, there were 242 talmidim studying in Lomzhe (yeshiva report, Jan. 19, 1939 [MWP/Lomzhe]).

3. "The rebuke" is the popular name given to this Torah portion because it includes threats of a dire fate for the Jewish people.

4. Rabinowitz, "Yeshivat," 226. See also Rosenstein, *Ahavat*, 293.

5. Kadosh Elul, 214; Surasky, "Derech," 29.

6. Edelstein, *Rabbi*, 44–45; Edelstein, "BiYmey," 327–28; *TJO* (Dec. 1970): 21. The German attack on Brisk began the next day, on September 14.

7. Stein, *Pinkas*, 172; Ben-Mordechai, "Metivta," 332; Berenstein, *Yeshivat*, 128; Blumental, *Mir*, 582; Weintraub, *BeSufa*, 260.

8. Levin, *Tekufa*, 13. Regarding the Molotov-Ribbentrop Pact and its secret codicil, see Sontag and Beddie, *Nazi-Soviet Relations*, 76–78.

9. Kadosh Elul, 214; Edelstein, *Rabbi*, 45–46 (cf. *TJO* [Dec. 1970]: 21–22); Rabinowitz, "Yeshivat," 226.

10. Yoshor, *HeḤafetz Ḥayim*, 745; Zariz, "Yeshivat," 212 (cf. *IdL*, Dec. 11, 1939); Pekier, *From Kletsk*, 26.

11. Rottenberg, *Bikkurei*, 12. See Edelstein, *Rabbi*, 45–46; Shapiro, *Go*, 85; Gershuni, *Yehudim*, 150; Weintraub, *BeSufa*, 262, 268; Epstein, "Yeshivat Mir," 117; Pekier, *From Kletsk*, 27. The roshei-yeshiva of Baranovitch, who had fled to Mir, returned to their town before Yom-Kippur (Berenstein, *Yeshivat*, 129).

12. Shapiro, *Soviet Treaty*, 213–14 (the following sections of the treaty dealt with the principles of mutual assistance, including maintaining limited Soviet ground and air forces on certain points in Lithuania to defend its borders); Sontag and Beddie, *Nazi-Soviet Relations*, 78, 105–7.

13. Arad, "Rikuz," 166; Warhaftig, *Palit*, 26; Gilboa, *Confess!*, 20.

14. Epstein, "Yeshivat Mir," 117. See also Hertzman, *Escape* 11. Cf. Benshalom, *BeSa'ar*, 152–53; Warhaftig, *Palit*, 28. The news of the treaty was broadcast on the day following its signing, on October 11.

15. Epstein, "Yeshivat Mir," 117; Hertzman, *Escape* 11–12; Parush, *Orot*, 50–51; Berenstein, *Yeshivat*, 1065. See also Buksboim, *Sefer*, 57.

16. Pekier, *From Kletsk*, 27, 30–32. See also Surasky, *Ohr*, II, 245–46. Rabbi David Rappaport (1890–1941), a Talmud instructor in the Ohel-Torah Yeshiva of Baranovitch, had left his yeshiva as well and accompanied the Kletsk group to Vilna.

17. Even-Ḥen, *BeReshit*, 12–15; Edelstein, "BiYmey," 331–32; Zariz, "Yeshivat," 212; Va'ad-Hatzala, *Ḥurbn*, 142, 145; Warhaftig, *Palit*, 31, 141; Weintraub, *BeSufa*, 265.

18. Levin, *Tekufa*, 188.

19. Bruk, *Gevilei*, 244; "HaRav R' David Bliacher," 172; Weintraub, *BeSufa*, 270; Semiatitzky, *Ner*, 8; Levin, *Novarodok*, 43; Rabinowitz, "Yeshivat," 217, 227. The other yeshivot-gedolot in areas under German rule were the Novardok Yeshiva in Ostrovtsa and the Torat-Ḥayim and Beit Yosef yeshivas in Warsaw.

20. Va'ad-Hatzala, *Ḥurbn*, 147–48; letter: Grodzensky to Rosenberg, Dec. 19, 1939 (IRC/2/67); Gar, *Azoy*, 49; Warhaftig, *Palit*, 28; Berenstein, *Yeshivat*, 1067; Parush, *Sharsheret*, VI, 219; Rabinowitz, *Pinsk*, 289; Even-Ḥen, *Tenu'a*, 87; *YIVO Bletter* 17, no. 3 (1941): 280; Porat, "Rikuz," 8. Their number continued to grow until it reached approximately 2,200, as appears in table 7.1 in the next section.

21. Porat, "Rikuz," 8; Bauer, "Pe'ulot," 177 (who mentions about 2,065 members of the pioneer movements); Arad, "Rikuz," 168–69; Shpizman, *Ḥalutzim*, 30; Gershuni, *Maḥbarot*, 90. Ḥalutzim were pioneers preparing for agricultural settlement in Eretz-Yisrael.

22. Warhaftig, *Palit*, 32; Epstein, "Yeshivat Mir," 117–18; Rotstein, *Aḥiezer*, 49; Va'ad-Hatzala, *Ḥurbn*, 152.

23. Shapiro, *Go*, 54 (English source).

24. Hertzman, *Escape*, 15. Regarding Beit-Shmuel Yeshiva, see *BaDerech*, Feb. 21, 1936; Eliḥai, *HaMizrahi*, 89–90; Evron, *Ḥinuch*, 229.

25. Epstein, "Yeshivat 'Sha'ar haTorah'," 303–4; Guttentag, "Eshed," 160; Edelstein, *Rabbi*, 47; *IdL*, Nov. 24, 1939.

26. Epstein, "Yeshivat Mir," 118–19; Kossovsky-Shaḥor, *Igrot*, I, 286; Hertzman, *Escape*, 14, 18; Va'ad-Hatzala, *Ḥurbn*, 147; *IdL*, Dec. 22, 1939; Agudas-haRabonim, *Tetikayts-Baricht*, 5; Bauer, "Pe'ulot," 177; Porat, "Nesibot," 56; Levin, "Yerushalayim," 110; *Vyriausybės Žinios* 684 (Dec. 21, 1939): 832–33; Surgailis, *Antrojo*, 43, 148; Barak (Brik), "Pelitey," 359–62. See also *HaTzoffe*, Feb. 8, 1940; *Der Keidaner*, Jun. 1, 1940. Regarding the need for bribes, see Klibansky, "HaYeshivot," 351n84.

27. Surasky, *Ohr*, II, 251; Kossovsky-Shaḥor, *Igrot*, I, 286; Pekier, *From Kletsk*, 15; Agudas-haRabonim, *Tetikayts-Baricht*, 5. For the reasons for the delay, see Klibansky, "HaYeshivot," 351n89.

28. Kossovsky-Shaḥor, *Igrot*, I, 288–89. See also Barak (Brik), "Pelitey," 361; Rotstein, *Aḥiezer*, 50.

29. Rottenberg, *Bikkurei*, 12. See also Va'ad-Hatzala, *Ḥurbn*, 150.

30. Rottenberg, *Bikkurei*, 12; Rosenstein, *Ahavat*, 294; Va'ad-Hatzala, *Ḥurbn*, 147–48.

31. According to the order of columns: Forverts, Nov. 23, 1939; Va'ad-Hatzala, *Ḥurbn*, 147–48; letter: Warhaftig to HaMizraḥi, Mar. 26, 1940 (ARZ/6/223). The number of the Remayle Yeshiva refers to three local yeshivas with no numerical separation between them. The number in brackets of the Brisk Yeshiva is taken from Va'ad-Hatzala, *Ḥurbn*, 169 (because this yeshiva is missing in the list of the beginning of 1940). For a discussion of the total number of students, see Klibansky, "HaYeshivot," 353n101.

32. "HaRav R' Pesaḥ Pruskin," 228; Hed, "Beit Ulpena," 327; Even-Ḥen, *Tenu'a*, 150; Hirschprung, *Fun Natzishen*, 215; Warhaftig, "Baayat," 3; *IdL*, Apr. 22, 1940. Ninety-nine talmidim studied in the Vilna branch of Radin (list of talmidim, Feb. 29, 1940 [VHY/509]), similar to the numbers of Pinsk and Lomzhe.

33. Even-Ḥen, *BeReshit*, 20, 27, 45–46; Shapiro, *Go*, 56–58; "Ich Ver"; Va'ad-Hatzala, *Ḥurbn*, 147; Rottenberg, *Bikkurei*, 12; Pekier, *From Kletsk*, 37; Zariz, "Yeshivat," 214; Yoshor, "HaRav R' Yehoshua Levinson," 307; Nekritz, "Yeshivot," 287. Testimonies to the tranquility in other yeshivas see in Klibansky, "HaYeshivot," 355.

34. Letter: Finkel to The Jewish Agency, Jan. 16, 1940 (CZA, certificates/3477). See also Berenstein, *Yeshivat*, 222.

35. See Warhaftig, *Palit*, 149.

36. Letter of Mar. 10, 1940 (Kossovsky-Shaḥor, *Igrot*, I, 294). See also ibid., 283, 286, 292; letter: Shapiro to Finkel, Dec. 26, 1939 (CZA, certificates/3477); Meizlish, "Igrot," 17–18; Epstein, "Yeshivat Mir," 118; Zuroff, "HaTzibur," 49, 63; Pekier, *From Kletsk*, 36.

37. Warhaftig, *Palit*, 138; Even-Ḥen, *Tenu'a*, 158, 165.

38. Letter: Warhaftig to "Torah vaAvoda," Apr. 18, 1940 (ARZ/6/223). See also Gardi, *Pirkei*, II, 164; letters: Warhaftig to Shapiro, Feb. 18, 1940 (ARZ/6/223), and Langbort to The Jewish Agency, Apr. 7, 1940 (CZA, certificates/3477); Weintraub, *BeSufa*, 283; Eliash, "HaYeḥasim," 327, 399. The approach of Rabbi Grodzensky was common among Bundist and Zionist leaders as well (Warhaftig, *Palit*, 42; Liss, *Reuven Rubinstein*, 87).

39. Grossman, *Ki Im*, 52; Surasky, *HaRav miPonivezh*, I, 68. See also Warhaftig, *Palit*, 146–47; Eliash, "Hatzalat," 160n37; Zuroff, "HaTzibur," 63.

40. Letter: Finkel to Shapiro, Jan. 28, 1940 (CZA, certificates/3477).

41. Warhaftig, *Palit*, 150. See also Warhaftig, *Ḥidushei*, "Instead of Introduction"; Epstein, "Yeshivat Mir," 120–21.

42. Epstein, "Yeshivat Mir," 121–22; Berenstein, *Yeshivat*, 223–25, 269, 392. See also Warhaftig, *Palit*, 50–51, 62–63, 149, 151. In April 1940 the Germans invaded Denmark and Norway and closed off the maritime access of Lithuania to the Baltic Sea. In May 1940 they

occupied Holland and Belgium, closing the exit by air. On the possibility of an alternate route towards the east, see the letter: Warhaftig to Shapiro, Apr. 18, 1940 (ARZ/6/223); Barak (Brik), "HaMisrad," 303; Friedlender, "Din," 1.

43. Zuroff, *The Response*; Eliash, "HaYeḥasim"; Eliash, "Hatzalat." See Letter: Leavitt to Sebeleff (JDCIA, f. 732).

44. See more on this in chapter 3.

45. *HaPardes* 13, no. 8 (1939): 1–3; *HaPardes* 13, no. 9 (1939): 4–9; *DMZ*, Sep. 17, 1939. See also Rakeffet-Rothkoff, *The Silver Era*, 188; Yoshor, "Nasich," 11–12.

46. *HaPardes* 14, no. 3 (1940): 3; *HaPardes* 14, no. 4 (1940): 3; Va'ad-Hatzala, *Ḥurbn*, 13H, 42H, 166–70, 174; Bunim, *A Fire*, 77; Zuroff, "HaTzibur," 52–58, 65, 67–72; "Ich Ver."

47. Eliash, "Hatzalat," 132, 134–42, 160–61; Goldman, "Rabbi Herzog's," 7–8. See also Va'ad-Hatzala, *Ḥurbn*, 248.

48. Even-Ḥen, *Tenu'a*, 12.

49. Even-Ḥen, *BeReshit*, 14–15.

50. Regarding the noninclusion of the Beit-Shmuel Yeshiva in the lists of Va'ad-HaYeshivot, see Klibansky, "HaYeshivot," 353n100.

8

UNDER SOVIET RULE

Lithuania, like its Baltic counterparts Latvia and Estonia, stood like an isolated island of tranquility in the eye of the storm of armed conflict in the west and brutal annexation of Polish territories in the south and east. In fact, at certain points in Lithuania, the Soviets maintained limited ground and air forces for defense in accordance with the mutual assistance treaty, but their presence was not noticeable. Nevertheless, the relative quiet did not deceive many of the Jews of that country, nor did it deceive the refugees who had already experienced the direct results of war, and the general atmosphere in Lithuania was fraught with tension and concern.[1]

Indeed, after a short while, this political anomaly ended. It all began on May 25, 1940, with a sharply accusative memorandum issued by Soviet foreign minister Vyacheslav Molotov (1890–1986), in which he criticized Lithuania regarding the disappearance of two Russian soldiers from their garrison in its territory. In conversations that he held with the Lithuanian prime minister and foreign minister in the following days, he raised additional harsh claims of violations of the mutual assistance treaty between the two nations, and on June 14 he presented the Lithuanian foreign minister with an ultimatum comprised of three demands:

1. To try the Lithuanian minister of the interior and the director of the defense ministry for their direct responsibility for actions against the Soviet garrison.

2. To establish a government that is capable of fulfilling the mutual assistance treaty between the two countries.
3. To allow the Soviet army free and immediate entry into Lithuania in order to enforce the mutual assistance treaty and deal with any opposition to the garrison.

The government of Lithuania was required to reply to these demands by the next day. Before dawn on Saturday June 15, President Antanas Smetona (1874–1944) was still trying to form a new government that would be more acceptable to the Soviet Union. However, already on that Saturday, a large number of tanks went out of the Soviet garrison, moving toward Kovna. They went past the city and moved on in the direction of the western border. Smetona, who did not expect this step, escaped that very day with his family to Nazi Germany. About two days later, a "people's government" was established in Lithuania, headed by a temporary president, Justas Paleckis (1899–1980), a pro-Soviet Lithuanian journalist. An attorney from Telz, Mečislovas Gedvilas (1901–1981), known for his support for communism, was appointed interior minister. This was the initial stage in the steps that were taken to transform Lithuania into a Soviet republic.

On July 14, elections were held for the "people's *seimas*," in which a single party, the Communist and Non-Party Union, was presented, and as expected it won by an almost total majority. Already at its first session on July 21, the elected seimas decided on Soviet rule in Lithuania. Following the request of the people's government, Lithuania was included as a republic in the Union of Soviet Socialist Republics (USSR) on August 3, 1940, and a Soviet council of people's commissars headed by Mečislovas Gedvilas took the place of the government.[2]

These rapid and dramatic developments aroused mixed reactions among the Jews: on the one hand, they increased the feeling of the need to flee Lithuania at any cost; on the other hand, they created great alarm and paralysis. In less than a month from the Soviet invasion, on the night of July 11, there were widespread arrests throughout Lithuania of individuals connected to the Smetona government and to organizations that did not toe the Soviet line. This action increased the concerns of the residents, especially the refugees. The tensions and distress among the talmidim of the migrant yeshivas were expressed in the words of one student:

> Terror froze our blood and we felt that the place was closing in on us. All, especially Torah students, were seized by fear and trembling, and every sick heart began to feel the expected danger, and all of our thought without cease was only how to flee and escape this narrow place that is burning under our feet. Many were desperate to be saved from a state that is locked and shut, but due to the great faith that even if a sharp sword is placed on one's neck, one should not refrain from prayer—we did not abstain from entreating God to have mercy on the remnants of the scholars, and take us out of the straits and open the gate that is shut.[3]

The great fear felt among the yeshiva talmidim was not baseless. The new rulers seemed to threaten not only the possibility of the students leaving Lithuania but also their continued Torah study there, and they sensed that the Soviets, from whom they had escaped not long ago, would soon capture them in their new refuge as well.[4]

On September 7, 1940, the Supreme Soviet of the USSR issued a decree that granted Soviet citizenship to all the inhabitants of Lithuania, and consequently their exit from its borders was forbidden. At the same time, the refugees were considered a source of ferment and agitation as well as an impediment to public order, and the authorities wished to be rid of them if possible.[5] This discriminatory attitude caused, among other things, conduct on the part of the migrant yeshivas that was different from that of the local yeshivas, even though they all were equally afraid of the Russians, and the Soviet policies toward them were identical. The local yeshiva students had few expectations about receiving exit permits from their country; at most they could hope for a positive outcome from external rescue efforts. In contrast, the various reactions of the migrant yeshivas show the ambivalence that the refugees felt toward the new situation developing in Lithuania. This chapter will examine these reactions of the yeshivas—whether they dared to continue in their efforts to leave or remained isolated and exposed to the decrees of the Soviet authorities.

DISPERSAL OF THE YESHIVAS

The new regime began to vigorously transform Lithuania and immediately shut all the organizations and propaganda mouthpieces that were not communist. Afterward it turned to deal with the economic aspects of the old capitalist order and on July 26, 1940, announced the nationalization of the banks and industry. The next stage focused on the persecution of religious institutions.[6]

At the end of July and the beginning of August, several yeshivas received the order to vacate their premises. On July 31 the Telz Yeshiva was obliged to turn over its building to local authorities, who designated it as a military medical facility for neurological patients. The yeshiva moved into the building of the mechinah, but that was soon confiscated as well for use as a dormitory for a vocational school that had just been established. This time the yeshiva located itself in the large beit-midrash and remained there until the end of the winter semester of 1941. A similar fate met the Slabodka Yeshiva. The authorities took over its new building, which was not yet prepared for holding classes. Not content with that, they also confiscated the building that housed the active yeshiva. Its talmidim were forced to move to a building that stood opposite to it, which housed the Ohel-Moshe Yeshiva-ketana, and there were those who even preferred to spread out among the local synagogues, either because they were instructed to do so by the yeshiva administration or due to their personal initiative, so as to continue to study far from prying eyes while maintaining contact with the Musar-mashgiaḥ and the actual rosh-yeshiva, Rabbi Avraham Grodzensky.[7]

Other yeshivas suffered even more at the hands of the new regime and were obliged to leave not only their buildings but also their towns. They were permitted to continue with their studies, but in smaller groups and in small towns far from important population centers. One of these was the Mir Yeshiva, which was ordered to leave Keidan. Its administration immediately mobilized to deal with the situation and set up a yeshiva students' committee, whose job was to divide the baḥurim into groups. The departure from the town was set for the first day of the Hebrew month of Av, August 5, 1940. After morning prayers, the talmidim gathered for the last time in the beit-midrash where they had studied, and they parted with an emotional and tear-filled recitation of psalms in the presence of many of the local residents. A group of baḥurim led by Rabbis Ḥayim Shmuelevitz (1902–1979) and Yeḥezkel Levenstein moved to the town of Krakinove, and other groups went to Krok and Remigole. A fourth group, led by the senior talmid Leib Malin, was told to return to Vilna and stay there. However, the difficulties in the big city caused the baḥurim to go back after about one month and settle in Shatt, near Keidan. Rabbi Eliezer-Yehudah Finkel himself was wary of being overly noticeable and decided to stay far from his talmidim and settle with his secretary in an isolated town, Grinkishok. From there he continued to deal privately with the maintenance of the students and their rescue.

The Mir baḥurim organized themselves in batei-midrash in the small towns and lodged in the homes of the residents almost secretly. The mashgiaḥ, Rabbi Levenstein, chose to join the members of the new group in Shatt, and his great influence upon them can be seen in the testimony of one of the talmidim: "That month of Elul left such a great impression upon us so that even several years later . . . that short time was one of the most outstanding."[8] He did not neglect the other groups; despite his fragile health and physical difficulties in the conditions on the road at that season of the year, he made the effort to visit those groups once every two weeks in order to give talks of Musar and encouragement to their students.[9]

In August 1940, the Kletsk Yeshiva also had to leave its place. Unlike Mir, where groups of its students scattered to towns in close proximity to Keidan, the administration of Kletsk chose to move away from Yaneve to the region bordering Latvia. The older talmidim migrated to Duksht, another group headed by the Musar-mashgiaḥ Rabbi Yosef-Leib Nenedik settled in Dusiat, and the rest, led by the Rabbis Aharon Kotler and Elazar Shach, moved to Salok. In that same month, the Ohel-Torah Yeshiva of Baranovitch migrated from Trok; its administration and some of its students settled in the adjoining town of Semilishok, whereas other groups of its charges moved to Zhosle and even went as far as Kupishok. Other yeshivas also felt the changes in the air; the Torat-Ḥesed Yeshiva of Baranovitch moved from Tavrig to the adjacent smaller town of Shkudvil, and some of Mezritch talmidim left Nementchin and settled in Shirvint.[10]

It was not only the yeshivas that had migrated that were obliged to leave their host towns. Even the local Telz Yeshiva, which had already twice changed its location, had to disperse its students into several groups. During Pesaḥ 1941, while the yeshiva was on holiday vacation, the local authorities commandeered the large beit-midrash—the last place where the yeshiva had been located—to use as a club. They instructed the residents not to prepare any more rooms for the baḥurim who were expected

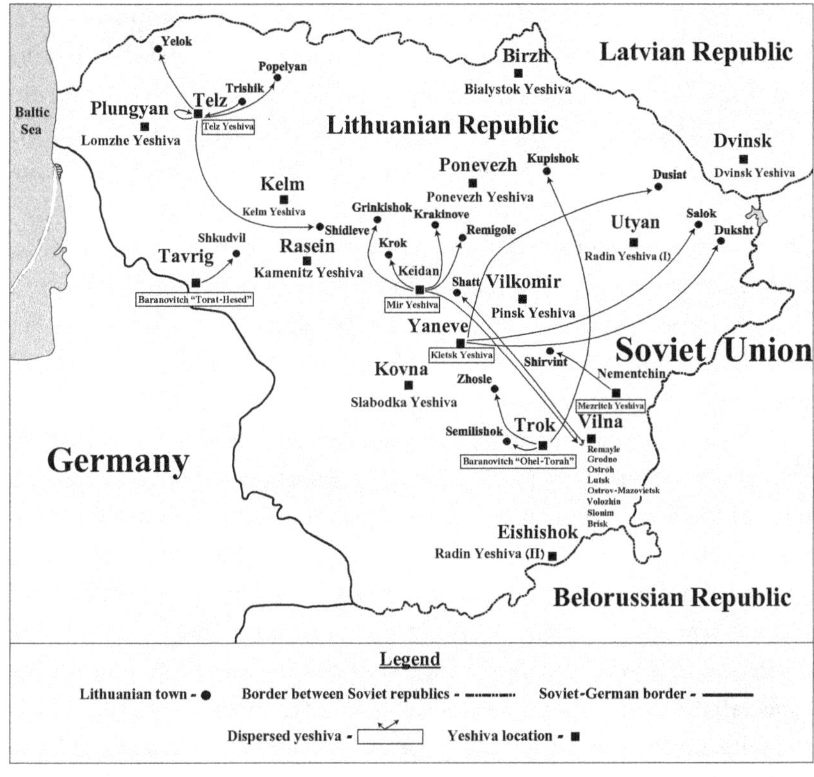

MAP 8.1.

Dispersal of the yeshivas in the Lithuanian province in the Soviet period.

to return to Telz for the summer semester. After investigation through the appropriate channels, the yeshiva administration received a hint from above to scatter into smaller groups to not attract unnecessary attention. Rabbi Avraham-Yitzḥak Bloch assembled the representatives of the talmidim for consultation, and it was decided to divide the students into groups and settle them in a number of towns. A senior or outstanding talmid was put in charge of each group, and the rosh-yeshiva and the Talmud instructors visited the various groups to teach and guide them. In this way, studies went on almost in secret until the Germans entered Lithuania.[11] Map 8.1 shows the dispersion and relocation efforts of the yeshivas.

This partially clandestine learning proves that the Soviets did not forbid study in the yeshivas, although they expended efforts to make it difficult for the talmidim. Why did the yeshivas mentioned have to leave their towns while others were exempt from this fate? The number of their students was not the deciding factor, because the Kamenitz Yeshiva, located in the county seat of Rasein and known for its considerable size, was not disturbed in its studies. There is reason to assume that the attempts to harm the yeshivas did not arise from an organized policy but rather were a result of instructions from the local authorities who were apparently autonomous in their decisions. In any case, from that point on, a sense of persecution was felt in the yeshivas that had experienced the heavy hand of the Soviets and even in those that still remained undisturbed.[12]

A few of the yeshivas' administrations found a need to encourage the baḥurim and spiritually prepare them for the expected developments in light of the Soviet continued takeover of life in Lithuania. Rabbi Azriel Rabinowitz of Telz interrupted his own regular studies to instruct his young talmidim for many hours in proper behavior during times when *mesirut-nefesh* (self-sacrifice) was required. Indeed, at that time the theme of self-sacrifice for Torah observance was a common one in other yeshivas, especially those that were part of the Novardok movement. After one of the talks on this subject given by Rabbi Shmuel Weintraub in the Pinsk Yeshiva, which had settled in Vilkomir, the Torah scrolls were taken out of the holy ark, and the talmidim committed themselves to never neglect the study of Torah. A similar event occurred in the Bialystok Yeshiva in Birzh; one of its young administrators, Rabbi Nisan "Bobroisker" Tzelniker, even composed a special verse on mesirut-nefesh and adapted a popular Russian tune in order to allow its singing without interference.[13]

An additional painful blow was dealt to these already low spirits with the death on Friday, August 9, 1940, of Rabbi Ḥayim-Ozer Grodzensky, the spiritual father of the migrating yeshivas, who saw to all their needs in the interwar period in general and particularly when they fled to Lithuania. Their talmidim felt an obligation to participate in his funeral, which was to take place in Vilna two days hence, and rented trucks to arrive there on time. Despite the watchful eyes of the Soviet authorities, they joined the masses filling the streets to accompany Rabbi Grodzensky to his final resting place.[14]

OVERSEAS RESCUE EFFORTS

The Soviet occupation significantly worsened the material condition of the refugees. After several months, the JDC, which had helped them greatly, was forced to cease its activities in Lithuania due to the American government's opposition to transferring funds to that country. Without the organized support of this vital group and other aid organizations, the yeshiva students were in danger of starvation, and only the assistance of local Jews made it possible for them to hold on. However, besides their material problem, the issue of their rescue from the Soviet regime, under whose protection they had unwillingly come, hovered over them like a dark shadow.[15]

The rapid developments awakened the centers of activity on behalf of the yeshivas in the United States and the Land of Israel. Two of the main participants acting on their behalf were mentioned in the previous chapter: Va'ad-Hatzala, which assisted them especially from a material standpoint, and the chief rabbi of the Land of Israel, Rabbi Yitzḥak-Isaac Herzog, who used his influence on the British government in an attempt to bring the yeshiva students to Eretz-Yisrael. It would seem that the Soviet occupation strengthened the feeling of urgency of these forces and this time harnessed them to the task of the physical rescue of the roshei-yeshiva and their talmidim, as well as the attempt to move their yeshivas, whether to the Land of Israel or the United States.

Rabbi Herzog chose not to travel to London this time, apparently out of the urgency of the situation. At the end of July and in early August 1940, he wrote to senior British officials requesting the immigration of the talmidim of the displaced yeshivas to Palestine to save them from spiritual destruction at the hands of the Soviet regime. The response of the new colonial secretary, Lloyd George (1879–1941), was swift and negative. Rabbi Herzog did not despair, and two months later the chief rabbinate, which was under his authority, requested 1,500 certificates in the immigration quota for students for the period of October 1940–March 1941. This request was not fulfilled either, even partially, because the British had decided not to issue immigration permits at all for the aforementioned period. Rabbi Herzog's efforts at that critical time were fruitless due to the British policy of strict enforcement of the "White Paper."[16]

In the United States, the Jewish community's awakening to action was slower. After news of the continued existence of the yeshivas under the new Soviet regime arrived, the Rabbinical Council of America considered it sufficient to issue a call on August 13, 1940, for material aid. However, a change occurred quite soon, and intensive activity was put into motion in order to rescue the yeshivas. The first to be in contact with officials in Washington regarding this subject were Tze'irei Agudat-Yisrael (the youth branch of Agudat-Yisrael); Va'ad-Hatzalah followed suit, and both organizations successfully obtained many emergency entry permits to the United States. The allocation of visas for the Torah scholars of the Jewish people was not only a matter of physical rescue. The heads of the Va'ad saw their arrival in the United States as an opportunity, for the first time since the days of mass immigration, to create a true spiritual revolution among American Jewry. It would seem that this attitude motivated the Va'ad to concentrate its activities in bringing Torah figures to the United States and refraining from aiding parallel rescue efforts that were not congruent with these goals. This is what also caused the Va'ad to focus its efforts on rescuing rabbis and roshei-yeshiva, and the long lists of students that were in its hands were neglected.[17]

ATTEMPTS TO LEAVE

The Soviet occupation proved to Rabbi Eliezer-Yehudah Finkel that in his unusual activist efforts to rescue his yeshiva, he was more correct than his counterparts, and this understanding caused him to increase his attempts to obtain the immigration certificates that he desired so much. The sense of urgency is apparent between the lines of the letter he wrote to the Jerusalem branch of Agudat-Yisrael on July 8, 1940, about three weeks after Lithuania was occupied: "Let us emphasize that you should not wait until there is a possibility of obtaining [certificates] for the entire number of talmidim, but rather, what can be obtained immediately—you should obtain immediately, because one should rush, but let it please be for a goodly number [of talmidim]."[18]

While Rabbi Finkel and his students were waiting with bated breath for a reply from Jerusalem, a rumor began to circulate in Kovna on July 22, 1940, that a talmid of the Telz Yeshiva from Holland, Naḥum-Zvi Gutvirt, and another few people received visas to the Dutch Curacao Islands from the honorary Dutch consul in Lithuania, Jan Zwartendik (1896–1976). This provided a ray of hope that the refugees would be able to leave Lithuania by way of the Far East. Zeraḥ Warhaftig made efforts to spread this information among the refugees and convince them of its reality. Later, he wrote:

> It was not easy to motivate the masses of refugees to come to Kovna, to stand in line for hours, and afterwards even for days, to pay quite a large sum, eleven *lit*, a sum that equaled the weekly support the Joint provided each refugee, in order to receive a stamp on a passport that promised nothing. Many ridiculed and dismissed the entire mission as absurd. Indeed, the Dutch pseudo-visa in itself was worthless. It was merely an illusion . . . I did not delude myself, nor did I delude the masses of refugees, but I maintained that in our situation one has to seize any chance, and it was worthwhile to make the effort to obtain the Dutch permit, the "visa" to Curacao, and on the basis of this permit to obtain a Japanese transit visa.[19]

Talmidim of the Mir Yeshiva immediately heard about this "odd" plan of action, and in those difficult and tense days, it raised both hopes and controversy in the yeshiva, which was still located in Keidan. Yosef-David Epstein, the yeshiva secretary, wrote, "Most of the yeshiva students had never heard of Curacao, and even Japan was strange to them. Who thought about such distant lands and such strange nations—this was unimaginable. The nervous tension of the baḥurim and their burning desire to leave made even this strange plan acceptable. But when it was presented to the administration—it encountered difficulty. The rosh-yeshiva saw aliyah to Eretz-Yisrael as his soul's desire. The impatience of the yeshiva students towards the distant possibility of aliyah brought them closer to this strange plan of wandering across far-away Asia."[20] Positive answers from the Land of Israel were not forthcoming, and the talmidim who saw no hope in continuing to wait for them insisted on not missing the new opportunity that had presented itself.

"The ambassador of the yeshiva," Eliezer Portnoy, requested that Gutvirt look into Zwartendik's willingness to provide Curacao visas to all of the Mir students as a group. As a result of the consul's consent, the Polish passports of the baḥurim were sent to Kovna and were given over to his care. It took about a week to sign them all, and then the way was open to approach the Japanese consulate. Moshe Zupnik, a talmid from Frankfurt, was chosen for this task, and he succeeded in convincing the consul, Chiune Sugihara (1900–1986), to give Japanese transit visas to Curacao to the entire large group of yeshiva students. Moreover, Sugihara even allowed Zupnik to sit in the consulate offices from August 5, 1940, and stamp all the passports himself while his friends were evacuating Keidan.[21]

At the same time, Rabbi Aharon Kotler was not idle either. He understood that the tranquil atmosphere in the towns where the groups of students from his yeshiva were being housed did not reflect the difficult situation. The negative replies to his requests that arrived from Eretz-Yisrael spurred him on to find alternate emigration solutions for his charges, and he decided to send a few of his talmidim who were in the town of Salok to Kovna and Vilna to follow up on them. The baḥurim soon found out about the Japanese transit visas, and they returned and spoke about them to their friends. The low price was what caused most of them to be suspicious of this solution, and they refrained from taking any concrete steps at that point to advance their leaving Lithuania.[22]

Indeed, this solution seemed quite strange, and it was apparently not a practical one. Japanese transit visas were worthless without an exit permit from the USSR, and obtaining the latter seemed to be an impassable obstacle. A breakthrough occurred when two talmidim of the Mir Yeshiva—who had Japanese visas and immigration permits to the United States—received Soviet authorization and succeeded in exiting Lithuania for Japan, apparently in August 1940.[23]

How was it that the Soviet regime agreed to permit leaving the USSR? Already in the beginning of 1940, Rabbi Herzog had asked the Soviet ambassador in London, Ivan Maisky, to obtain transit permits to Palestine for the yeshiva students living in independent Lithuania. After the Soviet occupation of the country, on his own initiative Zeraḥ Warhaftig contacted government officials in Kovna and requested an exit permit in principle from Soviet Lithuania to Japan for Polish refugees. These two uncoordinated requests were dealt with on the highest levels in Moscow. After examining all the interests involved in this matter, a positive decision arrived in July 1940—revolutionary in terms of the traditional policies of the Soviet Union—and this encouraging decision was passed on to Warhaftig on August 9, 1940.[24]

The actualization of the plan for leaving Lithuania was the cause for deliberation and anguish among the refugees in general and particularly among the yeshiva administrators, due to the fear of a Soviet trap. The concerns of the roshei-yeshiva regarding this issue led to their critical conclusion not to endanger their talmidim by presenting an exit request to the authorities. Whether this conclusion was expressed as a binding decision or whether it simply reflected their understanding of the situation, it determined the entire fate of the Lithuanian yeshiva world. As a result of these concerns, that world was doomed.[25]

The baḥurim of Mir did not accept this group approach. They again put pressure upon their rabbi and this time insisted upon presenting their request for exit permits to the authorities despite the great danger involved. Indeed, Rabbi Finkel realized that all his efforts with his acquaintances and friends in Eretz-Yisrael had been fruitless, and that even the yeshiva's supporters in the United States had not produced any results. However, he did not wish to act against the general policy of his colleagues and needed to deliberate further on this matter, which seemed fateful to him. In the end, he arrived at a sort of compromise: his charges were permitted to present their requests on their own accord without any opposition from the administration. This was an historic decision on the part of the Mir Yeshiva.[26]

The talmidim who received the right to decide on their own did not hasten to carry out their decision. It is natural that they also experienced profound soul-searching, personally and as a group. In October 1940, they decided to risk their lives and approach the authorities with requests for exit permits. These decisive and difficult moments were described by the yeshiva secretary in his picturesque language: "When the news of the decision of the Mir students to present a request to leave arrived at the other yeshivas—there was a terrible feeling. They were really afraid that they [the Mir baḥurim] were about to bring down disaster upon all the students of Torah and to bring about an end to the yeshivas. But great strengths arose at that time among them, and lifted them above all hesitations, disparagements and threats."[27]

About one month before the students' decision, as a result of the change of Soviet policy, official emigration offices were opened in the NKVD buildings in Kovna and Vilna. There, it was possible to present requests to leave the USSR. Unlike the success of the Mir Yeshiva with the deputations of Poland, Holland, and Japan, it was unable to act as a unit with the Soviet authorities. The NKVD required the personal appearance of each individual who requested an exit permit, and even the rosheiyeshiva themselves were obliged to go to the Kovna offices. Those who went there were required to fill out request forms and wait for days until their case was decided. Indeed, in December 1940 the first yeshiva students were called. The baḥurim who arrived at the intimidating office were surprised to receive positive answers to their requests from the NKVD representatives.[28]

At the same time, in late December 1940, a passage from the USSR to the Land of Israel opened through Turkey—for those who had British immigration certificates. Rabbi Finkel decided to choose this shortened path due to his belief in his ability to exert influence from within Eretz-Yisrael to save his yeshiva, for which he predicted many difficulties upon its arrival in Japan. With an exit permit from the Soviet Union in hand, he departed Lithuania and set out toward Odessa and Istanbul. Lacking any alternative, personnel changes took place in the yeshiva's leadership at one of its most difficult times, and the young Rabbi Ḥayim Shmuelevitz, Rabbi Finkel's son-in-law, became its head.[29]

Not all the yeshiva students were able to make the journey to the East together because the process of calling all the baḥurim to the NKVD offices took several weeks. Each group of talmidim that received permits from the NKVD prepared to depart on its own, and tickets to Vladivostok, a city in the southeast of the USSR near the Sea of Japan, were purchased at the train station in Kovna for a reasonable price, seven hundred rubles. However, this convenient arrangement soon went awry. The Soviets decided to derive economic benefit from releasing the refugees from Lithuania and gain foreign currency that was vital to the country. The sale of tickets was transferred to Intourist, an official government agency that dealt with tourists. In January 1941, it began to demand the payment of about $170 per ticket—an amount that would have been appropriate for American visitors—in foreign currency that was forbidden to be held in the Soviet Union.[30]

Such a high price was beyond the reach of most of the talmidim. The general sense of confusion on the eve of the exodus from Lithuania, compounded by the short validity of the exit permit, was described by the yeshiva's secretary:

> The eyes of the talmidim were directed at this time towards collective effort on the part of the yeshiva. Their expectations were first and foremost focused on the rosh-yeshiva. A vigorous demand from all directions, from the yeshiva students was that he use all the ways and means: to demand [funds] from the yeshiva's office in New York, to contact the Joint, to request loans from local sources. The rosh-yeshiva also felt helpless. The money needed to be found in a number of days, and where can one possibly obtain a sum of $50,000? . . . . A flood of telegrams burst forth—to the yeshiva office from the rosh-yeshiva, to relatives and friends from individual yeshiva students.[31]

The fate of the yeshiva fell upon the shoulders of the young Rabbi Ḥayim Shmuelevitz. However, the solution for its rescue was not in his hands at all. The key was in the hands of Rabbi Avraham Kalmanowitz, the yeshiva's representative in the United States. He was already famous for his exceptional energy and the great benefit that he had brought the yeshiva in the many trips that he took on its behalf. Indeed, all of its hopes were focused upon him. Rabbi Kalmanowitz described what had occurred from his own point of view: "I will never forget what happened to me on that eve of the holy Sabbath [January 10, 1941] . . . when I received tens of telegrams in one day from the rabbi and the talmidim about matters that tear the heart and kidneys: 'A numbers of hours, have mercy, help, hurry, borrow, use our food as collateral, send tickets to Intourist. We will never forget'."[32]

Rabbi Kalmanowitz did not disappoint this time either. Following the emergency appeals of the yeshiva, he gathered the relatives of the talmidim who lived in the United States for an urgent meeting. Truly, they succeeded in raising most of the money required, and within two weeks the sum was transferred to the Intourist offices.[33]

The yeshiva students set off. This was not a short trip; after passing through Minsk and spending a few days in a prestigious Moscow hotel, it took another ten days on the Trans-Siberian Railway to Vladivostok. One of the talmidim on the voyage described it:

> It was a good trip and there were facilities for sleeping. The railway officers supplied us with bread, herring and warm water with crystal sugar. The

> *Bnei-Yeshiva* [talmidim] also brought along additional foods. The coaches were heated during the entire trip due to the extreme cold weather outside. . . . We had a steady *minyan* [prayer quorum] and we learned. The students took along numerous *seforim* [books] from the yeshiva library, in addition to their personal copies. One member of the group even took along a *Sefer-Torah* [Torah Scroll]. On the entire trip we were accompanied by the men of the NKVD. They did not leave us for a minute, until we passed the Russian border.[34]

In February 1941 the departure of most of the yeshiva students from Lithuania was completed, and in this way about 230 talmidim of the Mir Yeshiva were rescued. Only one group of thirty baḥurim living in the town of Shatt remained in its place and did not leave.[35]

The vigorous activity surrounding the exodus of the students of Mir, and at the same time of other refugees, was not concealed from the eyes of the other yeshivas. Did the success of so many people from Poland in reaching Japan change the yeshivas' passive approach? Some of them did become convinced that independent action in leaving Lithuania was very important, and they tried to correct their lack of activity in the past. In the beginning, their talmidim were required to obtain passports, Curacao visas, and Japanese transit visas for themselves. The trouble was that the great delay prevented them from acting in a systematic and relatively straightforward manner. The consulates in Kovna were already closed at the end of August 1940, and great creativity was required to obtain the vital paperwork. Apparently most of them could not make up for lost time and did not have a chance to take advantage of the generous and lenient opportunities that the Soviet authorities offered the refugees.[36]

This is what happened, for example, to the talmidim of the Kamenitz Yeshiva in Rasein. From the time that the rumor spread there that in Kovna, Polish documents were being issued to the refugees in lieu of passports, they turned to the heads of the yeshiva and asked them for guidance, but the latter decided to prevent any organized action. Due to this negative attitude, no further steps were taken in reference to departure, even after the Curacao visas became well-known. In the course of time, the baḥurim came to understand that the members of the yeshiva administration, with the exception of the mashgiaḥ, received exit permits, and therefore they decided to elect an administration committee of three members as well as a team of ten talmidim whose task was to search for a way out of Lithuania. The members of this team found out that the Dutch consul had already left Kovna, and in their distress, they contacted the Dutch consulate in Stockholm. It sent a package of Curacao entrance permits even though the Kamenitz students did not have Polish passports. The baḥurim succeeded in obtaining the remaining documents in roundabout ways and through a long and exhausting process. When they had all the required documents, they set out, well-dressed, for Kovna in order to request Soviet exit permits. But there they met bitter disappointment. There was a notice on the door of the NKVD offices that by order of the commissar for internal affairs, the issuing of exit permits had been discontinued. The disappointed talmidim were obliged to return to Rasein, and all they could do was continue with their regular studies.[37]

It would seem that the students of the Bialystok and Radin Yeshivas went through a similar process. Among the Radin talmidim were those who succeeded in obtaining exit permits before the authorities ceased issuing them.[38]

The exception among the aforementioned yeshiva students were the talmidim of Kletsk, or at least the members of its group in the town of Salok. When the Soviet emigration offices were opened, they understood that the inexpensive Japanese transit visas were in fact real, and they may have missed the opportunity to leave Lithuania. However, they did not attempt, nor were they allowed to actively pursue a solution to their problem, because in Salok they lived in the shadow of their rabbi, Aharon Kotler, one of the architects of the general passive policy of the yeshiva heads. Change was expected only after a dramatic event that occurred on a Friday in November 1940 that shattered the illusory calm in the town. That day, three members of the secret police broke into Rabbi Kotler's office and ordered him to report to their headquarters. After a short interrogation, he was released, but the seriousness of his situation became clear to him. He decided to increase his efforts to leave Lithuania because he already had an immigration certificate for the Land of Israel and even a recommendation for a visa to the United States. As soon as he obtained the missing documents—a Japanese transit visa and an exit permit from the Soviet Union—he departed Salok. Many local Jews escorted him to the railroad station in Vilna. His talmidim parted from him in tears and hoped he would act on their behalf from overseas. In early January 1941, he was already on his way to Japan, and from there he succeeded in reaching the United States.

Rabbi Kotler's intensive efforts to leave Lithuania did not spur on his students in Salok to find alternate solutions. Instead, they began to deliberate about their future, and many even considered returning to their towns in Poland that were under Soviet rule. Opposing this was their desire to remain together and face the coming evil with their combined strength. One can assume that they also pinned their hopes upon Rabbi Kotler's efforts on their behalf. Indeed, a short time after he arrived in the United States, he succeeded in obtaining visas to Chile for all of his talmidim, but this was a considerable time after the emigration offices of the NKVD in Lithuania had been closed, and hopes for their departure from the country evaporated. The baḥurim in Salok remained there for Purim and Pesaḥ 1941 with no one from the yeshiva's administration, and only the local rabbi and the town's Jews were there to cheer them up.[39]

Unlike the case of the Mir Yeshiva and its timely and up-to-date actions, the late awakening of the other yeshivas prevented the organized rescue of their talmidim, and only a few succeeded in leaving Lithuania. Even those fortunate baḥurim encountered the obstacle of procuring dollars for purchasing train tickets to Vladivostok. Nevertheless, they acted wisely, avoided the Intourist offices in Kovna, and bought tickets in local currency in Vilna or Riga; when these tickets were no longer being sold there, they bought them in Moscow and, later on, even in other train stations on the way to Vladivostok. These resourceful talmidim succeeded in reaching Japan, and there they mixed in with the Mir Yeshiva. But unfortunately they were the minority among the yeshiva students.[40]

In contrast to the possibilities of rescuing the yeshivas that had migrated to Lithuania—possibilities that were nearly untapped—the way out of that country was closed to the local yeshivas. The involuntary Soviet citizenship denied their students any hope of obtaining exit permits, even if they possessed visas to the United States or certificates to go to Palestine. Nevertheless, the heads of the yeshivas in Lithuania worked tirelessly to save their talmidim. Rabbi Yosef-Shlomo Kahaneman, who succeeded in reaching the Land of Israel prior to Pesaḥ 1940, began in the summer of 1941 to erect a yeshiva building in Bnei-Brak in the hope of making it into a base for rescuing his talmidim from Ponevezh—whose fate at that time was concealed from him—and as a means for convincing the Mandatory authorities to issue them certificates. Similar to these efforts, the heads of the Telz Yeshiva decided to send Rabbis Eliyahu-Meir Bloch and Mordechai Katz to the United States at the beginning of September 1940 in an attempt to rescue the yeshiva and at the same time to set up a continuing yeshiva in the Free World. But these attempts, which were intended to rescue talmidim who were Lithuanian citizens, were futile from the very beginning because they clashed with one of the fundamental principles of the Soviet regime.[41]

DEPARTURE OF THE YESHIVA HEADS

Rabbi Aharon Kotler's aforementioned efforts to procure for himself the necessary documents in order to be saved from hostile authorities and the teary farewell of his talmidim at the Vilna train station were not unique episodes in the yeshiva world at that time. Many roshei-yeshiva decided to do so, and when they departed Lithuania, they left most of their students behind. In order to better understand the scope of this phenomenon, table 8.1 shows the managements of the migrating yeshivas after the closing of the Soviet emigration offices in the beginning of 1941.

It is noteworthy that most of the heads of the migrating yeshivas left Lithuania with certificates or visas, which they had succeeded in obtaining.[42] This widespread phenomenon of leaving the majority of the talmidim behind without any possibility of rescue in the yeshivas' most difficult hour raises one of the painful issues of that time. It should be noted that the isolation of the yeshiva students from their families transferred parental responsibility to their rabbis, and the departure of the roshei-yeshiva was liable to arouse feelings of neglect and vulnerability to the arbitrariness of the Soviet authorities among the young people. One could explain the phenomenon of the departure of the roshei-yeshiva from Soviet Lithuania as a function of their desire to personally spur on the decision-makers to issue certificates or visas for their talmidim. But this explanation is lacking in view of the prominence of the yeshivas that initiate the table—Kletsk, Kamenitz, and even Grodno—whose all instructors and heads left, leaving the mashgiḥim in charge of the students who remained. This

Table 8.1. The administration of the yeshivas in the beginning of 1941

	Left Lithuania		Remained in Lithuania	
Yeshiva	**Rosh-yeshiva**	**Yeshiva directors**	**Rosh-yeshiva**	**Yeshiva directors**
Kletsk	Aharon Kotler	instructor: Elazar Shach		mashgiaḥ: Yosef-Leib Nenedik
Kamenitz	Reuven Grozovsky	instructors: Moshe Bernstein and Ya'akov-Moshe Leibowitz		mashgiaḥ: Naftali-Ze'ev Leibowitz
Grodno	Moshe Shatzkes	director: Moshe-Mordechai Shkop		mashgiaḥ: Shlomo Harkavy director: Yeshaya Hindes
Lomzhe	Yeḥiel-Mordechai Gordon [was in the United States at the outbreak of war]		acting rosh-yeshiva: Yehoshua-Zelig Ruch	mashgiaḥ: Moshe Rosenstein instructors: Shabtai Vernikovsky, Leib Pruskin and Yehoshua-Isaac Kostyokovsky
Bialystok	Avraham Yoffen			mashgiḥim: Yisrael Movshovitz and Nisan Tzelniker instructor: Nisan Potashinsky

Table 8.1. (*continued*)

	Left Lithuania		**Remained in Lithuania**	
Yeshiva	**Rosh-yeshiva**	**Yeshiva directors**	**Rosh-yeshiva**	**Yeshiva directors**
Pinsk	Shmuel Weintraub			mashgiaḥ: Yeraḥmi'el Shulman instructor: Yosef Rozental director: Shalom Rabinowitz
Radin	Mendel Zaks			mashgiaḥ: Eliezer-Ze'ev Kaplan instructors: Avaraham Trop and Mordechai-Isaac Burland director: Yehoshua Levinson
Slonim	Shabtai Yogel			mashgiaḥ: Avraham-Zvi Listovsky
Remayle (Vilna)			Yisrael Levovitz	instructors: Efraim-Zvi Bialostotsky and Ze'ev Segal
Mezritch			Shmuel Panitch	
Torat-Ḥesed Baranovitch			Avraham-Shmuel Hirschowitz	
Volozhin			Ḥayim Valkin	

question is sharpened in light of the earlier reluctance and even outright opposition of the heads of the migrant yeshivas to any independent action at all on the part of the talmidim to facilitate their own rescue. After the fact, it became clear that were it not for this opposition, it would have been possible to save most of them.[43]

It would seem that the key to understanding this phenomenon can be found in the words of Rabbi Elḥanan Wasserman in a letter to his brother in Eretz-Yisrael, during the period of Lithuanian independence in 1940: "I have no intention of leaving the yeshiva [in Trok] and going to the Land of Israel on my own, but it is impossible to move the yeshiva to the Holy Land since they do not permit men from eighteen to fifty to go from Riga, all the more so it is impossible to travel through Germany. Nevertheless, I wish to obtain certificates for myself and my sons, in the case that we may suddenly have to leave our present location."[44] Assuming that these words represented the opinion of his colleagues as well, it seems that the efforts of the roshei-yeshiva should be divided into two stages. The first was in the period of independent Lithuania, during which they wished to ensure for themselves rescue permits only in case of emergency. The vanguards who received emigration certificates to Palestine within the first quota were the heads of Mir, Kamenitz, and Kletsk yeshivas. They aspired to bring their talmidim to the Land of Israel, and the heads of Kamenitz and Kletsk did not even take advantage of the personal permits that they had and delayed their use to a later emigration quota in the hope of taking their students with them. In the second quota for April–September 1940, additional certificates were allocated to the heads of the Bialystok and Pinsk yeshivas, as well as for the members of the administration of Grodno, Kletsk, and Kamenitz. But the only one who tried to take advantage of the permit that he had in the period of Lithuanian independence was Rabbi Eliezer-Yehudah Finkel. Opposition to this step came from his colleague Rabbi Yeḥezkel Levenstein in particular; the mashgiaḥ of the Mir Yeshiva was of the opinion that the obligation of its head was to be with his talmidim, and his absence was liable to endanger the yeshiva's very existence. Indeed, when Rabbi Finkel's plan was not carried out due to his wife's injury, the mashgiaḥ saw this as proof for the rightness of his position. He himself never considered leaving the yeshiva, and a short time before Lithuanian independence was dissolved, he wrote, "I can obtain a visa to

Eretz-Yisrael, and it is ready even now in the consulate in Kovna, but of course I am not even thinking of this."[45]

The second stage began after the Soviet occupation of Lithuania. It may be that the confiscation of the buildings of some yeshivas and scattering a number of them to towns appeared to their heads as omens that their continued long-term existence was hopeless. They were familiar with the stories of persecution and arrest of rabbis and roshei-yeshiva in the USSR in the 1920s, as well as the shutting of the yeshivas that were still active there at that time. The senses that they had developed as refugees during the current war aroused fears that they and their families would be arrested by the authorities and sent to Siberia. When they saw that there was no possibility of taking their many students out of Lithuania, they felt that all they could do was to save themselves, and those among them who had connections tried to take others from the yeshiva administration with them.[46]

The fate of the heads of the local yeshivas in Lithuania and Ohel-Torah of Baranovitch was different. They had Lithuanian or Latvian citizenship and could not leave the Soviet Union even had they wanted to do so, because the Soviet citizenship had been imposed on them.[47] Just a few of them were outside Lithuania when the war broke out and were forced to stay in place. However, even the Ponevezh rosh-yeshiva who received a diplomatic passport from the Lithuanian government and reached the Land of Israel or the faculty members of the Telz Yeshiva, who got special Soviet permits for their mission to the United States, were more naïve than their counterparts of the migrating yeshivas. They left their wives and their many children behind because they did not suspect that those would be harmed in Lithuania during the war time.[48] But neither they nor the heads of the migrant yeshivas ever imagined that by their exodus from Lithuania, they had saved themselves from imminent annihilation.

ARREST AND DEPORTATION

Up until the closing of the emigration offices, several thousand refugees succeeded in leaving the USSR, among them talmidim of the Mir Yeshiva and a few from other yeshivas. All the rest were faced with the choice by the authorities of accepting Soviet citizenship or foreign refugee status.

A similar policy was instituted the previous year in western Belorussia and Ukraine. In an edict that was issued there on November 29, 1939, automatic Soviet citizenship was assigned to all the local residents, and the choice of accepting this was given to refugees from western Poland. Most chose not to actualize this privilege that was granted them, and consequently the NKVD set up "refugee rehabilitation committees" in April–May 1940. These committees obligated them to choose between Soviet citizenship according to the edict or repatriation to their homes in the area of German occupation. Surprisingly, most of the Jewish refugees signed up for the latter option. However, instead of acceding to their request, the authorities arrested them on June 29, 1940, and after a short time exiled them to the interior of the Soviet Union. Of course, the news of the expulsion of more than two hundred thousand Jews spread throughout Lithuania by way of letters from relatives and friends, and therefore the refugees in this country were quite aware of the significance of the choice placed before them.[49]

The talmidim of the migrant yeshivas were also faced with the same dilemma. The baḥurim of the Kletsk Yeshiva who were in Salok were ordered by the district official to come to his headquarters in the town of Azherena in May of 1941. In the forms that they were given to complete, they were asked to choose between remaining in the Soviet Union or leaving, and even to specify the country which they preferred. The students understood that their fate was hanging in the balance, and their answer would likely determine their future for the better or the worse. After discussing the matter among themselves, they all decided to leave the Soviet Union and emigrate to one of the countries preferred by them—the United States, the Land of Israel, or Chile. On June 13 they were summoned once more to fill out forms, this time in the office of the local mayor. They were required to declare in writing concerning their interest in Soviet citizenship and were given three hours to make their decision. After deliberating and discussing the issue among themselves, the majority decided to give a negative reply. Only two of the baḥurim chose to sign that they agreed to accept Soviet nationality out of fear that they could not bear the hardships of Siberia that were in store for them if they refused, preferring to return to their towns in western Belorussia. At the conclusion of the formal signing, the talmidim returned home to get organized for the coming Sabbath. A similar procedure went on with the Bialystok Yeshiva in Birzh, and probably with other migrant yeshivas as well.[50]

On that Friday night and the early hours of Saturday, June 14—one year since Lithuania was occupied—deportation of individuals who were unwanted by the regime began in all the areas annexed by the USSR. About twenty thousand were expelled from Lithuania alone, among them several thousand Jews.[51]

Among the candidates for deportation were also refugees who refused Soviet citizenship, including the students from the migrant yeshivas. During that night and the following days, a widespread hunt was organized for them in the towns. A talmid from Kamenitz described what he saw before him when he went to visit the Knesset-Yisrael Yeshiva of Slabodka a few days later:

> I arrived at the yeshiva at noontime. Across the street, there was a huge sign posted: "One Who Does Not Work Does Not Eat. . . ." In this case it was a direct insult and threat to the school's faculty and students. Inside the building I was astonished to find everything littered and in disarray. I sat down on a bench to rest a bit, but just then a man poked his head in the doorway and whispered to me, "The police raided this place last night, and again this morning. They're arresting everyone. Run, young man, run!"[52]

Obviously, the authorities looked among the baḥurim of Slabodka for refugee students from Poland to arrest and deport them, and these young men tried to hide during the arrests. Many of the talmidim from the other migrant yeshivas did the same. Students of the Kamenitz Yeshiva in Rasein, where the planned arrests were already known, looked for hiding places for themselves. Nevertheless, half of them were seized by the NKVD and taken with the mashgiaḥ by freight train to a labor camp in the Komi Republic. In the Bialystok Yeshiva in Birzh, the authorities succeeded in arresting about one hundred talmidim and the mashgiaḥ and sent them to forced labor in Siberia. Before dawn, on the Sabbath of June 14, the talmidim in Salok, who on the day before had refused Soviet citizenship, were also arrested. They were allowed to return from the local police station to their rooms to take necessary items and then were sent by buses to the train station in Duksht. They were put on a freight train there, and on Tuesday morning it set off for Siberia. When the hunt after refugee students was over, the local yeshivas could continue on with their regular schedules. In this way, the studies in Slabodka returned to normal until the Sabbath of June 21, 1941.[53]

The sounds of German bombing, which began to be heard well the next morning, were the first sign of the reality of war in Lithuania. Late on Tuesday, German shock troops entered Kovna, and in a very short time Lithuania fell into German hands like a ripe fruit. Only a single group of local talmidim succeeded in being saved—some baḥurim of Telz who studied in Trishik and decided to attempt to cross the border into Russia. Nearly all those who remained in Lithuania were cruelly murdered by the Lithuanians and the Germans.[54]

SUMMARY

The Soviet occupation of Lithuania was predictable in many ways, but nevertheless it caught Jews by surprise and made many of the refugees shudder. The rapid actions of the new regime to enforce its policies, among them the confiscation of the yeshiva buildings and the scattering of a number of the educational institutions to small towns, paralyzed their heads. The roshei-yeshiva chose to act extra cautiously and oppose all organized activity by their talmidim, whether obtaining visas or requesting exit permits from the Soviet authorities. After a short time, it became clear that their concerns were exaggerated, and the various permits did indeed make it possible to leave the Soviet Union and even reach Japan. The consequences of this policy of the yeshiva heads are revealed in the dismal picture shown by the data related to those leaving Lithuania.

A short time after the Soviets occupied Lithuania, a unique constellation was formed for a limited time of just over one month. During this period it was possible to obtain substitute Polish passports, Curacao visas, and transit visas to Japan with no limits. These documents were even given out to entire groups by the consuls on request. At this time the gates of the USSR were surprisingly open, and in a unique step its authorities allowed the Polish refugees who had the proper permits to leave. This arrangement let about 1,200 of them to emigrate to the Land of Israel by way of Turkey, and about three thousand went to the Far East. Among the latter, there were less than four hundred yeshiva students, including approximately 230 talmidim of the Mir Yeshiva, and some sixty baḥurim from Ḥachmei-Lublin and Tomchei-Temimim yeshivas. These statistics show that the number of survivors among the students of the Lithuanian yeshivas was tiny.[55]

The exception among the roshei-yeshiva was Rabbi Eliezer-Yehudah Finkel, whose burning desire to take his yeshiva out of Lithuania motivated him to deviate from their general policy of passivity. The determination of the rescue team of Mir, which employed every required means to advance the possibility of leaving, and the silent support of their rabbi joined together for the success of the yeshiva's near-total rescue and the maintenance of its organizational framework after it left Lithuania. The students of the other yeshivas did not realize how vital it was to establish special rescue teams either due to a lack of initiative or the lack of support from their rabbis, who actually opposed taking the necessary steps. When many of the baḥurim began to wake up, it was already too late to go through the entire obstacle course of obtaining permits before the Soviet emigration offices closed in Lithuania.[56]

In contrast to the talmidim, their roshei-yeshiva were granted certificates to emigrate to the Land of Israel or visas to the United States, and thanks to their position, most of them succeeded in obtaining the necessary transit visas to receive exit permits from the USSR in time. Those who were able to leave Japan and reach the United States established there a rescue committee of their own. In their first announcement to the press on August 8, 1941, they proudly noted the Torah learning in their yeshivas in Lithuania under conditions of privation and fear: "The evil of our most stubborn enemies and all their furious attacks have not succeeded in making our Torah students deviate from their holy task. . . . This gives us confidence that even now, in the most tragic worldwide catastrophe, the students of Torah are united and carry the banner of the Torah. Therefore, there is no room for despair, and no justification or basis to doubt the existence of the tents of Torah of 'Yavneh and its sages' on the other side of the sea."[57] These roshei-yeshiva imagined that the success of their disciples to withstand Soviet oppression would repeat itself during the Nazi occupation. However, when their words were published, a minority of their students were already in labor camps throughout the Soviet Union; whereas the majority of the talmidim were no longer alive or would shortly meet their deaths in cruel and unusual ways.[58]

NOTES

1. Gar, *Azoy*, 47. Soviet bases had been set up in four towns (ibid., 48).

2. Ibid., 55–56, 60–75, 85–86.

3. Karpenshprung, *Divrei Mordechai*, preface. See also Gar, *Azoy*, 83; Va'ad-Hatzala, *Ḥurbn*, 214; Gar, *Umkum*, 28. Cf. Shtark, *Tahapuchot*, 35.

4. Pekier, *From Kletsk*, 40; Hertzman, *Escape*, 12. Cf. Surasky, *Marbitzei*, III, 242.

5. Geilke, *Das Staatsangehörigkeitsrecht*, 340; United Nations, *Laws*, 31.

6. Levin, *Tekufa*, 261; Gar, *Azoy*, 82, 103.

7. Levin, "Ḥofesh," 176; Gifter, "Yeshivat," 186; Oshri, "Yeshivat," 163. See also *HaTzoffe*, Sep. 29, 1940; Weintraub, *BeSufa*, 285.

8. Berenstein, *Yeshivat*, 1042.

9. Ibid., 397, 444–46; Epstein, "Yeshivat Mir," 119–20; Hertzman, *Escape*, 35–36.

10. Testimonies: Orlansky, Waldschein; Surasky, *Ohr*, II, 256, 273; the testimonies of Shmuel Levin and Feivel Musnitzky (KoC/86), and Sarah Einbinder-Deitch (KoC/137); Pekier, *From Kletsk*, 45; letter: Kotler to Rosenberg, Oct. 2, 1940 (IRC/3/63); Farbstein, *MiTelz*, 147–48, 179; Stein, "Shkudvil," 1863. Regarding the study locations of Tavrig and Nementchin, see table 7.1. Rabbi Shach (1899–2001) was a Talmud instructor in Luninets and Kletsk Yeshivas.

11. Gifter, "Yeshivat," 186–87; "HaRav R' Avraham Yitzḥak," 33; Farbstein, *MiTelz*, 204–7; testimony: Melamed.

12. *HaTzoffe*, Sep. 29, 1940. Cf. *HaTzoffe*, Jan. 15 and 23, 1941; letters: Kleinerman to Rosenberg, Aug. 21, 1940 (IRC/2/67), and Kostyokovsky to Rosenberg, Sep. 1, 1940 (IRC/3/110).

13. Weintraub, *BeSufa*, 291–92; Weintraub, *Devar Shemu'ah*, "Tziyun leNefesh" section; Kaplan, "HaRav," 121. See also *Hatzoffe*, Jan. 30, 1941. Regarding the song of the Bialystok Yeshiva in Birzh, see Klibansky, "HaYeshivot," 370n39.

14. Pekier, *From Kletsk*, 41–42; Bergman, *Lulei*, 238; Weintraub, *BeSufa*, 288; Kossovsky, "Letoledot Rabeinu," 271.

15. Rottenberg, *Bikkurei*, 13; letter: Kotler to Rosenberg, Oct. 2, 1940 (IRC/3/63); Bauer, "Pe'ulot," 180; Beckelman, "Polish Refugees," 51; Edelstein, "BiYmey," 341–42.

16. Eliash, "Hatzalat," 145–46, 156.

17. Va'ad-Hatzala, *Ḥurbn*, 17H, 50H, 198, 201–3, 236, 256–58; students' lists (CRC-224/18); Warhaftig, *Palit*, 195–96, 207; Eliash, "Hatzalat," 146–47; Bauer, "Pe'ulot," 182; Zuroff, "HaTzibur," 135; *DMZ*, Aug. 13, 1940.

18. Parush, *Sharsheret*, VI, 286.

19. Warhaftig, *Palit*, 102–3. See also pages 100–101; *Hamodi'a*, Sep. 24, 1999. Cf. the testimony of the couple Levin (OHD/V101/44).

20. Epstein, "Yeshivat Mir," 121. See also Berenstein, *Yeshivat*, 390.

21. Berenstein, *Yeshivat*, 252, 381, 394–98. See also Epstein, "Yeshivat Mir," 122–23; Hertzman, *Escape*, 32; Warhaftig, *Palit*, 74, 108, 111; Levine, *In Search*, 5; Sugihara's List (published from the archives of the Japanese foreign ministry in Tokyo).

22. Pekier, *From Kletsk*, 40, 137; Warhaftig, *Palit*, 153. Cf. Hirschprung, *Fun Natzishen*, 236; Segalowitz, *Gebrente Trit*, 180–81; *HaTzoffe*, Jul. 13, 1941.

23. Epstein, "Yeshivat Mir," 121–22. See also Warhaftig, *Palit*, 122.

24. Warhaftig, *Palit*, 120–22, 125–26; Goldman, "Rabbi Herzog's," 8. See also Levin, *Tekufa*, 231–33; Porat, "Nessibot," 60–62; Even-Ḥen, *Tenu'a*, 179–80.

25. Edelstein, "Do'ḥ," 144; Even-Ḥen, *Tenu'a*, 164; Zuroff, "Hatzalat," 68. Cf. Rabinowitz, *Bleter*, 130–31.

26. Shapira, "Yeshivat Mir," 5; Berenstein, *Yeshivat*, 442–43; Even-Ḥen, *Tenu'a*, 165.

27. Epstein, "Yeshivat Mir," 123. See also Hertzman, *Nes*, 64–65; Rottenberg, *Bikkurei*, 15; Even-Ḥen, *Tenu'a*, 165.

28. Friedlender, "Din," 2; Ben-Natan, *BiTenu'a*, 14; Warhaftig, *Palit*, 127, 152, 258 (document from Sep. 20, 1940); Berenstein, *Yeshivat*, 270–71, 275, 381, 398; Hertzman, *Escape*, 39 (who was inexact); Hirschprung, *Fun Natzishen*, 239. NKVD was the People's Commissariat for Internal Affairs, established in 1934, which was responsible for internal security and also population registration.

29. Barak (Brik), "Pelitey," 370; Warhaftig, *Palit*, 116, 152–53; Kalmanowitz, *Kulmos*, 99; *HaPardes* 15, no. 6 (1941): 45; Va'ad-Hatzala, *Ḥurbn*, 249–50.

30. Regarding other costs of travel, see Klibansky, "HaYeshivot," 377n76–77.

31. Epstein, "Yeshivat Mir," 123–24. See also Hertzman, *Escape*, 42–43; Berenstein, *Yeshivat*, 289.

32. *HaPardes* 15, no. 4 (1941): 7.

33. Hertzman, *Escape*, 43; Epstein, "Yeshivat Mir," 124; Karpenshprung, *Divrei Mordechai*, preface. Cf. Levi, "HaRav," 93.

34. Hertzman, *Escape*, 48–49 (English source). See also Berenstein, *Yeshivat*, 448.

35. *HaPardes* 15, no. 4 (1941): 8; *HaPardes* 15, no. 6 (1941): 45–47; Epstein, "Yeshivat Mir," 124. For a discussion of those who remained, see Klibansky, "HaYeshivot," 378–79, n. 85–86.

36. Warhaftig, *Palit*, 105–7; Friedlender, "Din," 2; Sugihara's List (see note 21 of this chapter).

37. Shapiro, *Go*, 58–62 (cf. *TJO* [May 1973]: 23); Even-Ḥen, *BeReshit*, 48–49, 63; the testimony of Volbe (YVA/O.3/3044); "Ich Ver"; Berenstein, *Yeshivat*, 397; testimony: Garber.

38. Nekritz, "Yeshivot," 288; Farber, "R' Leiballe," 100.

39. Pekier, *From Kletsk*, 47–50, 52–53; Warhaftig, *Palit*, 178 (Kotler's letter to Warhaftig, Dec. 3, 1940), 215–16. See also Zuroff, "Hatzalat," 68.

40. Hertzman, *Escape*, 44–45.

41. Shoshana, "HaYeshiva," 290, 294–95; Summary of the Bloch-Wischnitzer talk, 1944 (MWP/Cleveland Yeshiva); Bloch, "Di Telzer Yeshive," 629–30; Gershuni, *Yehudim*, 158; Surasky, *HaRav miPonivezh*, II, 72, 78, 84; *HaTzoffe*, Feb. 20, 1941.

42. Regarding two more heads of the migrant yeshivas who intended to leave Lithuania, see Klibansky, "HaYeshivot," 382n104. In the absence of Rabbi Yeḥiel-Mordechai Gordon, who was in the United States on behalf of his yeshiva and was forced to remain there when the war broke out, his brother-in-law Rabbi Yehoshua-Zelig Ruch was the substitute head of the Lomzhe Yeshiva.

43. See Warhaftig, *Palit*, 214, 216; *Yeshurun* 8 (2001): 176; *TJO* (Jun. 1970): 18. Regarding a similar phenomenon relating to Zionist activists and the young pioneers, see Klibansky, "HaYeshivot," 383n108. Compare to the different approach of Rabbi Ḥayim Shmuelevitz when the Mir Yeshiva was in Japan: *Hapardes* 15, no. 4 (1941):7; Hertzman, *Escape*, 62–63; Even-Ḥen, *Tenu'a*, 300.

44. Surasky, *Ohr*, II, 253.

45. Levenstein, *Or Yeḥezkel*, 40. See also Shapira, "Yeshivat Mir," 4; Warhaftig, *Palit*, 138–39.

46. For more about the dilemma facing the roshei-yeshiva, see Farbstein, *BeSeter*, 189–90.

47. Soviet Latvian citizenship prevented Rabbi Elḥanan Wasserman from receiving an exit visa (Surasky, *Ohr*, II, 271–73; Warhaftig, *Palit*, 227). Rabbi Dov Zuchovsky (1898–1960), a Musar-mashgiaḥ in Slabodka, was the only one from the local yeshivas who left Lithuania with a regular certificate thanks to his Palestinian citizenship.

48. Apart from Rabbis Kahaneman of Ponevezh and Bloch and Katz from Telz, also Rabbi Yitzḥak-Isaac Sher of Slabodka was outside of Lithuania at the time; he went for a cure in Switzerland in 1939 and remained there at the start of the war until his aliyah to Eretz-Yisrael. His son-in-low, the Talmud instructor Rabbi Mordechai Shulman, was on a fundraising mission in the United States when the war broke out, and stayed there. Rabbis Sher and Shulman left their wives and children in Lithuania as well.

49. Friedlender, "Din," 1–2; Litvak, "HaShilton," 63–65, 68; Levin, *Tekufa*, 210–12; Zak, *Knecht*, 57, 77–78, 134–35.

50. Nekritz, "Yeshivot," 288; Pekier, *From Kletsk*, 53–55.

51. Langleben-Klibansky, *MiYarketei Tzafon*, 80H–110H; Dieckmann, *Deutsche besatzungspolitik*, 153–54. Levine's figures seem to be inflated in *Pinkas Hakehillot*, 88.

52. Shapiro, *Go*, 70–71 (English source; see *TJO* [Jun. 1970]: 18).

53. Testimonies: Kremerman and "Man of Kovna"; Oshri, "Yeshivat," 163 (who was not exact regarding the date); Nekritz, "Yeshivot," 288; Hurwitz, *Madregat haAdam*, 5; Pekier, *From Kletsk*, 55–63; Shapiro, *Go*, 62, 199; Gershuni, *Yehudim*, 159; Parush, *Sharsheret*, VI, 215; letter: Gold to "HaMizraḥi" members, Mar. 15, 1940 (DSA). Cf. Fortman, "Bnei Torah," 8; interview with Rabbi Isaac Osband, Sep. 13, 1946 (BC-ostland 9-125B 9-126A).

54. Testimony: Fortman; interview with Rabbi Isaac Osband, Sep. 13, 1946 (BC-ostland 9-125B 9-126A); Shoshana, "HaYeshiva," 292; Farbstein, *MiTelz*, 219–26; Klibansky, "Jewish Resistance."

55. Levin, *Ḥurbn Eirope*, 225, 229; Berenstein, *Yeshivat*, 415–16; Zuroff, *The Response*, 195–96; Hertzman, *Escape*, 54; Barak (Brik), "Pelitey," 370; Zuroff, "Hatzalat," 73; Warhaftig, *Palit*, 182.

56. Even-Ḥen, *Tenu'a*, 168–69.

57. *DMZ*, Aug, 8, 1941 (from Yiddish). See Va'ad-Hatzala, *Ḥurbn*, 203; Warhaftig, *Palit*, 138–39, 204–5, 221. "Yavneh and its sages" refers to the yeshiva established in Yavneh for the sages of the Land of Israel after the Roman conquest of Jerusalem and the destruction of the Temple there.

58. Regarding some of the cruel and unusual ways, see Klibansky, "Jewish Resistance."

EPILOGUE

YESHIVA IDENTITY

At the same time that the basic characteristics of the Lithuanian yeshiva became fixed before the First World War, this institution also acquired its own special identity, which was further clarified in the following years. Already during that war, this identity was expressed in the yeshiva through the solidarity of the older students and their decision to remain together. However, its complete reflection could be seen in the interwar period, when despite material and emotional difficulties, the yeshiva and most of its talmidim functioned as a consolidated unit. This identity, which derived its strength and vitality principally from the changes that occurred in the Lithuanian yeshiva during those years between the two world wars, will be elucidated in this final section.

The rapid developments that took place among Eastern European Jewry in the last decades of the nineteenth century made their mark on the Torah world in the cultural milieu of Lithuanian Jews as well. Modernization, practical ambitions, and the Haskalah movement brought about the closing of many study kibbutzim that were spread out among town batei-midrash, and the few that remained nearly disappeared by the end of the nineteenth century under the influences of Russian socialist movements that had penetrated the Jewish street. In contrast, the yeshivas were better protected against the new winds of change because of the ordered organizational structure that characterized them and the supervision exercised over their students. However, they were not immune to outside influences. Their vulnerability was uncovered in the first decade of the twentieth century when the Bund and Zionist movements succeeded in making inroads among their talmidim and even caused the near collapse of a number of the yeshivas. Few years later, the reactionary policies of the Russian Empire moderated the revolutionary spirit among the youth and brought about the return to the regular program in the yeshivas. These Talmudic institutions continued to stabilize also thanks to the restraint-inspiring Musar teachings that had been introduced into their curriculum.

At the end of the First World War far-reaching changes took place in the yeshivas' habitat. The trend toward secularization, which accelerated during the war, was expressed by the spread of attitudes oriented toward practicality and productivity among the wider Jewish community. Cultural autonomy in the new states of Poland and Lithuania facilitated the implementation of these attitudes by offering free choice among varied educational frameworks. Jewish gymnasia that offered a general and Jewish studies program alongside training for a productive future provided an alternative to the famous Torah-study institutions. The yeshivas were no longer considered by the masses as intellectually elite institutions, and the majority of young people who aspired toward broadening their education chose to distance themselves from yeshiva studies. The rabbi of Lomzhe, Rabbi Moshe Shatzkes (1882–1959), described the attitude toward yeshivas (which he defined as "the workshops where the Jewish soul and the nation's future is created"): "Nearly no one is interested in them or in maintaining them, and no one is concerned about the fate of the sons-builders, who sacrifice themselves upon the altar of the Torah."[1]

Only a few of the young people in the towns chose to enroll in the Torah educational track that began in the yeshivot-ketanot. There were young men who did so to appease their parents, and when they completed their studies at age seventeen or eighteen, they went on to academic studies or joined the workforce to make a living. Thus, the decision of a yeshiva-ketana graduate to enter a yeshiva-gedola was made out of choice and personal conviction. But even one who chose this path confronted obstacles in the fulfillment of his aspirations. The economic constraints of the yeshivot-gedolot and the desire of their heads to maintain a balance in the ages of the talmidim made it difficult to be accepted to them, and during the end of the 1920s and the early 1930s, this led to the almost total closing of the gates of the yeshivas in Polish Kresy. The young candidates had to beg, exert pressure upon the roshei-yeshiva, and sometimes enlist the influence of prominent people in order to be accepted. The answer to their request seemed to some of them a matter of life or death, as can be seen from one letter to Va'ad-HaYeshivot: "This affects my entire spiritual life, for if, Heaven forfend, the gates of the yeshiva are closed to me, in the middle of my [spiritual and intellectual] ascent, what will my future be? And also the past? This is the fourth year that, thank God, I study on my own, and now where? Your honors will surely fulfill my request."[2] Indeed, sometimes the roshei-yeshiva were obliged to be flexible in their policies and accept these young candidates.[3]

It is certain that those baḥurim who were steadfast in their desire, and in the end were accepted to the yeshiva, ascribed a great deal of importance to their institution and saw their studies as an essential condition for adapting a religious way of life and the basis for their future vocation. This process of "filtration" therefore created a yeshiva student body whose members were of a uniform type. This uniformity was further strengthened through the process of aging that took place among the talmidim. In the past, talented bar-mitzvah boys were common among the older students. However, a short time after the First World War, a significant change took place when pedagogical and economic factors led to the division of the yeshivas into yeshivot-ketanot and yeshivas for older students. The grouping of baḥurim according to age increased the age of the talmidim in the yeshivot-gedolot, and in the 1930s there were nearly no students aged seventeen or younger, and even eighteen-year-olds were a minority group there. The unstable and vulnerable adolescent age, which in the past had found its marked expression in severe disturbances in the yeshivas, did not manifest itself any more in that decade among the young students, whose personalities were undergoing advanced processes of consolidation.[4]

The uniformity previously described gave those new talmidim a feeling of self-confidence in the unsupportive and sometimes unsympathetic surroundings. These feelings of assurance were bolstered by two outstanding phenomena that occurred in their midst: the consistent increase in the crowding in the study halls, creating a sense that the yeshivas were in demand, and the flocking of foreign talmidim to the Lithuanian yeshivas. Up until the First World War, only a few students found their way to these yeshivas from other European countries. The war and the Bolshevik revolution created the phenomenon of migrant baḥurim from Russia and Ukraine who stood out in the yeshivas that had returned from their wartime exile. However, the local students considered them to be talmidim who had been forced to join the yeshivas due to the severe conditions under the Soviet regime and found it difficult to see their heroic actions as the result of free choice. This was not the case of the students from America and Central Europe. They appeared in the yeshivas of Poland and Lithuania, aspiring to deepen their Torah knowledge and receive rabbinical ordination. Most of them were high school or even university graduates, came from middle-class families, and in the eyes of the locals seemed to be affluent and well-to-do. Their sacrifice of the comfortable and prosperous lifestyle that they had enjoyed in their countries of origin and their choice to come and study in yeshivas, of which the majority were located in small and neglected towns where material conditions were quite poor, instilled a feeling of pride in the local talmidim. These local baḥurim had suffered numerous insults from their counterparts from the towns of Lithuania and Poland who scorned them for choosing "nonproductive" yeshiva studies. The "wealthy" high school and university graduates from overseas choosing the yeshiva as the proper place for their professional training proved to the locals the true worth of their education.

Needing to increase their level in basic knowledge, the foreign students required the help of their Polish and Lithuanian fellow talmidim and hired them as private tutors. Besides the considerable income that these services generated for needy local baḥurim, which helped them a great deal, this shared activity had a significant influence on their characters. The need of the foreign students for assistance in their studies increased the self-worth of the local teachers and reinforced the importance of their scholarly achievements in their own eyes. Moreover, the opportunity to express their abilities in the field of teaching and influencing others strengthened their own feeling that someday they would be able to work to change the spiritual situation in their own hometowns. In addition, the daily conversations with the foreign students, who had a high school or university education, exposed these provincial baḥurim—who came from godforsaken little towns in Lithuania or Poland—to Western and modern modes of thinking, helping them widen their horizons and adopt a broader view of life and the world.[5]

It would therefore seem that this new talmid, with his strengthened self-image, no longer needed any justification to explain his choice of the yeshiva course of study. However, his positive and encouraging attitude toward his studies and his yeshiva was likely to be maintained for a limited time only. As time passed, his enthusiasm and excitement would wane due to the material and emotional hardships that he would encounter in the time that he was far away from his family, as well as from his realistic view of the future that awaited him after completing his course of study. The young man would begin to notice the older baḥurim around him, in their late twenties and early thirties. Quite a few of them had chosen to study in their yeshiva for many years because they found no appropriate solution to their aspirations in the outside world. This situation was not a good portent for the young talmid who had just begun to make progress in his learning. It is reasonable to assume that thoughts about the efficacy of the path that he had chosen were likely to arise and even bring about the decision to change the course of his life.[6]

It was at these crossroads of decision that the Musar supervisors appeared, and it was their concern to strengthen the spirit of the baḥurim and reinforce the essentiality and faith in the correctness of their choice. A recognizable change took place in the status of the mashgiḥim in the transition to the interwar period. The revolutionary consciousness that was an inseparable part of youth in the Jewish street at the end of the nineteenth century and the beginning of the twentieth century was reflected in the yeshivas by the talmidim's sharp opposition to Musar teachings. They saw in its imposition a clear attempt at tightening supervision over them and limiting their freedom of action, and the struggle against it expressed their rebelliousness toward the administrators of their institutions. Under these circumstances the mashgiaḥ, the most faithful representative of the Musar movement, was incapable of exerting his full influence on the students. After the First World War, these conditions underwent fundamental change. Revolutionary attitudes no longer had a place in the atmosphere of freedom that spread over the countries where the yeshivas were located, and Musar teachings ceased to be a point of contention and an excuse for quarrelling with the administration. Moreover, in the 1920s Musar teachings were also introduced into the Lithuanian yeshivas, which had previously not adopted them. The figure of the mashgiaḥ became an accepted and leading one in the yeshiva, unlike in the past, when this position had been forced on its students, and some of them avoided coming in contact with him. The mashgiaḥ knew each one of his charges and his abilities, accomplishments, aspirations, and problems, and he acted to help the talmidim in their difficulties and existential issues and direct them in the path that was right in his eyes. His public Musar talks were replete with influential psychological effects and dealt with, among other things, the role of the yeshiva baḥur in the changing surroundings and his mission upon going out into the world of action one day. The penetrating impression of these talks not only crystallized the young students' worldview but also rallied the entire group of talmidim around their yeshiva.[7]

This feeling of solidarity among the students also had another source: their sense of commitment to the yeshiva. Many of its talmidim came from small towns and belonged to the lower middle socioeconomic class. As the economic situation in Eastern Europe worsened, their families had trouble assisting them, and they became material burdens on their yeshiva. Its administration not only paid most of the cost of room and board but also attempted to fulfill most of their needs—shoes and clothing, medical expenses, and even exemption from military service. Such all-encompassing aid gave the students a feeling that they were an integral part of the yeshiva and heightened their identification with it.[8]

It is therefore not surprising that in the period between the world wars, even when the baḥurim were actually hungry for bread, most continued to rally around their yeshivas. Even more, a short time after the outbreak of the Second World War, young students and older ones, who studied in the Lithuanian yeshivas in Poland, chose to leave their families in Polish Kresy and fled as a group toward Vilna; there and afterward in the towns of Lithuania, they continued to study together. This type of solidarity existed in the local and migrant Lithuanian yeshivas even under the harsh conditions from the time of the Soviet domination of Lithuania until the Nazi conquest.

ORGANIZATIONAL REVOLUTION

A principal and obvious change in the yeshiva world in the interwar period took place in the field of organization. In the introduction to this book, different types of yeshivas were mentioned that were active in the Lithuanian Jewish cultural milieu in the middle of the nineteenth century. These included those yeshivas that were supported by local communities as well as two supracommunity yeshivas located in Volozhin and Mir. On the eve of the First World War, this picture was reversed, and most of the yeshivas had become supracommunity institutions. In the interwar period, there were very few that did not follow this pattern, and they were all in the Polish Kresy. These were the three new Hasidic Lithuanian yeshivas, which were under the sponsorship of Hasidic rebbes and supportive Hasidic communities, and apparently there were also several yeshivas of the old-fashioned type. In the discussion about the customary practice of inheritance, I wondered whether the Yeshiva of Brisk would still be considered a community institution from the time it was reestablished after the war, or perhaps it was only the death of its childless rosh-yeshiva that made it dependent on the community. Either way, the local rabbi determined those who were appointed to positions there in the 1930s, and the situation was the same in the Remayle Yeshiva in Vilna. Could the Slonim Etz-Ḥ ayim Yeshiva still be considered a community institution? The impression is that it received no exceptional support from the community, and its head operated it according to his will without any outside interference. In any case, these aforementioned yeshivas received valuable support from outside aid committees, and it would therefore seem that they had lost their community character to one degree or another and become similar to their supracommunity counterparts.

The more essential change was specific to the yeshivas in the Polish Kresy. Close to the First World War, there were approximately thirty yeshivot-gedolot in the Russian Empire and Poland, and each one of them operated independently and without any organizational or economic connection to the others. Even "daughter yeshivas" such as Slutsk, which was established on the initiative of Slabodka, or Shklov, which was reopened by the rosh-yeshiva of Slutsk, were not administratively or financially dependent upon the "mother yeshivas." After the war, all of the yeshivas in Lithuania and Poland continued to function completely independently. However, the poor Kresy regions had a difficult time creating a strong economic base for the many yeshivas located within them, in particular due to the economic crisis that struck Europe in the beginning of the 1920s and the decrease of support from the United States in those years. A solution was found in 1924 to their situation through the founding of an umbrella committee, Va'ad-HaYeshivot. For the first time a dedicated organization was formed whose role was to take care of the economic aspects of a large group of yeshivas. The right to conduct fundraising campaigns throughout the Polish Kresy was exclusively passed on to the Va'ad, and it set up an impressive hierarchical system for collecting donations in 350 communities. The funds raised were divided among the Kresy yeshivas according to set allocation percentages, and these made basic maintenance possible, although sometimes with great difficulty.[9]

The innovative role of the Va'ad was not limited to these economic matters. It also had full responsibility for the streaming of the yeshiva-ketana graduates to yeshivot-gedolot at the end of each term according to quotas that it set, and only through its referrals was it possible for new young talmidim to be accepted to the Kresy yeshivot-gedolot. This ambitious role of Va'ad-HaYeshivot deviated from the "modest" role designated for it at its founding meeting in Vilna in 1924: to serve as the central economic organization for all the Kresy yeshivas. The expansion of its responsibilities and its development into a miniature modern ministry of education placed the Va'ad in a position of significant influence and power. But beyond the power it gained as an active instrument in economically strengthening the yeshivas and its influence on their activities, the novel feature in its existence was expressed in limiting the absolute ownership of the roshei-yeshiva of their institutions. Exclusive authority, which in the past had been in their hands, including fundraising within their areas and the acceptance of new students, was taken away from them and transferred to a common suprayeshiva organization. From that point on, the Va'ad was the body that concentrated an important portion of the economic and organizational administration of all the Kresy yeshivas.

This hierarchical framework was not copied in Lithuania. Four years after Va'ad-HaYeshivot was established, the editors of the Orthodox periodical *HaNe'eman*, which was published in Telz, expressed their wish: "How fine it would be if those that fear Heaven, directors of the yeshivot-gedolot and ketanot [in Lithuania] would speak among themselves and establish Va'ad-HaYeshivot like in occupied Lithuania [the areas under Polish control]. Experience has shown that in this way they would succeed much better than if each one acts on his own."[10] Indeed, the yeshivas in Lithuania encountered a conflict of interests, and their income was harmed when they raised funds within the narrow borders of their country. Nevertheless, the yeshiva heads preferred to act without any interference in their independent work. It can be assumed that they did not rejoice at the prospect of any change for the same reasons that some of the roshei-yeshiva opposed the establishment of Va'ad-HaYeshivot in Kresy. Still, the small number of yeshivas in Lithuania did not justify the impressive and revolutionary organizational solution of establishing a suprayeshiva body.[11]

A GOLDEN AGE?

One of the surprising turning points in the history of the Lithuanian yeshivas was the growth of their student population at the end of the 1920s and even more so in the 1930s (a period that was particularly oriented toward productivity when many alternative educational institutions and training programs were available to Jewish youth in Poland and Lithuania). Does this fascinating development show that the interwar period was the "golden age" and heyday of the Lithuanian yeshivas? The answer to this question will be based on quantitative data. A survey of the student population of the yeshivot-gedolot in 1937 indicates that there were approximately 4,100 talmidim studying in all of them that year.[12] This data is surprising because the number of yeshiva students before the First World War was estimated at five thousand, ostensibly a decrease of approximately 20 percent in the transition from one period to another.[13] However, this simplistic comparison is inappropriate because the figures from these two periods relate to different student age groups. Before the First World War, young lads studied in yeshivot-gedolot alongside older baḥurim. This situation underwent an essential change after the war due to the establishment of numerous yeshivot-ketanot for younger students, as well as the increase in the age of the youngest talmidim in the yeshivot-gedolot. At the end of the 1930s, the limit was eighteen or nineteen, and the younger students found their place in the yeshivot-ketanot. Either way, taking into account the change in the age of the talmidim, no significant variation can be seen in the size of the student population between the period before the First World War and the period before the Second World War. This fact indicates that in both of these periods, many of the yeshivas took the opportunity to fill their ranks as much as economics allowed, and because there was no significant growth in the number of yeshivas after the war, it is not possible to expect a marked change in the total number of students.[14]

At the end of each semester, the large number of yeshivot-ketanot created a vast pool of new graduates that massed at the gates of the yeshivot-gedolot. The policy of enrolling only a few new students on the part of the yeshivot-gedolot due to economic constraints, along with the extended years of study of older, senior baḥurim there, caused the lines of yeshiva-ketana graduates waiting at their gates to be accepted to lengthen, as can be seen in a letter that the head of the yeshiva-ketana in Radin, Rabbi Mordechai-Dov Reitblatt, wrote to Va'ad-HaYeshivot: "I hereby inform you that the number of yeshiva-ketana graduates who must be accepted to the yeshiva-gedola is four: three of them, their time to be accepted to yeshiva-gedola has come, but they were rejected because of crowding [in the yeshivot-gedolot] until now, but it is impossible to delay them further. The fourth has also studied for an additional term, therefore it is impossible to delay these four any longer."[15]

I have no statistical data about those who applied to yeshivot-gedolot, but the primary sources show that in certain years, there were many dozens of applicants from the graduates of the yeshivot-ketanot. The yeshivot-gedolot found it difficult to keep pace with such an entrance of new students, and the unavoidable consequences were soon to come. Rabbi Avraham-Shmuel Hirschowitz, rosh-yeshiva of Torat-Ḥesed of Baranovitch, described the situation: "The talmidim are knocking on the doors of the yeshivas, but no one opens them, and many baḥurim are forced as a consequence to end their studies. Thus, they push them, God forbid, into a stormy sea, and they are dragged off by the tide."[16] Indeed, many of the yeshiva-ketana graduates were forced to leave the yeshiva world.[17]

The answer to the question posed previously is therefore not unequivocal. In the interwar period, the yeshivas ceased to be at the center of Jewish life in Poland and Lithuania and were relegated to the sidelines of public interest. For that reason, they were insufficiently supported by their towns, and their number did not increase significantly in comparison to the number of yeshivas before the First World War. Under these circumstances, filling of the classrooms of the yeshivas and closing the doors to new students actually lent to the feeling that the yeshiva world was flourishing, but this flourishing was quite limited. Yet Orthodox personalities made sure to preserve the tradition of Torah study by establishing yeshivot-ketanot in the area of the Lithuanian Jewish cultural milieu and also in the regions of Vohlin and the Kongresówka. Even if these yeshivas were not successful in attracting the majority of Jewish youth, a few students from each town and its environs were sufficient to fill the classrooms of the yeshiva-ketana, which had only a few dozen places at most, and in a few years that formed a pool of graduates ready to study in the yeshivot-gedolot.

It is doubtless that the potential of this world to grow would have been great if it had been possible to actualize that potential under the difficult conditions of the time. If it had not been for the economic limitations that tied the hands of the yeshivas, they would have grown significantly. Moreover, in Poland and perhaps in Lithuania, another few yeshivas would have been set up, where many graduates of the yeshivot-ketanot who found it difficult to be accepted could have studied.[18] It would seem that the head of the yeshiva-ketana in Eishishok did not exaggerate when he addressed the puzzlement of the representative of Va'ad-HaYeshivot at the tiny number of students in his yeshiva: "If they would announce in public that they are accepting [graduates to the yeshivot-gedolot]—then the talmidim [in the yeshivot-ketanot] would increase to an amazing degree."[19]

FROM THEN UNTIL NOW

In the interwar period, the Lithuanian yeshivas succeeded in gaining a foothold in Eretz-Yisrael through establishing branches. A few yeshivas of a similar type were also set up in Europe and the United States by graduates of the Lithuanian system of learning. However, the principal yeshiva world continued to be concentrated in Eastern Europe. With the outbreak of war in 1939, its continuous activity was interrupted. Most of that world found refuge in Lithuania until the Nazis invaded and annihilated it. Among the few survivors, there were roshei-yeshiva who had managed to arrange their departure from Soviet Lithuania before the Nazi conquest, most of the talmidim of Mir, and individuals from other yeshivas who reached Japan, as well as yeshiva groups that were deported by the Soviets to labor camps in Siberia and survived. This was the end of the story of the Lithuanian yeshivas; only a tiny few of their type remained in the Land of Israel and America.

Nevertheless, after the Second World War, it was possible to see the growth of yeshivas similar to the ones that had been destroyed, and they even bore the same names. These new yeshivas were established upon the initiative of roshei-yeshiva or talmidim who had survived the Holocaust and felt a need and sense of mission to rebuild the Lithuanian yeshiva world.[20] There was a novel and outstanding element in its new life—the shift of its center of gravity from its traditional location in Eastern Europe to Eretz-Yisrael and the West—and it would seem that in these new places, trends that had begun in the Old World in the years before the Shoah were further emphasized.

Earlier it was stated that had it not been for the severe financial constraints, there were two parallel trends that could have been expected in the Lithuanian yeshivas in their traditional locations: the continuous growth of the number of their talmidim, and the establishment of additional yeshivas in the Kresy and perhaps in Lithuania as well. It is possible to observe these processes in the Lithuanian yeshivas in Israel. They are markedly growing larger in size as compared to their forerunners, and in a few, thousands of talmidim study, especially overseas students. Most of these Israeli Torah-study institutions have daughter yeshivas scattered throughout the country, and these expand the ability to absorb more graduates of yeshivot-ketanot.

However, it is not only due to the lack of economic obstacles that these processes of continuity are taking place. They draw their vitality particularly from changes that are the result of the rapid growth of Ḥaredi society and its place in Israel. Many years have passed since the yeshivas in Israel served only as fortresses of preservation and protection against the influences of the street. The yeshiva track has become an essential and required part of the way of life of Ḥaredi society. Acceptance to one of the famous Lithuanian yeshivas is therefore a quasireligious aspiration for baḥurim and an obvious condition for social advancement and a successful match. This is the explanation of the increased demand for these yeshivas and their rapid growth. The story of their impressive renewal is not part of this book, but one can conclude from it that due to the economic, social, and political situation in Israel, which is so different from that of the past, these yeshivas in Israel are realizing the unfulfilled vision of the "founding fathers" in Lithuania and Poland.[21]

* * *

In one of his conversations, Meir Bar-Ilan, the youngest child of the Netziv and a graduate of the Volozhin and Telz Yeshivas, expressed his thoughts to his interlocutor: "The Ḥasidic movement succeeded in eternalizing itself. A vast and multi-branched literature was written, and is still being written, about every Ḥasidic stream, about each rebbe's court and every sort of Ḥasidic experience and custom. History and documentation, thoughts as well as stories and poems—Ḥasidism immortalized and immortalizes itself, and perhaps from this its salvation of renewal will spring. However, we, the Mitnagdim, have not merited the discovery of the great treasures that were kept in the treasure-house of the great Torah-centers, which were hidden in the small towns of Poland and Lithuania."[22] Years have passed, and even the Mitnagdim have begun here and there to immortalize their great rabbis and the Talmudic institutions of the past. The contribution of this book is the first systematic effort at providing the factual foundation for getting to know the Lithuanian yeshivas in an era that the Torah world's collective memory defines as the golden age of its history. These yeshivas, where unique personalities of Torah giants taught and dedicated talmidim studied, went through extreme changes and turbulence in those interwar years, beginning in exile and wandering in the First World War and ending in blood and deliberate murder in the Second World War. Much more will be certainly told of this yeshiva world. May my work be one part of a great edifice.

NOTES

1. Idelevitz, *Sefer haYovel*, 45. "Sons-builders" was a rabbinic play on words ("*banim-bonim*"; see Babylonian Talmud, Berachot 64a).

2. Postcard: Reif to Va'ad-HaYeshivot, May 16, 1932 (VHY/373).

3. See Golan, *HaLaila*, 203–4; testimony: Garber; Nishri, *Me'ir*, II, 10.

4. See Gardi, *Pirkei*, I, 53; Assaf, "Shenot," 36; Stampfer, Shalosh Yeshivot, 230.

5. Testimony: YBB. Cf. *HaKerem* (1887): 67.

6. Zaritzky, *HaEsh*, 120.

7. Cf. Assaf, "Shenot," 43. It is therefore reasonable to assume that the dropout rate of yeshiva graduates to nontraditional frameworks significantly decreased relative to the high dropout rate before the First World War.

8. Rozental, *Torah*, 127.

9. Cf. *Sinai* 91 (1982): 170.

10. *HaNe'eman* 8 (1928): 3; the letters "Va'ad-HaYeshivot" are with wider spacing in the original.

11. Compare to the founding of a central committee for the numerous yeshivot-ketanot in Lithuania in the letter: Schnaider to Haffkine Foundation, Feb. 23, 1939 (MWP/Va'ad-yeshivot-ketanot).

12. This number includes approximately 3,300 yeshiva students in Poland (report of expenditures, Dec. 22, 1936 [VHY/1107]) and 800 in Lithuania and Latvia.

13. See introduction, near note 19.

14. At first glance, it is possible to see a relative increase of the numbers of talmidim when comparing the two periods, because geopolitical changes disconnected a portion of Russian and Ukrainian Jewry from the areas where the yeshivas were located in the interwar period. However, an examination of the yeshivas in the period before the First World War indicates that only a limited percentage of their talmidim came from the area that was to be annexed by the Soviet Union.

15. His postcard, Apr. 13, 1932 (VHY/511).

16. Letter: Hirschowitz to Va'ad-HaYeshivot, May 11, 1929 (VHY/13).

17. See Poupko, *Michtavei*, 250; Desler, *Shenot*, II, 217.

18. See the opinion of Rabbi Eliezer-Yehudah Finkel in the second chapter, near note 1. A similar opinion was expressed in letter: Va'ad-HaYeshivot to Sokolovsky, Nov. 6, 1929 (VHY/46).

19. Letter: Sorotzkin to Va'ad-HaYeshivot, Dec. 29, 1933 (VHY/117). See also *DoV*, Apr. 20, 1934.

20. For example, Rozovsky, *Zichron*, 570–72.

21. See Friedman, "Al haNissim," 434–40.

22. Krone, *Morai*, 162.

APPENDIX: BRIEF BIOGRAPHIES

B

Baksht, Aharon (1869–1941)—Born in Ivye, Vilna Province; educated in the Volozhin, Slabodka, and Kelm Yeshivas. Prior to the First World War, he served as rabbi and rosh-yeshiva in Shadeve, Kovna Province. After the war, he served as rabbi in Suvalk and Lomzhe, Poland, and from 1929 onward in Shavl, Lithuania.

Bliacher, David (1890–1943)—Born in Uman, Kiev Province; educated in the yeshivas of Knesset-Yisrael of Slabodka and Novardok. During the First World War, he headed the Kiev Yeshiva. In 1921 he set up a central Novardok Yeshiva in Mezritch, Poland, and served as its head.

Bloch, Avraham-Yitzḥak (1891–1941)—Born in Telz, Kovna Province; son of Rabbi Yosef-Leib Bloch; educated in his yeshiva in Telz. In 1921 he was appointed Talmud instructor there, and in 1929 he inherited his father's positions as rabbi of Telz and head of its yeshiva.

Bloch, Yosef-Leib (1860–1929)—Born in Rasein, Kovna Province; educated in the Kelm and Volozhin Yeshivas; son-in-law of Rabbi Eliezer Gordon. When his father-in-law was chosen as rabbi of Telz and the head of its yeshiva in 1883, he was appointed Talmud instructor in that yeshiva.

In 1902 he resigned from his position and served as rabbi and rosh-yeshiva in Vorne, and later in Shadeve in the province of Kovna. In 1910 he inherited his father-in-law's positions in the Telz rabbinate and in its yeshiva.

Broyde, Simḥa-Zissel (1824–1898)—born in Kelm, Kovna Province; educated in the yeshiva of Rabbi Yisrael Lipkin in the Nevyazher Kloyz in Kovna; foremost among his talmidim. In 1866 he established a religious school for boys in Kelm, and in 1876 he moved it to Grobin, Courland Province. In 1886 he was forced to close it due to health reasons, and from that time on served as the head of the Kelm Yeshiva.

E

Epstein, Moshe-Mordechai (1866–1934)—Born in Baksht, Vilna Province; educated in the Volozhin Yeshiva. He was appointed in 1893 as a Talmud instructor in the Slabodka Yeshiva, and from 1897 he was its single head. From 1909 he also served as rabbi of the town of Slabodka. In 1928 he resigned from his positions to head the Hebron branch of Knesset-Yisrael, which he had established four years earlier. After the 1929 riots there, he moved his yeshiva to Jerusalem.

F

Finkel, Eliezer-Yehudah (1878–1965)—Born in Kelm, Kovna Province; son of Rabbi Notte-Hirsch Finkel; educated in the yeshivas of Kelm, Telz, Slabodka, Slutsk, the kibbutz of Brisk and Hlusk; son-in-law of Rabbi Eliyahu-Baruch Kamai of Mir. In 1906 he was appointed as Talmud instructor in the Mir Yeshiva, and from 1917 he served as its head. In 1941 he was successful in reaching Eretz-Yisrael, and he established the Mir Yeshiva in Jerusalem.

Finkel, Notte-Hirsch (1849–1927)—Born in Rasein, Kovna Province; disciple of Rabbi Simḥa-Zissel Broyde of Kelm. In 1877 he established a kollel in Slabodka, and in 1882 he founded the Slabodka Yeshiva and served as its Musar supervisor. He went on aliya to Eretz-Yisrael in 1925.

G

Gordon, Eliezer (1841–1910)—Born near Svir, Vilna Province; educated in the yeshivas of Rabbi Yisrael Lipkin in Vilna and Kovna. In 1874 he was appointed as rabbi of Kelm and set up a yeshiva there. In 1883 he began to serve as rabbi of Slabodka, and in the same year he was appointed as rabbi of Telz and rosh-yeshiva in that town. He died in London during a fundraising trip for his yeshiva.

Gordon, Yeḥiel-Mordechai (1882–1964)—born near Trok, Vilna Province; educated in Knesset-Israel Yeshiva of Slabodka; son-in-law of Rabbi Eliezer Shulevitz of Lomzhe. In 1907 he was appointed as Talmud instructor in the Lomzhe Yeshiva, and in 1923 he became its head. In 1926 he established a branch of the yeshiva in Petaḥ-Tikva.

Grodzensky, Avraham (1882/4–1944)—Born in Warsaw; educated in the yeshivas of Lomzhe, Radin, and Knesset-Yisrael of Slabodka. In 1925 he was appointed as Musar supervisor in the Slabodka Yeshiva. From 1939 he served as substitute rosh-yeshiva as well, in the absence of Rabbi Yitzḥak-Isaac Sher, who went for a cure in Switzerland and remained there at the start of the war.

Grodzensky, Ḥayim-Ozer (1863–1940)—Born in Ivye, Vilna Province; attended Eishishok Kibbutz and Volozhin Yeshiva. In 1887 he was appointed as halachic authority in Vilna and became the patron of the local Remayle Yeshiva. In 1896 he established a study kibbutz in Vilna for rabbinical training. In 1924 he was one of the founders of Va'ad-HaYeshivot in Polish Kresy and served as its head.

H

HaCohen, Yisrael-Meir (Poupko; 1838/9–1933)—Born in Zhetl, Grodno Province; studied in Vilna. In 1865–1869 he served as the head of the Vasilishok Yeshiva in the Province of Vilna. In 1869 he set up a study kibbutz, which eventually developed into the Radin Yeshiva. He became well-known through his work Ḥafetz-Ḥayim (1873) on the laws of malicious speech and slander. In 1924 he initiated the establishment of Va'ad-HaYeshivot in Polish Kresy.

Ḥasman, Leib (1869–1935)–Born in Ivye, Vilna Province; educated in Slabodka, Kelm, and Volozhin Yeshivas. In 1896 he was appointed as Musar-mashgiaḥ in the Telz Yeshiva. In 1902 he was chosen to serve as rabbi in Ludvinove in Suvalk Province and from 1906 was rabbi in Stutchin in Vilna Province, where he established a yeshiva. In 1926 he went on aliyah to Eretz-Yisrael, and he served as Musar-mashgiaḥ in the Knesset-Yisrael Yeshiva in Hebron and Jerusalem.

Hirschowitz, Avraham-Shmuel (1894–1941)—Born in Telz, Kovna Province; as a child, he lived in Talsen, Courland Province. In the mid-1920s he was appointed as rosh-yeshiva of Torat-Ḥesed of Baranovitch. At the onset of the Second World War, he escaped with his Hasidic Lithuanian yeshiva to Vilna and settled it in the town of Tavrig.

Hurwitz, Yosef-Yozel (1848–1919)—Born in Plungyan, Kovna Province. Under the influence of Rabbi Yisrael Lipkin, he left his business and joined the Kovna Kollel. In 1896 he founded the Novardok Yeshiva. During the First World War, he went into exile with his yeshiva to Homel and set up a network of Novardok-style yeshivas in Russia and Ukraine.

K

Kahaneman, Yosef-Shlomo (1886–1969)—Born in Kul, Kovna Province; educated in the yeshivas of Telz and Novardok; member of the Kodshim Kollel in Radin. In 1911 he was appointed as rabbi of Vidz in Vilna Province and opened a yeshiva-ketana there. In 1919 he was chosen as rabbi of Ponevezh, established a yeshiva-gedola there, and headed it. In 1940 he arrived in the Land of Israel and shortly afterward founded the Ponevezh Yeshiva in Bnei-Brak.

Kamai, Avraham-Hirsch (1859–1941)—Born in Shkud, Kovna Province; son and disciple of Rabbi Eliyahu-Baruch Kamai. He was appointed rabbi of Keidan in Kovna Province in 1911 and of Mir, Minsk Province, from 1917. When the Mir Yeshiva returned from the First World War exile, he also served there as a Talmud instructor.

Kook, Avraham-Yitzḥak HaCohen (1865–1935)—Born in Griva, Courland Province; educated in Volozhin Yeshiva. He served as rabbi in Zheimel, Kovna Province and later in Boisk, Courland Province. He was appointed rabbi of Jaffa and the colonies in 1904 and of Jerusalem in 1919. In 1921 he was chosen as Ashkenazi Chief Rabbi of the Land of Israel. In 1923 he founded Mercaz HaRav Yeshiva in Jerusalem.

Kotler, Aharon (1891–1962)—Born in Sislevitch, Grodno Province; educated in Knesset-Yisrael of Slabodka and Slutsk Yeshivas; son-in-law of Rabbi Isser-Zalman Meltzer. In 1915 he became a Talmud instructor in the Slutsk Yeshiva. In 1921 he established a branch of the yeshiva in Kletsk, Poland, and from 1925 he served as its official rosh-yeshiva. In 1941 he succeeded in immigrating to the United States, and in 1943 he was appointed as the head of Beth Medrash Govoha in Lakewood, New Jersey.

L

Leibowitz, Baruch-Ber (1870–1939)—Born in Slutsk, Minsk Province; attended Volozhin Yeshiva. He was appointed rabbi of Hlusk, Minsk Province, and a yeshiva developed around him. From 1904 he was the rosh-yeshiva of Knesset Beit-Yitzḥak.

Levenstein, Yeḥezkel (1884–1974)—Born in Warsaw; talmid in the yeshivas of Lomzhe, Radin, and Kelm. He served as Musar supervisor in the yeshivas of Mir and Kletsk and the Petaḥ-Tikva branch of Lomzhe, and after the death of Rabbi Yeruḥam Levovitz in 1936, he filled that position once again in Mir. During the Second World War, he successfully reached Japan along with his yeshiva.

Levovitz, Yeruḥam (1873–1936)—Born in Luban, Minsk Province; educated in the yeshivas of Slabodka and Kelm; member of the Kodshim Kollel in Radin. He served as Musar supervisor in the yeshivas of Radin,

Mir, Slabodka, and Ponevezh, and from 1924 he filled that position once more in Mir.

Lipkin, Yisrael (1810–1883)—Born in Zhager, Kovna Province. Served as a Talmud instructor in Remayle Yeshiva in 1840 for a short while, as a rosh-yeshiva in a small yeshiva in the Zaretche suburb of Vilna until 1848, and from that point on in the yeshiva in the Nevyazher Kloyz in Kovna. Founder of the Musar movement. In 1857 he moved to Germany, and in 1880 he spent two years in Paris. In his last months, he led the Jewish community of Königsberg.

M

Meltzer, Isser-Zalman (1870–1954)—Born in Mir, Minsk Province; educated in Volozhin and Radin Yeshivas. In 1893 he was appointed Talmud instructor in the Slabodka Yeshiva, and in 1897 he established the Slutsk Yeshiva; he served as its rosh-yeshiva and later also the rabbi of Slutsk. In 1923 he fled Slutsk and headed the Kletsk Yeshiva. In 1925 he settled in the Land of Israel and became the head of Etz-Ḥayim Yeshiva in Jerusalem.

N

Nenedik, Yosef-Leib (?–1941)—Born in Soḥovola, Grodno Province; educated in Telz and Kelm Yeshivas. Served as Musar-mashgiaḥ in the yeshivas of Braynsk, Lomzhe, and Radin before the First World War. During the war he was the Musar supervisor in the Grodno Yeshiva, and after the war he was the Musar supervisor in Ponevezh and Kobrin. From 1935 he served in that position in Kletsk.

P

Pruskin, Pesaḥ (1880–1939)—Born in Kobrin, Grodno Province; educated in the yeshivas of Radin, Slabodka, Kelm, and Slutsk. Served as temporary Musar supervisor in the Slutsk Yeshiva, and as rosh-yeshiva in Shklov and later in Amtchislav, Mohilev Province. In 1923 he established the Kobrin Yeshiva and headed it. From 1924 he was rabbi of Kobrin as well.

R

Rabinowitz, Yitzḥak-Ya'akov (1854–1919)—Born in Shershev, Grodno Province. In 1879–1880 he was a talmid of the rabbi of Brisk, Yosef-Ber Soloveitchik. In 1888 he was appointed as a rosh-yeshiva in the communal Bialystok Yeshiva, and one year later he served as the rosh-yeshiva of Slabodka. He was chosen as the rabbi of Gorzd in 1893 and of Ponevezh, Kovna Province, in 1895. In 1911 he founded a small yeshiva in Ponevezh. In the First World War, he went into exile with the yeshiva. After the war, he returned to Ponevezh but died there from typhus.

Reines, Yitzḥak-Ya'akov (1839–1915)—Born in Karlin, Minsk Province; educated in the Volozhin Yeshiva and the Eishishok Kibbutz. Served as the rabbi of Shukian, Kovna Province, and later of Sventchian, Vilna Province. In 1882 he established a yeshiva in Sventchian; it was in existence for two years. In 1884 he became rabbi of Lida, Vilna Province. In 1902 he founded the Mizrachi Religious Zionist Movement in Vilna, and in 1905 he established the Lida Yeshiva.

Ruch, Yehoshua-Zelig (1880–1941)—Born in Rakishok, Kovna Province; studied in Knesset-Yisrael Yeshiva of Slabodka; son-in-law of Rabbi Eliezer Shulevitz of Lomzhe. He was appointed as Talmud instructor in the Lomzhe Yeshiva. From 1933 he served as substitute rosh-yeshiva in the absence of his brother-in-law Rabbi Yeḥiel-Mordechai Gordon, who was in the United States on behalf of his yeshiva and was forced to remain there when the war broke out.

S

Sarna, Yeḥezkel (1890–1969)—Born in Horodok, Minsk Province; educated in the yeshivas of Maltch, Knesset Beit-Yitzḥak of Slabodka, Telz, Knesset-Yisrael of Slabodka, and the exiled Radin Yeshiva; son-in-law of Rabbi Moshe-Mordechai Epstein. In 1924 he established the Knesset-Yisrael branch in Hebron and served as Talmud instructor and acting director there and later in Jerusalem. In 1934 he became the official rosh-yeshiva there.

Shapiro, Avraham-Duber (1870–1943)—Born in Kobrin, Grodno Province; educated in the Volozhin Yeshiva; son-in-law of Rabbi Yeruḥam-Leib Perelman (known as the "Gadol from Minsk"). Served as rabbi in Smolevitch in the province of Minsk, and from 1913 served as rabbi in Kovna. From 1919 he was also the head of the Rabbis' Association of Independent Lithuania, and he later served as its honorary president.

Sher, Yitzḥak-Isaac (1879–1953)—Born in Hlusk, Minsk Province; educated in the yeshivas of Hlusk, Volozhin, and Slabodka; son-in-low of Rabbi Notte-Hirsch Finkel. He served as Talmud instructor in the Knesset-Yisrael Yeshiva in Slabodka, and in 1928 he was appointed as its head. When the Second World War broke out, he was recuperating in Switzerland. He made aliyah to the Land of Israel, and in 1947 he established Slabodka Yeshiva in Bnei-Brak.

Shkop, Shim'on (1860–1939)—Born in Turets, Minsk Province; educated in the Mir and Volozhin Yeshivas. In 1886 he became Talmud instructor in the Telz Yeshiva. From 1903 he served as rabbi of Maltch, Grodno Province, and set up a yeshiva there; from 1906 he did the same in Braynsk, Grodno Province. In 1920 he was appointed head of the Grodno Yeshiva.

Shorin, Yoel (1862/71—1927)—Born in Lochvitza, Poltava Province; educated in the Volozhin Yeshiva. In 1897 he established a yeshiva in Berezhnitsa in Vohlin Province, and two years later he moved it to Zvhil in the same province. In 1919/1921, he led his yeshiva's escape to the town of Korets in Poland.

Shulevitz, Eliezer (1848–1931)—Born in Kolne, Lomzhe Province (Poland); attended Eishishok Kibbutz and Volozhin and Kelm Yeshivas. In 1883 he founded the Lomzhe Yeshiva. In 1923 he made aliyah to the Land of Israel.

Sokolovsky, Moshe (1868/70–1931)—Born in Rozhinoy, Grodno Province. In 1896 he became a Talmud instructor in the Brisk Yeshiva, and in 1901 he was appointed as its head. After the First World War, he rehabilitated his Talmudic institution and served as its rosh-yeshiva.

Soloveitchik, Ḥayim (1853–1918)—Born in Volozhin, Vilna Province; son and disciple of Rabbi Yosef-Ber Soloveitchik; son-in-law to Rabbi Raphael Shapiro. In 1881 he was appointed as Talmud instructor in the Volozhin Yeshiva, and in 1892 he was appointed rabbi of Brisk in Grodno Province.

Soloveitchik, Yitzḥak-Ze'ev (1886–1959)—Born in Volozhin, Vilna Province; son and disciple of Rabbi Ḥayim Soloveitchik. In 1918 he was appointed as rabbi of Brisk, Poland. In 1941 he succeeded in reaching Eretz-Yisrael.

T

Trop, Naftali (1871–1928)—Born in Grodno; student in the yeshivas of Kelm, Slabodka, and Telz. In 1900 he was appointed as Talmud instructor in the Ohr-haḤayim Yeshiva-ketana in Slabodka, and from 1904 he served as the head of the Radin Yeshiva.

V

Vitkind, Hillel (1889–1974)—Born in Amdur, Grodno Province; talmid in the Novardok Yeshiva. After the First World War, he assisted in the establishment of a central Novardok yeshiva in Warsaw. In 1930 he set up a Novardok yeshiva in Jaffa, and two years he later relocated it in Tel-Aviv.

W

Wasserman, Elḥanan (1875–1941)—Born in Birzh, Kovna Province; attended Telz Yeshiva and the kibbutz of Brisk, and from 1907 the Kodshim Kollel in Radin. From 1903 to 1904, he headed a yeshiva in Amtchislav in the Mohilev Province, from 1910 he headed a yeshiva-ketana in Brisk, and from 1916 he headed the part of Radin Yeshiva in Smilovitch. In 1921 he reestablished and headed the Ohel-Torah Yeshiva of Baranovitch.

Weintraub, Shmuel (1886–1943)—Born in Proskurov, Podolia Province; educated in Novardok, Telz, and Slutsk Yeshivas. In 1918 he became the head of the Novardok Yeshiva in Berditchev, Ukraine. In 1922 he moved with the yeshiva to Poland, and after a number of stops along the way in this country, he settled the yeshiva in Pinsk in 1927. During the Second World War, he succeeded in reaching the Land of Israel.

Y

Yoffen, Avraham (1884/7–1970)—Born near Pinsk, Minsk Province; educated in the yeshivas of Slutsk and Krinik; son-in-law of Rabbi Yosef-Yozel Hurwitz. He served as Talmud instructor in the Novardok Yeshiva, and during the First World War, he was the head of that yeshiva in Homel. In 1919 he inherited the position of head of the Novardok yeshiva network from his father-in-law. In 1921 he set up a central Novardok yeshiva in Bialystok, Poland, and served as its head. During the Second World War, he succeeded in immigrating to the United States and established Beit-Yosef Yeshiva there.

Yogel, Shabtai (1875–1958)—Born in Piesk, Grodno Province; studied in Eishishok Kibbutz and Volozhin Yeshiva. From 1906 he headed Slonim Yeshiva. During the Second World War, he succeeded in reaching Eretz-Yisrael and established a yeshiva in Ramat-Gan.

Z

Zelmans, Avraham (1882–1940s)–Born in Mir, Minsk Province; talmid in the Novardok Yeshiva. In 1916 he was appointed as head of a Novardok yeshiva in Rostov-on-Don. In 1922 he founded a central Novardok yeshiva in Warsaw and served as its head.

Zusmanovich, Yosef (1894–1941)—Born in Jerusalem; educated in the yeshivas of Etz-Ḥayim of Jerusalem, Ponevezh, and Telz; son-in-law to Rabbi Moshe-Mordechai Epstein. From 1924 he filled his father-in-law's positions as rabbi in the Slabodka suburb and as Talmud instructor in Knesset-Yisrael Yeshiva. In 1928 he was nominated as the rabbi of Slabodka suburb by a portion of its inhabitants, and from 1931 he served as its official rabbi. In 1937 he was chosen as rabbi of Vilkomir, Lithuania.

GLOSSARY

admor (pl. *admorim*)—Hasidic grand rabbi, spiritual leader of a Hasidic dynasty
aliyah—immigration to the Land of Israel
avrech (pl. *avrechim*)—married yeshiva or *kollel* student
ba'al-bayit (pl. *ba'alei-batim*)—literally: householder, layman, in contrast to rabbis and scholars
baḥur (pl. *baḥurim*)—young man, yeshiva student
bar-mitzvah—Jewish coming of age ritual for boys
beit-din—court
beit-midrash (pl. *batei-midrash*)—study hall
birzhe—stock exchange
dayyan (pl. *dayyanim*)—rabbinical court judge
derasha—address, sermon
Eretz Yisrael—the Land of Israel
gabai (pl. *gaba'im*)—beadle, official of a Torah-study institution/synagogue/study hall
ḥabura (pl. *ḥaburot*)—small student study group in a yeshiva
halacha (pl. *halachot*)—Jewish law
ḥaluka—literally: distribution; monthly stipend
ḥalutz (pl. *ḥalutzim*)—pioneer preparing for agricultural settlement in the Land of Israel
Haskalah—Enlightenment
ḥeder (pl. *ḥadarim*)—literally: room; traditional Jewish elementary school
illuy (pl. *illuyim*)—prodigy
kibbutz (pl. *kibbutzim*)—group

- study *kibbutz* (pl. study *kibbutzim*)—study group
- *kibbutz* class—the upper class of the yeshiva, whose students had already reached the level of independent study

kloyz—synagogue/study hall, usually named after its founder
kollel (pl. *kollelim*)—Talmudic institution for married graduates of the yeshivas
mashgiaḥ (pl. *mashgiḥim*)—supervisor
matmid (pl. *matmidim*)—diligent student

mechinah—a branch of a yeshiva with a preparatory program
mitnagdim—the historic opponents of Hasidism, mainly the followers of Rabbi Eliyahu, the "Vilna Gaon," in the cultural environment of Lithuanian Jewry
mitzvot—Torah precepts and commandments
Musar—Jewish ethics
rebbe (pl. *rebbes*)—see *admor*
rosh-yeshiva (pl. *roshei-yeshiva*)—yeshiva head
seder (pl. *sedarim*)—study session
shtiebl (pl. *shtieblach*)—small, informal prayer house
sugya (pl. *sugyot*)—topic in Talmud study
talmid (pl. *talmidim*)—student
Talmud-Torah—a community school for children
Torah liShma—Torah study for its own sake
Va'ad-HaYeshivot—Yeshiva Committee
yeshiva-gedola (in pl. *yeshivot-gedolot*)—senior yeshiva for older students
yeshiva-ketana (in pl. *yeshivot-ketanot*)—junior yeshiva for younger students
Yishuv—pre-State Jewish community in the Land of Israel
- New *Yishuv*—modern and often secular, Zionist settlement of the Land of Israel
- Old *Yishuv*—old Jewish communities, whose members had continuously resided in or had come to the Land of Israel in the earlier centuries to live pious life in the Holy Land

BIBLIOGRAPHY

ARCHIVES AND COLLECTIONS

AJJDCA—21/32 Collection, American Jewish JDC Archives, New York
AJYP—Autobiographies of Jewish Youth in Poland (RG 4), YIVO Archives, New York
ARZ—Archive of Religious Zionism, Bar Ilan University, Ramat Gan
BC—Boder Collection, Voices of the Holocaust, Illinois Institute of Technology, Chicago
CAHJP—The Central Archives for the History of the Jewish People, Jerusalem
CRC—Central Relief Committee Records, Yeshiva University Archives, New York
CZA—The Central Zionist Archives, Jerusalem
DSA—David Safier Archives (private), Lawrence, New York
IRC—Israel Rosenberg Collection (ARC 98), Jewish Theological Seminary Archives, New York
JDCIA—JDC Israel Archives, Jerusalem
KoC—Koniuḥowsky Collection (O.71), Yad Vashem Archives, Jerusalem
LCSA—Lithuanian Central State Archives, Vilnius
LHA—Luba Ḥarlap Archives (private), Jerusalem
LJC—Lithuanian Jewish Communities (RG 2), YIVO Archives, New York
MPTA—Rabbi Mordechai Pinḥas Teitz Collection, Rivkah Blau-Teitz Archives (private), United States
MWP—Mark Wischnitzer, Papers, 1927–1955 (RG 767), YIVO Archives, New York
NWC—Nissan Vaxman Collection (ARC. 4* 1714), National Library Archives, Jerusalem
OHD—Oral History Division, The Institute of Contemporary Jewry, The Hebrew University of Jerusalem
SEA—Shlomo Eitan Archives (private), Jerusalem
VHY—Va'ad-HaYeshivot (RG 25), YIVO Archives, New York
YLKA—Yehudah Leib Kogan Collection, Family Kogan Archives (private), Jerusalem
YVA—Yad Vashem Archives, Jerusalem

NEWSPAPERS AND PERIODICALS

DIdS—Di Idishe Shtime, Kovna
DIdV—Dos Idishe Vort, New York
DMZ—Der Morgn Zhurnal, New York
DoV—Dos Vort, Vilna
IdL—Idisher Lebn, Kovna-Telz
TJO—The Jewish Observer, New York

BOOKS, STUDIES, AND ARTICLES

Abraham, Zvi J. "HaYeshivot beHungariya haNirḥava." In *Mosedot Torah beEiropah beVinyanam u'veḤurbanam*, edited by Samuel K. Mirsky, 435–47. New York: Ogen Publishing House of Histadrut Ivrit of America, 1956.

Agranovsky, Genrich, and Sid Z. Leiman. "Three Lists of Students Studying at the Volozhin Yeshiva in 1879." In *Turim: Studies in Jewish History and Literature: Presented to Dr. Bernard Lander*. Vol. 2, edited by Michael A. Shmidman, 1–24. New York: Touro College Press, 2008.

Agudas-haRabonim. *Tetikayts-Baricht fun Agudas-haRabonim 5694–5700*. Kovna, 1940.

Agudat haRabbanim. *Sefer haYovel shel Agudat haRabbanim haOrtodoksiyim deArtzot-haBerit veKanada: LiMelot Esrim veḤamesh Shanim leHivasda (1902–1927)*. New York: Oriom Press, 1928.

Alon, Gedalia. "Yeshivot Lita." In *Meḥkarim beToledot Yisrael biYmey Bayit Sheni u'veTekufat haMishna vehaTalmud*. Vol. 1, 1–11. Tel Aviv: HaKibbutz haMe'uḥad, 1957.

Alperovitz, Yitzḥak. *Telz (Lita): Matzevet Zikaron leKehila Kedosha*. Tel Aviv: Irgun Yotzei Telz beYisrael, 1984.

Altshuler, Mordechai. "HaNisayon Le'argen Kinus Klal-Yehudi beRusia Aḥar haMahapeicha." *He'avar* 12 (1965): 75–89.

———. *HaYevsektsiya biVrit haMo'atzot (1918–1930): Bein Le'umiyut leKomunizm*. Tel Aviv: HaMachon leYahadut Zemaneynu, 1981.

Arad, Yitzḥak. "Rikuz haPelitim beVilna Erev Milḥemet haOlam haSheniya." *Yad Vashem* 9 (1973): 165–75.

Ascher, Abraham. "Interpreting 1905." In *The Revolution of 1905 and Russias Jews*, edited by Stefani Hoffman and Ezra Mendelsohn, 15–30. Philadelphia: University of Pennsylvania Press, 2008.

Assaf, David. *Derech haMalchut: R' Yisrael meRuzhin uMekomo beToledot haḤasidut*. Jerusalem: Shazar Center, 1997.

Assaf, Simḥa. "Shenot haLimudim Sheli biYeshivat Telz (5665–5668)." *He'avar* 2 (1954): 34–45.

Atlas, Shmuel. "Der Derech haHavone in der Litvishe Yeshives." In *Lite*. Vol. 1, edited by Mendel Sudarsky, Uriyah Katzenelenbogen, Yitzḥak Kissin, and Berl Cohen, 605–14. New York: Jewish-Lithuanian Cultural Society Lite, 1951.

Ayalon, Ben-Tsiyon Ḥ., ed. *Sefer-Zikaron liKehilat Meytchet*. Tel Aviv: Irgun Yotzei Meytchet beYisrael u'veḤutz-laAretz, 1973.

Ayalon-Baranik, Ben-Tsiyon Ḥ., ed. *Pinkas Ostro'oh: Sefer-Zikaron liKehilat Ostro'oh*. Tel Aviv: Irgun Oley Ostro'oh beYisrael, 1960.

Ba'al-Maḥshavot. "Grobin (Perek leToledot haTenu'a haMusarit)." Part II. *He'avar* 2 (1918): 89–107.

Bacon, Gershon C. *The Politics of Tradition: Agudat Yisrael in Poland, 1916–1939.* Jerusalem: Magnes, 1996.

Baksht, Aharon Y. *Lev Aharon: Ma'amarei Maḥshava beTorat haMusar.* Jerusaelm: Netzaḥ, 1982.

Balosher, Aba. *Ḥayim Naḥman Bialik beVolozhin, Volozhin biBialik: Zikaron leḤaver-Yeshiva sheHaya veEinenu Od, u'leYeshiva* sheHayta *veEinena Od.* Kovna, 1935.

Barak (Brik), Zvi. "HaMisrad haEretzyisraeli beLita." In *Yahadut Lita.* Vol. 2, edited by Refael Ḥasman, 291–304. Tel Aviv: Igud Yotzey Lita, 1972.

———. "Pelitey Polin beLita baShanim 1939–1941." In *Yahadut Lita.* Vol. 2, edited by Refael Ḥasman, 353–70. Tel Aviv: Igud Yotzey Lita, 1972.

Baricht fun der Idisher Seim-Fraktziye fun II Litvishn Seim (1923–1926). Kovna: Idisher Seim-Fraktziye (Y. Kuznitsky and L. Beilis Press), 1926.

Barkai, Binyamin Y. "Naḥalat Binyamin: Yomanim." In *Naḥalat Binyamin Sefer Zikaron: Sheurim veSiḥot miMaranan veRabanan Rashei Yeshivot Telz uSlabodka-Hevron,* edited by Shmuel Barkai, 1–148. Jerusalem, 2005.

Bauer, Yehudah. "Pe'ulot Hatzala Derech Vilna." *Yad Vashem* 9 (1973): 177–83.

Beckelman, Moses W. "Polish Refugees Eastward Bound." *Jewish Social Service Quarterly* 18, no. 1 (1941): 50–54.

Ben-Artzi, Shmuel. "Bein Yotzer leYitzro (Sipuro-Viduyo haTeragi shel Rav, Pelit haShoah)." *Mabu'a* 26 (1994): 9–46.

———. *Shivti: Arba'a Sipurim meḤayei Ba'aley-haMusar haNovardekaiyim biYeshivot "Beit Yosef" beḤu"l.* Jerusalem: Kiryat Sefer, 1967.

———. "Te'unat Derachim." *Mabu'a* 4 (1967): 9–30.

Ben-Mordechai, A. "Metivta Rabbata 'Ohel Torah' deBaranovitch." In *Mosedot Torah beEiropah beVinyanam u'veḤurbanam,* edited by Samuel K. Mirsky, 247–90. New York: Ogen Publishing House of Histadrut Ivrit of America, 1956.

Ben-Natan, Refael. *BiTenu'a Aḥat: Zichronot, Hagigim veDivrey Torah.* Tel Aviv: Moreshet, 1991.

Ben-Yemini, Sh. "In der Malchus fun Toire." In *Sefer haZikaron shel haYeshiva haGedola "Kness-set Beit Yitzḥak" beKamenitz deLita (Polin),* edited by Yehudah A. Karp, 26–35. Warsaw, 1938. Reprint, Jerusalem: Yeshivat Kamenitz, 2004.

Benshalom, Bentsiyon. *BeSa'ar beYom Sufa: Pirkey Polin.* Tel Aviv: Massada, 1944.

Berenstein, Avraham, Yom-Tov Forgas, and Yonah Naveh, eds. *Yeshivat Mir: HaZeriḥa beFa'atei Kedem.* Vol. 1–3. Bnei Brak: Merkaz Prager—Machon leMoreshet Yisrael, 1999.

Berenstein, Moshe. *Hegyonot: Inyanim Shonim.* Vol. 1–2. Jerusalem: Ḥorev, 1953.

Berezovsky, Shalom N. *Zikaron Kadosh: LeZecher Maran haKadosh Admor MohaRShD"I Z"l Hy"d miSlonim-Baranovitch.* Jerusalem: Beit Avraham Yeshiva, 1967.

Berger, Ludwig. "HaMivneh haSotzyali-haKalkali shel Yahadut Polin (1918–1939)." In *Beit Yisrael bePolin: MiYamim Rishonim ve'ad liYemot haḤurban.* Vol. 1, edited by Yisrael Haylperin, 200–215. Jerusalem: HaMaḥlaka leInyanei haNo'ar shel haHistadrut haTziyonit, 1948.

Berger, Shulamit Z. *An Inventory to the Records of the Central Relief Committee.* Vol. 2. New York: Yeshiva University Archives, 1999.

Bergman, Asher. *Lulei Toratcha: Uvdot uMa'asim Me'alfim lefi Seder Parashiyot haTorah meRaban shel Yisrael haGaon heḤasid haAmiti Maran Rabi Elazar Menaḥem Man Shach Ztz"l.* Bnei Brak, 2002.

———. *Orḥot Ḥasidecha*. Bnei Brak, 1999.

———. *Shimush Ḥachamim*. Bnei Brak, 2001.

Berkovitz, Yosef. *Ḥelkat Yosef*. Bnei Brak, 1959.

Berlin, Meir. *MeVolozin ad Yerushalayim: Zichronot*. Vol. 1–2. Tel Aviv: Yalkut, 1940.

Berman, Ya'akov. *Siḥot uFirkei Zichronot: Al Toledot Yehudei Mizraḥ Eiropa baMaḥatzit haRishona shel haMe'ah haEsrim*. Jerusalem, 1976.

Bialoblotsky, Shmuel. "Merkezey haTorah beLita." In *Yahadut Lita*. Vol. 1, edited by Natan Goren, Leib Garfunkel, Raphael Ḥasman, Dov Lipetz, Eliyahu Segal, Yisrael Kaplan, and Reuven Rubinstein, 185–205. Tel Aviv: Am haSefer, 1959.

———. "R' Itzelle miPonivezh." In *Yahadut Lita*. Vol. 1, edited by Natan Goren, Leib Garfunkel, Raphael Ḥasman, Dov Lipetz, Eliyahu Segal, Yisrael Kaplan, and Reuven Rubinstein, 394–97. Tel Aviv: Am haSefer, 1959.

Bideleux, Robert, and Ian Jeffries. *A history of Eastern Europe: Crisis and Change*. London: Routledge, 1998.

Bihm, Adolph. *HaKeren haKayemet leYisrael*. Reworked by Adolph Pollak. Jerusalem: HaLishka haMerkazit shel haKeren haKayemet leYisrael, 1939.

Billadi, Yitzḥak. "Toledot Mishpaḥat Goelman." In *Ohel Rachel: Perakim meḤayea'h shel Marat Rachel Billadi A"h*, 79–204. Jerusalem, 1991.

Blau, Rivkah. *Learn Torah Love Torah Live Torah: Harav Mordechai Pinchas Teitz, the Quintessential Rabbi*. New Jersey: Ktav, 2001.

Bloch, Eliyahu M. "Di Telzer Yeshive." In *Lite*. Vol. 1, edited by Mendel Sudarsky, Uriyah Katzenelenbogen, Yitzḥak Kissin, and Berl Cohen, 623–30. New York: Jewish-Lithuanian Cultural Society Lite, 1951.

Bloch, Shlomo Z. *HaTzadik Rabi Shlomo: Rabi Shlomo Zalman Bloch Z"l (Talmid Muvhak le'haKadosh Ba'al Ḥafetz Ḥayim Z"l)*. Jerusalem, 1990.

Blumental, Naḥman, ed. *Mir*. Jerusalem: Entziklopedia shel Galuyot, 1962.

Boi-Komitet. *Heichal haTereh Yeshivas "Knesses Yisroel": Der Nayer Binyen fun Slabodker Yeshive*. Kaunas-Vilijampole: Boi-Komitet, 1935.

Breuer, Mordechai. *Eida uDeyokanah: Ortodoxiya Yehudit baRaich haGermani (1871–1918)*. Jerusalem: Shazar Center, 1991.

———. *Oholei Torah: HaYeshiva Tavnitah veToledoteyah*. Jerusalem: Shazar Center, 2004.

Brezin, Aba Z. *Tzum Yidishn Folk: Di Geshichte un Bedaytung fun di Yeshive "Knesses Yisroel" in Ḥevron*. Jerusalem: Yuda A. Weiss Print, 1929.

Brown, Benjamin. "Gadlut haAdam veHaktanato: Temurot beShitat haMusar shel Yeshivat Slobodka." In *Yeshivot uVatey Midrashot*, edited by Immanuel Etkes, 243–71. Jerusalem: Shazar Center, 2006.

———. *HaḤazon Ish: HaPosek, haMa'amin uManhig haMahapecha haḤaredit*. Jerusalem: Magnes, 2011.

Broydes, Yitzḥak. *Vilna haTziyonit veAskaneyah: Sefer Zichronot uTe'udot al Pe'ulot Ḥovevey Tziyon vehaTziyonim beVilna (miShenat 1881–1924)*. Tel Aviv: Histadrut Oley Vilna vehaGalil beTel Aviv, 1939.

Bruk, Ben-Tsiyon, and David Zaritzky, eds. *Gevilei Esh: Siḥot, Musar veDivrei Hagut meEzvonam shel Gedolei uKedoshei Yeshivot "Beit Yosef"—Novharodok sheNispu baShoah*. Jerusalem: Yeshivat Beit Yosef Novharodok, 1973.

Buksboim, Yosef, ed. *Sefer haZikaron liChvodo u'leZichro shel Rabeinu haGadol Maran Rabi Ḥayim Shmuelevitz Zt"l Rosh Yeshivat Mir*. Jerusalem: Moriyah, 1980.

Bunim, Amos. *A Fire in his Soul: Irving M. Bunim, 1901–1980: the Man and his Impact on American Orthodox Jewry*. Jerusalem: Feldheim, 1989.

Carlebach, Esriel. "Mussar: Notizen zur Geschichte einer Bewegung." *Jahrbuch der Jüdisch-Literarischen Gesellschaft* 22 (1931–1932): 293–393.

Cohen, Berl. "HaḤinuch haIvri beLita haAtzma'it." In *Yidishe Shtet, Shtetlech un Dorfishe Yishuvim in Lite biz 1918*, 719–45. Brooklyn, NY: Simcha Graphic Associates, 1991.

Committee of the Jewish Delegations. *The Pogroms in the Ukraine under the Ukrainian Governments (1917–1920): Historical Survey with Documents and Photographs*. London: Committee of the Jewish Delegations, 1927.

Daniel, S., ed. *HaSar Ḥayim-Moshe Shapira: Dyokano shel Medinai Dati*. Tel Aviv: Yad Shapira, 1980.

Deinard, Efraim. *Zichronot Bat Ami*. Vol. 1. St. Louis, MO: Moinester Printing Company, 1920.

Desler, Eliyahu E., ed. *Sefer haZikaron Beit Kelm*. Vol. 1. Bnei Brak: Siftei Ḥachamim, 2002.

Desler, Reuven D. *Shenot Dor vaDor: Asufat Genazim*. Vol. 1–II. Jerusalem: ArtScroll/Mesorah, 2000–2004.

Dieckmann, Christoph. *Deutsche besatzungspolitik in Litauen 1941–1944*. Göttingen: Wallstein, 2011.

Dinur, Ben-Tsiyon. *BeOlam sheShaka: Zichronot uReshumot miDerech Ḥayim (1884–1914)*. Jerusalem: Bialik Institute, 1958.

Domb, Asher. "Pirkei Ḥayim." In *Torat Yeḥi'el: Ḥidushim uVe'urim beSugyot haSha"s u'veInyanim Shonim*, by Yeḥi'el Vilensky, 1–38 (at the end of the book). Jerusalem: Mechon Hadrat Yerushalayim, 2003.

Domb, Cyril. *Memories of Kopul Rosen*. London: Carmel College, 1970.

Don-Yiḥye, Yehudah L. "BiYeshivat Volozhin (kitei Zichronot)." Part I. *Netiva* 11, no. 28–29 (1936): 4.

Druck, David. *R' Levy Ginzburg: Yaḥaso, Ḥayav uSefarav*, translated by M. Maisels. New York: P. Shoulson, 1934.

Drushkovitz, Avraham. *Sha'arei Hora'a*. Kovna: Y. Kuznitsky and L. Beilis, 1933.

Dubnov, Shim'on. *Pinkas haMedina: Pinkas Va'ad haKehillot haRashiyot biMedinat Lita*. Berlin: Ayanot, 1925.

Dvoretz, Yisrael Z. *HaGaon Rabi Moshe Mordechai Epstein: Ḥayav uFe'ulotav*. Tel Aviv: Netzaḥ, 1944.

Edelstein, Ya'akov. "Do'ḥ Ishi al Hatzala biTekufat HaShoah." *Gesher* 112, no. 1 (1985): 142–44.

———. "Keitzad Avra Yeshivat Slabodka leḤevron?" *Kivunim* 16 (1982): 103–6.

Edelstein, Yitzḥak. "BiYmey Sufa," compiled by Dina Porat. *Gal-Ed* 3 (1976): 325–59.

———. *Rabi Baruch Dov Leibovitch: Ḥayav uFe'ulotav*. Tel Aviv: Netzaḥ, 1957.

Eidenu: Ḥoveret Meyuḥedet shel "Hedenu" leZichro shel Rabeinu haGadol haGaon R' Shlomo Poliachek Zatz"l (haIluy miMeytchet). New York: Talmidei Yeshivat R' Yitzḥak Elḥanan, 1929.

Eisenstadt, Moshe E. "Yeshivat Volozhin (miZichronot Yemey Ne'uray)." *He'avar* 14 (1967): 159–72.

Eisenstein, Miriam. *Jewish Schools in Poland 1919–39*. New York: Kings Crown, 1950.

Eisner, Isi J. "Reminiscences of the Berlin Rabbinical Seminary." *LBI Year Book* 12 (1967): 32–52.

Elberg, Simḥa. *Varsha shel Ma'ala: Perakim miMasechet-Pela'im sheNirkema beTochechey Birat Polin Lifney haShoah*. Bnei Brak: Netzaḥ, 1969.

Eliash, Shulamit. "Hatzalat Yeshivot Polin sheNimletu leLita beReshit haMilḥama." *Yalkut Moreshet* 32 (1982): 127–68.

———. "HaYeḥasim Bein haRabanut haRashit leEretz-Yisrael vehaShilton haMandatori (1936–1945)." PhD diss., Bar-Ilan University, 1979.

Eliḥai, Yosef. *HaMizrahi uTenu'at Torah veAvoda bePolin 1928–1939*. Jerusalem: haSifriya haTsiyonit, 2001.

Endlin, Neḥemia. *Oif di Vegn fun Partizaner Kamf*. Tel Aviv: Komitet fun Gevezene Yidishe Partizaner un Untergrunt-Kemfer fun Kovner Getto, 1980.

Engelman, Morris. *Four Years of Relief and War Work by the Jews of America, 1914–1918*. New York: The Schoen Printing Company, 1918.

Epstein, Moshe M. *Levush Mordechai*. Vol. 1. Warsaw, 1901; Vol. 2. Jerusalem, 1929.

Epstein, Yosef D. "Yeshivat Mir." In *Mosedot Torah beEiropah beVinyanam u'veḤurbanam*, edited by Samuel K. Mirsky, 87–132. New York: Ogen Publishing House of Histadrut Ivrit of America, 1956.

Epstein, Zelig. "Yeshivat 'Sha'ar haTorah' biGrodna." In *Mosedot Torah beEiropah beVinyanam u'veḤurbanam*, edited by Samuel K. Mirsky, 291–305. New York: Ogen Publishing House of Histadrut Ivrit of America, 1956.

Etkes, Immanuel. "Bein Lamdanut leRabanut beYahadut Lita shel haMe'ah ha-19." *Zion* 53, no. 4 (1988): 385–403.

———. *Rabbi Israel Salanter and the Mussar Movement: Seeking the Torah of Truth*, translated by Jonathan Chipman. Philadelphia-Jerusalem: Jewish Publication Society, 1993.

———. *The Gaon of Vilna: The Man and His Image*, translated by Jeffrey M. Green. Berkeley: University of California Press, 2002.

———. "Yeshivot Lita biRe'i Sifrut haZichronot." In *Yeshivot Lita—Pirkei Zichronot*, edited by Immanuel Etkes and Shlomo Tikochinski, 9–56. Jerusalem: Shazar Center, Dinur Center, and the Hebrew University in Jerusalem, 2004.

Etkes, Immanuel, and Shlomo Tikochinski, eds. *Yeshivot Lita—Pirkei Zichronot*. Shazar Center, Dinur Center, and the Hebrew University in Jerusalem, 2004.

Ettinger, Shmuel. *Bein Polin leRusia*. Jerusalem: Shazar Center and Bialik Institute, 1995.

Etzion (Holtzberg), Yitzḥak R. "HaZerem haḤinuchi 'Yavneh' beLita." In *Yahadut Lita*. Vol. 2, edited by Refael Ḥasman, 160–65. Tel Aviv: Igud Yotzey Lita, 1972.

Even-Ḥen, Ya'akov. *BeReshit haSufa: Sipurim*. Jerusalem: Mabu'a, 1986.

———. *Tenu'a biSe'arat Milḥama (Derech Vilna leYisrael)*. Tel Aviv: Moreshet, 1984.

Evron, Dov. *Ḥinuch beMa'avako: LiDe'muto shel haḤinuch haYehudi, haDati-Le'umi bePolin, Bein Shetei Milḥamot haOlam*. Jerusalem: Sifriyat Elinar, 1988.

Ezraḥi, Shulamit. *HaMashgi'aḥ R' Meir: Toledot Ḥayav shel Maran haGaon haTzadik Rabi Meir Ḥadash Ztz"l*. Jerusalem: Feldheim, 2002.

Ezrat Torah. *Luaḥ haYovel shel Ezrat Torah: liMelot Esrim Shana laMosad Ezrat Torah (15 beElul 5675–5695)*. New York: Moinester Publishing Company, 1936.

———. *Sefer haZikaron me'haMosad Ezrat Torah*. New York, 1919.

———. *Zikaron baSefer*. New York: Ezrat Torah Al Yad Agudat haRabbanim, 1922.

Farber, Kalman. *Olkeniki Radin Vilna: MiYomano shel Ben Torah baShoah uLefane'ah*. Jerusalem, 2007.

———. "R' Leibale Minsker Hy'd." *Shema Yisrael Zechor* 7 (1986): 98–100.

Farbstein, Ester. *BeSeter Ra'am: Halacha, Hagut uManhigut biYemei haShoah*. Jerusalem: Mossad haRav Kook, 2002.

———, ed. *MiTelz Ad Telz: Yomano shel haRav Ḥayim Stein 1939–1944*. Jerusalem: HaMerkaz leḤeker haShoah beMichlala Yerushalayim, 2015.

Fichman, Ya'akov, ed. *Bialik*. Tel Aviv: Va'ad haYovel beHishtatfut hotza'at Omanut, 1934.

Finkel, Eliezer Y. "Kol Kore! Beit Ulpana Ravta Yeshivat Mir, Av 5682." *VHY/371* (Summer 1922).

Finkelstein, Louis, and Alexander Marx. "Necrology: Cyrus Adler." *Proceedings of the American Academy for Jewish Research* 10 (1940): 1–2.

Fishman, David E. "Musar and Modernity: The Case of Novaredok." *Modern Judaism* 8, no. 1 (1988): 41–64.

———. "The Musar Movement in Interwar Poland." In *The Jews of Poland Between Two World Wars*, edited by Yisrael Gutman, Ezra Mendelsohn, Jehuda Reinharz, and Chone Shmeruk, 247–71. Lebanon, NH: University Press of New England, 1989.

Fletcher, John M. "University Migrations in the Late Middle Ages, with Particular Reference to the Stamford Secession." In *Reform and Resilience: Universities in Transition 1300–1700*, edited by James M. Kittleson and Pamela J. Rebirth, 163–89. Columbus: Ohio State University Press, 1984.

Fortman, Moshe. "Bnei Torah miLita sheAmdu beMivḥan haEimim." *Beit Ya'akov* 26 (1961): 18–19.

Frank, Yehudah L., ed. *Esah Einai el heHarim*. Tel Aviv, 2004.

Frankel, Jonathan. *Crisis, Revolution, and Russian Jews*. New York: Cambridge University Press, 2009.

Friedland, Pesaḥ. "HaGaon R' Moshe Mordechai Epstein Ztz'l." *HaTor* 14, no. 2 (1933): 6–8.

Friedlender, Yosef. "Din veḤeshbon al Matzav haAliya beVilna baḤodashim Yuli 1940–Yanuar 1941." *CZA, S6/1542* (Feb. 20, 1941): 1–4.

Friedman, Eliezer E. *Sefer haZichronot (1858–1926)*. Tel Aviv, 1926.

Friedman, Menaḥem. "'Al haNisim'—Periḥato shel Olam haTorah (haYeshivot vehaKollelim) beYisrael." In *Yeshivot uVatey Midrashot*, edited by Immanuel Etkes, 431–42. Jerusalem: Shazar Center, 2006.

———. *Ḥevra vaDat: HaOrtodoxia haLo-Tziyonit beEretz-Yisrael 1918–1936*. Jerusalem: Ben Zvi Institute, 1978.

"Fun Amerikaner Universitetn in di Poilishe Yeshives." In *Mir*, edited by Naḥman Blumental, 529–32. Jerusalem: Entziklopedia shel Galuyot, 1962.

Gar, Yosef. *Azoy iz es Geshen in Lite: Tzu der Geshichte fun der Sovetisher Memsholeh 1940–1941*. Tel Aviv: HaMenorah, 1965.

———. *Umkum fun der Yidisher Kovne*. Munich: Farband fun Litvishe Yidn in der Amerikaner Zone in Daitchland, 1948.

Gardi, Natan. *Pirkei Ḥayim shel Ḥalutz Dati*. Vol. 1–2. Tel Aviv: HaMaḥlaka leHasbara biChtav shel haMiflaga haDatit Leumit HaMizraḥi-HaPoel HaMizraḥi, 1973–1979.

Garfunkel, Leib. "HaMa'avak shel Yehudei Lita al Zechuyot Leumiyot." In *Yahadut Lita*. Vol. 2, edited by Raphael Ḥasman, 35–72. Tel Aviv: Igud Yotzei Lita, 1972.

———. "MeIgra Rama leVira Amikta." In *Yahadut Lita*. Vol. 2, edited by Raphael Ḥasman, 28–34. Tel Aviv: Igud Yotzei Lita, 1972.

Geilke, Georg. *Das Staatsangehörigkeitsrecht der Sowjetunion*. Frankfurt am Main: Alfred Metzner, 1964.

Gelbart, Shmuel. *Di Groise Yeshive Toras Ḥesed in Lodz: Ihre Shefer un Boyer*. Lodz: Mesorah, 1929.

Gelber, Natan M. "Korot haYehudim bePolin meReshit Ḥalukatah ve'ad Milḥemet haOlam haSheniya." In *Beit Yisrael bePolin: MiYamim Rishonim ve'ad liYemot haḤurban*. Vol. 1, edited by Yisrael Ḥaylperin, 110–27. Jerusalem: HaMaḥlaka leInyanei haNo'ar shel haHistadrut haTziyonit, 1948.

Gelbstein, Rachel. "HaMishna haḤinuchit shel Tenuat haMusar." *Darkeinu baḥinuch* 1 (1993): 81–167.

Gerlitz, Menaḥem M., ed. *Ḥidushei haGR"Ḥ haShalem beSugiyot haSha"s al Seder haDapim: Masechet Bava Metzia*. Jerusalem: Oraita, 1995.

Gershuni, Aharon E. *Yahadut beRussia haSovyetit: LeKorot Redifot haDat*. Jerusalem: Mossad haRav Kook, 1961.

———. *Yehudim veYahadut biVrit haMoatzot: Yahadut Russia miTekufat Stalin ve'ad haZeman haAḥaron*. Jerusalem: Feldheim, 1970.

Gershuni, Yehudah. *Maḥbarot shel Na'ar: 1939*. Beit Zera, 1997.

Gershuni, Yehudah. *Sha'arei Tzedek: Derashot veDivrei Maḥshava*. Jerusalem, 1995.

Gerstenkorn, Yitzḥak. *Zichronotai al Bnei-Brak*. Vol. 1–2. Bnei Brak: P. Even Print, 1942–1946.

"Geschichtlicher Ueberblick der Entwicklung der Mirer Jeschiwah." *MWP*: 1–6.

Gibraltar, Yitzḥak E. *Yasor Yisrani: Pirkei Hod uShevivim al Kovna beTifartah ve'al Ḥayei ha-Ruaḥ shePiku Bah*. Vol. 1. Bnei Brak, 2007.

Gifter, Mordechai. "Yeshivat Telz." *In Mosedot Torah beEiropah beVinyanam u'veḤurbanam*, edited by Samuel K. Mirsky, 169–88. New York: Ogen Publishing House of Histadrut Ivrit of America, 1956.

Gilboa, Yehoshua A. *Confess! Confess!: Eight Years in Soviet Prisons*, translated by Dov Ben-Aba. Boston: Little, Brown, 1968.

Gliksman, Devorah. *A Tale of Two Worlds: Rabbi Dovid and Rebbetzin Basya Bender: The Bridge Between the Yeshivah-Bais Yaakov Worlds of Pre-War Europe and Post-War America*. Brooklyn, NY: Mesorah, 2009.

Golan, Yehudit. *HaLaila Eino Afel*. Jerusalem: Feldheim, 1998.

Goldberg, Hillel. *Israel Salanter, Text, Structure, Idea: The Ethics and Theology of an Early Psychologist of the Unconscious*. New York: Ktav, 1982.

Goldman, Jacob. "Rabbi Herzog's First Rescue Journey." *Niv Hamidrashia* (1964): 5–11.

Gordon, Avraham Y. *Nefesh Ḥaya*. Bnei Brak, 1991.

Gotlieb, Naftali Z., ed. *Zichronotay: Pirkei Zichronot Mas'irim uMeratkim, miYalkuto shel haGaon haḤasid haAmiti, Ish haMesirut-Nefesh, miGedolei haRabbanim shel Yahadut Russiya haMa'atira, haRav haGaon Naḥum Shemarya Sasonkin Ztz"l*. Jerusalem, 1988.

Gotlieb, Shmuel N. *Oholei-Shem*. Pinsk: M. M. Glouberman, 1912.

Grade, Ḥayim. "Talmidei-Ḥachomim in der Lite." Part 1, *Di goldene Keit* 90 (1976): 5–34; Part 2, *Di goldene Keit* 94 (1977): 5–33.

———. *The Yeshiva*. Vol. 2: Masters and Disciples, translated by Curt Leviant. Indianapolis: Bobbs-Merrill, 1977.

———. *Ya: Lider*. Vilna: Farlag fun B. Kletskin, 1936.

Graubart, Yehudah L. *Sefer Zikaron: Reshumot Miymei haMilḥama haAḥrona—veHashkafot Shonot uMichtavim*. Lodz: Mesorah, 1926.

Greiniman, Shmuel. *Ḥafetz Ḥayim al haTorah*. New York: Metivta Tiferet Yerushalayim, 1943.

Grinbaum, Aharon. *The American Joint Distribution Committee and the Yeshivoth: History, Observation, Reports*. Jerusalem: Joint Israel, 1974.

Gringauz, Samuel. "Jewish National Autonomy in Lithuania (1918–1925)." *Jewish Social Studies* 14, no. 3 (1952): 225–26.

Grodzensky, Ḥayim O. *Aḥiezer.* Vol. 4. Likutim. Bnei Brak, 1986.

Grodzinsky, Avraham. *Torat Avraham: Ma'amarim veSiḥot miKitvey Yado*. Bnei Brak: Yeshivat Kollel Avrechim Torat Avraham, 1978.

Grodzinsky, Yehoshua L. *Shevilim: Ba'ayot Ḥinuch, Tarbut veLashon*. Tel Aviv: Yavneh, 1956.

Gross, Binyamin. "Al Tefisat Olamo shel R' Ḥayim meVolozhin." *Bar-Ilan* 22–23 (1988): 160–91.

Grossman, Reuven. *Ki Im . . .: Tziyunei Derech beToledot Ḥayav uMishnato haRuḥanit shel Maran haGaon Rabi Mordechai Ze'ev Shulman Zt"l Rosh Yeshivat "Knesset Yisrael" Slabodka Bnei-Brak*. Petaḥ Tikva, 1983.

Gugenheim, Claude A., ed. *Letters From Mir: A Torah World in the Shadow of the Shoah*, translated by C. L. Latham. New York: Orthodox Union Press, 2014.

Guttentag, Naḥum M., ed. "Eshed haNeḥalim." In *Sefer Zikaron liChvodam uleZichram shel haRav Avraham Vaysfish Z"l veRa'ayato haTzadeket Marat Shoshana Z"l*. Jerusalem, 1992.

HaHitagdut. *Ḥoveret likrat haAsefa*. Bialystok: HaHitagdut biYeshivat Beit Yosef Bialystok, 1937.

HaMerkaz haOlami. *Keren haTorah shel Agudat Yisrael*. Vienna: HaMerkaz haOlami shel Keren haTorah, 1925.

"HaRav R' Avraham Yitzḥak Bloch—Telz." In *Eleh Ezkerah: Osef Toledot Kedoshei 5700–5705*. Vol. 1, edited by Yitzḥak Levin, 26–33. New York: HaMachon leḤeker Ba'ayot haYahadut haḤaredit, 1956.

"HaRav R' David Bliacher—Mezritch." In *Eleh Ezkerah: Osef Toledot Kedoshei 5700–5705*. Vol. 6, edited by Yitzḥak Levin, 169–73. New York: HaMachon leḤeker Ba'ayot haYahadut haḤaredit, 1965.

"HaRav R' Elḥanan Wasserman—Baranovitch." In *Eleh Ezkerah: Osef Toledot Kedoshei 5700–5705*. Vol. 1, 82–91. New York: HaMachon leḤeker Ba'ayot haYahadut haḤaredit, 1956.

"HaRav R' Pesaḥ Hurwitz—Kletsk." In *Eleh Ezkerah: Osef Toledot Kedoshei 5700–5705*. Vol. 7, edited by Yitzḥak Levin, 221–24. New York: HaMachon leḤeker Ba'ayot haYahadut haḤaredit, 1972.

"HaRav R' Pesaḥ Pruskin—Kobrin." In *Eleh Ezkerah: Osef Toledot Kedoshei 5700–5705*. Vol. 7, edited by Yitzḥak Levin, 225–29. New York: HaMachon leḤeker Ba'ayot haYahadut haḤaredit, 1972.

Harkavy, Zvi. *MeImrei haZvi (Kuntress I): Divrei Halacha, Kitvei Yad uMeḥkarim Toraniyim*. Jerusalem, 1980.

Hartglass, A. "Milḥamot Yehudei Polin al Zechuyoteihem haEzraḥiyot vehaLeumiyot." In *Beit Yisrael bePolin: MiYamim Rishonim ve'ad liYemot haḤurban*. Vol. 1, edited by Yisrael Haylperin, 128–51. Jerusalem: HaMaḥlaka leInyanei haNo'ar shel haHistadrut haTziyonit, 1948.

Ḥasman, Yehudah L. *HaOr Yahel: Iyunim beMusar veYirat Hashem*. Vol 1. Tel Aviv: Netzaḥ, 1954.

Haylperin, Yisrael. "Reshito shel Va'ad Medinat Lita." *Zion* 3, no. 1 (1938): 51–57.

Hed, Shlomo. "Beit Ulpena Ravta deKobrin." In *Mosedot Torah beEiropah beVinyanam u'veḤurbanam*, edited by Samuel K. Mirsky, 325–327. New York: Ogen Publishing House of Histadrut Ivrit of America, 1956.

Helmreich, William B. *The World of the Yeshiva: An Intimate Portrait of Orthodox Jewry*. New Jersey: Ktav, 2000.

Henkin, Eitam S. *Ta'aroch Lefanai Shulḥan: Ḥayav, Zemano uMifalav shel haRi"m Epstein Ba'al Aruch haShulḥan*. Jerusalem: Maggid, 2019.

Herschberg, Avraham S. *Pinkes Bialystok: Grunt-MaTeryaln tzu der Geshichte fun di Yidn in Bialystok biz noch der Ershter Velt-Milḥome*. Vol. 2. New York: Gezelshaft far Geshichte fun Bialystok, 1950.

Hertzman, Elchonon Y. *Escape to Shanghai*, translated by Chaim. U. Lipschitz. New York: Maznaim, 1984.

———. *Nes haHatzala shel Yeshivat Mir*. Jerusalem, 1976.

———. *Olam haMusar vehaDa'at: Leket Ma'amarim beMusar vaDa'at, beEmuna u'veḤinuch*. Bnei Brak, 2003.

Ḥigger, Moshe. *Sam Ḥayim: Sipurim uMa'amarim*. Jerusalem: Rubin Mass, 1990.

Hirschprung, Pinḥas. *Fun Natzishen Yomertol (Zichroines fun a Palit)*. Montreal: The Eagle Publishing, 1944.

Histadrut Talmidei Yeshivat Slabodka. *Kinus Histadrut Talmidei Yeshivat "Knesset Yisrael" Slabodka*. Kovna: S. Yoselevitch Print, 1937.

Hoffman, Joshua. "Rav Kook's Mission to America," *Orot* 1 (1991): 78–99.

Holtzman, Avner, ed. *Ḥayim Naḥman Bialik: HaShirim*. Or Yehudah: Devir, 2005.

Hurwitz, Aryeh L. *Zichronot Meḥanech Ivri*. Vol. 1. Jerusalem: Lishkat haḤinuch beBoston veHotza'at haSefarim M. Newman, 1960.

Hurwitz, Yosef Y. *Madregat haAdam beTikun haMidot*. Poltava, 1918. Reprint, Yeshivat Mezritch, 1932.

———. *Madregat haAdam: miMa'amarei Admor haGaon haḤassid Moreinu haRav Y. Hurwitz Ztz"l sheDiber be'haYeshivot deNovhardok*. Jerusalem: HaTeḥiya Press, 1964.

Hutner, Yitzḥak. *Paḥad Yitzḥak: Igrot uMichtavim*. New York: HaMossad Gur Aryeh, 1991.

"Ich Ver Na vaNad." *YVA-O.17/66*: 1–7.

Idelevitz, Moshe M., ed. *Sefer haYovel liChevod Rabeinu . . . Shim'on Yehudah haCohen Shkop Shelit"a . . . liMelot Ḥamishim Shenot Avodato haPoriya al Sede Harbatzat haTorah*. Vilna 1932. Reprint, Bnei Brak: Netzaḥ, 1977.

Jungreiss, Yitzḥak E., "Yeshivat Ḥatam Sofer biPresburg." In *Mosedot Torah beEiropah beVinyanam u'veḤurbanam*, edited by Samuel K. Mirsky, 449–515. New York: Ogen Publishing House of Histadrut Ivrit of America, 1956.

Kadosh Elul: *Eimat haDin veḤerdat haMishpat veAvirat Ḥodesh Elul vehaYamim haNora'im biMeḥitzatam shel Gedolei uMe'orei haDorot uVa'alei haMusar Ztz"l*. Jerusalem, 1995.

Kalmanovitch, Avraham. *Kulmos haLev: Da'at Torah veSa'arot Ruaḥ*. Jerusalem, 1996.

Kanyevsky, Avraham Y. *Toledot Ya'akov: Toledot Ḥayav veHanhagotav shel Maran haGaon heḤasid Rabeinu Ya'akov Yisrael Kanyevsky Ztz"l Baal ha"Kehilot Ya'akov."* 2nd ed. Bnei Brak, 1995.

Kaplan, Pesaḥ. "HaRav R' Azriel Rabinovitch—Telz." In *Eleh Ezkerah: Osef Toledot Kedoshei 5700–5705*. Vol. 5, edited by Yitzḥak Levin, 116–22. New York: HaMachon leḤeker Ba'ayot haYahadut haḤaredit, 1963.

Karlinsky, Ḥayim. *HaRishon leShoshelet Brisk: Toledot Ḥayav uFe'alav shel haGaon Rabi Yosef-Dober haLevi Soloveitchik Ztz"l Rosh Yeshiva beVolozhin veAba"d beArim Slutsk uBrisk*. Jerusalem: Mechon Yerushalayim, 1984. Reprint, 2004.

Karp, Yehudah A. *Sefer haZikaron shel haYeshiva haGedola "Knesset Beit Yitzḥak" beKamenitz deLita (Polin)*. Warsaw, 1938. Reprint, Jerusalem: Yeshivat Kamenitz, 2004.

Karpenshprung, Mordechai. *Divrei Mordechai*. Brooklyn, NY: Balshon, 1954.

Katz, Dov. *Divrei Hagut uRe'ut: Ma'amarim*. Vol. 1–2. Jerusalem, 1979, 1981.

———. "Maran R' Yeḥezkel Sarna Ztz"l: Perakim leToldotav." In *Aḥar He'asef: Me'asef Zikaron leAdoneinu Moreinu veRabeinu Geon haTorah vehaMusar Ish Ḥai Rav Pealim Mekavtze'el miMekimei Ulah shel Torah veYirah beEh"k Maran Rabi Yeḥezkel Sarna Ztz"l*, edited by Naftali M. Kravitz, 144–58. Jerusalem: Ḥebron Yeshiva, 1971.

———. *Pulmus haMusar: Musaf leSidrat "Tenuat HaMusar."* Jerusalem: Weiss Print, 1972.

———. *Tenuat HaMusar: Toledote'ah, Ishe'ah veShitote'ah*. Vol. 3. Tel Aviv: Avraham Tziyoni, 1967. Vol. 4–5. Tel Aviv: Re'em Print, 1978.

———. *Toledotai (Mahadura Mishpaḥtit)*. Jerusalem, 1981.

Katz, Reuven. *Sha'ar Reuven: Davar belto*. Jerusalem: Hotza'at haSefarim haEretz-Yisraelit, 1952.

Katzenelson-Nochimov, Tzipora. *Yitzḥak Katzenelson: Zayn Lebn un Shafn*. Buenos Aires: Tzentral-Farband fun Poilishe Yidn in Argentine, 1948.

Kaubrys, Saulius. *National Minorities in Lithuania: an Outline*, translated by Milda Dyke. Vilnius: Vaga, 2002.

Kenez, Peter. *Civil War in South Russia, 1918: The First Year of the Volunteer Army*. Berkeley: University of California Press, 1971.

Klibansky, Ben-Tsiyon. "'BeMakom sheYesh Ḥilul haShem Ein Ḥolkin Kavod LaRav'—Ma'amada shel Agudat haRabbanim beLita." *Zion* 75, no. 3 (2010): 313–46.

———. "HaYeshivot haLita'iyot beMizraḥ Eiropa Bein Shetei Milḥamot haOlam." PhD diss., Tel Aviv University, 2009.

———. "'Hitagdut haYeshivot Takif Olam uMelo'oh'—LiDemuta shel Itonut Novardok." *Kesher* 40 (2010): 115–25.

———. "Jewish Resistance in Provincial Lithuania in 1941." *Holocaust Studies* 26, no. 1 (2020): 38–61.

———. *KeTzur Ḥalamish: Tor haZahav shel haYeshivot haLita'iyot beMizraḥ Eiropa*. Jerusalem: Shazar Center, 2014.

———. "'Lama Ze Titraḥ—Kefotz Kan laNahar!'—HaMusar kaMa'ane haOrtodoksi haMuvhak laModerna." *Gal-Ed* 23 (2012): 15–58.

———. "'LeKadesh Shem Shamayim baOlam!'—LiDemuta shel haMahapecha haTelza'it." *Mayim Midalyav* 21 (2010): 25–64.

Kloizner, Yisrael. "Toledot haYehudim beLita." In *Yahadut Lita*. Vol. 1, edited by Natan Goren, Leib Garfunkel, Raphael Ḥasman, Dov Lipetz, Eliyahu Segal, Yisrael Kaplan, and Reuven Rubinstein, 23–123. Tel Aviv: Am haSefer, 1959.

Kol, Shmuel. *Eḥad beDoro: Korot-Ḥayav, Ma'avako uFa'olo shel Rabi Yosef Shlomo Kahaneman haGaon miPonivezh Ztz"l*. Vol. 1–2. Tel Aviv: Orot, 1970.

Kossovsky, Yitzḥak. "Letoledot Rabeinu." In *Me'asef Beit-Midrash*, edited by Meir Karelitz, 261–71. Tel Aviv: Yeshivat Geonei Volozhin, 1941.

Kossovsky-Shaḥor, Ya'akov. *Igrot R' Ḥayim Ozer: Kovetz Igrotav shel Maran Raskbh"g haGaon Rabi Ḥayim Ozer behaG"r David Shlomo Grodzensky Ztz"l*. Vol. 1–2. Bnei Brak, 2000–2001.

Krakovsky, Menaḥem. *Arzei haLevanon: Kovetz Derashot*. Vilna: G. Kletskin Print, 1936.

Kravitz, Naftali M., ed. *Aḥar He'asef: Me'asef Zikaron leAdoneinu Moreinu veRabeinu Geon haTorah vehaMusar Ish Ḥai Rav Pealim Mekavtze'el miMekimei Ulah shel Torah veYirah beEh"k Maran Rabi Yeḥezkel Sarna Ztz"l*. Jerusalem: Ḥebron Yeshiva, 1971.

Kremerman, Eliyahu. *Beurei Mishpat: Ḥidushim uVe'urim beInyanei Sh"A Ḥoshen Mishpat Simanim 28–60*. Jerusalem, 1993.

Krone, Moshe. *Ishim veNiḥoḥim: Magid Siḥot*. Tel Aviv: Moreshet, 1992.

———. *Morai veRabotai, Aḥai veRe'ai: Pirkei Zichronot*. Tel Aviv: Moreshet, 1987.

Kruk, Yosef. *Taḥat Diglan shel Shalosh Mahapechot: Ishim uTnuot beDori*. Vol. 2. Tel Aviv: Maḥbarot leSifrut, 1970.

Landoi, Betzalel. *Yeshivot Lita uPolin—miVolozhin ve'ad haShoah*. *Maḥanayim* 78 (1963): 34–45.

Langleben-Klibansky, Gitta. *MiYarketei Tzafon: Milḥemet Hisardut shel Tze'ira Yehudiya miLita al Gedot Okyanus haKeraḥ haTzefoni*. Elkana: Ḥeker Yahadut Lita, 2013.

Leoni, Eliezer, ed. *Korets (Vohlin): Sefer Zikaron liKehilateinu sheAlah Ale'ah haKoret*. Tel Aviv: Irgun Yotzei-Korets beYisrael, 1959.

Leshovitz, Katriel, ed. *Volkovisk: Sipurah shel Kehila Yehudit-Tziyonit*. Tel Aviv, 1988.

Levenstein, Yeḥezkel: *Or Yeḥezkel*. Bnei Brak, 1976.

Levi, Moshe, ed. *Yeshivat 'Knesset Ḥizkiyahu' Kefar Ḥasidim: Yovel Hih, 50 Shana liYesud haYeshiva haKedosha*. Kefar Hasidim: Yeshivat Knesset Ḥizkiyahu, 1999.

Levi, Yosef. "HaRav R' Eliezer Aryeh Lichtenstein—Laḥva." In *Eleh Ezkerah: Osef Toledot Kedoshei 5700–5705*. Vol. 6, edited by Yitzḥak Levin, 91–97. New York: HaMachon leḤeker Ba'ayot haYahadut haḤaredit, 1965.

Levin, Dov. "Ḥofesh Dati Mugbal ve'al Tenai (MeḤayei haDat shel Yehudei Lita taḥat haShilton haSovieti, 1940–1941)." *Sinai* 79 (1976): 164–80.

———, ed. *Pinkas Hakehillot: Lita*. Jerusalem: Yad Vashem, 1996.

———. *Tekufa beSograyim 1939–1941: Temurot beḤayei haYehudim baEzorim sheSupeḥu liVrit haMo'atzot biTeḥilat Milḥemet haOlam haSheniya*. Tel Aviv: HaMachon leYahadut Bat Zemanenu, Beit Loḥamei haGeta'ot vehaKibbutz haMe'uḥad, 1989.

———. "Yerushalayim deLita keMiklat Ara'i liFelitim Yehudim beMilḥemet haOlam haSheniah." In *Umah veLashon: Sefer Zikaron liProf. Aryeh Tartakover*, edited by Menaḥem Zahari, Ḥayim Rabin, Yeshayahu Haran, Nissan Harpaz, and Michael Zand, 95–114. Jerusalem: Haberit haIvrit haOlamit vehaKongres haYehudi haOlami, 1986.

Levin, Meir. *Novarodok: A Movement That Lived in Struggle and Its Unique Approach to the Problem of Man*. New Jersey: Jason Aronson, 1996.

Levin, Pinḥas. *Toledot Agudat Yisrael: Hartza'a shel Kevod haRav Pinḥas haCohen Levin Shelit"a—Nisan 5731*. Jerusalem: Mechon Beit Ya'akov leMorot Yerushalayim, 1980.

Levin, Shalom D., ed. *Zichron haRasha"z Guraryeh: Hitkatvuto im K"k Admor Moharayat"z N"e*. Brooklyn, NY, 2004.

Levin, Yitzḥak. *Ḥurbn Eirope: Gezamelte Ma'amorim*. New York: Mechon Meḥkar liVe'ayot Batar-haMilḥama shel haYahadut haDatit, 1948.

Levine, Hillel. *In Search of Sugihara: The Elusive Japanese Diplomat Who Risked His Life to Rescue 10,000 Jews from the Holocaust*. New York: Free, 1996.

Levinsky, Yom-Tov. "Pirkei Havai meḤayei haYeshiva haLita'it: Al haYeshiva haGedola beLomzhe lifnei Yovel Shanim." *Maḥanayim* 78 (1963): 52–59.

———, ed. *Sefer Zikaron liKehilat Lomzhe*. Tel Aviv: Irgun Oley Lomzhe beYisrael, 1953.

Levinson, Avraham. *HaTenu'a haIvrit baGolah*. Warsaw: HaEksekutiva shel haBerit haIvrit haOlamit beLondon, 1935.

Levinthal, Dov A. *The World Famous Yeshiva College of Telshe, Lithuania*. 1929.

Levovitz, Yeruḥam. *Da'at Torah: Limudei Musarei haTorah me'et Rabeinu haGaon haḤasid Ohr Olam Maran Yeruḥam HaLevi Levovitz Ztz"l asher Limed Larabim baYeshiva haKedosha deMir*. Vol. 5 (2). Jerusalem: M. Greenberg Print, 1995.

Lichtenstein, Kalman, ed. *Degel Naftali: Kovetz Ḥidushei Torah Mukdash leZichrono shel Maran haGaon haTzadik R' Naftali Ze'ev haCohen Leibowitz Ztz"l*. New York: Yeshivat Kamenitz, 1958.

Lichtenstein, Kalman and Yeḥezkel Rabinowitz, eds. *Pinkas Slonim*. Vol. 1. Tel Aviv: Irgun Yotzei Slonim beYisrael, [1961].

Liekis, Šarūnas. *"A State within a State?": Jewish Autonomy in Lithuania 1918–1925*. Vilnius: Versus aureus, 2003.

Lipetz, Dov. "HaḤinuch haIvri vehaTenuah haIvrit beLita haAtzma'it (1920–1940)." In *Yahadut Lita*. Vol. 2, edited by Raphael Ḥasman, 113–29. Tel Aviv: Igud Yotzei Lita, 1972.

Liss, Avraham, ed. *Reuven Rubinstein*. Tel Aviv: Igud Yotzei Lita beYisrael, 1971.

Litvak, Yosef. "HaShilton haSovieti veHatzalat Yehudim 'Polaniyim' u'Ma'araviyim'." *Beḥinot* 2–3 (1972): 47–80.

Lohr, Eric. "The Russian Army and the Jews: Mass Deportation, Hostages, and Violence during World War I." *Russian Review* 60, no. 3 (2001): 404–19.

Lomzhe Yeshiva. *Keren Pardes-haTorah: Notzera beMatarah Levases et Kiyuma shel Yeshivat Lomzhe bePetaḥ-Tikva*. Petaḥ Tikva: Pardes-haTorah, 1927.

Lunsky, Ḥaikel. *MeHageto haVilna'i: Tipusim uTzelalim, Ketuvim leItot baTzarah*. Vilna: Agudat-haSofrim vehaZhurnalistim haIvrim beVilna, 1921.

Mahler, R. *Toledot haYehudim bePolin (ad haMe'ah ha-19)*. Merḥavya: HaKibbutz haArtzi Hashomer Hatsair, 1946.

Mandelboim, David A. *Yeshivat Ḥachmei Lublin: HaYeshiva uMeyasda Mahara"m Shapiro Ztz"l*. Vol 1–2. Bnei Brak: HaMachon leHotza'at Sefarim she'al-yad HaMerkaz leIdud Mifalei Tarbut uMeḥkarim Toraniyim beYisrael, 1994.

Margaliot, Yeshaya. Z. *Amudei Arazim*. Jerusalem: HaMa'arav Press, 1932.

Mark, Ya'akov. *Gedolim fun Unzer Tsayt: Monografyes, Ḥarakter-Shtrichen un Zichreines*. New York: Oriom Press, 1927.

Mashbitzky, Efraim R. "Achsaniyot shel Torah (MiZichronotai me'haYeshiva beValozhin)." Part 2. *BaDerech* (June 8, 1934).

Matthäus, Jurgen. "German *Judenpolitik* in Lithuania during the First World War." *LBI Year Book* 43 (1998): 155–74.

Mazeh, Ya'akov. *Zichronot*. Vol 1. Tel Aviv: Yalkut, 1936.

Meizlish, Penina. "Igrot veEduyot beInyanei Hatzala 1939–1944." In *Pedut: Hatzala Biymei haShoah*, edited by Nathaniel Katzburg, 15–114. Ramat Gan: Bar-Ilan University, 1984.

Meler, Shim'on. Y. *'HaRav miBrisk': Toledot Maran Ri"z haLevi*. Vol. 1–2. Jerusalem, 2004.

———. *Igrot Maran Ri"z haLevi 'HaRav miBrisk.'* Jerusalem, 2008.

Meltzer, Yeda'el. *BeDerech Etz haḤayim: MiToch Masechet Toldotav, Hanhagotav ufa'olo shel Rabeinu haGadol Raban shel Yisrael, Sar haTorah veAmud haYirah Maran Rabi Iser Zalman Meltzer Ztz"l Ba'al 'Even haEzel.'* Vol 1–2. Jerusalem: Arzei haḤen, 1986.

Menes, Abraham. "Patterns of Jewish Scholarship in Eastern Europe." In *The Jews: Their History, Culture, and Religion*. Vol. 1, edited by Louis Finkelstein, 376–426. New York: Harper and Brothers, 1960.

Mirsky, Samuel K. "MeArchiyono shel R' Yitzḥak Blazer Z"l." *Talpiot* 5, no. 1–2 (1950–1951): 135–39.

Mishkinsky, Moshe. "Fun der Mirer Yeshive—Tzu Yidisher Dichtung: Zichreines un Impresiyes Tzum Ondenk fun Ḥayim Semiatitzky." Part 1, *Lebns-Fragn* 489–490 (1993): 16–17; Part 2, *Lebns-Fragn* 491–492 (1993): 19–20.

Mohrer, Fruma. *RG 25—Vaad Hayeshivot (Wilno, Poland): Records 1847, 1892, 1924–1940*. New York: YIVO, 1982.

Morgenshtern, Aryeh. *HaShiva liYerushalayim: Ḥidush haYishuv haYehudi beEretz-Yisrael beReshit haMe'ah haTesha-Esreh*. Jerusalem: Shalem, 2007.

Murphy, Curtis G. *From Citizens to Subjects: City, State, and the Enlightenment in Poland, Ukraine, and Belarus*. Pittsburg, Pa: University of Pittsburg Press, 2018.

Nadler, Aharon (Allan). "HaSinteza beḤasidut Slonim Bein Ḥasidut leLimud Torah beNusaḥ haMitnagdim." In *Yeshivot uVatei Midrashot*, edited by Immanuel Etkes, 395–415. Jerusalem: Shazar Center, Dinur Center and the Hebrew University in Jerusalem, 2007.

Naḥmani, Shimshon, and Naḥum Ḥinitz, eds. *Pinkas Slutsk uVenote'ah*. Tel Aviv: Va'ad haSefer, 1962.

Nekritz, Daniel. *Lev haAri: Siḥot Musar uFirkei Ḥayim shel Rabi Yehudah Leib Nekritz Ztz"l*. Vol 1. Brooklyn, NY: Fink Graphics, 1992.

Nekritz, Yehudah L. "Yeshivot Novardok." In *Mosedot Torah beEiropah beVinyanam u'veḤurbanam*, edited by Samuel K. Mirsky, 247–90. New York: Ogen Publishing House of Histadruth Ivrith of America, 1956.

Netzer, Shlomo. *Ma'avak Yehudei Polin al Zechuyoteihem haEzraḥiyot vehaLeumiyot (1918–1922)*. Tel Aviv: Tel Aviv University, 1980.

Nishri, Aharon Ḥ. *Me'ir Einei Yisrael*. Vol. 1–6. Bnei Brak: Me'ir Einei Yisrael, 1998–2003.

Nissenboim, Yitzḥak. *Alei Ḥeldi: 5629–5689*. Warsaw: Grafia Press, 1929.

Olitzky, Leib. *Yeshive-Layt*. Tel Aviv: Y. L. Peretz, 1968.

Oshri, Efraim. *Ḥurbn Lite*. New York: HaRav A. Oshri Buch Komitet, 1951.

———. "Yeshivat 'Knesset Yisrael' biSlobodka." In *Mosedot Torah beEiropah beVinyanam u'veḤurbanam*, edited by Samuel K. Mirsky, 133–68. New York: Ogen Publishing House of Histadrut Ivrit of America, 1956.

Ovsey, Yehoshua. *Ma'amarim uReshimot*. New York: Ohel, 1947.

Oyerbach, Natan R., ed. *Zichronot haRav Moshe Oyerbach Ztz"l*. Jerusalem: haMa'ayan, 1982.

Parush, Menaḥem. *Sharsheret haDorot baTekufot haSo'arot*. Vol. 1–6. Jerusalem, 2001.

Parush, Mordechai. *Orot miMir: LeToledot Ḥayav uFe'alav shel haGaon R' Eliezer Yehudah Finkel Ztz"l, Banav veḤatano ztz"l Mamshichei Darko beHanhagat Yeshivat Mir baAretz u'veḤu"l*. Jerusalem, 1996.

Pekier, Alter. *From Kletsk to Siberia: A Yeshivah Bachur's Wanderings during the Holocaust*. New York: Mesorah, 1985.

Pevzner, Yevgenia. "Yevreiskiy Komitet Pomoshchi Zhertvam Voiny (1914–1921)." *Tirosh* 10 (2010): 141–54.

Pipes, Richard. "Catherine II and the Jews: The Origins of the Pale of Settlement." *Soviet Jewish Affairs* 5, no. 2 (1975): 3–20.

Plotnick, Pesaḥ. *Divrei Ḥachamim*. Warsaw: Feder Print, 1934.

Poliachek, Ḥaya R. "Goral ha'Ketavim." In *Ḥidushei ha'Iluy miMeytchet: Shi'urim beMasechtot haSha"s*, by Shlomo Poliachek, after preface. Jerusalem: Mossad haRav Kook, 1974.

Pomerantchik, Aryeh. *Yehege haAryeh*. Petaḥ Tikva, 1999.

Porat, Dina. "Nesibot veSibot leMatan Vizot-Ma'avar Sovietiyot liFelitei Polin haYehudiyim beVilna baShanim 1940–1941." *Shevut* 6 (1979): 54–67.

———. "Rikuz haPelitim haYehudiyim beVilna baShanim 1939–1941—Ma'amatzei haYetzi'ah." MA thesis, Tel Aviv University, 1973.

Poupko, Aryeh L. *Michtavei haRav Ḥafetz Ḥayim Ztz"l: Korot Ḥayav, Derachav, Nimukav veSiḥotav*. Warsaw: Hutner, 1937.

Rabiner, Ze'ev A. *HaRav Rabi Yehudah Leib Fayn Ztz"l*. Tel Aviv: Ayalon Print, 1973.

———. *Maran Rabeinu Meir Simḥa Cohen Ztz"l*. Tel Aviv: Ayalon Print, 1967.

Rabinowitz, Ya'akov, ed. *Bleter fun Yidish Lite*. Tel Aviv: HaMenorah, 1974.

Rabinowitz, Yisrael. "Yeshivat Lomzhe." *In Mosedot Torah beEiropah beVinyanam u'veḤurbanam*, edited by Samuel K. Mirsky, 217–27. New York: Ogen Publishing House of Histadrut Ivrit of America, 1956.

Rabinowitz, Yosef Y. *Birkat Yitzḥak: Seridei Ḥidushim al haSha"s*. Jerusalem: Beit Yetomim Diskin Print, 1950.

Rabinowitz, Ze'ev, ed. *Pinsk: Sefer Edut veZikaron liKehilat Pinsk-Karlin*. Vol. 1, part 2. Tel Aviv: Irgun Yotzei Pinsk-Karlin biMedinat Yisrael, 1977.

Rabinowitz-Teomim, Eliyahu D. *Seder Eliyahu: Toledot haGaon Rabbi Eliyahu David Rabinowitz-Teomim (HaAderet)*. Jerusalem: Mossad haRav Kook, 1984.

Rakeffet-Rothkoff, Aaron. *The Silver Era in American Jewish Orthodoxy: Rabbi Eliezer Silver and His Generation*. Jerusalem: YU Press, 1981.

Ran, Leizer, ed. *Yerushalayim deLita: Me'uyar uMeto'ad*. Vol. 2. New York: Vilno Album Committee, 1974.

Rand, Asher Z., ed. *Toledot Anshei Shem: Meyuḥad leToledot haRabbanim vehaAdmorim haMefursamim sheNismechu miGeonei veTzadikei Eiropa*. Vol. 1. New York, 1950.

Reines, Moshe. "Achsaniyot shel Torah." *Otzar haSifrut* 3 (1889): 5–35.

Research Institute on Peace and Post-War Problems. "Jews of Lithuania." In *The Jewish Communities of Nazi-Occupied Europe*. New York: American Jewish Committee, 1944.

Reznick, Avraham A. *Klei Sharet: Shu"t Ḥidushei Halachot uVe'urei Sugyot*. Netanya, 1957.

Riff, Yitzḥak Z. *Ner Yitzḥak: Ḥidushei Torah uVerurei-Halacha*. Tel Aviv: Dov Guterman Print, 1957.

Rivkind, Yitzḥak. "Yeshivat Ponivezh." *Hatzefira* (Aug. 26, 1913): 2–3.

Rolnik, Yosef. *Zichreines*. New York: Waldon Press, 1954.

Rosen, A. "HaGaon Rabi Shim'on Shkop sheHekim Dor shel Gedolei Rashei HaYeshivot." *Beit-Ya'akov* 66 (1964): 10–11, 15.

Rosenblum, Yonason. *Reb Ya'akov: The Life and Times of HaGaon Rabbi Ya'akov Kamenetsky*. Brooklyn, NY: Mesorah, 1993.

Rosenstein, Moshe. *Ahavat Meisharim*. Jerusalem, 2002.

———. *Yesodei haDa'at*. Vol. 1, Warsaw: Hutner, 1935; Vol. 2, Bilgoraj: N. Kronenberg Print, 1938.

Rotstein, Shmuel. *Aḥiezer: HaGaon Rabeinu Ḥayim Ozer Grodzensky miVilna—Ḥayav uFe'ulotav*. Jerusalem: Netzaḥ, 1942.

Rottenberg, Moshe. *Bikurei Aviv: Ḥidushim uVe'urim beSugiot haSha"s*. St. Louis: Quality Printing and Publishing Company, 1942.

Rozental, Ḥayim S. *HaRav haDome leMalach: Ketzot Derachav baKodesh shel Raban shel Yisrael, Marana veRabana haGaon Rabi Baruch Dov Leibovitz Ztz"l*. Jerusalem, 2005.

———. *Torah Yevakshu miPi'hu: Divrei Yame'ah shel Yeshivat "Sha'ar haTorah" biGrodna, Polin, veRosha, Maran Rosh Rashei haYeshivot, Sar haTorah vehaYir'ah haGaon Rabi Shim'on Yehudah haCohen Shkop Ztz"l*. Jerusalem, 2000. Reprint, 2006.

Rozental, Shabtai D., ed. *HaZvi Yisrael: Maran haGaon Rabi Zvi Pesaḥ Frank Ztz"l Mara deAtra diYerushalem*. Jerusalem: Mechon haRav Frank, 1971.

Rozin, Aaron. "HaYeshuv haYehudi beMinsk baShanim 1917–1941." In *Minsk Ir VaEm: Korot-Ma'asim-Ishim-Havai*. Vol. 2, edited by Shlomo Even-Shoshan, 7–105. Tel Aviv: Kiryat Sefer, 1985.

Rozovsky, Michel D. *Zichron Shmuel: MiTorato shel Rabeinu haGadol haGaon haAmiti Maran Rabi Shmuel Rozovsky Ztz"l*. Jerusalem, 1985.

Salant [Lipkin], Yisrael. *Etz Peri*. Vilna: Yehudah Leib Metz Print, 1881.

Salmon, Yosef. *Do Not Provoke Providence: Orthodox in the Grip of Nationalism*, translated by Joel A. Linsider. Boston: Academic Studies Press, 2014.

———. "Reshit Reforma biYeshivot Mizraḥ Eiropa: Ma'amatzav shel haRav Reines biShenot haShemonim laMeah she'Avra." *Molad* 4, no. 19–20 (1971): 161–72.

Samet, Moshe. *HeḤadash Asur min haTorah: Perakim miToledot haOrtodoxia*. Jerusalem: Dinur Center and Carmel, 2005.

Samson-Rabinowitz, Rachel. *A Jubilee of Watching: The Story of HaRav Chayim Eliezer Samson*. Jerusalem: Feldheim, 1994.

Samsonowicz, Henryk. "Polish Politics and Society Under the Jagiellonian Monarchy." In *A Republic of Nobles: Studies in Polish History to 1864*, edited and translated by Jan K. Fedorowicz, 49–69. Cambridge: Cambridge University Press, 1982.

Sar haTorah: Korot haḤayim shel Maran haGaon haGadol Zekan Rashei haYeshivot Rabeinu Yeḥiel Michel Feinstein Ztz"l. Jerusalem, 2004.

Sarna, Ya'akov Ḥ., ed. *Daliyot Yeḥezkel*. Vol. 5. Jerusalem: Mossad Haskel, 2003.

Sarna, Yeḥezkel. Transcription of a Recording of the Memoirs of Rabbi Yeḥezkel Sarna (SEA).

Sasson, Natan S., ed. *Naḥalat Avot: Asufat Te'udot uChetavim miGinzei Mispachat Sasson*. Jerusalem: Mechon Ahavat Shalom, 2007.

Schechter, Yehudah L. *Zichronot R' Zeraḥ Barnet: Supru Al Yado*. Jerusalem: Moriah Print, 1929.

Schmukler, Moshe S. *Toledot Rabeinu Ḥayim miVolozhin—Ḥayav, Zemano, Sefarav vehaYeshiva haGedola*. Vilna: S. F. Garber, 1909.

Schwadron, Shalom M., ed. *Lev Eliyahu*. Vol. 1. Jerusalem: HaVa'ad leHotza'at Kitvei Maran Z"l, 1983.

Schwartz, Bat-Shevah. *BeOd Laila*. Bnei Brak: Ganzach Kiddush Hashem, 1997.

Schwartz, Betzalel, and Yisrael Ḥ. Billitzky, eds. *Kobrin*. Tel Aviv: HeḤadash Print, 1951.

Schwartz, Daniel. "Bein Berlin, Lita vehaMizraḥ haRaḥok: Al Kama Shu"t ve'Tikun beHashmata'." *Kiryat Sefer* 64, no. 3 (1992): 1077–87.

Schwartzbord, Moshe E. *BaKodesh Ḥaz292iticha: Petitim miShulḥan Gavo'ah*. Bnei Brak, 1996.

Scott, Hamish M. *The Emergence of the Eastern Powers, 1756–1775*. Cambridge: Cambridge University Press, 2001.

Segal, Y. *VeEleh Toledot Yitzḥak: Olamam shel Gedolim*. Bnei Brak, 1999.

Segalowitz, Z. *Gebrente Trit: Ayndrikn un Iberlebungen fun a Plitim-Vanderung*. Buenos Aires: Tzentral-Farband fun Poilishe Yidn in Argentine, 1947.

Semiatitzky, Ḥayim. *Oisgeshtrekte Hent*. Warsaw: Literarishe Bleter, 1935.

Semiatitzky, Naftali H. *Ner leYitzhar: Kolel Ma'amrei Musar Hitorerut Hergeshim uDerushim Naim al Seder haTorah uMo'adei haShana*. Bnei Brak, 1989.

Sh-o, S. "God vMirskom Yeshibot." *Perezhitoye Sbornik* 4 (1913): 220–241.

Shabad, Tzemaḥ. "Der Onheib fun 'YEKOPO' (Bletlech Zichreines)." In *Oif di Ḥurves fun Milḥomes un Mehumes: Pinkes Fun Gegnt-Komitet "YEKOPO" in Vilne (1919–1931)*, edited by Moshe Shalitt, 574–603. Vilna: Gegnt-Komitet YEKOPO, 1931.

Shalitt, Moshe. *Oif di Ḥurves fun Milḥomes un Mehumes: Pinkes Fun Gegnt-Komitet "YEKOPO" in Vilne (1919–1931)*. Vilna: Gegnt-Komitet YEKOPO, 1931.

Shapira, Ben-Tsiyon. *Igrot leRa'aya"h: Kevutzat Michtavim shel Gedolei haZeman el Tel-Talpiyot Maran haRav Avraham Yitzḥak haCohen Kook Ztz"l Ab"d Iha"k Yerushalayim Tvbb"a uMarah deAtra deYisrael*. Jerusalem: HaMachon leHotza'at Sefarim a"d haRatziy"a Ztz"l, 1986. Reprinted with additions, Jerusalem: HaMachon leHotza'at Sefarim a"d haRatziy"a Ztz"l, 1990. Page references are to the 1986 edition unless otherwise noted.

Shapira, Shalom Z. "Yeshivat Mir beGolat Shanḥai." *Beit-Ya'akov* 170–71 (1974): 4–5.

Shapiro, Chaim. *Go, My Son.* Jerusalem: Feldheim, 1989.

Shapiro, Leonard. *Soviet Treaty Series.* Vol. 2. Washington, DC: Georgetown University Press, 1955.

Shapiro, Moshe S. "R' Itzele Ponevezher." In *Lite.* Vol. 1, edited by Mendel Sudarsky, Uriyah Katzenelenbogen, Yitzḥak Kissin, and Berl Cohen, 577–82. New York: Jewish-Lithuanian Cultural Society Lite, 1951.

———. *R' Moshe Shmuel veDoro: Kovetz Masot veIgrot Me'ezvono shel haRav Moshe Shmuel Shapiro Z"l.* New York, 1964.

Shazar, Zalman. *Kochvei Boker: Sippurei Zichronot uFirkei Masa.* Tel Aviv: Am Oved, 1974.

Sheinfeld, Shabtai. *HaKnesi'ah haGedola haSheniya shel Agudat Yisrael.* Vienna: HaMerkaz haOlami shel "Agudat Yisrael" beVina, 1929.

Shelli, Meir. "Resisei Telz." In *Sadot vaLev: Perakim beDerech Ḥayav uMifal'o shel Avraham Hartzfeld,* edited by Shim'on Kushnir, 422–32. Tel Aviv: Sifriyat haSadeh, 1962.

Sher, Yitzḥak A., ed. *Beit Yisrael: A"d Yisud Kolel Avrechim Gedolei Torah veYirah biSlobodka.* Kovna: Mankus Print, 1922.

Shoshana, Avraham. "HaYeshiva beHitpat'ḥutah: Pirkei Tolada veHa'aracha." In *Sefer Yovel haMe'ah shel Yeshivat Telz, Limelot Me'ah Shana liYesud haYeshiva 1875–1975.* Brooklyn, NY: Empire Press, 1976.

Shoshkes, Ḥayim. *Lender un Shtet (Rayze Ayndruken).* Vilna: Farlag fun B. Kletskin, 1930.

Shpizman, Leib. *Ḥalutzim baMaḥteret u'vaKrav: Pirkei Meri uGevura shel Yehudim biYemei Shilton haNatzim beEiropa,* translated by Moshe Hurwitz. Jerusalem: Kiryat Sefer, 1964.

Shtark, Yehoshu'a. *Tahapuchot haGoral.* Jerusalem, 2008.

Shulman, B. "HaRuaḥ haMahapchanit baYeshivot (Telz veShadov 1906–1909)." *He'avar* 12 (1965): 134–46.

Shulvass, Moshe A. "HaTorah veLimudah bePolin veLita." In *Beit Yisrael bePolin: MiYamim Rishonim ve'ad liYemot haḤurban.* Vol. 1, edited by Yisrael Haylperin, 13–35. Jerusalem: HaMaḥlaka leInyanei haNo'ar shel haHistadrut haTziyonit, 1948.

Shulzinger, Moshe M. *Peninei Rabeinu Avi haEzri.* Bnei Brak, 2002.

Shurin, Yisrael. *Morei haUmah.* Vol. 3. Efrat, 2000.

Silman, Yoḥanan. "Torat haNefesh beHaguto shel R' Yisrael Lipkin (miSalant)." *Bar-Ilan* 11 (1973): 288–304.

Slouschz, David S. "Toledot Ḥayai." *He'avar* 5 (1957): 29–43.

Slutsky, Yehudah. "Diyunei Mo'etzet haMinisterim haRusit beVitul Teḥum haMoshav laYehudim (August 1915)." *He'avar* 13 (1966): 41–58.

———. *HaItonut haYehudit-Rusit baMe'ah haEsrim (1900–1918).* Tel Aviv: HaMachon leḤeker haTefutzot, 1978.

———. *HaItonut haYehudit-Rusit baMe'ah haTesha-Esreh.* Jerusalem: Bialik Instite, 1971.

Solomon, Norman. "The Analytic Movement in Rabbinic Jurisprudence: A Study in One Aspect of the Counter-Emancipation in Lithuanian and White Russian Jewry from 1873 Onwards." PhD diss., University of Manchester, 1966.

Sontag, Raymond J., and James S. Beddie, eds. *Nazi-Soviet Relations 1939–1941: Documents from the Archives of the German Foreign Office.* Washington, DC: Department of State, 1948.

Sorotzkin, Elḥanan. "HaRav R' Avraham Zvi Kamai—Mir." In *Eleh Ezkerah: Osef Toledot Kedoshei 5700–5705.* Vol. 3, edited by Yitzḥak Levin, 37–41. New York: HaMachon leḤeker Ba'ayot haYahadut haḤaredit, 1959.

———. "HaRav R' Yitzḥak Elḥanan Valkin—Antopol." In *Eleh Ezkerah: Osef Toledot Kedoshei 5700–5705*. Vol. 6, edited by Yitzḥak Levin, 278–81. New York: HaMachon leḤeker Ba'ayot haYahadut haḤaredit, 1965.

Spector, Shmuel. "Va'ad Yehudei Lita." In *Yahadut Lita*. Vol. 1, edited by Natan Goren, Leib Garfunkel, Raphael Ḥasman, Dov Lipetz, Eliyahu Segal, Yisrael Kaplan, and Reuven Rubinstein, 124–37. Tel Aviv: Am haSefer, 1959.

Stampfer, Shaul. *Families, Rabbis and Education: Traditional Jewish Society in Nineteenth-Century Eastern Europe*. Oxford: Littman Library of Jewish Civilization, 2010.

———. *Lithuanian Yeshivas of the Nineteenth Century: Creating a Tradition of Learning*, translated by Lindsey Taylor-Guthartz. Oxford: Littman Library of Jewish Civilization, 2012.

———. "Marital Patterns in Interwar Poland." In *The Jews of Poland Between the World Wars*, edited by Yisrael Gutman, Ezra Mendelsohn, Jehuda Reinharz, and Chone Shmeruk, 173–97. Hanover, NH: University Press of New England, 1989.

———. "Shalosh Yeshivot Lita'iyot baMeah haTesha-Esreh." PhD diss., The Hebrew University in Jerusalem, 1981.

Stefansky, Naḥum. *MiMir Netiv Meir: MiMishnato shel haRav Aryeh Binah Ztz"l*. Jerusalem, 2003.

Stein, Avraham S., ed. *Baranovitch: Sefer Zikaron*. Tel Aviv: Irgun Yotzei Baranovitch beYisrael, 1954.

———, ed. *Pinkas Kletsk*. Tel Aviv: Irgun Yotzei Kletsk beYisrael, 1960.

Stein, Ḥayim. "Shkudvil un Ir Umkum." In *Lite*. Vol. 1, edited by Mendel Sudarsky, Uriyah Katzenelenbogen, Yitzḥak Kissin, and Berl Cohen, 1861–66. New York: Jewish-Lithuanian Cultural Society Lite, 1951.

Stern, Yeḥiel M. *Gedolei haDorot*. Vol. 1–3. Jerusalem: Mechon Minḥat Yisrael, 1996.

Stone, Daniel. *The Polish-Lithuanian State: 1386–1795*. Seattle: University of Washington Press, 2001.

Strigler, Mordechai. "Farshverer (Dertzeylung)." Parts 1–2, *Idisher Kemfer* 45 (1964), serialized in issues 1550–1558, 1572–1580.

———. *Geklybene Droshes Farn Folk*. Bilgoraj, 1938.

Surasky, Aharon. "Derech Eitan." In *HaMusar vehaDa'at al haTorah, Bereshit*, by Avraham Yoffen, 7–32. Jerusalem: Friedman Press, 1976.

———. *HaRav miPonivezh: Pirkei Ḥayim veYetzira shel Geon Yisrael Abir haRo'im Marana veRabana Rabi Yosef Shlomo Cahaneman Ztz"l*. Vol. 1–3. Bnei Brak: Machon Ḥayei Yahadut Lita, 1999.

———. *Marbitzei Torah uMusar: BiYeshivot Nusaḥ Lita miTekufat Volozhin ve'ad Yameinu*. Vol. 1–4. Tel Aviv: Hamerkaz leIdud Meḥkarim Toraniyim beYisrael, 1976.

———. *Ohr Elḥanan: Sipur Ḥayav uKetzot Derachav shel Rabeinu haGaon haKadosh Rabi Elḥanan Bunem Vaserman Hy"d Rosh Yeshivat "Ohel Torah" Baranovitch*. Vol. 1–2. Los Angeles: HaYeshiva haKedosha Ohr Elḥanan, 1978.

———. *Rabi Shim'on veTorato: Korot Ḥayav veShitato haTalmudit shel haGaon haAdir Rabi Shim'on Yehudah haCohen Shkop Ztz"l*. Bnei Brak: Netzaḥ, 1973.

Surgailis, Gintautas. *Antrojo Pasaulinio Karo Pabėgėliai ir Internuotieji Lenkijos Kariai Lietuvoje (1939 09–1940): Monografija*. Vilnius: Generolo Žemaičio Lietuvos Karo Akademija, 2005.

Szajkowski, Zosa. "Concord and Discord in American Jewish Overseas Relief, 1914–1924." *YIVO Annual of Jewish Social Sciences* 14 (1969): 99–158.

———. "Jewish Relief in Eastern Europe 1914–1917." *LBI Year Book* 10 (1965): 24–56.

Tau, Yeshayahu M., ed. *Sefer haZikaron leMaran ha"Paḥad Yitzḥak" Ztz"l liChvodo u'leZichro shel Hod Kevod Adonenu Morenu veRabenu Ks"t Maran haGaon Rabi Yitzḥak Hutner Ztz"l.* Brooklyn, NY: HaMossad Gur Aryeh, 1997.

Teitelbaum, Aaron. "Report on Jewish Educational Institutions in Eastern and Central Europe and Palestine Submitted to Dr. Cyrus Adler." *CRC-104/2* (January 27, 1927): 1–40.

Tikochinski, Shlomo. "Darchei haLimud biYeshivot Lita baMe'ah haTesha Esreh." MA diss., The Hebrew University of Jerusalem, 2004.

———. *Lamdanut Musar veElitizm: Yeshivat Slabodka miLita leEretz Yisrael.* Jerusalem: Shazar Center, 2016.

Tory, Avraham. Geto Yom Yom: Yoman Mismachim miGeto Kovna. Jerusalem: Bialik Institute and Tel Aviv University, 1988.

Trop, Naftali. *Ḥidushei haGrana"t haShalem al Sidrei Nashim Nezikin.* Jerusalem: Orayta, 1989.

Trunk, Yeḥi'el Y. *Poiln: Zichroines un Bilder*. Vol. 3. New York: Unzer Tzayt, 1946.

United Nations. *Laws Concerning Nationality*. New York: United Nations, 1954.

Unterman, Isser Y. "Torah Meḥazeret al Achsaniya Shela (MiZichronot Alumai)." In *Sefer haYovel liChevod Rabeinu . . . Shim'on Yehudah haCohen Shkop Shelit"a . . . liMelot Ḥamishim Shenot Avodato haPoriya al Sede Harbatzat haTorah*, edited by Moshe M. Idelevitz, 12–20. Vilna: D. Krejnes Press, 1936. Reprint, Bnei Brak: Netzaḥ, 1977.

Va'ad HaAretz. *Der Idisher Natzional-Rat in Lite: Baricht Vegn Zayn Tetikayt 1920–1922.* Kovna: Arbet Print, 1922.

Va'ad Hatzala. *Ḥurbn un Retung: Di Geshichte fun "Va'ad Hatzole" in Amerike.* New York: Va'ad Hatzole Buch Komitet, 1957.

Va'ad HaYeshivot. *Pinkas haTormim haTemidim leTovat Va'ad HaYeshivot.* Vilna, 193-.

Vagshel, Aharon. *Yaḥid veDoro: Toledotav veOrḥot Ḥayav shel haGaon haTzadik Rabi Mordechai Zuckerman Ztz"l.* Vol. 1. Jerusalem, 2011.

Valach, Shalom M. "HaMaor haGadol: MiToledot Ḥayav shel haGaon haTzadik Rabi Ḥayim Zaytchik Ztz"l uMorashto leDorot." In *haMe'orot haGedolim: Kavei Ohr veTe'urim miDeyokanam shel haIshim haMusariyim Yotzrei Tenu'at haMusar uFe'uloteihem*, by Ḥayim E. Zaytchik, 1–14. Jerusalem, 1994.

———. *Shmuel beKorei Shemo: Toledot Ḥayav shel haGaon haTzadik Rabi Shmuel Weintraub Ztz"l Rosh Yeshivat "Beit Yosef" deNovhardok Pinsk veAba"d Karlin.* Bnei Brak, 1990.

Vaxman, Nissan. "BiMeḥitzat he'Ḥafetz-Ḥayim' Ztz"l (Arba'im Shana liFetirato)." *Shana beShana* (1974): 419–32.

———. "HaGaon R' Eliezer Yehudah Finkel Z"l." *Shana beShana* (1967): 409–26.

Vigodsky, Ya'akov. *In Shturm (Zichreines Fun di Akupatziye-Tzaytn).* Vilna: Farlag fun B. Kletskin, 1926.

Vilensky, Ze'ev, ed. *Kuntres Yonat Elem: Ḥidushei Torah, Be'urim, He'arot veHe'arot me'haRav haMano'aḥ haKadosh haGaon haMefursam Beḥir haYeshivot R' Yona Karpilov Hy"d miMinsk, Russia.* Bnei Brak: Yeshivat Yonat Elem, 1989.

Vozner, Shai A. *Ḥashiva Mishpatit biYeshivot Lita: Iyunim beMishnato shel haRav Shim'on Shkop.* Jerusalem: Magnes, 2016.

Vunder, Meir. "HaYeshivot beGalitziya." *Moriah* 18, no. 3–4 (1992): 95–100.

Warhaftig, Yeruḥam. *Ḥidushei Yeruḥam al haRambam.* Jerusalem: Ḥorev Print, 1945.

———. *Shalmei Yeruḥam: Ḥidushim uVe'urim al haRambam beInyanei Kodshim.* Jerusalem: Zuckerman Print, 1941.

Warhaftig, Zeraḥ. "Baayat haPelitim haYehudim beLita (Sekira)." *CZA, S26/1384*: 1–4.

———. *Palit veSarid biYmei haShoah*. Jerusalem: Yad Vashem, 1984.

Weinberg, Jechiel. "Die Jeschiwoth in Rußland." *Jeschurun* 3, no. 2 (1916): 107–26.

Weintraub, Lipa, ed. *BeSufa u'veSe'ara: Toledot Ḥayav shel haGaon haTzadik Rabi Shmuel Weintraub Ztz"l Rosh Yeshivat "Beit Yosef" deNovhardok Pinsk veAba"d Karlin*. Bnei Brak, 2000. Reprint, Bnei Brak, 2005.

———. *Devar Shemu'ah: Kolel Be'urim, Ḥidushim veHe'arot al Kama Inyanim veSugyot miMasechet Bava Metzia*. Bnei Brak, 1960.

Wischnitzer, Mark. "Di Banayung fun Yeshives in Mizraḥ-Eirope noch der Ershter Velt-Milḥome." *YIVO Bleter* 31–32 (1948): 9–36.

———. "Ḥomer leToledot haYeshivot beEiropa haMizraḥit (biShenot 1919–1939)." Part II, *Talpiot* 5, no. 3–4 (1952): 603–18; Part IV, *Talpiot* 6, no. 3–4 (1955): 739–49.

Y., L. "Zichreines fun a Sanitar." In *Vilner Zamelbuch*. Vol. 2, edited by Zemaḥ Shabad, 65–91. Vilna: N. Rosental Print, 1918.

Yablonsky, Nisan. *Nitzanei Nisan: Ma'amarim Yekarim beFilpulah shel Torah, haNe'emarim beLimud Shi'urim lifnei Talmidei Yeshiva, Meyusadim al Masechtot haSha"s, Gam Eizo She'elot uTeshuvot beHalacha*. St. Louis, MO: Moinester Printing Company, 1930.

Yadler, Ben-Tsiyon. *BeTuv Yerushalayim: Zichronot meḤayei Yerushalayim uGedole'ah baMe'ah haAḥrona*. Bnei Brak: Netzaḥ, 1967.

Yakobzohn, Binyamin Z. *Esa De'i le'meRaḥok: Pirkei Zichronot*. Bnei Brak: Netzaḥ, 1967.

———. *Zichronot*. Jerusalem: HaMaerkaz leSifrut Ḥaredit beEretz-Yisrael, 1953.

Yisraeli (Kula), Ya'akov. *Beit Karlin Stolin*. Tel Aviv: Keren Ya'akov veRachel (Penina), 1981.

Yoshor, Meir M. "Epilogue." In *Netiv Yam*. Vol. 1, by Yeḥiel M. Gordon, 128–30. Jerusalem: Histadrut Talmidei Yeshivat Lomzhe, 1955.

———. "HaRav R' Eliezer Ze'ev Kaplan—Radin." In *Eleh Ezkerah: Osef Toledot Kedoshei 5700–5705*. Vol. 3, edited by Yitzḥak Levin, 127–32. New York: HaMachon leḤeker Ba'ayot haYahadut haḤaredit, 1959.

———. "HaRav R' Yehoshua Levinson—Radin." In *Eleh Ezkerah: Osef Toledot Kedoshei 5700–5705*. Vol. 3, edited by Yitzḥak Levin, 302–7. New York: HaMachon leḤeker Ba'ayot haYahadut haḤaredit, 1959.

———. *HeḤafetz Ḥayim: Ḥayav uFa'olo*. Bnei Brak: Netzaḥ, 1997.

———. "Nasich beMamlechet haTorah." In *Netiv Yam*. Vol. 2, by Yeḥiel M. Gordon, 1–18. Jerusalem: Histadrut Talmidei Yeshivat Lomzhe, 1970.

———. *The Chafetz Chaim: The Life and Works of Rabbi Yisrael Meir Kagan of Radin*. Brooklyn, NY: Mesorah, 1997.

Zagranitchniy Komitet Bunda. *Doklad po Yevreiskomu Voprosu, Prikazy Vlastey, Razniye Dokumenty: Istoriya Odnovo Pogroma*. Geneva?: Zagranitchniy Komitet Bunda, 1916.

Zak, Avraham. *Knecht Zenen Mir Geven*. Buenos Aires: Tzentral-Farband fun Poilishe Yidn in Argentine, 1956.

Zak, Shim'on. "HaYeshivot beLita u'vePolin." In *Netivot haḤinuch: Kovetz Pedagogi-Pesichologi*, edited by Fishel Schneerson, Ya'akov Levi and Dalya Levin, 98–107. Tel Aviv: Histadrut haMorim beEretz-Yisrael, 1945.

Zaks, Zvi. H. *Michtavim uMa'amarim miMaran Rabeinu Ba'al he'Ḥafetz Ḥayim Ztz"l*. Vol. 2. Jerusalem: Yeshivat Ḥafetz Ḥayim meRadin, 1990.

Zalkin, Mordechai. "'Ir Shel Torah'—Torah veLimudah baMerḥav haIroni haLita'i baMe'ah haTesha Esreh." In *Yeshivot uVatei Midrashot*, edited by Immanuel Etkes, 131–61. Jerusalem: Shazar Center, Dinur Center and the Hebrew University in Jerusalem, 2007.

———. "'Ortodoxei haIr'? LiShe'elat Kiyuma shel Ortodoxia beLita baMe'ah haTesha Esreh." In *Ortodoxia Yehudit: Hebetim Ḥadashim*, edited by Yosef Salmon, Aviezer Ravitzky, and Adam S. Ferziger, 427–46. Jerusalem: Magnes, 2006.

———. "'SheYihye Kulo Ivri': Reshet haḤinuch 'Yavneh' beLita Bein 'Ḥinuch Ḥaredi' le'Ḥinuch Ivri.'" In *Zechor Davar leAvdecha: Asufat Ma'amarim leZecher Dov Rapel*, edited by Shmuel Glick, 121–43. Jerusalem: Michlelet Lifshitz, 2007.

Zaltzman, Shlomo. *Min he'avar*. Tel Aviv, 1943.

Zaritzky, David. *HaEsh haMitlakaḥat*. Jerusalem: Aleh, 1984.

———. *Lema'alah min haShemesh*, translated by N. Ginton. Tel Aviv: Avraham Tziyoni, 1954.

———. *Torat haMusar: Mivḥar Siḥoteihem, Imroteihem veToledoteihem shel Gedolei haMusar*. Tel Aviv: Moriah, 1959.

Zariz, David. "Yeshivat Radin." In *Mosedot Torah beEiropah beVinyanam u'veḤurbanam*, edited by Samuel K. Mirsky, 189–216. New York: Ogen Publishing House of Histadruth Ivrith of America, 1956.

Zeidman, Hillel. "HaRav Yosef Zusmanovitch—Slabodka." In *Eleh Ezkerah: Osef Toledot Kedoshei 5700–5705*. Vol. 5, edited by Yitzḥak Levin, 28–35. New York: HaMachon leḤeker Ba'ayot haYahadut haḤaredit, 1963.

———. *Ishim sheHikarti: Demuyot meAvar Karov beMizraḥ Eiropa*. Jerusalem: Mossad haRav Kook, 1970.

———. "Yeshivat Ḥachmei Lublin." In *Mosedot Torah beEiropah beVinyanam u'veḤurbanam*, edited by Samuel K. Mirsky, 393–413. New York: Ogen Publishing House of Histadruth Ivrith of America, 1956.

———. "Yeshivat 'Knesset Beit Yitzḥak' deKaminitz." In *Mosedot Torah beEiropah beVinyanam u'veḤurbanam*, edited by Samuel K. Mirsky, 307–24. New York: Ogen Publishing House of Histadruth Ivrith of America, 1956.

Zemba, Avraham. "'Shtiblach' beVarsha." In *Mosedot Torah beEiropah beVinyanam u'veḤurbanam*, edited by Samuel K. Mirsky, 355–61. New York: Ogen Publishing House of Histadrut Ivrit of America, 1956.

Zevin, Shlomo Y. *Ishim veShitot: Shurat Ma'amarim al Ishei Halacha veShitoteihem baTorah*. Tel Aviv: Avraham Tziyoni, 1958.

Zilber, Binyamin Y. *Torat haYir'ah*. Jerusalem, 1954.

Zilber, Marcus. "HaHanhaga haPolitit haYehudit beVilna vehaMaḥloket al Demuta shel haMedina haLita'it haMitgabeshet, 1915–1918." *Historiya* 33 (2014): 117–56.

Zilberg, Moshe. "Kat haNovhardoka'im (Zichronot)." Part 1, *Ha'aretz* (Dec. 26, 1932): 2; Part 2, *Ha'aretz* (Dec. 28, 1932): 2.

Zinowitz, Moshe. *"Etz Ḥayim": Toledot Yeshivat Volozhin, More'ah, Ḥaye'ah, Talmide'ah veToratah*. Tel Aviv: Mor, 1972.

———. *Ishim uKehilot*. Tel Aviv: Dr. Rivkah Ruckenstein-Zinowitz, 1990.

———. *"Mir": Toledot Yeshivat Mir, More'ah, Ḥaye'ah, Talmide'ah veToratah*. Tel Aviv: Mor, 1981.

Zolf, Falk. *Oyf Fremder Erd: Bletlech fun a Lebn*. Ṿinipeg: Israelite Press, 1945.

Zuckerman, Baruch. *Zichreines*. Vol. 1–2. New York: Farlag "Idisher Kemfer" un Farband Bicher-Farlag, 1962–1963.

Zuroff, Efraim. "Hatzalat Talmidei Yeshivot Polin derech haMizraḥ haRaḥok biTekufat HaShoah." *MiDor Dor* 1 (1979): 49–76.

———. "HaTzibur haOrtodoxy beArtzot-haBerit veḤurban Yahadut Eiropa: Va'ad haHatzala shel haRabbanim haOrtodoxim beArtzot-haBerit biTekufat haShoah (1939–1945)." PhD diss., The Hebrew University of Jerusalem, 1997.

———. *The Response of Orthodox Jewry in the United States to the Holocaust: The Activities of the Vaad ha-Hatzala Rescue Committee, 1939–1945*. New York: Michael Scharf Publication Trust of the Yeshiva University Press, 2000.

Zusman, Yosef. *Kuntres Ḥibat haKodesh*. Ponivezh, 1914; Riga, 1916 (SEA).

Zusmanovitch, Yosef. *Kuntres Mishpat Yerushat Misrah*. Kovna: Laime Print, 1928.

———. *Teru'at Melech*. Keidan: S. Movshovitz Print, 1937.

ORAL TESTIMONIES

(Next to the name of each witness is his educational institution and the location and date of the testimony.)

Ben-Artzi, Shmuel—Mezritch Yeshiva (Jerusalem, May 11, 2004)

Ben-Porat, Yehudah—Kelm Yeshiva (Jerusalem, Mar. 7, 2005)

Bronznik, Naḥum—Telz Yeshiva (Jerusalem, Nov. 19, 2003)

Fortman, Moshe—Telz, Ponivezh, Kletsk-Yaneve, and Kelm Yeshivas (Bnei Brak, Jan. 1, 2003)

Garber, Yisrael—Kamenitz Yeshiva (Jerusalem, Jun. 7, 2005)

Ḥamiel, Ḥayim Yitzḥak—Lomzhe and Warsaw Beit Yosef Yeshivas (Jerusalem, Jun. 2, 2005)

Karno, Yisrael—Telz Yeshiva (Jerusalem, Jan. 13, 2003)

Klibansky, Menaḥem—Slabodka Yeshiva (Tel Aviv, 1988)

Kremer, Azriel—Slabodka Yeshiva (Jerusalem, Jul. 29, 2003; Sep. 2, 2003)

Kremerman, Zalman—Telz and Slabodka Yeshivas (Jerusalem, Jan. 11, 2003)

"Man of Kovna"—Ateret Zvi Yeshiva-ketana in Kovna (Jerusalem, Aug. 20, 2003)

Margalit, Moshe—Novardok and Pinsk Yeshivas (Bnei Brak, Feb. 15, 2004)

Melamed, Avraham—Telz Yeshiva (Ramat Gan, Dec. 24, 2002)

Orlansky, Yisrael—Mezritch-Nementchin Yeshiva (Jerusalem, Feb. 2, 2004)

Shurin, Yisrael—Telz Yeshiva (Efrata, Mar. 23, 2003)

Volbe, Shlomo—Mir Yeshiva (Jerusalem, Dec. 30, 2002)

Waldschein, Refael—Baranovitch Yeshiva (Jerusalem, Feb. 9, 2004)

YBB—Baranovitch and Mir Yeshivas (Jerusalem, Nov. 11, 2004)

Zuckerman, Mordechai—Radin and Kelm Yeshivas (Jerusalem, Dec. 26, 2002)

INDEX

Note: Page numbers in *italics* indicate a figure or a table.

BEN-TSIYON KLIBANSKY is Lecturer at Efrata College in Jerusalem. A native of Lithuania, a senior electronics engineer, and formerly innovative technology-intensive project manager, he is a researcher and editor in the history of Lithuanian Jewry.

CPSIA information can be obtained
at www.ICGtesting.com
Printed in the USA
LVHW111309250522
719727LV00002B/7

9 780253 058492